I0112421

DRAMA OF DEMOCRACY

DRAMA OF DEMOCRACY

POLITICAL REPRESENTATION IN MUMBAI

Lisa Björkman

UNIVERSITY OF MINNESOTA PRESS

MINNEAPOLIS • LONDON

Every effort was made to obtain permission to reproduce
material in this book. If any proper acknowledgment has not been included here,
we encourage copyright holders to notify the publisher.

The lyrics from "Yeh jo Public Hai" are copyright
Anand Bakshi and reprinted with permission.

Portions of chapter 1 were originally published as "'You Can't Buy a Vote':
Meanings of Money in a Mumbai Election," *American Ethnologist* 41,
no. 4 (2014): 617–34, doi:10.1111/amet.12101; copyright 2014 by the
American Anthropological Association.

Copyright 2025 by the Regents of the University of Minnesota

Drama of Democracy: Political Representation in Mumbai is licensed
under a Creative Commons Attribution-NonCommercial-NoDerivatives 4.0
International License (CC BY-NC-ND 4.0):
https://creativecommons.org/licenses/by-nc-nd/4.0/.

Published by the University of Minnesota Press
111 Third Avenue South, Suite 290
Minneapolis, MN 55401-2520
http://www.upress.umn.edu

Available as a Manifold edition at manifold.umn.edu

ISBN 978-1-5179-1893-4 (hc)
ISBN 978-1-5179-1894-1 (pb)

A Cataloging-in-Publication record for this book is available from
the Library of Congress.

Printed in the United States of America on acid-free paper

The University of Minnesota is an equal-opportunity educator and employer.

for democracy

Contents

Abbreviations

AIMIM	All India Majlis-e-Ittehadul Muslimeen (All India Council for Unity of Muslims)
APCR	Association for Protection of Civil Rights
BAC	Bombay Aman Committee
BJP	Bharatiya Janata Party (Indian People's Party)
BMC	Brihanmumbai Municipal Corporation
BMMA	Bharatiya Muslim Mahila Andolan (Indian Muslim Women's Movement)
CAA	Citizenship Amendment Act
HBKL	Hum Bharat ke Log (We the People of India)
IMSD	Indian Muslims for Secular Democracy
JIH	Jamaat-e-Islami Hind
JNU	Jawaharlal Nehru University
MHADA	Maharashtra Housing and Area Development Authority
MLA	Member of Legislative Assembly
MNS	Maharashtra Navnirman Sena
MP	Member of Parliament
NCP	National Congress Party
NGO	Nongovernmental organization
NPR	National Population Registry

NRC	National Registry of Citizens
RPI	Republican Party of India
RSS	Rashtriya Swayamsevak Sangh
RTI	Right to Information
SRA	Slum Rehabilitation Authority

Introduction

"The Real Show"

On October 5, 2022, in the Indian city of Mumbai,[1] a crowd estimated between 100,000 and 250,000 gathered inside central Mumbai's iconic Shivaji Park.[2] Following a blistering oration by the recently ousted chief minister, Uddhav Thackeray—in which he warned that India was drifting toward "dictatorship and slavery" and denounced Maharashtra's new chief minister, Eknath Shinde, and his newly formed government as "parasites" and "traitors"—the event's organizers burned an effigy fashioned in the likeness of Ravana, the mythical nine-headed demon and primary villain of the Hindu epic Ramayana. The effigy was crafted from cardboard boxes—each of Ravana's nine heads was made from a box, and the demon's box-body was emblazoned with the number 50. The significance of both the boxes and the number 50 was clear enough: Shinde had recently defected from Uddhav Thackeray's leadership, taking with him just enough of the party's sitting legislators to cause Maharashtra's Thackeray-led coalition government to collapse.[3] After forging a coalition with the Shiv Sena's erstwhile allies—India's ruling Bharatiya Janata Party (BJP)—Shinde and his cohort proceeded to form a new government in Maharashtra, now with Shinde as chief minister. The Marathi word for "box" (khoka) has another, widely known meaning, ubiquitous in Bombay gangster films as an underworld reference to one crore (ten million) presumably ill-gotten rupees;[4] the 50 inscribed on the khoka-bodied Ravana was an allusion to the fifty crore rupees[5] that each of the legislators aligned with Maharashtra's new chief minister was rumored to have been awarded in exchange for the mass defection that had split

1

the long-ruling Shiv Sena party and deposed Thackeray from the chief minister's seat. The defectors are trying to "kill democracy," Thackeray warned the animated throngs; "Will you become their slaves?"[6]

At first glance, this October 2022 Mumbai gathering appears to be of a piece with broader worldwide trends wherein, across the world and political spectrum, democracy seems to have moved out of the electoral booth and into the open: the 2011 global Occupy movement saw crowds gathering in cities worldwide to denounce global plutocracy in the name of "the 99 percent"; furious throngs assembled in Minneapolis following the 2020 police murder of George Floyd, condemning the rot of structural racism that belies the American facade of liberty and equality, and fueling Black Lives Matter protests in cities across the globe;[7] in 2019, Hong Kongers gathered in a series of protest demonstrations demanding "liberation" from rule by Beijing in the wake of electoral reforms and a new extradition law;[8] in January 2023, after ten weeks spent camping outside military headquarters in Brasília, thousands of supporters of Brazil's

Figure 1. Effigy in the likeness of Ravana at a 2022 rally in Shivaji Park, Mumbai. Still from Asian News International (@ANI), "#WATCH | Maharashtra: Shiv Sena (Uddhav Thackeray faction) performs 'Ravan Dahan' at Shivaji Park in Mumbai, on the occasion of #Dussehra," X, October 5, 2022, https://x.com/ANI/status/1577684110516318209.

far-right former president Jair Bolsonaro stormed government buildings demanding that the military overturn the elections.[9] While the content of claims, grievances, and goals of mass political gatherings varies
dramatically, similarities in form and figuration have led to popular and
scholarly speculation about a global-level crisis of representative democracy—with assembled crowds interpreted as a sign that institutionalized
processes and procedures by which a democratic people is meant to constitute and govern itself have become insufficient to the task of channeling the political passions of our times.[10]

While political passions are breeching the levees from both left and
right, some have wondered whether the work of transforming such passions into enduring political formations somehow comes more easily to
right-wing authoritarian leaders than it does to left-leaning liberals who
would defend democratic rights and freedoms: pro-democracy movements of the Arab Spring were brutally crushed in both Tunisia and
Egypt, where dictatorships made a swift return; the global Occupy upris-
ings against American corporate capitalism, which seemed a watershed
movement at the time, are characterized a decade later as a mere "aster-
isk in the history books;"[11] the long-awaited Euro-American reckoning
with structural racism and the enduring legacies of slavery and imperialism that Black Lives Matter mobilizations seemed to herald is drown-
ing in a rising tide of ethnonationalist authoritarianism on both sides
of the Atlantic. Citing similarities between contemporary and historical
authoritarian mobilizations, political historian Ruth Ben-Ghiat points
out that whipping up political emotions and assembling "communities
of belonging" in the form of impassioned crowds is the bread and butter
of authoritarianism: "In Trump's case, he even gave them apparel, he
gave them slogans. This is what the fascists did. This is what Meloni's
doing, the neo-fascist prime minister in Italy." For proponents of liberal
democracy, Ben-Ghiat notes, the "proper content" of politics is not "cheering crowds" but rather "policy solutions."[12] Indeed, while antidemocratic
crowds swell, the global trend on the political left seems to be in the opposite direction: the more passionate and unreasonable the authoritarian
right becomes, the more the left seems reduced to fact-checking. "Today's
electoral left is highly cerebral," writes pundit Anand Giridharadas. "It
is suspicious of the politics of passion. It doesn't do emotional appeals.
It doesn't have much of a role for music, for the body, for in-person

communing in public spaces, for catchy slogans, for arresting visuals."[13] Is there some sort of natural affinity between political style and substance? Does liberal democracy speak the language of rationality and sincerity, while political emotion, imagery and embodiment properly belong to the authoritarian right? How, in other words, ought the relationship between political form and political content be construed? Such questions comprise the conceptual stakes of this book.

Back in Mumbai, in decrying the illegitimacy of Maharashtra's newly formed government, the words of freshly ousted chief minister Uddhav Thackeray indeed seem to recall the now-famous speech delivered by defeated American president Donald Trump on January 6, 2021, just before insurrectionary crowds claiming to be "the real people" stormed the U.S. Capitol vowing to "save our democracy."[14] And yet, whereas Trump's gathering was a precursor to insurrectionary violence that attempted (and nearly succeeded) to actually subvert the laws and procedures of American democracy, Thackeray's event concluded rather differently: at the end of the evening, the appreciative and energized throngs filed tidily out of the venue, hopped into trains or cars, and headed home. Which is to say: unlike Trump's rally-goers, the Mumbai crowd was not exhorted to literal rebellion (immediate or otherwise) by Thackeray's words; rather, the allegations of treachery, the burning of the cheekily crafted fifty-khoka Ravana, the passionate proclamation of democracy's demise—all was interpreted in light of its particular context: the Hindu festival of Dussehra.

Marked in a myriad of ways across India, Dussehra is perhaps best known for the widespread dance-theater performances and dramatic public reenactments at outdoor fairs and open gatherings of the Hindu epic Ramayana—a genre of festival-theater known as Ramlila.[15] Dussehra (also known as Vijayadashmi, which means "day of victory") celebrates the god Ram's victory over the demon Ravana at the end of the Ramayana with performative enactments of the vanquishing of evil—the lighting of bonfires and burnings of effigies of the demon. The Shiv Sena has convened Dussehra gatherings (Dusshera melava in Marathi) at Shivaji Park, situated in Central Mumbai's Marathi-speaking heartland, every year since 1966[16]—which was the same year the organization was established by Uddhav Thackeray's father, Balasaheb Thackeray. The park and the party share a namesake in the seventeeth-century Maratha warrior king Chhatrapati Shivaji Maharaj, and every Dussehra, Shiv Sena supporters travel from all corners of Maharashtra to gather in Shivaji Park, in order to listen to rousing orations about the continuing injustices inflicted on Marathi-speaking "sons of the soil," about the Shiv Sena's plans for setting things right, and finally to celebrate inexorable victory over such evils with the burning of Ravana effigies. In 2022, however, for the first time ever, Mumbai witnessed not one but two Shiv Sena Dussehra gatherings: five kilometers from Shivaji Park, at the open grounds of Bandra-Kurla, Maharashtra's new chief minister, Eknath Shinde, addressed his own crowd from a stage that bore a remarkable resemblance to the one at Shivaji Park where Uddhav Thackeray was passionately denouncing Shinde and his assembled associates as treasonous turncoats: same bow-and-arrow iconography; same cartoon tiger; same party name—शिवसेना (Shiv Sena)—inscribed on each of the two podiums (see Figures 3 and 4).

While making and breaking coalitions is certainly nothing new in Maharashtra (or in India), this time things were different.[17] This time the defecting legislators did not seek to leave the party behind, but rather to take it with them; Shinde had declared his breakaway faction to be the "real" Shiv Sena. With a municipal by-election on the horizon, and with all eyes on the high-stakes Mumbai election expected later that year,[18]

Figure 2. Media coverage of competing Shiv Sena rallies convened by political rivals Uddhav Thackeray and Eknath Shinde. Still from Mirror Now, "Uddhav Thackeray vs Eknath Shinde | How Dussehra Festival Became a Political Faceoff in Maharashtra." YouTube video, October 7, 2022, https://www.youtube .com/watch?v=7QkHYCvIYfU.

Figure 3. Shiv Sena tiger imagery at Uddhav Thackeray's Dussehra rally. Video still from Mirror Now, "Uddhav Thackeray vs Eknath Shinde | How Dussehra Festival Became a Political Faceoff in Maharashtra," YouTube video, October 7, 2022, https://www.youtube.com/watch?v=7QkHYCvIYfU.

Figure 4. Shiv Sena tiger imagery at Eknath Shinde's Dussehra Rally. Video still from @mieknathshinde, Instagram, October 12, 2022, https://www.instagram .com/reel/CjnO_6yuo_6/?hl=en.

Shinde had approached the courts, laying claim to the party's name and iconography, and requesting that Thackeray be denied the right to use the Shiv Sena name as well as its bow-and-arrow symbol in the upcoming polls. The courts referred the matter to the Indian Election Commission, and it was in this context that—while everyone waited with bated breath for an official decision on which of the two factions would be officially recognized by the Election Commission as "the real Shiv Sena"— Dussehra rolled around, prompting the two spectacular gatherings that one major media house described as "grand Sena shows."[19]

In the days leading up to Dussehra, each of the two Shiv Sena camps went so far as to post video "trailers" for their upcoming performances on their Facebook and Twitter pages. And on the day itself, media coverage of the two events recounted anxious efforts by a rapt public to work out which of the two was the "real" Shiv Sena: "A Sena versus Sena show of strength," wrote Shoumojit Banerjee in the English-language daily *The Hindu* the day before the rallies, describing the high stakes: "While the legal battle is not over, party cadre and observers concur that the size of crowds at the Dussehra rallies will settle the issue."[20] Indeed, with the notion that crowds might lend credence to one or the other faction's claim to be the party's true avatar, much attention was paid by media reporters on the work of assembling and displaying the crowds, and to their appearance and composition. Commentators described how both Shinde and Thackeray had given functionaries "quotas" and "targets"—numbers of people each party worker would bring to the rally—so that the each of the grounds would appear to the cameras to be packed to the point of bursting. And yet, since the two venues have different capacities, the point was not absolute numbers but rather the creation of what reporters described as overflow "optics":[21] journalists reported that each camp's quota was carefully calculated so that the eventual crowd would "spill over" each ground's official capacity.

Meanwhile, in order to offset any notion that the gatherings weren't "authentic," and to counter the widespread rumors that chartered buses had been prearranged to transport far-flung, cash-compensated crowds to rallies, media interviews with rally-goers sought to demonstrate the "real" character of their support for their chosen rally: "All the people you can see here today are the real Shiv Sainiks," one Thackeray supporter told a reporter; "'All those who came walking for Uddhav Thackeray from other cities are the true Shiv Sainiks. We haven't been paid to come here. We paid for our own tickets and we came,' she said, as she and her fellow supporters flashed their local train tickets."[22] Displaying a keen fluency in the way the performances were being discussed and evaluated, the women flashing their ticket stubs for the media cameras were doing their bit to shape the narrative. If political parties conventionally compete to represent people (and are evaluated for the extent to which they do so), here the situation is curiously inverted, with crowds of people competing to represent a party.

Two hundred fifty thousand people gather in a public park for a blistering invective alleging the illegitimacy of the sitting government, punctuated by a triumphant torching of an effigy of evil. And yet far from the critique of the institutions and procedures of electoral democracy that such a scene would appear to present, all these events are internal to the democratic process, comprising alliance-making and party formation in the run-up to election. Not only were the battles to perform also battles to become "the real Shiv Sena," but popular evaluations of the efficacy of those performances were interpreted as signs of what might be expected in the upcoming municipal elections. One New Delhi Television Ltd. (NDTV) reporter thus summed up his assessment: "They've both been releasing teasers but the rally itself is the teaser. Because the real movie, real picture is [the Municipal Corporation] election. . . . Mumbai ka king kaun? [Who is Mumbai's king?] That's the fight being fought on these maidans [grounds]."[23]

The competing Dusshera rallies gesture toward a two-part paradox that animates this book. The first part is that, far from seeking to obviate the institutions and procedures of representative democracy, these crowds assembled precisely with the goal of being accorded official state recognition. The embodied crowd, in other words, is not counterposed with the formal institutions of democracy and representation but rather is itself the very site and substance of representation. And the second part is that it is precisely by signaling theatricality (using the form of a Ramlila and seeking out particular media optics and audience interpretation) that the political actors (both onstage orators and the participant audiences) sought to establish their "realness."

Drama of Democracy is about this two-part paradox, where representation is not the opposite of the real but instead is where reality is enacted, encountered, and evaluated. If representational sign is not contrasted with performative act—if representation is not counterposed with "direct" democracy but rather is where democracy "really" happens—then how are performative bids to represent (to be) evaluated? This book demonstrates the extraordinary fluency in this evaluative work in Mumbai, where people of all walks of life are remarkably astute at navigating and assessing political signs and representations, endlessly discussing and debating possible meanings of the city's dense material-semiotic ecologies—whether words or images, cash or crowds, fliers or flowers. In Mumbai, the evaluative criterion of representation is not whether something is sign or substance, or even whether people are deemed to utter truths or falsehoods. Rather, what matters is whether and how some performance is perceived to activate and actuate the social relations and political subjectivities that it professes to display. *Drama of Democracy* explores the aesthetic and affective resonances of representation, where embodied political performances are encountered and evaluated in real time, from within the sociomaterial landscapes and contexts of enactment.[24] Understanding representation in this way—as real-time embodied performance—invites and impels a consideration of the material substance of representation together with the very forms of language-based political communication with which things like heady crowds or illusory images tend to be counterposed. This book demonstrates ethnographically how public orations and meetings; traditional and social media; pamphlets and texts in a myriad of languages and printed scripts; quieter communications such as private conversations; images and artistic renderings or nonlinguistic sign-vehicles (say, cash, food, or flowers)—how all of these are at once sign and substance of representation.

The research for this book animated a rather straightforward puzzle: the evaluative concepts and discourses animating popular and scholarly appraisals of "democracy in crisis" (Indian or otherwise) bear little resemblance to how Mumbaikars navigate and evaluate the promises and perils of political life.[25] India has a paradoxical relationship with widespread notions of democratic crisis. On the one hand, the world's most populous democracy has in recent years presided over undeniably antidemocratic trends: vertiginous rise in social and economic inequality, attended by gloves-off majoritarianism and sharp constrictions of democratic freedoms (especially press freedoms). In 2021 the U.S.-based

advocacy organization Freedom House demoted India's democratic status from "free" to "partly free," citing the shrinking of civil liberties and
denial of constitutionally guaranteed "fundamental rights."[26] And yet
alongside these troubling trends, observers note that democracy in contemporary India is practiced with ever-greater vigor: electoral participation and partisan engagement has only expanded in recent years, with
women, gender minorities, and people of oppressed castes and classes
turning out in ever-higher numbers to cast their votes in regularly held
elections.[27] India presents an enigma: even as democracy becomes more
exclusionary and unfree, Indian voters place their hopes and invest their
energies in electoral democracy and political representation as the means
and sites through which to contest those same injustices and unfreedoms.

Scholars of Indian democracy have tended to explain Indian voters'
energetic engagements with electoral politics in two (often interrelated)
ways: as a combination of patronage politics and identity-based political
mobilizations. In the former, electoral politics are described as the vehicle of targeted distributions of resources to narrow groups of constituents (as "clients"). In place of a tax-and-spend programmatic politics,
Indian democracy has been described as the institutionalized site of quid
pro quo contingent exchanges between elites (social, political, economic)
and otherwise-powerless masses who receive goods and services as a
condition of electoral support—sometimes described as "vote buying."
Scholarly accounts of this sort of conditional, election-mediated distributions of patronage goods are often combined with accounts of how
reified identity categories inform political loyalties—with ethnic, religious, and caste elites said to trade on a cynical form of identity politics.
And yet recent research reveals the limitations of such accounts of electoral democracy and party politics in India: a wave of new scholarship
has emphasized the extraordinary heterogeneity and dynamism of the
Indian electorate, whose political allegiances do not map predictably or
tidily onto identity categories. In combination with a robust secret ballot,
this means that it is not possible for community elites to monitor voter
compliance; and indeed (and as chapter 1 will show), for the most part
they don't even try.[28] So, how do Mumbaikars practice and evaluate political representation? *Drama of Democracy* explores this question ethnographically, revealing a terrain of representation very different from the

one upon which so much contemporary democratic theory and popular critique hinge.

Representation/Re-presentation

In order to situate this book's argument about representation, it will be helpful to attend to this fraught concept—and to distinguish it from the rather different notion that historian Paul Friedland characterizes as "re-presentation."[29] Contemporary scholarship on political representation often takes as a point of departure the classic formulation of Hanna Pitkin, whose influential 1967 book *The Concept of Representation* offered a deceptively simple definition: "Representation, taken generally, means the making present in some sense of something which is nevertheless not present literally or in fact."[30] Pitkin's book is concerned with the various ways in which the "sense of something" that is not present has been construed, and with the proper procedures and evaluative criteria for institutionalizing and assessing different forms of representation. Taking a Wittgensteinian "ordinary language" approach to representation, Pitkin asserts that in order to make sense of some word or concept, it is necessary to attend to the contexts in which the word is used. Pitkin thus identifies four distinct ways in which representation is invoked. "Formalistic representation" refers to the institutional arrangements by means of which political representatives are authorized and held accountable by their "not present" constituents. The other three kinds of representation that Piktin outlines—symbolic, descriptive, and substantive—describe other ways in which that which is "not present" is construed: if a representative acts in the interests of one's constituents, this is substantive representation; the representative who resembles the represented in some iconic sense is of the descriptive type; the representative who "stands for" a constituency's collective meaning (however understood) is said to represent symbolically. Pitkin's formulations spurred a generation of Anglo-American scholarship, with theorists debating the benefits and trade-offs of prioritizing one or another form of representation and assessing the proper procedures for measuring and assessing the responsiveness and accountability of representatives to those they profess to represent.

Contemporary global political churnings have provoked a scholarly rethinking of Pitkin's classic concept of representation. Political theorist

Ernesto Laclau notes that representation entails a "logical impossibility," since "perfect representation" would require "a direct process of transmission of the will of the represented, when the act of representation is totally transparent in relation to that will."[31] Transmission of the will, of course, requires that the individual "will" be fully constituted and independent of the process of representation, which is simply not the case: even if some individual interest (or "will") were to be transparently transmitted through institutionalized procedures of representation, that interest would become inscribed in "complex reality different from that in which the interest was initially formulated" such that the interest itself changes. Noting that the classic formulation problematically presumes not only individual wills but entire constituencies as existing "logically prior" to their representation, Laclau's formulation joins a "constructivist turn" in representation, attending instead to the recursive relationship between the representer and the represented.[32] Focusing on how the identity of "the people" is conjured into being through "performative practices" construes representation not as a fixed (election-mediated) relationship of authorization and accountability but rather as a dynamic practice and "claim" that asks "what representation does, rather than what it is."[33] Of course scholarly debates over what representation is or does or ought to do are bound up with the particular historical conjunctures in which such debates emerge. Political theorist David Plotke points out, for instance, how in a Cold War context, procedures of accountability and authorization took on a particular political salience, since holding competitive elections was what distinguished democracy (minimally construed) from communism.[34] Rather than sorting the pros and cons of the various sorts of representation generically understood (Descriptive is better! No, substantive!), Plotke questions a presumption at the heart of Pitkin's seminal formulation: the implicit counterposing of representation with presence (recall that representation for Pitkin is defined minimally as conveying something that is "absent").[35] It is democratic theory's preoccupation with representation as absence, in other words, that renders the embodied, fleshy presence of crowds so seemingly problematic.

This conceptual counterposing of representation with embodiment in contemporary democratic theory is largely a historical artifact, anthropologist Jason Frank notes, of the transition from royal to popular sovereignty during Western Europe's eighteenth-century Age of Democratic

Revolutions.[36] French theorist Claude Lefort describes the "empty space" opened up by the eighteenth-century dethroning of European monarchs and argues that power in modern democracy is thus, by definition, disembodied. The legitimacy of democratic authority, Lefort writes, "is based on the people; but the image of popular sovereignty is linked to the image of an empty place, impossible to occupy, such that those who exercise public authority can never claim to appropriate it. Democracy combines these two apparently contradictory principles: on the one hand, power emanates from the people; on the other, it is the power of nobody. And modern democracy thrives on this contradiction. Whenever the latter risks being resolved or is resolved, democracy is either close to destruction or already destroyed."[37] The seeming threat posed by the embodied crowd to contemporary democratic life is thus an existential one, inhering in the notion that in seeking to occupy the "empty space" proper to representation—in actually manifesting "the people"—the embodied crowd signals democracy's destruction.

Things were not always this way. Paul Friedland traces this counterposing of embodiment with representation in so much democratic theory to the interrelated transformations in notions of both political and theatrical representation that took place in Revolutionary-era France. Prior to the Enlightenment, Friedland's research demonstrates, people responded to political events (say, public oratory) in the same way they would if they were watching a play: with cheers and applause, or with disapproving whistles. This was because in both theater and politics, performance in pre-Enlightenment France was understood not as a representation of something absent but rather an act of actual incarnation: "re-presentation." Comparing premodern theater to the convening of the Estates General in pre-Revolutionary France, Friedland notes how at the theater, "a successful performance depended upon the actor's experiencing the passions of the character, on the actor's literally becoming the character for the duration of the play"; similarly, the convocation of the Estates General was a "political spectacle in which spirit took on flesh, in which political actors re-presented with their own bodies a mystical body that had no substance of its own."[38] The shared conception of representation underpinning premodern politics and theater—that is, not representation as absence but re-presentation as "the act by which an intangible body is literally made present in concrete form"—upends the commonly held presumption that the relationship between politics and theater is merely metaphorical: "Theater was not 'really' about politics any more than politics was 'really' about theater. Instead, theatrical and political representation were particular manifestations of the same underlying representative process."[39] Friedland thus tracks the implications for both theater and politics of an extraordinary eighteenth-century shift in the underlying concept of representation:

> The task of actors on both stages underwent a parallel redefinition: Theatrical actors were prevailed upon to represent their characters abstractly, in a manner that *seemed realistic* to the audience, rather than a manner that the actors experienced *as real*. And, at the same time, political theorists were slowly articulating a comparable reconceptualization of political representation. . . . Unlike previous political bodies that had claimed to *be* the French nation, the National Assembly merely claimed to speak on the nation's behalf.[40]

It is precisely the notion that modern representative democracy no longer entails being the nation but rather speaking on its behalf—the "disincorporation" of political power[41]—that leads to so much contemporary hand-wringing over the stubborn persistence of human bodies assembling in what ought to be the empty space of the sovereign.[42]

And yet contemporary Mumbai exhibits no such unease with embodiment or presence; on the contrary, as the Dusshera gatherings demonstrate, "incorporation" is the very criterion for evaluating the "realness" of representation in the first place. If "everything changed" in 1750, it seems Mumbai didn't get the memo.[43] And perhaps Mumbai is no exception; perhaps in the so-called West as well, the change was less complete and far-reaching than chroniclers (past and present) would have us believe. Indeed, as anthropologist William Mazzarella has pointed out, conventional diagnoses of the contemporary global-political conjuncture often say more about the problematic premises upon which such framings hinge than provide insight about the actual societal churnings they profess to describe; as concepts, in other words, they tend to be more normative than descriptive.[44] Noting that the term "populism" has been used to describe political movements as disparate as Trumpism, Occupy, and even Gandhi's "Quit India" struggle to cast off British rule, Mazzarella points out that "populism" is better understood as a go-to word that observers periodically deploy when historical conditions bring to the surface contradictions that are actually inherent to the project of liberalism:[45] the uneasy coexistence of political and legal equality with the actual fact of discrimination and domination; the legal enshrining of equal rights alongside their unequal enforcement; the humanist celebration of individual reason as the locus of political subjectivity alongside actual practices of political representation/re-presentation that are (still) shot through with affect and aesthetics, embodiment and incarnation, theatricality and performance. Which is to say, while it may well be true that Western political observers' normative conceptions of representation changed during Europe's Age of Democratic Revolutions—that extraordinary moment of global churning to which so much contemporary democratic theory can be traced—the uptake and internalization of those norms appears to have been somewhat uneven. And not merely in Mumbai (or India), where such conceptualizations of both theater and politics appear rather beside the point (except perhaps in some elite bourgeois pockets), but perhaps also in those Western seats of "modernity" where representative democracy is so often held to be in crisis.

Democracy's Other Histories

Contemporary diagnoses of the embodied character and affective entailments of mass politics as excessive of the institutionalized procedures of democratic representation are an artifact of the methodological operationalization of the presumptions of liberal democratic theory: the constitution of a democratic people (the demos of democracy) by means of universal suffrage; the formation of political preferences through engagement in a liberal public sphere; the procedures of election as both the legal-institutional mechanism by which representatives are authorized to carry out the mandate of the people as well as the mechanism by means of which representatives are held accountable to that mandate. Within this framework, embodiment is always already defined in opposition to the properly channeling of political preferences through the institutions and technologies of "public" communication and representation (conceptualized as absence).[46]

And yet while the Anglo-American world has rediscovered representation of late, seen from elsewhere these debates appear rather parochial.[47]

Dispensing with unhelpful anglophone preoccupations with "presence," historians and anthropologists working in postcolonial contexts have long attended to the contextual specificity of embodied practices of political assembly and have demonstrated how "putting people on the ground" accomplishes things politically—and that this set of performative practices is easily intelligible when not refracted through Eurocentric theory. In a rich historical account, for instance, Sandria Freitag distinguishes the "public sphere" of Western European state formation from what she calls the "public arenas" of colonial North India. Seeking to explain the emergence in North India of "politicised community identity" in the nineteenth century, Freitag explores how festivals, processions, and cultural spectacles ("crowds and rites, music and sword play, sacred space and sacred time . . . ritual, theater and symbol") provided the symbolic vocabularies by means of which "politicised community identity"—Hindu and Muslim in this case—were constituted and enacted. The "public arena," Freitag writes, provided an "alternative world to that structured by the imperial regime, providing legitimacy and recognition to a range of actors and values denied place in the imperial order."[48] It was in this space of the "public arena" that a transition from the face-to-face interactions and exchanges by means of which "relational communities" were constituted locally were transformed throughout the nineteenth century into to the broader "extra-local" identity categories of "Hindu" and "Muslim"— dynamics set in motion by new technologies of mass media and communication that historian Benedict Anderson calls "print capitalism."[49]

Similarly emphasizing the communicative entailments of embodiment, Lisa Mitchell's *longue durée* account of popular assembly in the Indian subcontinent from precolonial times to the present theorizes crowd gatherings as highly coordinated communicative acts—strategically employed to "broadcast" concerns into a public sphere, making "use of escalating strategies to create spaces of discursive contestation where interests can be raised and recognized enough to even be brought into public discussion."[50] Expanding a classic (Habermasian) notion of a "public sphere" to include mass politics, Mitchell insists that "the collective emptying and filling of public spaces for the purposes of gaining recognition, making representational claims, amplifying unheard voices, gauging public support for substantive agendas, vying to shape political decision-making, performing power, and holding elected officials accountable to their campaign commitments, is not only quite widespread, but also forms a fundamental feature of the way that democracy works in India between elections."[51] Mitchell points out that while Arab Spring or Occupy movement crowd events captured global media attention due to their construal as "spontaneous and exceptional, understood as rejecting existing state structures and seeking to create alternative sovereignties," contemporaneous assemblies of much larger (even staggering) scale in the southern Indian state of Telangana—assembling to call attention to elected representatives' unfulfilled campaign promises—failed to register globally as newsworthy, because such crowd events are "understood in India as neither spontaneous nor exceptional in form."[52] Mitchell's *long durée* account demonstrates how embodied mass politics is itself a material technology of political communication, and one that has a democratizing impetus—employed strategically and instrumentally by marginalized citizens, not as a challenge to the state, but rather (and on the contrary) to get its attention—making grievances heard by state officials, who are thereby held accountable to their constituents.

Beginning not with eighteenth-century Europe but rather at a much earlier moment and in the Indian subcontinent, such alternate genealogies of democracy render untenable the broad-brush reduction of contemporary political churnings to the abiding contradictions of liberalism, and gesture toward rather different questions (both normative and empirical) of the global political contemporary—inviting not democratic diagnosis but conceptual curiosity. Indeed, noting the "semantic or cultural emptiness" of the concept of political representation, anthropologist Jonathan Spencer points out that while "we all know there is a link between representative and represented, what form that link may take" is an empirical question.[53] *Drama of Democracy* takes up this question—and invitation—through an ethnographic account of political representation as embodied performance.

Performance and Performativity

While I will have much to say about the concept of "performance" in the chapters to come, it will be helpful here to briefly introduce how I use the term in this book, to outline how my usage relates to the vast body of extant scholarship on political performance and performativity, and to lay out the conceptual stakes in putting these ideas to work in a study of democracy. The theatrical and performative dimensions of social and political life have long attracted the attention of anthropologists and sociologists, with classic works interested in symbolic dimensions of political spectacle, as well the regime-legitimizing and (re)integrative work of performative enactment that Victor Turner famously termed "social drama."[54] Notwithstanding much internal debate and disagreement, anthropological work on political theater and spectacle is united by the basic idea that performance isn't merely an aesthetic genre of entertainment but a practice that actually does something. This notion—that performance has effects in and on the world—has come to be known as performativity.

First outlined by British philosopher of language J. L. Austin, in a series of lectures published in 1962 titled *How to Do Things with Words*, the concept of the "performative" refers to the idea that words accomplish the very thing that they describe: "I do" pronounced in the context of a marriage ceremony, for instance, or "I apologize" in an attempt at relational repair. The idea that words do things fueled a generation of anthropological scholarship, interested largely in the role of performance in reproducing and preserving "traditional" social order and in shoring up power arrangements—especially in moments of crisis. For Alfred Radcliffe-Brown, writing in the 1960s, "the function of any recurrent activity, such as the punishment of a crime, or a funeral ceremony, is the part it plays in the social life as a whole and therefore the contribution it makes to the maintenance of the structural continuity."[55] Radcliffe-Brown's "functionalist" theory of public life and state ceremony was critiqued by Clifford Geertz, whose influential work on the Balian "theatre state" (Negara) insisted on the priority of individual meaning-making subjects, where the "dramaturgy of state ritual" enacts shared cosmologies of belief: "theatre [is] designed to express a view of the ultimate nature of reality," Geertz writes, "to shape the existing conditions of life to be consonant with that reality . . . and, by presenting it, to make it happen—make it actual."[56] Geertzian "dramaturgy of state ritual" is performative insofar as it actualizes the worldview that it expresses.

Geertz's use of the word "ritual" points to the question of efficacy: what is a "ritual," and what makes it effective?[57] How, moreover, is ritual efficacy to be assessed? Questions of efficacy are at the front and center of Austin's formulation, which distinguishes between two kinds of performatives: those that actually accomplish their intended effects (Austin calls these "happy" or "felicitous" performatives) and those that fail to produce their objects (performatives that are "unhappy" or "infelicitous"). Speakers' intentions (what Austin calls illocution) may or may not line up with whatever outcome (or perlocution) is effected by some utterance. Assessing whether an Austinian performative has succeeded or failed thus hinges on knowing a speaker's intentions.[58] But can one really know another's (or even one's own) intentions?

This matter of intention was the crux of French philosopher Jacques Derrida's critique of Austin's concept of the performative. Derrida pointed out that in making sense of how words produce meaningful effects, what matters is not what the speaker may or may not have intended (if the speaker even thought about it) but instead what Derrida calls iterability: whether some performative articulates "forms of language that are already in existence before the speaker utters them." Performatives "work," Derrida suggests, through the repetition and citation of linguistic signs that are already meaningful.[59] Derrida developed the notion of performativity as a way to describe how particular social subjects are actually produced through the repetition and citation of words and actions that are already laden with meaning.

Derrida's notion of performativity has been taken up scholars of politics as a way to describe how particular social subjects and collective political identities are produced through words and actions—what Judith Butler describes as "reiterative and citational practice by which discourse produces the effects that it names," and what Lisa Wedeen calls a "structural logic" whereby national identity is summoned into being through practices of declaration.[60] Wedeen demonstrates that political spectacles are not mere displays of power but rather (and citing Geertz's discussion of the Balian "theatre state") are performative "instances of that power."[61] By "denaturalizing" political identities, Wedeen powerfully demonstrates how political relationality is enacted (rather than merely symbolized) by performance. Similarly drawing on Derrida's notion of "citationality" and Butler's formulation of the "performatively constituted" character of subjectivity, Thomas Blom Hansen's account of political spectacle in 1990s Mumbai describes "public rituals" (protests, rallies, roadblocks) as "citational practices, drawing on a vast reservoir of popularized national history and religious myths and imagery."[62] "Strategic performance," Hansen suggests, is the semiotic grammar through which political authority in Mumbai is articulated. "To be someone, to enjoy respect and authority is not a given fact," Hansen writes, "but needs to be reproduced through reiterative performances of various kinds."[63]

While such formulations are attentive to the performative character of political spectacle, accounting for the citational syntax of a "public ritual" does not explain when and how a performative iteration communicates and actuates the authority it sets out to produce; as Charles Morris puts it, making a Peircean point, "something is a sign only because it is interpreted as a sign of something by some interpreter."[64] To account for this requires ethnographic attention to the material enactment of political spectacle as performance. And as Irving Goffman reminded us long ago, performance must also consider the question of audience.[65] Understanding performative effect means attending to what people do with some sign: Do they take photos and share over social media? What do they say about it? Do they deride it? Quote it? Laugh at it? Making sense of performance effects requires attending to how signs are taken up and set in motion in ever-changing ways by a myriad of audiences—whether known or unknown, intended or unintended. Attending to such practices of articulation pushes past intractable questions of intention and efficacy and asks instead about the next sign.

Far from a mere methodological quibble, this shift in attention has decisive implications for a study of politics: while studying political performativity yields important insights into the production of political subjectivities and the (re)production of authority, in the absence of attention to the performance question of audience—without attending to how performatives are perceived, evaluated, and rearticulated in ways that might be illegible to (or even subvert) authors' designs (if and when such designs exist)—political performativity finds only authoritarianism. And this is because thinking about performativity without attending to questions of audience "assumes that a display of power is power," rather than admitting the possibility that a display of power is a farce or is later ridiculed or even goes unnoticed.[66] Understanding whether and how political performativity inhabits either authoritarianism or democracy requires attending to how people respond to performances—which is a matter of methodology. *Drama of Democracy* operationalizes a notion of performance that attends methodologically to questions of audience evaluation and "uptake."[67] This methodological move allows us to see how in Mumbai, performance pervades political life across the ideological spectrum—producing and inhabiting a lively terrain of relationality, contestation, and public debate that is proper to democracy.

Drama of Democracy takes up theater theorist Richard Schechner's deceptively simple proposition notion that "performance" entails embodied practices of showing: "The more clearly you show what you are doing," Schechner writes, "the more obviously you are performing."[68] Italian semiotician Umberto Eco recalls a thought experiment posed by Charles Peirce: "What kind of sign could have been defined by a drunkard exposed in a public place by the Salvation Army in order to advertise the advantages of temperance."[69] While Peirce himself declined to answer the puzzle, Eco's own formulation is powerfully suggestive:

> As soon as he has been put on the platform and shown to the audience the drunken man has lost his original nature of "real" body among real bodies. He is no more a world object among world objects—he has become a semiotic device; he is now a sign. . . . He stands for the category he belongs to [i.e., a drunk]. There is no difference, in principle between our intoxicated character and the word "drunk."[70]

Yet, Eco notes, while words and things are both signs, they are not the same. There is, Eco suggests, "something that distinguishes our drunkard from a word": while a word is "actively produced," our drunkard, who already existed, has simply been displayed. Eco identifies this modality of signification as ostention: "ostention is one of the various ways of signifying, consisting in de-realizing a given object in order to make it stand for an entire class." Ostention, Eco insists, is "the most basic instance of performance." The chapters ahead demonstrate how material practices of ostention—what I call "ostentatious display"[71]—are a key dimension of the semiotic field within which virtuosity in the arts of political mediation and efficacy are performed.[72] Words are unreliable in Mumbai, where spoken promises and written rules do not go far in rendering recognizable the means by which the material necessities of everyday life are produced.[73] In this context, we see that more orchestrated and staged an event appears, the more persuasive and real it is as a sign of the orchestrator's authority; as Eco writes, "the elementary mechanisms of human interaction and the elementary mechanisms of dramatic fiction are the same."[74]

The concept of "ostention" ("de-realizing a given object in order to make it stand for an entire class") calls attention to the materiality of sign vehicles and to the embodied character of performance as re-presentation. "Like written and spoken languages," media scholars Margrit Pernau and Imke Rajamani write, "images, sounds, smells, tastes, shapes, and movements are cultivated into meaningful sign systems that form the media through which concepts are communicated, shaped, and changed."[75] Pernau and Rajamani's formulation pushes past the persistent mind-body dualisms that would characterize embodied sensation as sites of "pure feeling," unmediated by rational, language-based concepts. On the one hand, this offers up a critique of "strong" versions of "affect" theory, and on the other hand, of the dyadic approach of Saussurean semiotics, which is inattentive to the material and sensory affordances of sign vehicles.[76] Indeed, through a shared anthropological attention to the irreducible materiality of social life, scholars working in somewhat separate fields of linguistic anthropology, multisensory ethnography, and psychoanalytic ("affect") theories have converged (from their different perspectives) in a resounding critique of the persistent mind-body dualisms that haunt each of their respective fields: in his repudiation of "strong" versions of neo-Spinozian affect theory (and clear-eyed statement on what the notion of affect might be "good for"), Mazzarella explains how the notion of affect "implies a way of apprehending social life that does not start with the bounded, intentional subject while at the same time foregrounding embodiment and sensuous life." Similarly, Lauren Berlant, reflecting on what Clough describes as an "affective turn" in the social sciences, points out how the notion of affect "brings us back to the encounter of what is sensed with what is known and what has impact in a new but also recognizable way." Affect, Donovan Schaefer writes, is "the missing link between discursive regimes and bodies, the arterial linkages through which power is disseminated. 'The present' is not an assemblage of texts and knowledges, bloodless discursive inscriptions on the body, but a felt sense out of which political circumstances emerge."[77] Affect, in other words, conveys knowledge much like semiosis[78]—an insight that allows us to dispense with the unhelpful performativity/performance distinction.

And indeed, back in Mumbai, we can see how the 2022 Dusshera gatherings were at once performative and performance. On the hand, each of the crowds sought—through the embodied act of gathering—to performatively incarnate the "real Shiv Sena." And at the same time, the crowds were also a carefully curated variety of show, performed for innumerable potential and actual audiences: the media, the Indian Election Commission, the myriad mobile phone cameras who produced and circulated a bazillion digital images that evening. And of course, audience assessments regarding which of the two shows was more compelling (in its performance of becoming) would help decide which faction would actually be institutionally empowered (i.e., would legally become) the "real" Shiv Sena—which was of course the whole point. Because official recognition would accord those associated with the winning faction a desired identity and advantage in the upcoming election—a spectacular competition to represent.

Theorizing from Mumbai

The received framings of political theory, as this book shows, cannot account for the actually existing conceptual vocabulary through which Mumbaikars evaluate political life. Taking such evaluations into account, this book attends to the terms and categories by means of which Mumbaikars themselves appraise and "problematize" everyday political practices and processes of democratic representation.[79] Each of the book's five ethnographic chapters (interspersed with three scene-setting interludes) explores a distinctive domain of representation in Mumbai, each anchored by a related conceptual concern: meanings of money in relation to electoral accountability; political aesthetics and enjoyment; believability of words; material mediations of citizenship and belonging; the instability of image-representations and the partisan perils and political possibilities that such semiotic slippage affords. Each chapter explores the evaluative talk that surrounds a problematizing concept-keyword and attends as well to the array of subsidiary signs (words, things, concepts) that comprise the material and ideational terrain that the keyword's ambivalence mediates.[80] Attending to this material-discursive terrain of moralizing discourse and mediation, and treating evaluative terms of problematization as political-theoretical concepts in their own right, allows for an ethnographic account of the stakes—social, ethical, material, practical—of contemporary Mumbai's political life.

The first chapter, "Cash," follows election-season flows of money through the city, exploring the work that money performs in producing and reconfiguring sociopolitical relations of power and material authority in the run-up to the high-stakes event of the municipal election. The chapter is animated by the puzzle that while reportedly unprecedented sums of money changed hands in the run-up to polling, in the electoral district where the research for this chapter focused, the candidate who won a landslide victory actually spent minimally. Pushing past liberal hand-wringing over "vote buying," "corruption," and "clientelism," ethnographic attention to the actual practices of election-season gifting and exchange demonstrates instead how money animates intricate, highly speculative social and informational chains of association by means of which relations of representation are produced, instantiated, and maintained over time—and how these relations are the means by which material contestations and substantive citizenship claims are articulated and made good; "you can't buy a vote," as one seasoned campaign worker explains. Instead, as the chapter demonstrates, election-season cash accomplishes a few interrelated kinds of work. Money is shown to produce enduring sociopolitical networks (gifts of cash work much like any other gifted good in producing relations of debt and obligation), and gifts of cash perform semiotic work, signaling access to powerful networks of knowledge, resources, and authority. Election-season cash simultaneously inhabits these various registers. And yet the materiality of money as an infrastructure of communication invariably leads to semiotic slippage between and among the registers, fueling suspicions about "vote buying" in a rumor-infused environment.

The second chapter dives into the theatrical register of contemporary Mumbai's political life, anchored by moralizing talk about natak—a Hindi-Urdu-Marathi word that refers simultaneously to the performance of something and to the real-time, embodied practices entailed in a show's performative enactment.[81] Natak is a word that signals performance traditions and practices that are concerned with the conveying of emotions—as opposed to being primarily about narrative (as in the Greek-origin theatrical traditions as framed in Aristotle's *Poetics*). The chapter explores natak through its real-time enactments, focusing attention on the assembling of a large-scale campaign rally on the final day of election campaign season. Rather than counterposing "theatricality" with "authenticity," the chapter instead demonstrates how the rally produces an "image." The evaluative criterion of popular assembly, in other words, is not whether a crowd event is deemed to be authentic or mediated, or even whether conveners are deemed to utter truths or falsehoods. Rather, what matters is whether a materialized crowd-image resonates in a way that renders compelling and believable the authority and virtues of an event's conveners, and thereby actuates the social relations and political subjectivities that it professes to represent.

Chapter 3 is about the evaluation of words. Tracing talk about what is (and is not) to be "believed," the ethnography focuses on the weeks and months of communicative and relational work leading up to the final rally that comprises the subject of chapter 2: the chowk sabhaas (street-corner meetings), the multilingual paper pamphlets, the public oratory at "public meetings" and "stage shows," the door-to-door campaigns and late-night "mouse meetings," the formation of WhatsApp groups and circulation of digital videos—language-mediated communicative-relational work that was "on stage" during the mass gathering. Indeed, while the final rally itself was spatially and temporally bounded performance, the show itself indexes a vast and heterogeneous communicative landscape within which language plays a key role. The chapter probes ethnographically the relationship between particular words and material landscapes within which "belief" is crafted—demonstrating how words are evaluated not merely for their (semantic) "truth" value but instead pragmatically, in light of the myriad of semiotic resources available in a communicative situation.[82]

The fourth chapter, "Kaaghaz," attends to the recursivity between materially embodied mass gatherings and the images of those crowd events that are produced and circulated, especially over social media using mobile phone cameras. Focusing on a particular mass gathering that took place in December 2019 at August Kranti Maidan in Mumbai, in opposition to a new, highly exclusionary amendment to India's citizenship laws, the chapter focuses on the material affordances of kaaghaz and khoon—of paper and blood—as each relates to ambivalences over representations of "The People of India." Probing the conflict over kaaghaz's contradictory meanings—at once vehicle of "authenticity" and as well as of "mere representation"—the chapter demonstrates how these contradictions are mediated by the affordances of kaaghaz itself: paper facilitates the enacting of collective subjectivity by virtue of the relational encounters that paper's embodied materiality allows. Focusing on the vagaries of paper, the chapter troubles what is sometimes posed as a binary relationship between digital platforms such as WhatsApp—the immediacy and intimacy of which counterintuitively are often said to produce an effect of direct, unmediated communication—and the real-time, material modes of political assembly that are the staple of Mumbai's political vocabulary. Rather than counterposing the real and the virtual, the chapter's ethnography of kaaghaz attends to the broad spectrum of materials comprising the infrastructure of representation—paper placards, city streets, proximate bodies, mobile phones, digital images—yielding insight into the recursive relations between the material infrastructures of embodied crowds and those of their circulating image-representations.

Chapter 5, "Politics," centers on the anxious efforts by religious leaders, political activists, and party networks to curate crowd-images and manage their metapragmatics.[83] The accounts focus on efforts to convene or conclude (or sometimes altogether prevent) mass gatherings in light of the partisan perils wrought by the unstable affective resonances of crowd-images once put into circulation. As one interlocutor puts it: "The protests were becoming politicized." Ethnographic attention to the elaborate behind-the-scenes work of gathering official permissions and securing the resources to facilitate the protest gatherings (or prevent them) demonstrates the tortuous and uneven relationship between behind-the-scenes mediations and the (onstage) image-events that they facilitate. Ubiquitous evaluative talk about the "political" character of the protests gestures toward the ambivalent role (and possibly suspect motives) of political leaders in facilitating protest gatherings. The evaluative criterion, the chapter demonstrates, is not whether gatherings are spontaneous or mediated; instead, what matters is whether gatherings signal robust and reliable political alliances or are merely flash-in-the-pan, cynical mobilizations of mass affect in service of the narrow "interest" of political elites. Assessments (and allegations) regarding the "political" and "interested" character of crowd-images points to general uneasiness about mobilizations and deployments of mass affect, and evaluative discourse is concerned with attributing, claiming, or disavowing responsibility for to some or another image-event. The chapter probes the stakes of such evaluations, which are not dismissive of party politics as such (far from it);

rather, the political party comes into view as representation par excellence: a dense web of social and material relations facilitating communication, access to resources, and social belonging.

The inspiration for this book is rather straightforward: Mumbaikars put representative democracy to work toward ever-creative ends, displaying facility and fluency in the performative arts of political communication and representation. *Drama of Democracy*'s ambition is to chart a path through some of the conceptual impasses of the global present, where political representation tends to be evaluated according to its adherence to liberal precepts of absence: appraised for verisimilitude and account-ability to an absent subject or else dismissed as dangerous deceptions or emotional manipulations. Drawing on Mumbai's communicative cre-ativity, theatrical acumen, and conceptual wealth, this book instead offers up an alternate evaluative vocabulary based on practices of representation as incarnation and embodiment. Theorizing from Mumbai thus opens new questions and concepts by means of which the political churnings of the global contemporary might be understood.

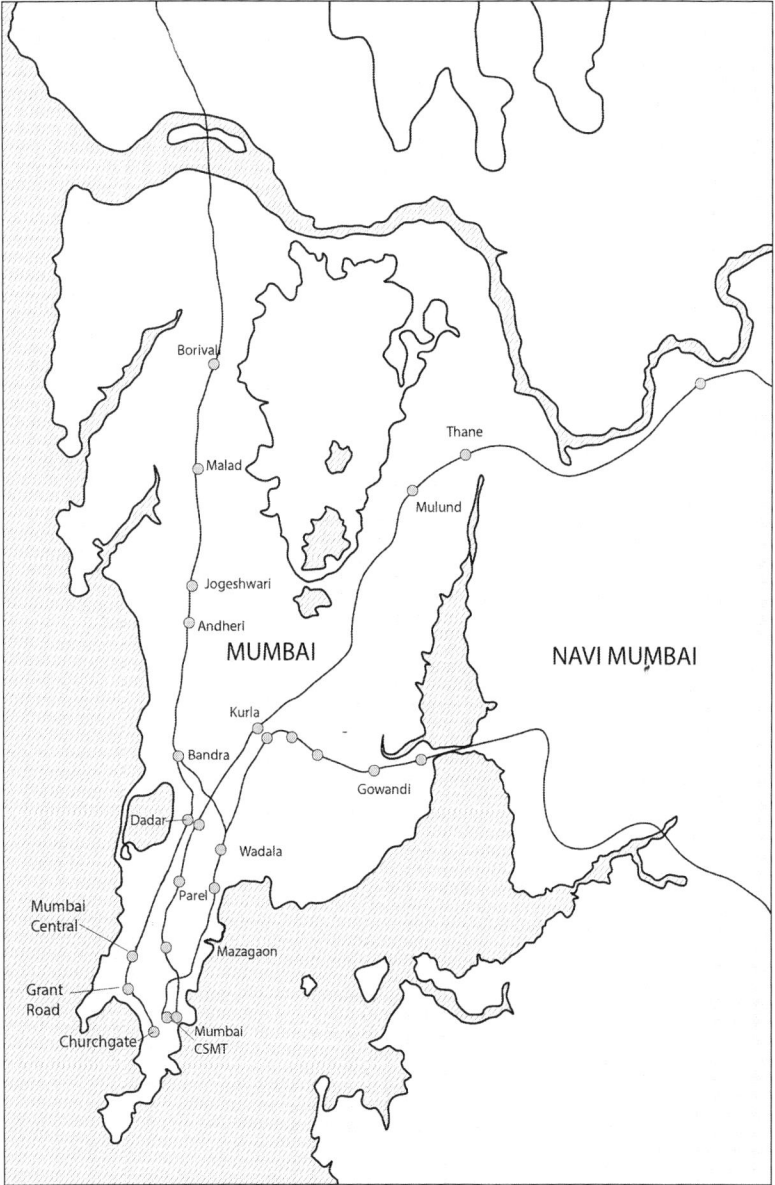

Map 1. Map of Mumbai local train lines (city and suburbs). This to-scale rendering of Mumbai depicts the locations of stations mentioned throughout the book.

Interlude I

Mediating "Slum"

On February 8, 2012—a week before polling day in the run-up to Mumbai's 2012 municipal corporation election—I received a frantic phone call from Seema, the candidate on whose ultimately unsuccessful bid to municipal office my research attention that winter focused.[1] Please come to her home straight away, Seema said; she had something "serious" to talk about. When I arrived, she served me tea and nervously explained that the copartisan MLA (Member of the State Legislative Assembly) in whose district Seema was contesting—a man named Mastan Aziz, popularly known as Mastanbhai, who by all accounts had been responsible for Seema's having been awarded the National Congress Party (NCP) ticket—had phoned her that morning, instructing her to ask her "university friend" (me) to make an official press statement declaring that we were, in fact, "friends." Seema explained that an opposition party candidate, a man named Shaffir (who was not only Seema's next-door neighbor but also a not-too-distant relative by marriage), had been spreading rumors about her tenure as elected councilor in an area I'll call Chikoowadi—a nearby constituency where Seema currently held elected office but from which she was now ineligible to recontest due to changes in the district's gender and caste reservations.[2]

I had been back in Mumbai for a few months already when Seema's call came that February morning, following up on lingering questions from my previous research—which had been about everyday politics of water provisioning and access.[3] That earlier work, carried out between 2008 and 2010 for my doctoral dissertation, had focused on what I had

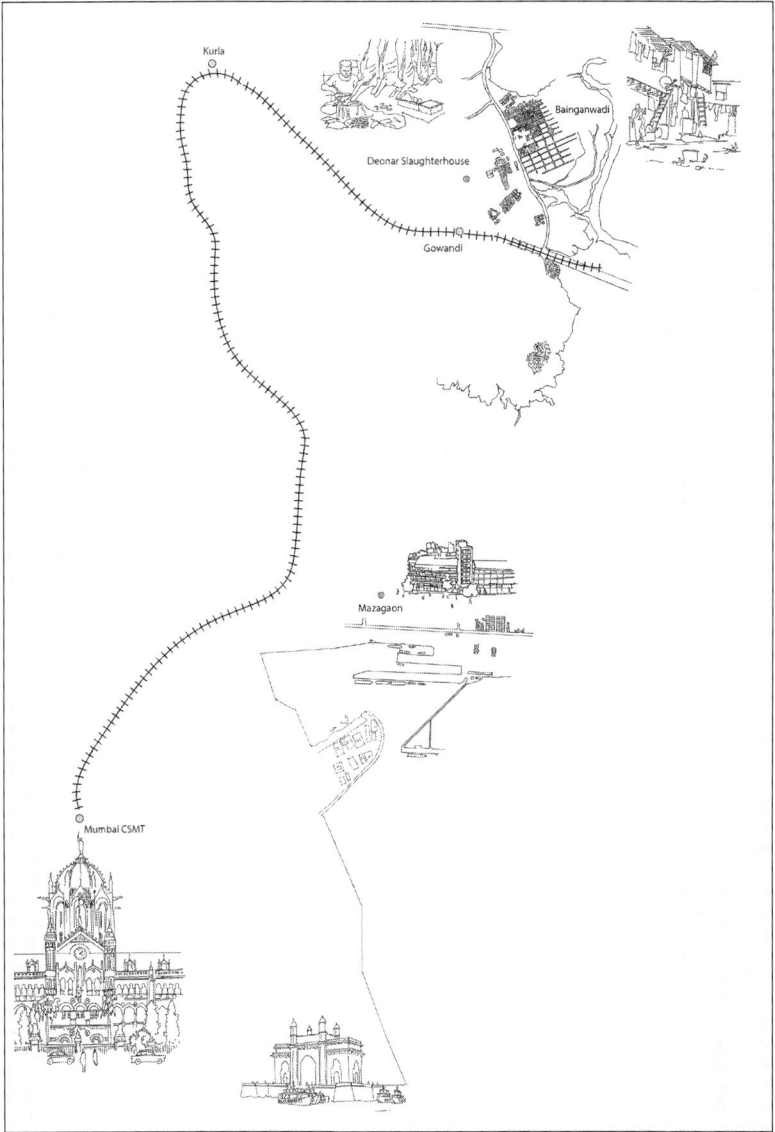

Map 2. Locations of places mentioned in Part I in relation to proximate train stations. See Map 1 for location of these stations within the city as a whole.

initially—and wrongheadedly—been thinking of as a sort of "informal politics": the everyday material processes and practices by means of which Mumbaikars actually made everyday substantive claims to urban resources (say, water) but which existed (by definition) outside the official institutions and rhythms of democracy and bureaucracy. Once in Mumbai, however, this tidy analytical divide between "formal" institutions and "informal" infrastructural practices readily collapsed under ethnographic inquiry; everyday material authority and urban expertise, I quickly discovered, are intimately intertwined with the formal institutions, offices, and rhythms of democracy and bureaucracy. As I wrote in the conclusion of my book *Pipe Politics*, which was based on that research:

> The intricate webs of knowledge, trust, and authority that shape informal political interventions can be (and increasingly are) articulated precisely through the formal institutions of electoral democracy, official procedures of municipal governance, and sometimes even policy frameworks that they challenge and reconfigure. This is not a politics of concession, corruption, or clientelism, nor is it a politics of subaltern resistance or revolution. This is representative politics in full swing, whereby claims to urban land and resources are fought out on the battleground of electoral democracy. The result is not necessarily a prettier, more just or equitable city but rather one whose future is hotly contested.[4]

I headed back to Mumbai in 2011–12 to study this "battleground of electoral democracy"—to learn more about the material-infrastructural politics of elections—for what would become (although I didn't realize it at the time) the first phase of a decade-long study for this book.

I chose to focus the initial phase of research on an area of the city with which I was already somewhat familiar—a low-income neighborhood I'll call Daulat Nagar, which is situated in the swampy reclaimed areas of Mumbai's eastern suburbs. I selected Daulat Nagar on the suggestion and invitation of Seema herself. Seema was a sitting member of Mumbai's Municipal Corporation—known as the BMC[5]—an elected city councilor, or nagarsevak—a word that literally means "city servant" but in Mumbai is glossed (in English) as "corporator." Seema and I had gotten to know one another over the years I'd spent trailing plumbers and engineers around her incumbent district in Chikoowadi. Over years of regular contact and conversation, our research relationship settled into an easy familiarity and mutual appreciation: we were women of roughly the same age, each navigating an overwhelmingly male-dominated city and society. Notwithstanding the dramatic differences in our life trajectories and circumstances, our connection was one of mutual respect and curiosity. I'd been struggling to gain reliable access to an election campaign in Chikoowadi and had asked Seema for advice. She shrugged and offered: Why not just follow her campaign in Daulat Nagar instead?

Sitting in her living room that February morning in 2012, a few days before polling, Seema nervously explained to me that Shaffir and his campaign team had been spreading rumors that she was infamous in her incumbent district in Chikoowadi for making official "complaints" to the municipal authorities about "unauthorized constructions" and then extorting cash payments from residents in exchange for withdrawing the complaints. Seema recounted anxiously how reports that she was a virtuoso player of this "complaint natak" (complaint game)—a not-uncommon pastime in Mumbai—was spreading through Daulat Nagar like wildfire.[6] Mastanbhai hoped that a press statement about Seema's "friendship" with an international scholar affiliated with an esteemed area university might be helpful in propping up the candidate's flagging reputation.[7]

Seema's (and Mastanbhai's) desperate appeal and frantic effort to rescue Seema's reputation gestures toward some of the most pressing issues confronting voters not only in Daulat Nagar but in Mumbai's popular neighborhoods more generally—neighborhoods that tend to be treated for policy purposes as "slums," and thus are often associated (inaccurately) with ideas of illegality. Although the word *slum* is frequently used in Mumbai interchangeably with terms like *encroachment* and *illegal area,* there is nothing in the 1971 Maharashtra Slum Areas (Improvement, Clearance and Redevelopment) Act's (hereafter Slum Act) official definition of "slum" that associates this category of settlement in Mumbai with formality or legality of tenure claims, with planning or lack thereof. Legally speaking, the Slum Act allows to be "declared" a slum "any area [that] is or may be a source of danger to the health, safety or convenience of the public of that area or of its neighborhood, by reason of the area having inadequate or no basic amenities, or being insanitary, squalid, overcrowded or otherwise."[8] The declaration of a neighborhood as a "slum" does not distinguish "legal" from "illegal" land use; rather, it renders a neighborhood eligible for various "improvement" schemes and facilitates public invest-ment in underserved neighborhoods.

The vagaries and contradictions of the policy frameworks governing built space and material infrastructures in areas of Mumbai treated as slums means that the built fabric of such neighborhoods is profoundly vulnerable to the vagaries of "law enforcement." To unpack what this means in practice, consider Daulat Nagar, a residential and small-scale-industrial neighborhood in Mumbai's eastern suburbs, home at the time of research to anywhere between 100,000 and 300,000 people (estimates vary). It was created as a municipal resettlement colony in 1976, when the Emergency-empowered municipal authorities issued a demolition notice to the nearby neighborhood of Indira Nagar (itself a resettlement colony), citing a need to reclaim the municipally owned land for another "public purpose."[9] Indira Nagar's households were each officially allotted ten-by-fifteen-foot "plots" on a swampy swath of public land on the edge of the city—an area that had been zoned in the Development Plan for "pub-lic housing." The official record (a thick file of correspondences among various public and private offices between 1972 and 2014) reveals that land on which Daulat Nagar is situated was supposed to be leased to the residents of Indira Nagar upon registration of cooperative housing soci-eties; however, a tussle over the details of a hastily executed land exchange (in the context of the Emergency) between two government bodies re-sulted in a forty-year bureaucratic tussle between residents and various state offices over the status of the official lease. In the interim half cen-tury, and in step with the city more generally, the neighborhood's popu-lation and housing stock grew.

Meanwhile, the policy framework by means of which Daulat Nagar residents might have obtained an official land lease and entered the Dis-trict Collector's Register as a cooperative housing society—alongside myriad other means by which tenure claims might be articulated—were occluded by a new policy discourse and framework that treats the neigh-borhood as a slum. This means that even though the neighborhood has never been "declared" a slum, which would render it officially govern-able according to the Slum Act, the contemporary political climate is such that the neighborhood is treated by municipal authorities, for pol-icy purposes, as a slum; Daulat Nagar was even surveyed in conjunction with the Government of Maharashtra's 1999 Slum Survey. When I asked

at the office of the District Collector how the surveyors had decided
which of Mumbai's neighborhoods to include in the slum survey, an officer who had been involved with that survey recalled: "We surveyed illegal
areas." When I pointed out that Daulat Nagar (like many other surveyed
areas) is not actually illegal, the officer nodded his agreement but shrugged
helplessly: "But . . . it seems illegal." He elaborated that of course they only
surveyed illegal-seeming single-story structures, not (actually or seemingly) illegal multistory buildings. While it's true that many (perhaps most)
high-rise buildings in Mumbai are constructed without proper authori-
zations, he explained, multistory illegal buildings cannot be surveyed as
"slums," because, well, "how can you bring a building under a slum redevelopment scheme?" It is not formal or legal evaluation, but rather
aesthetic judgments of a neighborhood—its suitability for demolition;
the displaceability of its residents—that renders it legible as a "slum."[10]

Treating Daulat Nagar as a slum effectively restricts the kinds of material investments that can be made in the neighborhood's built environment—its structures and infrastructures—to wholesale demolition and
redevelopment under a market-driven Slum Rehabilitation Scheme.[11]
Under this policy framework, the land in question would be handed over
to a private developer, who would rehouse "eligible" residents (i.e., those
able to marshal the requisite battery of documentary proofs of eligibility) in multistory tenement buildings; in exchange, the developer would
be rewarded with generously increased development rights on land freed
up by the verticalization of the neighborhood. A great many Daulat Nagar
residents express no interest in such a scheme, not least because of the
ongoing battle over their own rights to the land, but also because rehous-
ing under a Slum Rehabilitation Scheme would shrink living spaces while
rendering workshops and commercial enterprises unviable. In this reconfigured policy context, any material investment in the built space and
infrastructures of the area—the homes, workshops, water taps, indus-
tries, and businesses of this industrious middle-class neighborhood—
are rendered vulnerable to complaints of "illegality," where the question
of what is "legal or illegal" is a political rather than an empirical question.

In a transformed political-economic context in which the business
of land, real estate, and construction are among the most lucrative in
the city (as in the world more generally), the question of who can reside,
build, produce goods, and do business in the city—where and how—is no

small matter. The rumors of Seema's "complaint natak" in Chikoowadi gesture toward the broader political and economic context and stakes of municipal elections in Mumbai's lower-income neighborhoods, where the vast majority of the city's electorate resides. The activities leading up to polling day in 2012 must therefore be understood in relation to the sociomaterialities and political economies that infuse everyday life in Mumbai beyond election season, that is, the sociopolitical and material-infrastructural contexts that regular elections punctuate.

Given the legal vagary and contradiction that characterizes everyday life in Mumbai's popular neighborhoods, both production and mainte-nance of a neighborhood's physical form and infrastructure, as well as all manner of business activity, generally involves some kind of media-tion by someone who has access to various kinds of knowledge and resources that are necessary for navigating the physical, legal, and eco-nomic opacities of the city.[12] For instance, brokers are particularly sought after when some required work requires residency proof: a new water connection, for example, or inclusion in a Slum Rehabilitation Scheme. This is especially true for the vast numbers of people living as renting tenants, for whom residency proof is exceedingly difficult to procure.[13] In such cases, official applications are generally believed to have a better chance of being processed if they are accompanied by a letter from a politically connected person (e.g., a police officer or an elected official) verifying the address of the applicant. More important than the office or official position implied in the signature are the networks of power and authority that are implied in any particular signature. A powerful inter-mediary, for instance, has no need for a corporator's signature, and con-versely, an unknown corporator can accomplish very little without their army of brokers. A common popular and scholarly misconception is to assume that authority inheres in the post itself. But the direction of influ-ence is the inverse, with the authority that an elected corporator is able to wield stemming from the fields of knowledge, authority, and influ-ence from which they were elected.[14] Self-proclaimed "social workers," or karyakartas, will therefore often have working relations with an area's elected corporator, even if a karyakarta is affiliated with—and had even campaigned for—a candidate from another political party.

A note on terminology: the mediating work described here is gener-ally described simply as kam, a Hindi-Marathi-Urdu word that translates

as "work," with the person doing the work described as either a karyakarta—which translates as "doer" or "worker"—or else using the English-
origin term *social worker*. While the work of karyakartas is at the heart of
city politics, the term itself, significantly, is politically neutral; even when
a person maintains a longtime affiliation with a particular party, he or
she is often referred to either as a karyakarta or according to his or her
trade or field of specialization: "plumber," "building contractor," "pani-
walla" (water vendor), or, "social worker."[15] Although there are of course,
longtime karyakartas who overtly claim party affiliation and hold party
posts, in practice (as chapter 1 demonstrates) the partisanship even of
self-proclaimed party loyalists is quite fluid at the local level. The number of young people self-identifying as "karyakartas" and "social workers"
has dramatically expanded in recent years; as one young Daulat Nagar
resident put it, "These days, everyone's a social worker!"

The scope of activity locally described as "social work" is not limited to
mundane, household-level issues. Ambitious social workers—particularly
those with political aspirations of their own—set their sights on the resources of the municipal corporation, seeking to direct flows of investment
(particularly infrastructural investment) toward their neighborhoods.[16]
Self-styled "plumbers," for instance, have enormous amounts of influence in the municipal water department, where their knowledge of local
infrastructural networks frequently exceeds that of municipal engineers.
The official expertise of state officials often stems directly from the intimate material knowledge of local social workers. Since the authority
that an elected corporator wields stems from the fields of knowledge and
authority from which they were elected, the question of who among
social workers is given a party ticket comes into focus—as does the question of how electoral victories are then accomplished (or sought to be
accomplished) by producing, reconfiguring, performing, and displaying local-level relational networks and reservoirs of trust. It is to these
questions—and to the role of cash in this election-season work—that
chapter 1 turns.

1

Cash
"You Can't Buy a Vote"

پرچار प्रचार *praćār* [S], s.m. Coming or going forth; appearing; being in actual use, currency; diffusion, spread, promulgation; appearance, manifestation, publication, disclosure, publicity, notoriety.

—Platts, *A Dictionary of Urdu, Classical Hindi, and English* (1884)

On the eve of Mumbai's February 2012 municipal corporation election, a prominent English-language daily urged its elite readership to "be ready to wash your clothes and utensils this week [as] your maid might announce all of a sudden that she is going on leave." The city's vast fleet of domestic service providers, the article explained, had been diverted from its dishwashing duties in the kitchens of the powerful, offered cash to "bunk work" in order to "gather as a crowd" for political rallies at the behest of candidates who sought to win votes through these cash "bribes."[1]

The 2012 Mumbai election was characterized by reportedly unprecedented flows of cash and was narrated by media-fueled rumors about hired crowds and purchased votes.[2] The "vote buying" idea sits at the heart of a broader popular (and scholarly) discourse—one prominent among Mumbai's English speaking elites—about the decline of democracy, the corruption and criminalization of politics, and the sorry state of a government propped up by the shortsighted whims of the city's "slum-dwelling" masses: "The politicians are interested only in the slums," one prominent anticorruption activist explained to me, "because slums are the largest vote bank." He continued: "See, those people are only interested in what little money they can get this month, not with things like

infrastructure that take years to complete. Slum dwellers vote only because they have a handout coming their way; they are concerned only
with their handout." Mumbai's future, it is feared, is being held hostage to
auctionable "banks" of voters in city slums.

Candidate (and party) beneficence at election time is certainly nothing new in Mumbai (or in India), where campaign-season distributions
of goods as well as particularistic benefits toward specific constituencies
have generally been described in popular and scholarly accounts as part
of a broader system of "patronage" said to have characterized Indian politics at least since Independence. The persistence of patronage in Indian
political life has been explained—with varying degrees of celebration,
resignation, and disdain—as evidence of the socially embedded, "vernacular" character of Indian democracy.[3] Yet unlike patronage giving, cash
transfers tend to be characterized in both popular and scholarly accounts
in a language of purchase.[4] With money as the medium of election-season
prestations, votes are said to be for sale.[5]

This chapter is animated by a puzzle: while election-season cash flow
in Daulat Nagar was indeed characterized by impressive flows of cash,
the final vote tally did not reflect monetary expenditure. That is, the candidate who spent the most came nowhere near winning the seat, while
the candidate who won a landslide victory did so with limited spending. The lack of correlation between monetary expenditure and electoral
outcome suggests that perhaps all the talk about "vote buying" is a lot of
nonsense: a cash-flush city simply got carried away, and anxious candidates threw money at voters thinking that they could buy votes—which
ultimately, they could not. Indeed, this line of explanation was frequently
offered—by voters and candidates alike—in the aftermath of the 2012
municipal election. Yet at the same time, a parallel discourse emerged
from the ranks of the party workers on whose ultimately unsuccessful
campaign my research had focused: the money had been mismanaged;
the wrong people had been put in charge of distributing money; favorit-
ism had been shown in cash distributions; and finally, not enough money
had been distributed. Given the lack of correspondence between total
expenditure and electoral outcome, how should these grumblings be interpreted? Do the impressive sums of cash that changed hands during 2012
election indicate the marketization of the vote? If not—and this chapter demonstrates that they do not—then how might we understand the

significance of cash at election time? What, in other words, is all that money doing if it is not buying votes?

While vote-buying theories portend the subversion of democracy by the cash-fueled churnings of "political machines,"[6] an ethnography of election-season cash must attend more broadly to the sociomaterial and semiotic landscapes within which elections occur, and to the shifting, contested, and continuously renegotiated relations of power, knowledge, and material authority within and through which election-time cash is set in motion. Election-season cash flows, this chapter demonstrates, do not work as purchase-like exchanges of money for votes, but instead animate intricate, contingent, highly speculative relational and informational networks by means of which political contestations and substantive citizenship claims are articulated. Actors involved with moving money have divergent and often conflicting aspirations, motivations, and agendas, within which money itself plays multiple roles simultaneously. First, to the extent that cash is put to work as a medium of purchase, the money is shown not to buy votes but rather—somewhat conventionally—to pay for a variety of campaign-related expenses, including (and perhaps less conventionally) to hire flag-bearers for participation in campaign rallies. Second, money is shown to be productive and performative of sociopolitical networks that infuse everyday life far beyond election day; gifts of money work—unsurprisingly—much like any other gifted good.[7] Pushing past both "market corruption"–style cash-for-vote theories (which portend the evacuation of democratic accountability) and culturalist notions of "generalized reciprocity" (in which exchange simply describes already-existing social ties), the chapter demonstrates how election-season cash flows are instead constitutive of robust relations of representation: of trust, sociality, and democratic accountability.[8]

Third, the chapter explores the significance of cash as the material form of such gifts. Interpretations of election-season cash as the marketization of the vote hinge upon long-standing scholarly debates over the extent to which money possesses, as anthropologists Jonathan Parry and Maurice Bloch put it, "an intrinsically revolutionary power which inexorably subverts the moral economy of 'traditional societies.'"[9] By introducing a single measure of value into social spheres previously governed by other moralities or logics of valuation, money is theorized as having the potential to transform previously non-purchasable things into equivalent, freely tradable commodities: "It is in the nature of a general-purpose money," as Paul Bohannan puts it, "that it standardizes the exchangeability value of every item to a common sale."[10] Theorists of money from Marx to Simmel have emphasized money's particularity as an object of exchange that renders "everything quantifiable according to one scale of value," and economic anthropologists have stressed the sociocultural effects of the introduction of money into previously non-economic spheres of life.[11] By rendering comparable—that is, measurable by equivalent units of value—objects and relations that were previously governed by other logics or systems of value, these systems and moralities are held to deteriorate. The implications of this "great transformation"[12] for sociocultural life has been both celebrated and condemned: on the one hand, money's "qualityless" quality has been feted for "freeing" people from oppressive gender, caste, or other "traditional" hierarchical institutions; on the other, this same qualitylessness has been cast as amorality, with money accused of undermining and disembedding other sociocultural institutions, relations and moral principles. Simmel writes: "If modern man is free—free because he can sell everything and free because he can buy everything—then he now seeks . . . in the objects themselves that vigor, stability and inner unity which he has lost because of the changed money-conditioned relationships that he has with them."[13]

Classic money theory counterposes the exchange of commodities with the giving of gifts: gift exchange, Christopher Gregory explains, is held to produce and shore up "personal qualitative relationships between the subjects transacting," while commodity exchange "establishes objective quantitative relationships between the objects transacted."[14] While economic anthropologists have challenged this formulation—pointing out, for instance, that gift giving itself can inhabit a logic of market exchange[15] while commodities too can have "social lives"[16]—readings of election-time flows of cash as "vote buying" are uncritically wedded to "great transformation" theories of money. The result has been a narrowing of the scope of inquiry to the question of how voter "compliance" with a presumed cash-for-vote purchase "contract" is generated under conditions of voter balloting.[17] Asking instead the ethnographic question concerning the indexical work of cash money allows other meanings of money to emerge.[18]

The accounts in this chapter demonstrate how election-season flows of cash simultaneously constitute a "system of values"[19] that enables exchange while also pointing to "transactional" histories that signal access to powerful networks of knowledge, resources, and material authority. Meanwhile, in its role as an actual "medium of real-time transaction,"[20] money's "irreducible materiality"[21] lends itself to semiotic slippage between these two registers, fueling suspicions about "vote buying" in an already rumor-infused environment. The accounts demonstrate how highly visible spectacles of election-season cash expenditure generate intense speculation and political (re)alignments in the run-up to election day. Suggestive of neither a heroic narrative of subaltern resistance to bourgeois capitalism nor a dystopic scenario of mass exploitation in which forces of "marketization" empty the act of voting of meaning, election-time cash instead is shown to articulate relations of representation: money flows through a deeply political landscape of contestation and material claims-making within which issues at the heart of Mumbai's modernity—land use, infrastructural investment, business prospects, entrepreneurial self-making—are contested and negotiated.

Corralling Karyakartas

Ineligible to recontest in her incumbent district in Chikoowadi due to the change in reservation, Seema began the 2012 election season almost entirely unknown to Daulat Nagar's forty thousand-voter-strong constituency. Seema was not alone; a newly implemented 50 percent seat-reservation requirement for women (up from 30 percent in 2007), in combination with the existing 30 percent caste-based reservation for candidates belonging to Other Backward Classes (OBC), Scheduled Castes (SC), or Scheduled Tribes (ST), unseated 70 percent of Mumbai's sitting corporators during the 2012 election, while frustrating the aspirations of scores of would-be candidates. Moreover, on top of the gender and caste reservations, all of Mumbai's major political parties formed pre-poll alliances during the 2012 municipal corporation election.[22] Thus, while party leadership hammered out seat-sharing agreements and candidate lists for the 227 electoral wards, reports emerged from across the city (stories reported on gleefully by the city's excitable media) of bare-knuckled jockeying and threats of defection, with multiple social workers in each ward claiming it was "their turn" to contest the election on the various party tickets.

Unmoored from an area where she—by her own estimate—commanded the loyalty of at least two thousand karyakartas, Seema had expressed to party higher-ups an interest in contesting from Daulat Nagar, where she had resided since marriage but where she was unknown as a social worker.[23] Seema was eventually awarded the National Congress Party (NCP) "ticket" in Daulat Nagar at the expense of at least four other social workers, each of whom claimed a right to the ticket. A longtime Congress Party social worker named Juned, for instance, was incensed that despite his years of work, the Congress Party leadership had ceded Daulat Nagar to NCP. As he saw it, the ticket was his rightful due—or at least that of his family; with the women's reservation, he had lobbied Congress leaders for a ticket in the name of a close relative. While Juned made his anger publicly known early on—boycotting party meetings and allowing rumors to circulate about which candidate might be on the receiving end of his electoral might—conversations with other social workers suggested that his huffing and puffing was largely for show, an effort to communicate to the newcomer that she needed him more than he needed her. Indeed, since Daulat Nagar falls within the boundaries of a legislative assembly district held by NCP leader Mastanbhai, it was hardly surprising that Daulat Nagar was given to NCP. "Why don't you call him?," a veteran Congress Party loyalist counseled Seema early on during the campaign, when Juned's allegiances were still up for grabs. The man explained that Juned himself had indicated that he was boycotting Seema's campaign only because she had not yet approached him "nicely," acknowledging his position and formally requesting an alliance (preferably accompanied by a cash gift). Seema, however, suspected that Juned was a lost cause, having heard that the Congress karyakarta had accepted a generous cash gift from a senior member of a third party from which she herself had been expelled shortly before accepting the NCP ticket: "[The party leader] has probably paid [Juned] a lot of money," Seema surmised; "I had a falling out with [the party leader] so now he's trying to defeat me in any way possible."

Another frustrated contender was Hasina, the area's former NCP corporator from two terms prior (the last time the seat was reserved for women). As one longtime party worker explained to me, Hasina had been confident that she was in line for the ticket again and had already spent months shoring up her social networks and mulling over possibilities for future collaborations, particularly with the party's ward president—a woman named Sushma. When rumors began to circulate that the ticket would go to Seema—an area newcomer—an incensed Hasina convinced Sushma to approach Mastanbhai with an ultimatum: if the ticket was given to Hasina then Sushma would throw her weight wholeheartedly behind the party; otherwise Sushma herself would contest the election as an independent candidate, taking along her loyal voters, composed largely of the hundreds of area women participating in the local savings groups (bachat khata) that Sushma facilitated, and a few hundred families involved in a Slum Rehabilitation Scheme that she was rumored to be organizing (in collaboration with Mastanbhai, who was known to have good connections inside the Slum Rehabilitation Authority).[24] When Seema was awarded the coveted NCP ticket, Hasina promptly declared independence, filing a candidature application on behalf of her niece (a budding social worker in her own right). Sushma, the NCP district president who had apparently been convinced by Hasina's confidence of being awarded the NCP nomination and had thus taken pains to distance herself from Seema, now phoned Seema in a panic to explain and mend fences: Hasina had only been using her, Sushma explained, and professed her loyalty only to Seema.

Seema thus began the campaign season not only entirely unknown but faced with a sociopolitical landscape riven with deep wounds and fissures from the bitter fights over the party tickets. In this context, the first order of business was to corral the support of the karyakartas, particularly those with Congress or NCP affiliations who were presumably amenable to alliance. Indeed, while Seema herself was unknown, her party was not; the NCP boasted a strong network of social workers, many having long-standing personal loyalties to Mastanbhai, the standing MLA. Once her NCP candidature was announced, Seema thus found herself under the tutelage of a sprightly, diminutive, seasoned social worker named Hakim. He specialized in water, and before his kidneys failed, he spent long hours at the local water department office, pushing papers and negotiating hydraulic favors for area residents. Hakim was well known in Daulat Nagar—for his temper, his impatience, and above all for his unwavering work ethic. One well-known story has Hakim waiting for a municipal work crew that he had summoned to unblock a clogged drain. When the crew failed to arrive by midday (thereby putting Hakim's reputation on the line), the exasperated social worker is said to have leapt into the open drain, clawing out the muck and filth with his bare hands.

Hakim's affiliation with Mastanbhai was long-standing, and his loyalty unwavering—particularly in the years since the MLA began picking up the bill for Hakim's monthly dialysis treatments. Indeed, not even when Hakim's own niece accepted a nomination from a rival party was Hakim's commitment to Seema's campaign called into question. This would not the first time that Hakim would manage a campaign for a newcomer: Hasina's own victory a decade earlier was widely attributed to Hakim's reputation and networking skills; before that, Hakim had installed a woman named Sowmya in office on behalf of the Janata Dal: "Hakimne usko jitaya" (Hakim made her win) was how Sowmya's victory was generally recounted.

Seema's status as a newcomer and an unknown personality rendered her campaign highly vulnerable to the forces of rumor. Thus, the very night after Seema's candidature was announced, Hakim counseled Seema that their first order of business was to sort out the troubled relations with local NCP and Congress karyakartas: Sushma, Hasina (and her niece-candidate), Juned, and another longtime NCP party worker named Sonu, who had unsuccessfully sought the NCP ticket for his wife. Most important were Sushma and Hasina, who seemed open to collaboration; Juned and Sonu, who were reported to already have aligned themselves with the Samajwadi Party campaign, were quickly dismissed as lost causes. Despite Hasina's declaration of her niece's independent candidacy, she had made it known (through carefully spread rumors) that she would withdraw the application if (and only if) Mastanbhai called her personally to seek her support for Seema's candidacy. As Seema explained to me, the only way that Hasina could rejoin the party while preserving her reputation and dignity (i.e., her reputation as having strong networks independent of her association with Mastanbhai and his party) would be if she could proclaim that Mastanbhai himself had recognized the extent of her influence among area voters and had thus personally requested that she withdraw her niece's candidacy. Mastanbhai, however, was having none of it; as he explained to a gathering of 150 or so party workers a week before polling day, "Hasina? The public rejected her. She asked for the ticket, but we did a survey in the area—her image was tarnished. . . . We told her: 'We'll give you other responsibilities and then next time we'll see.' She said okay, but then put up her niece!" The standoff between Mastanbhai and Hasina was never resolved, and Hasina did not withdraw her niece's candidacy.

As for Sushma, her reputation as a powerful social worker was rumored to have an extended reach—"Us ki public bahut hai" (She has a lot of public!), it was often said of Sushma—and owing to this reputed extent of Sushma's "public," Hakim counseled that Seema would do well to have Sushma on their side—or at least not campaigning against her.[25] Indeed, after Sushma's initial phone call—during which she had apologized and pledged her support for Seema—the NCP ward president had been conspicuously absent and difficult to reach, having yet to come and meet Seema in person. Seema had requested a meeting earlier that very afternoon, but Sushma had put her off, telling her to "come tomorrow." Sitting in Hakim's home late that first night, Seema rang up Mastanbhai to ask his advice: "Leave Sushma behind," he counseled. "We'll get a new ward president. She's out of the party." Seema, however, was not convinced and went to meet Sushma the following day. Mastanbhai had called a meeting of party workers for the following evening, Seema explained, and she needed a crowd; Sushma was, after all, known as the NCP ward president, and "her people" were needed.

Notwithstanding these intractable rifts, it was with some confidence that, with Hakim at the helm, Seema set out to build a network of support for her candidacy. On a breezy night early in the campaign, our entourage (composed of Seema's immediate family, me, and Hakim) followed Hakim to a meeting that he had arranged with a group of men—butchers by profession—in the shade of the ramshackle tin roof of the neighborhood's open-air market, where I observed the following exchange:

SEEMA: [addressing the men] What are your problems? Speak openly.

MAN A: Water!

HAKIM: Get your papers together and I'll arrange for new connections.

MAN A: We don't have papers.

HAKIM: Okay, there are other ways, but I can't talk about it here in the open. Come to my home, we'll talk at my home.

MAN B: [animatedly] And demolitions!

SEEMA: Have I ever taken your money? Never! See, I'll protect you, you can trust me.[26]

MAN B: [gesturing at the muddy, uneven ground] We want to build a new market hall, a pucca [permanent, solid] one. If you build it with your corporator fund, then no one can complain.

The legal status of built space and infrastructures sat at the heart of these area voters' concerns, and the meeting thus gestures toward two interrelated risks that voters were attempting to navigate, concerns on the mitigation of which the act of voting would ultimately speculate. First, did Seema have access to networks of power and authority that would enable her to successfully navigate the legal contradictions governing the built space and infrastructures of their neighborhood? Making rounds with Hakim—who was well known in Daulat Nagar for his success arranging municipal water connections for residents who might not be in possession of the right combinations of documentary "proofs" surely went some way (or at least attempted to) in producing some confidence that Seema's networks would extend inside key offices of the municipal corporation. But—and second—what was to say that Seema would use her authority and connections to make the apparatus of the state and the "law" work in their favor rather than to their detriment?

Local social workers and community leaders sought to mitigate these not-insignificant risks in the run-up to the election both by forging reciprocal relations of obligation between candidates and groups as well as by relying on already-existing signs of shared interest and identity. For instance, during rare moments when she was not busy in meetings arranged by Hakim, Seema proceeded in her campaign efforts by reaching to prominent leaders of community organizations having affiliations with her husband's family's regional and linguistic background (as well, of course, to individual members of her extended family itself).

We head over to the office of a neighborhood "welfare society"—an NGO run by members of a particular self-described "community" of Tamil-speaking Muslims—where we're greeted by five men. One of the men, who appears to be a leader of sorts, tell us that 70 percent of Daulat Nagar belongs to that particular "community." Since this is Seema's husband's "community," I had expected to be greeted warmly, but they're guarded and receive us with open skepticism: "We've never met you," the man says flatly; it seems like an accusation.[27] "I've been busy in Chikoowadi," Seema replies, without apologizing. The man responds—still a little coldly—that he'd heard there was a standing corporator in Chikoowadi now fighting the election here in Daulat Nagar; their society has held many events, but they didn't invite her because they didn't know her personally. Now I can't tell if they're accusing her or apologizing for not inviting her;

maybe both. Seema nods and repeats: "I've been busy in Chickoowadi."
They seem to soften a bit, but then one of the men who hasn't spoken yet
jumps in: "You're not going to run around making complaints about illegal construction and demanding money like Hasina did, are you?" "No,
no!" Seema says quickly, anxiously. "You can ask anyone in Chikoowadi
whether I did that—absolutely not. [The MLA] has offered me the ticket
[in his constituency] because of my good work in Chikoowadi." She smiles
and laughs a little nervously: "[The MLA] told me he'd be behind me with
a whip if I ever did that in his area." They seem to accept this and nod.
The first man says: "Okay, the main problems here are water, blocked
gutters, and we need more toilets." Seema nods; this is nothing surprising. Then suddenly the second man starts talking about their group's
programs—and now it seems they're selling themselves to Seema. "We've
given out schoolbooks, we gave out mutton on Eid, we give out sewing
machines . . . and we've never taken money from anyone!" Now it's Seema's
turn to nod. After we're outside I ask Seema to explain what the MLA
had said to her about unauthorized construction: "Is he opposed to making complaints and then collecting money? Does he instead want you to
make complaints and then actually follow through?" She shakes her head
vigorously: "No no," she says, "[Mastanbhai] has told me not to interfere;
he says it's not my job."

The palpable distrust that permeates this encounter is matched by the
anxiety that runs through the exchange. The society leaders, for their
part, tack back and forth between (on the one hand) trying to sell themselves to Seema—to convince the candidate, that is, of their standing in
the neighborhood, their status as benevolent patrons who "never take
money from anyone!"—and (on the other hand) attempting to assess,
under conditions of absolute uncertainty, what Seema may or may not
do if elected to office. The question posed to Seema—of whether she
would run around making "complaints"—was clearly not a literal question but rather a straightforward expression of the deep uncertainty and
anxiety that underpinned the decision of whom to support.

Seema spent much of the initial days of the campaign in this way,
rounding up social workers and other prominent people for an inaugu-
ral campaign meeting (organized by Mastanbhai), where the strength of
each's following would be assessed. The evening before the meeting thus
found us (at the invitation of a childhood friend of Seema's husband) in

the five-thousand-voter-strong area of Daulat Nagar known as Phule Nagar, where Seema addressed a gaggle of social workers, instructing each of them to bring at least fifty people to the gathering. "They'll be fed and paid," Seema explained, at the rate of two hundred rupees each per day, with the money given as a lump sum to each social worker, to be further distributed (or not) by each social worker as he or she saw fit. Thereafter, Seema continued, she would need these people to work for her—to accompany her on rallies.

People arrived in droves to the party meeting, and the two thousand chairs rented for the occasion quickly proved insufficient to accommodate the throngs of people, who stood in lines along the back wall. Seema was visibly relieved at the impressive turnout. Her sister Razia explained: "They're all karyakartas; this is a karyakarta meeting, not a public meeting. Most of the people here are paid to be here." Indeed, Razia and a few other of Seema's relatives were standing at the entryway of the school grounds and circulating through the rows of seats to write down the names of social workers and count the number of supporters that each had brought. Sushma—in her capacity as NCP district president—had promised to send a hundred women to the meeting. When Sushma's "hundred women" turned out to number around twenty, Seema's team set about speculating over whether this disappointing attendance was a sign of Sushma's weakness or of her lack of commitment to Seema's campaign. Such assessments of party worker strength and loyalty—indicated by the numbers of each party worker's "people" who turned up—was, Razia explained, the primary purpose of the meeting.

Yet extrapolating from the evening's events, the meeting served several other purposes simultaneously and held different meanings for different actors. For party higher-ups—most importantly, for Mastanbhai—such a large and elaborate event allowed for a performance of personal commitment to Seema's campaign and to signal longer-term interest in the goings-on of the neighborhood. The first half of the two-hour meeting was thus devoted to inviting onstage a parade of prominent party-affiliated social workers to be garlanded by Mastanbhai in the presence of the audience. The tone of the meeting was celebratory, with the audience's status as honored and invited guests signaled by an elaborately choreographed (and what would otherwise have been disproportionately time-consuming) distribution of wobbly little cups of scalding tea. Mastanbhai made it clear that he intended for Seema to win, and the pomp and ceremony with which he recognized and honored the social workers in the audience indicated that those among them who would help Seema win might in the future be able to leverage Mastanbhai's support—and his network of powerful contacts—in their future work.

Yet from the perspective of the social workers themselves, the meeting held a somewhat-different significance: "We need to show Mastanbhai how much strength we have," one young karyakarta explained. "He should see that we're getting him attention." Indeed, whatever Mastanbhai's intentions for the meeting, social workers described the meeting primarily as an opportunity to represent themselves to Mastanbhai and to Seema as important wielders of power and influence. By turning up with a large crowd, each social worker attempted to portray him- or herself as someone who commanded the confidence of many voters—someone to whom the party would be indebted in the event of a victory. Indeed, the goals of social workers (to demonstrate personal strength) could sometimes work at cross purposes with the needs of the campaign (to assess the strength of various social workers' loyal constituencies), insofar as the personal and political aspirations of individual social workers can lead not infrequently to the passing of misinformation to party higher-ups. As one karyakarta explained, "See, the lower-level workers are also looking out for themselves, so they have to make it seem like they are the important one." Pointing at a young boy who had just delivered tea, he continued: "If you're Mastanbhai and you come to me and I introduce you to this fellow here and I say, 'He's one of my men—he's a very big and important man in the neighborhood!,' now why would I do that? Because then Mastanbhai will think, 'Oh, what important and powerful people I have in my team!,' and I gain esteem. So, you see, sometimes the karyakartas don't give good information."

Given that such rallies seemed to offer mutual (if sometimes contradictory) benefit to both Seema's campaign and to various social workers, what should be made of the distribution of cash? At one level, the cash that Seema funneled through networks of area social workers functioned rather straightforwardly, as wage-like payments for the labor of accompanying Seema on rallies. Yet the work accomplished by cash distributions to social workers has another, more crucial dimension: as productive and performative of alliances between Seema and the social workers. Seema's campaign energies were largely devoted to intense relationship-building and alliance-forging activities, in which gifts, promises, and especially money played a central role in both assessing and producing loyalties.

The very night Seema's candidacy was announced thus found us snaking our way through the dark lanes of Daulat Nagar until we emerged in an open expanse on the edge of a marshland; we had been invited by a local "community leader" who had immediately reached out to Seema's cousin's uncle's brother—a man named Nasir, who lives in the area—to arrange the meeting:

> We duck into a small, anonymous-looking structure. Inside the tiny space at least thirty not-young men in tall green hats are seated on the floor, facing a small shrine at the front of the room, next to which is seated—on a large orange pillow—a large, imposing man in bright white elaborately embroidered tunic. Behind the seated men in the hats, the walls are lined with younger men—at least fifteen of them, casually dressed, social worker types. They're Elae Hadis, Seema's husband tells me, from Ajmer; there are probably about two thousand voters from their community here in Daulat Nagar. They're strong Congress supporters, he tells me, and they invited Seema as soon as they heard about her NCP candidacy.[28] We sit down in front of the man on the pillow, but he doesn't look at me or at Seema; he talks to the men—first to Nasir. Nasir hands the man on the pillow a thick wad of thousand-rupee notes, which he promptly refuses. Nasir laughs nervously, insisting, "It's just our donation—for renovations." The man on the pillow nods and directs Nasir to hand the cash to another man, seated behind us, who accepts the money and touches the notes to his forehead. The man on the pillow says to Seema's husband, "We won't run around for you, but Seema can count on the vote here." Seema hands the man on the pillow her business card and says, "If you have any work then call my man and we will be here in fifteen minutes; we live close by." The man on the pillow laughs as he accepts Seema's card and places it on the shrine: "Yes, we plan to call you; that's why we invited you and took your card."

This particular meeting seems to have served two purposes. First, in the context of widespread defections among Congress-affiliated karyakartas, the man on the pillow clarified to Seema any confusion over whether or not his people would vote for her, communicating to Seema that her future win would put her in debt directly to them. The meeting, in other words, firmed up an agreement: votes now in exchange for "work" over the next five years. The formal offering of a cash gift thus functioned neither to purchase the votes of the individuals in the room nor to carry any burden of reciprocity; votes were promised not in exchange for the money but rather for future work. The cash worked both as a performance of Seema's access to powerful, moneyed networks that would enable her to perform that future work, as well as a show of her personal generosity. By handing over cash—not in an envelope, moreover, but as a thick stack of notes—Seema demonstrated not only her beneficence but also—significantly—that she has the means, knowledge, and material resources to act on it.

Second, and at the same time, the man on the pillow made it clear to the senior members of his own community—as well as to the crew of neighborhood social workers lining the walls—that they were to support Seema. The man on the pillow's proclamation that the people of his community would not "run around" for Seema's campaign is thus significant. The solemn and stylized performance formalized the agreement, working to produce trust in both directions—by reassuring area social workers that they could advise their neighbors to support Seema in the confidence that, in the future, their work would get done, all the while demonstrating to Seema that, even though people from the area might not "run around" for the campaign, her future win would put her in their debt.

Prachaar

While members of this particular community would not openly campaign for Seema, the campaign experienced no dearth of manpower. During the two weeks leading up to polling day, Seema paid at the rate of 200 rupees per day for anywhere from fifteen to one thousand people (mostly women) to attend rallies and to accompany her on prachaar—the Hindi/Marathi word for *advertising* or *publicity* that is widely used during election season in reference to candidate-led parades around the neighborhood.[29] The prachaar crowds were "provided" by various social workers to whom Seema paid the cash at the end of each day, according to the number of people provided. Because most of the social workers were unknown, the immediate task of Seema's core team (made up exclusively of her immediate family) was to assess the credibility of the various social workers' claims. A telling predicament was posed when Seema received an invitation from a prominent social worker who was well known from the previous election to have supported the current councilor, Furqan—who, with the change in ward's gender reservation, was now running a campaign on behalf of his aged mother.

> Seema, her husband, his two friends—Aslam and Raju—and I head over to the home of a Tamil-speaking woman named Rookiya, who Seema tells me called her up that afternoon to request a meeting. We arrive at Rookiya's one-room home and some boys are there too—three of them, probably in their early twenties, maybe younger. They sit quietly on the floor nearby. Rookiya laughs easily and has a straightforward, honest way that makes me like her. She speaks confidently, convincingly, telling Seema in no uncertain terms, "I will make you win; whoever I support wins." She runs a few chit funds[30] in the area, so she's widely known and well trusted. But Aslam is skeptical: "Look," he says, "you worked with Furqan last time." She nods, unfazed, stating simply, "I'm not working with Furqan this time." Seema nods slowly. Rookiya promises to have her boys round up as many people as Seema needs for her campaign—for rallies, for distributing fliers, for door-to-door campaigns. "People listen to me," Rookiya tells Seema, repeating, "whoever I work for, that person wins." When we're outside again, Aslam turns to Seema's husband: "How do we know that [Furqan] hasn't come to her first? Maybe she's just calling Seema in order to pass informa-tion to Furqan." But Seema seems inclined to trust her: Rookiya's family is from the same village as Seema's husband, she points out; they had even spoken to one another in Tamil. "Maybe because of this link she'll feel some closeness and work for us." Her husband is pensive, concluding: "We can't trust her . . . but we can't let on that we don't trust her. We have to make sure that these people feel trusted."

Notwithstanding the need to "make sure that these people feel trusted," Seema did not call Rookiya back, and Rookiya did not call again. While it is quite possible that commonalities of linguistic and regional Tamil identity had informed Rookiya's initial effort to reach out to Seema and offer the services of her "boys," the social worker's closeness to Furqan made her untrustworthy.

As Seema's campaign swung into motion, her newly inaugurated campaign office was bombarded daily with social workers wishing to send their people on Seema's campaign rallies and processions:

> A woman walks into Seema's office and sits down. Seema greets her but doesn't know who she is. Is she going to help you?, I ask. Seema's husband shrugs: "We don't know. She says she'll help and that she has so many people." I ask, But how do you know how many "people" someone has?, I ask, and what does it mean to "have people" anyway? He shrugs: "Even we don't even know." Hakim asks the woman, "Who are your karyakartas?" She doesn't give any names—just gestures with her hand, "Down there, the butchers." Hakim instructs her to write down a list of her karyakartas and their contact information. She bobs her head, yes, yes. She continues: "Actually, I would have come earlier but I just found out about you— I just got the call." Hakim: "From who?" She becomes a little flustered, answering: "Actually, . . . I don't know his name." Hakim: "Just bring your karyakartas."

After a social worker appeared like this to announce that he or she had so many "people" behind her, one of Seema's men would go to "ask around" in the neighborhood where the self-proclaimed social worker professed to have support: What work has this person done? Do people really support this person? If the "survey" was promising, then Seema's team would have to settle on a number of the social worker's supporters that Seema would pay for participation in campaign rallies. Notably, since all the major campaigns were offering cash for a crowd, there is no reason to think that a person receiving money from one or another party would have any reason to be inclined to vote in any particular way. Indeed, while the rally participants of course needed to be paid for their labor (many people having taken time off from regular jobs in order to make themselves available for this work), the significance of the money inheres in the relationship between Seema (or Seema's team) and the social worker, rather than the voter. The long-term-relational (as opposed to immediate-exchange) function of the cash transfers was further demonstrated when one of Seema's men eventually spotted Sushma (the elusive NCP ward president) at a Samajwadi Party rally. On that particular day, Seema had employed forty of "Sushma's ladies." After some

Figure 5. Seema's campaign rally (prachaar) through the narrow lanes of the neighborhood. Photograph by the author, February 2012

handwringing over whether or not to pay these women for that day's work (she did eventually pay them), Seema explained to the women that their leader seemed to have switched parties and instructed them to please not return the following day; there were other social workers eager to send women in their place.

The relationship-forging work of these cash transfers recalls anthropology's long-standing interest in gift, reciprocity, and exchange. Marcel Mauss tells us that the giving of gifts, while appearing to be "voluntary, disinterested and spontaneous," is in fact "obligatory and interested."[31] As one or another party is necessarily in a state of obligation—since gifts are by definition not reciprocated immediately but only after the passage of time—gift giving, Mauss tells us, produces enduring (and asymmetrical) social relations mediated by indebtedness. Mauss's influential insight— that social relations are not a precondition of exchange but rather are constituted by gifting—is powerfully demonstrated and elaborated in anthropologist Webb Keane's ethnography of marriage exchange negotiations on the Indonesian island of Sumba.[32] Detailing the embodied, interactive contexts through which the social is actually worked out in practice, Keane shows that for the parties to an exchange, "the practical unity" of each group is itself "produced by the goal of constructing good relations with an affine":

> Formalized encounter such as the negotiation of marriage payments is an important locus not only for solidary action and acts of exchange but also for the display of the group as such, as it is physically assembled and represented as a united front to face the affine. It is also the preeminent site for naming relations, identifying actors, and specifying the nature of the relationships in play—many of which cannot be assumed concretely to pre-exist the scene of encounter. . . . Repeated cumulative scenes of encounter and exchange serve to give the alliance and its constituent parties a palpable form.[33]

Seema's negotiations with social workers can usefully be understood through Keane's formulation of exchange negotiations as "scenes of encounter," as it is precisely through such exchange-mediated displays of assembled crowds that transactional partners are "identified" and relationships with them "ratified."[34] Social workers, for their part, offer their support for Seema's campaign not (only) through verbal promises but by actually producing/performing the scope and strength of their "publics." It is not enough, in other words, for a social worker to simply declare that he or she "has so many people." Rather, the "practical unity" of the social worker's public is made manifest through "repeated cumulative scenes of encounter and exchange" that comprise the campaign season. By the same token, Seema's verbal promises of support for social workers' future (post-election) work are made "binding, efficacious, and serious" by cash gifts.[35]

That the money Seema gave to area karyakartas produces and inhabits enduring social relations (as opposed to mediating an immediate purchase contract in which a relationship begins and ends with the exchange of money) is evidenced in a few of the conflicts that emerged over election-time cash prestations. Seema had on one occasion tried to save money by inviting an influential social worker named Renu to come on a rally alone—without any of her people. Renu was incensed: "It will hurt my image if I do not bring my people!" In the end Seema conceded, agreeing to employ eight of Renu's "people." Renu attended with sixteen supporters in tow—all of whom were eventually paid in full. Seema shook her head helplessly as she explained to me why she had paid them all: as Renu had clearly stated, her reputation was on the line. By bringing the uninvited people, Renu had—intentionally or unintentionally—tested the strength of her budding relationship with Seema. By paying them all, in other words, Seema had openly demonstrated her commitment to Renu, thereby shoring up Renu's authority in her neighborhood. For her part, Seema well knew that if Renu were to lose the confidence of the twenty or so families over whom her opinion ostensibly held sway, then those families would not trust Renu's advice on voting day. Area voters would vote for Seema, after all, not because Seema had employed or paid them (indeed, any number of candidates or parties were willing to do that), but on Renu's advice.

Un-purchasable Loyalty

On February 15, a day before polling, one of Seema's men overheard a conversation between a rival party's social worker and a woman doing laundry in the lane outside her doorway. The exasperated woman had dismissed the young man: "All you people have been coming to our doors to tell us how to vote. But we listen to Rookiya." Indeed, on the final days before the election, Daulat Nagar's lanes were choked with spies. Seema's team had posted an estimated one hundred boys (one for every four lanes) throughout the area, where they loitered, listened, and sent text messages back to Seema's office with reports of which areas were safely "ours" and which needed some more "attention." When a message arrived that the hawa (wind) was blowing in the wrong direction in a particular area, Seema would reach out to her most trusted karyakartas in those areas, asking for introductions to key people (prominent social workers, heads of large families, doctors, teachers, or popular business owners— a cast of characters referred to by the campaign team as "mains") who might be able to turn the tide.[36] After the report that this particular area was loyal only to Rookiya, we headed back over to try and make amends. When we arrived, Rookiya spoke angrily: "I called you the first day and told you I wanted to work for you! But you never called back, so now I'm working for Furqan." It was too late. Two weeks earlier it might have been possible to build a relationship with Rookiya. By employing Rookiya's women and making after-hours home visits to prominent residents, Seema might have boosted Rookiya's standing in her neighborhood by establishing the strength of Rookiya's connection to the party of the standing MLA. But while Rookiya's people would quite possibly still have listened to her if she directed them (even at the last minute) to vote for Seema, Rookiya herself had no reason to believe that throwing her weight behind Seema would be good for her—or for her neighborhood— in the longer run. Seema had squandered Rookiya's offer of alliance, and Rookiya was deeply insulted by Seema's last-minute effort to win her support.[37] Rookiya's disdain at Seema's offer reveals how the materiality of tokens of exchange (cash in this case) renders their meanings susceptible to slippage among "alternative regimes of value."[38] At the start of the campaign season, Rookiya had invited Seema into an alliance that might be shored up with a cash gift. Seema's last-minute appeal, by contrast, introduced the short-term ethic of market exchange into the negotiation—a misrecognition of Rookiya's socio-ethical landscape that resulted in insult.

Money's "semiotically underdetermined" character, moreover, cuts both ways:[39] just as Seema could not convert Rookiya at the last minute, Seema herself proved unmovable by late-in-the-game offers of cash-lubricated loyalty. Only a few hours after we left Rookiya's house, Seema was summoned to another meeting, invited by someone whom she had not yet met. We walked into a room and were greeted by eight serious-faced men. One of them handed Seema a business card that indicated that they were from a small, unregistered political party. One man spoke, explaining that their group had forty or so members—meaning two hundred votes (at an average of five votes behind each member). Seema, exhausted (both physically and financially), asked the spokesman to "Speak directly. What do you want?" He responded: "fifty thousand." Seema shook her head. "Maybe if you had been with us for the past ten days for our rallies . . . but voting is tomorrow. How can we give you so much money for just one day?" "Not for work," the man explained, "we'll give you the list [of our voters]." Seema refused: "At this point that's too much to ask. I don't know where you've been these days, but you haven't been with us." The man insisted that they hadn't been with anyone. As we turned to leave, Seema whispered to me: "They were running around with RPI [Republican Party of India]; one of my men saw them."

Money as Sign

All of the major parties contesting the polls in Daulat Nagar were reported to have distributed cash to social workers in exchange for lists of voters during the final days of the campaign. In Seema's campaign these cash transfers functioned not as payments for votes per se but rather to shore up and affirm the alliances forged over the previous weeks of rallies, late-night negotiations, and chooa (mouse) meetings, a reference to the time of day in which such meetings tend to take place: late at night, when the mice run around. Social workers offering lists of voters did so not in conjunction with any compliance-enforcing mechanism (proposed or implied) but rather as a demonstration of their pull in the neighborhood, as well as to show area residents the strength of their alliance with Seema. While it is tempting to interpret cash transfers in purchase terms, that such cash disbursements work in the same semiotic register as the earlier-described display of notes to the Elae Hadis community is demonstrated in this account related to me by a party worker named Prakash:

> The day before the election, I asked [the candidate] for money to pass to
> someone in my area who told me she had thirty-one votes. I had a few

people like this. [The candidate] said: "Okay, I'll have [the people handling the money] call you." Then [the money man] said he'd give money but [the amount] wasn't enough; I said: "It's not possible, people are giving [much more]. How will I look?" He said, "Okay, I'll see," but then he didn't call back. The woman kept calling, asking me what to do. Finally, I said to her: "Give your votes to whomever you want—I can't get you the money." She told me she was going to give her votes to Furqan. In the end, whoever didn't know who to trust gave to their vote to Furqan, since they already knew his work.

This last phrase is telling: Prakash's inability to direct a flow of cash to the woman called into question his claims to have access to the networks of power, knowledge, and authority that are so crucial for navigating everyday life in the city. Prakash knew this and thus did not even attempt to convince the woman.

If money works not as the medium of purchase but rather as gifts that are productive and performative of enduring relations and alliances, then what is the significance of cash as the material substance of such gifts? In the context of Mumbai's elections, cash distributions have a third dimension as an index of access to the most crucial kind of urban knowledge: how to navigate the opacities, dangers, and promises of the city's little-understood but palpably real economies. Residents of Mumbai's non-elite neighborhoods—particularly young people who are eager for a foothold in the city's enigmatic economies—are constantly on the lookout for reliable knowledge that might be used in navigating this perilous but crucial dimension of urban life. Cash woos social workers and voters by signaling networks of access to the worlds of opportunity and promise inhering in a city's enigmatic economies. While the eventual landslide victory by Furqan's elderly mother was credited by person after person to the reach and strength of Furqan's networks—connections with local businesspeople, the municipal bureaucracy, the police, various party leaders—discussions of the strength of the campaign almost invariably involved reverent references to Furqan's own business and personal wealth. While few could account for the precise origins of his affluence or with what kind of business he might be involved in, the strength of his money-making networks was evidenced and signified both in the grand, three-story palazzo he had built at the heart of this working-class neighborhood as well as in his liberality with cash: cash for marriages and dowries, cash for school fees, cash for medical bills, cash for home repairs.[40] "He is always very charitable," one area resident explained. "That's how he made a name for himself."

Furqan's financial reputation has lent his authority an almost transcendental quality. "God has been so good to me!," he is rumored to have proclaimed during his 2007 bid for office, when he purportedly carpeted the neighborhood in cash. To explain this relationship between authority and munificence we might turn again to Mauss's discussion of potlatch among the Kwakiutl people of the American Pacific Northwest:

> [A chief] can keep his authority in his tribe, village and family, and maintain his position with the chiefs inside and outside his nation, only if he can prove that he is favorably regarded by the spirits, that he possesses fortune and that he is possessed by it. The only way to demonstrate his fortune is by expending it to the humiliation of others, by putting them "in the shadow of his name."[41]

Notably, Furqan's wealth was popularly ascribed to his translocal sociopolitical networks in much the same way as Mauss describes the display of personal fortune in potlatch—as evidence that he stood in the good graces of the city's inscrutable higher powers: various party leaders, the municipal bureaucracy, the state police and urban economies—that is, of inherently murky sources of material and supernatural authority. It is these networks that are held to have underpinned Furqan's business successes—successes evidenced by his displays of abundant wealth.

That cash is a (visible, material) sign of other kinds of (invisible, immaterial) resources is of course not very surprising. Yet the power of election-season cash in Mumbai is not contained by the exchange value printed on the bills; money, in other words, does not work as Bohannan famously described, to facilitate exchange of dissimilar goods by "standardiz[ing] exchangeability value of every item to a common sale."[42] Social theorists who have sought to complicate classic money theory provide some useful tools of analysis. Parry and Bloch, for instance, have argued that, in and of itself, money does not necessarily transform social relations the way Simmel has argued; such a line of reasoning, they suggest, is more an indication of the Western fetishism of money than of money's own properties—a fetishism that, they charge, has "been taken over somewhat uncritically by the anthropologist."[43] Rather than presuming that money causes and signifies a regime of "free convertibility" that "ushers in a world of moral confusion," Parry and Bloch suggest that "not only does money mean different things in different cultures, but . . . it may mean different things within the same culture."[44] They suggest that we might instead think of money as inhabiting "two related but separate transactional orders": "on the one hand," they write, "transactions concerned with the reproduction of the long-term social or cosmic order; on the other, a sphere of short-term transactions concerned with the arena of individual competition."[45] Indeed, as the accounts in this chapter show, the very same money can simultaneously inhabit these two "orders," with money flowing from Seema to social workers working—gift-like—to produce and reproduce longer-term sociopolitical networks (if not quite a "cosmic order"), while a portion of that very same money often is transferred to rally participants as transactional, wage-like payments.

Yet the third register that election-time cash inhabits—the semiotic— invites us to consider not only the temporality of money exchange but also money's communicative work and multiple meanings. Drawing on his ethnographic fieldwork about the centrality of monetary exchange to cultural life in the Republic of Palau (Micronesia), anthropologist Richard Parmentier identifies the connection between the "work" money does in producing and coordinating exchange transactions as well as the way money works to "demarcate, mediate, and emblemize social status and relations."[46] Parmentier emphasizes the necessary coexistence of both these dimensions of money—on the one hand, "the tendency to put money into play, to let it travel along important transactional paths," and on the other hand the amassing of large sums of wealth for periodic display.[47] At stake here is not simply a reenactment—through conspicuous demonstrations of wealth—of a past history of successful transactional relations, but a performative enactment—through actual real-time exchange—that one is a transactional partner worth engaging. As Parmentier explains, "a man thought to have financial resources who does not commit them when required . . . not only gains a reputation as being stingy, but the money he does hold will be devalued since others will not be eager to be financially involved with him." Cash transfers, in this sense, are at once performance and performative—working simultaneously as a sign of the "sedimented embodiment of accomplished power" and as the "transactional mechanism for its attainment."[48]

The performance/performative valence of election-season money exchange in Mumbai that I have described might usefully be explained in similar terms: while gifts of cash to karyakartas work to establish relations, the money itself is also a sign of "accomplished power." This also helps to account for the apparent paradox that while Furqan's electoral success was frequently attributed to the candidate's wealth, the 2012 campaign itself actually spent relatively little. A social worker who had campaigned for Furqan in the previous election (during which Furqan himself is rumored to have been quite liberal with cash) explained that this time around it was not necessary to actually distribute cash: "Furqan is the master of hype—even he just gives a hundred-rupee note, people run around saying, 'Furqan is distributing so much money!'" For Furqan, rumors of cash were as good as cash itself—the work of the cash being less that of actual exchange than of shoring up reputation. By the same token, for an unknown candidate like Seema, establishing a reputation for being in command of transactional networks of power and authority demanded—as Prakash's disappointed account suggests—that she put her money where her mouth is by producing hard cash itself.

"Everybody Flips"

The transfer of cash—both the giving and receiving—can thus be characterized as simultaneously a performance and a wager. As Prakash explained, "Giving money is a gamble because everybody flips. During a corporator election everyone flips at least once.[49] Sometimes people take money from one candidate and then distribute it in the name of another. But you have to try—if you spend money then maybe people will vote for you." For Seema, the "gamble" involved assessing various social workers' claims to command so many votes, and then to bet her limited resources on the right ones. For the social workers the game is no less risky, since the decision of which candidate to support has far-reaching consequences that last long after election day. Thus, the campaign loyalties of karyakartas remained quite fluid, even up to election day; during a rally three days before polling, I overheard one karyakarta laugh as he chastised his friend (who was at that moment wearing three NCP hats and a scarf), "Just work for one party, okay?," to which the boy responded,

"Party-warty kuch nahi hai! [I have no party!]." In this context, the weeks of campaigning—of sending supporters on rallies and presenting party lists in exchange for cash—must be understood not only as performative relationship-building facilitated by gift-like cash transfers but also as performances of access to networks of knowledge, authority evidenced by the cash itself. In Prakash's case, his inability to direct cash from Seema's campaign to the woman with the thirty-one votes led the woman to doubt that Prakash—and perhaps Seema herself—had sufficiently effective networks. Moreover, Prakash explained, this inability called Seema's "winnability" itself into question; if she was unable to produce the cash in this case, how many other social workers might she have also disappointed? It is quite likely that after this incident Seema lost not only the woman's thirty-one votes but also those of Prakash's entire network: as he himself put it, "Everyone flips at least once." Indeed, for a social worker like Prakash, who would live and do business in the neighborhood no matter who won, betting on the right candidate is of crucial importance. At issue here is not so much the risk of revenge by the victor against areas from which he or she did not win support, but rather the danger of putting someone incompetent, shortsighted, or vindictive at the helm of the ward.[50]

What Money Can Buy

Less than two years into her term as elected corporator, Furqan's ailing mother passed away. A by-election was called, and furious voters—who had so recently demonstrated their overwhelming support for Furqan but were now enraged at what was described as his "disappearance" following his mother's election[51]—handed a landslide victory to an independent candidate, a young man named Santosh whose wife had contested in 2012 on a Samajwadi Party ticket but who himself had recently been expelled from the Samajwadi Party after a video clip circulated through the city in which he appeared in police custody, demonstrating how—using a small machine—he had been "duplicating" credit cards. Santosh (whose wife had outflanked Seema in the 2012 election by a few hundred votes but had still garnered less than a third of the votes cast for Furqan's mother) had reportedly blanketed the neighborhood in cash in 2012; inside sources report that his campaign spent double what Seema's campaign had. When I had expressed to one of his social workers my shock at the scale of this misplaced investment, the man shook his vigorously: "No no! He didn't expect to actually win this time around. But see, before the election, he was known around here only as 'duplicate-note-wala Santosh'; but after the election he became 'election-wala Santosh!'"[52] Santosh used the 2012 election to whitewash his reputation, establishing himself as a generous and reliable benefactor; indeed, following his failed 2012 bid he hammered this point home by taking his entire contingent of campaign workers on a promised ("whether we win or lose") weeklong holiday to Goa. Following another cash-infused bid for office, Santosh won the 2014 by-election in a landslide. A longtime Congress-affiliated social worker summed up Santosh's victory like this:

> For a candidate, the most important things are to have contacts with the police and with the BMC [Brihanmumbai Municipal Corporation]. If you have *approach* with these two, then you get the people. Santosh is a known criminal—duplicate notes, duplicate credit cards, plenty of cash. There's so much corruption that people here want [to elect] someone who has plenty of money to pay the police and the BMC. And Santosh showed he had plenty of money—he gave money to the mains in each lane. See, there are groups that form at the time of elections, and Santosh was there—he was always around, talking to these groups, listening to their problems and making promises and paying them money, lots and lots of money. See, Santosh and his brother are in construction business. Construction is a lucrative industry and is also a great way to whiten money. But see, to succeed as a builder around here you need to keep your houses from getting torn down [by the authorities], and to do that you need contacts.

A local housing contractor named Karim explained to me what this means in practice. When he is preparing start new work, Karim tells me,

> I call up everyone—the corporator, local offices of political parties, the various departments [of the] municipal corporation, the police, everyone. But still, people from the neighborhood can complain—they can take a photograph and complain. When that happens, the BMC will call me and tell me to "manage that person." If that person is serious complainer—if they follow up on the complaint—then I have a problem; in this case the BMC will come and demolish a little bit. Then take their own photograph

proving that they have responded to the complaint with this demolition.[53]
But of course, then the BMC and the police officials are vulnerable, so
they tell me, "Go ahead but do the work fast." Speed is key to the success of
my work.

Being a successful contractor in Mumbai's popular neighborhoods—
where the contradictory and opaque regulatory frameworks governing
infrastructural investment amount to an ever-present vulnerability to
allegations of "illegality"—requires not only that a contractor maintain
networks of connections with local officials but also that in order to "do
the work fast" one must have reliable, on-demand access to all the materials required for construction: cement, sand, water, labor, and cash. These
are materials and resources that are difficult to procure—particularly
sand and water, the securing of which is legally and infrastructurally
complex. To be a successful contractor, in other words, requires elaborate networks of trust, not only in the neighborhood but throughout the
city and beyond.[54] Indeed, Karim tells me that although he calls himself
a "contractor," his role is really more that of a "point man."[55] He doesn't
manage the actual work of building and construction itself, he explains;
rather, he's the one with whom the client makes the "contract." I ask him
what he means by "contract," since, after all, much of the work over which
Karim presides has an ambiguous (sometimes even antagonistic) relation
to formal law and urban policy. In this context of legal contradiction and
vagary, what good is a contract? Karim takes out his smartphone and pulls
up a document. The document specified the details of the work to be
done—the scope of the work, the duration (move-out and move-back-in
dates), the cost—and is signed by both parties as well as a "witness"—
some person that both parties know, trust, and respect—to whom they
can appeal in case of any eventual dispute. Because of the legally ambiguous nature of the work, Karim tells me in impeccable English, "We don't
have it validated by courts or anything." For this reason, "reputation" and
"guarantee" are very important. "Other contractors, if there's a dispute,
maybe they run off with the deposit or something. But with me I've never
had a dispute. I keep goodwill with everyone." Maintaining "goodwill,"
Karim explains, is the essence of the work of being a "point man." In the
case of our contractor-turned-corporator Santosh, all of which is to say,
the imperviousness of his houses to the destructive forces of "complaint"

demonstrated the strength and reliability of his networks, signaling to area social workers and voters that Santosh might indeed be a very good person to represent them in the municipal corporation.

Cash as Infrastructure of Publicity

This chapter has demonstrated how cash is enlisted in three interrelated kinds of election-season work. First, money plays a rather conventional role in constituting a scale of value that enables commensuration and exchange—paying for things like flags or police permissions, or the labor of flag-bearing under the midday sun. Second, money produces enduring sociopolitical relations; gifts of cash work performatively—much like any other gifted good—producing relations of debt, reciprocity and trust. And third, cash performs semiotic work, signaling access to powerful networks of knowledge, resources, and authority. Election-season cash simultaneously inhabits these three registers: since it is common knowledge that many election-rally participants are paid for their participation, the size of the crowd indicates—among other things—the strength of the collective investment in putting on a good show. And at the same time, in its crowd-assembling modality, cash works as the crowd-show's infrastructure.

What does it mean to characterize cash as infrastructure? In a historical account of the word *infrastructure*—its introduction and absorption into the English language—anthropologist Ashley Carse points to the two-part contemporary meaning of infrastructure suggested in the word's *Oxford English Dictionary* definition. On the one hand, infrastructure is "a collective term for the subordinate parts of an undertaking." Something's infrastructure is its "substructure" or "foundation." And at the same time, "infrastructure" refers to particular phenomena in themselves: "the permanent installations forming a basis for military operations, as airfields, naval bases, training establishments, etc."[56] In the former part of the definition, infrastructure can be distinguished from concepts like "system" or "network" insofar as infrastructure (literally "that which is below a structure") explicitly signals a hierarchical relationship: an infrastructure is subordinate—spatially beneath or temporally prior—to whatever "undertaking" it facilitates. And at the same time, the word *infrastructure* entered English at a particular historical moment in order to describe something historically specific and concrete: NATO's international military program. Carse cites NATO's 1949 general secretary's clarification of the term's meaning in the context of 1949 Common Infrastructure Program:

> [infrastructure] has been adopted by NATO as a generic term to denote all those fixed installations which are necessary for the effective deployment and operations of modern armed forces, for example airfields, signal communications, military headquarters, fuel tanks and pipelines, radar warning and navigation aid stations, port installations and so forth.[57]

By conceptually holding together a wide variety of material phenomena previously imagined as distinct (say, pipelines and airfields), the concept of "infrastructure" enabled the conjuring into being of something entirely new: a "common" international military program. Carse points out how its imprecision and dual valence initially led to suspicion of the word and to derisive allegations of conceptual "promiscuity."[58] And yet the usefulness of "infrastructure" inheres precisely in the concept's promiscuousness. In Mumbai, we have seen how money is at once substructural to the undertaking of producing and shoring up the social relations that its circulation facilitates, while also (and necessarily) having a concrete material form that indexes historical relations; it is the skillful wielding of money's multiple valences that can bring into being new social relations and forms. And at the same time the dangers of semiotic slippage among the various registers leads to constant suspicion, rendering money—both cash and concept—inescapably subject to allegations of promiscuity.

I asked a longtime political party worker named Rakesh to explain to me the significance of cash-infused crowds at election rallies: "If everyone here knows that everyone else is paid," I asked, "then what's the purpose of the crowd? Everyone knows it's just a lot of natak [acting]!" "People need to see a crowd; they need to know how much public you have," Rakesh answered—using the English-origin word *public*. I pressed: "But . . . everyone knows you're paying the public!" Rakesh shrugged, "People don't mind that the public is paid. The public will come for money also, there's no shame in this. You look powerful if you can manage such a huge public! You show you're wealthy and strong by showing you can get the public." So, I asked, if the hordes are hired, then is the size of a crowd simply a proxy for the wealth of its organizers? Rakesh laughed and demurred: money alone can't gather a crowd. Rather, he explained that "to get the public, people must believe that you can get work done." He used the word *believe*. The crowd, in other words, indexes the scope and scale of public belief in a candidate's "capacity" and willingness to "get work done." Ethnographic attention to cash flows in election-season Mumbai—as well as to the moralizing talk that attend such flows—reveals that elitist readings of election-season cash as the obviating of substantive public discussion on matters of shared concern by a myopic, cash-poor electorate concerned "only with their handout" are misplaced.[59] Rather, cash is a crucial component of Mumbai's infrastructure of social relationality—a material-discursive technology whose circulation brings into being a myriad of possible and actual publics.

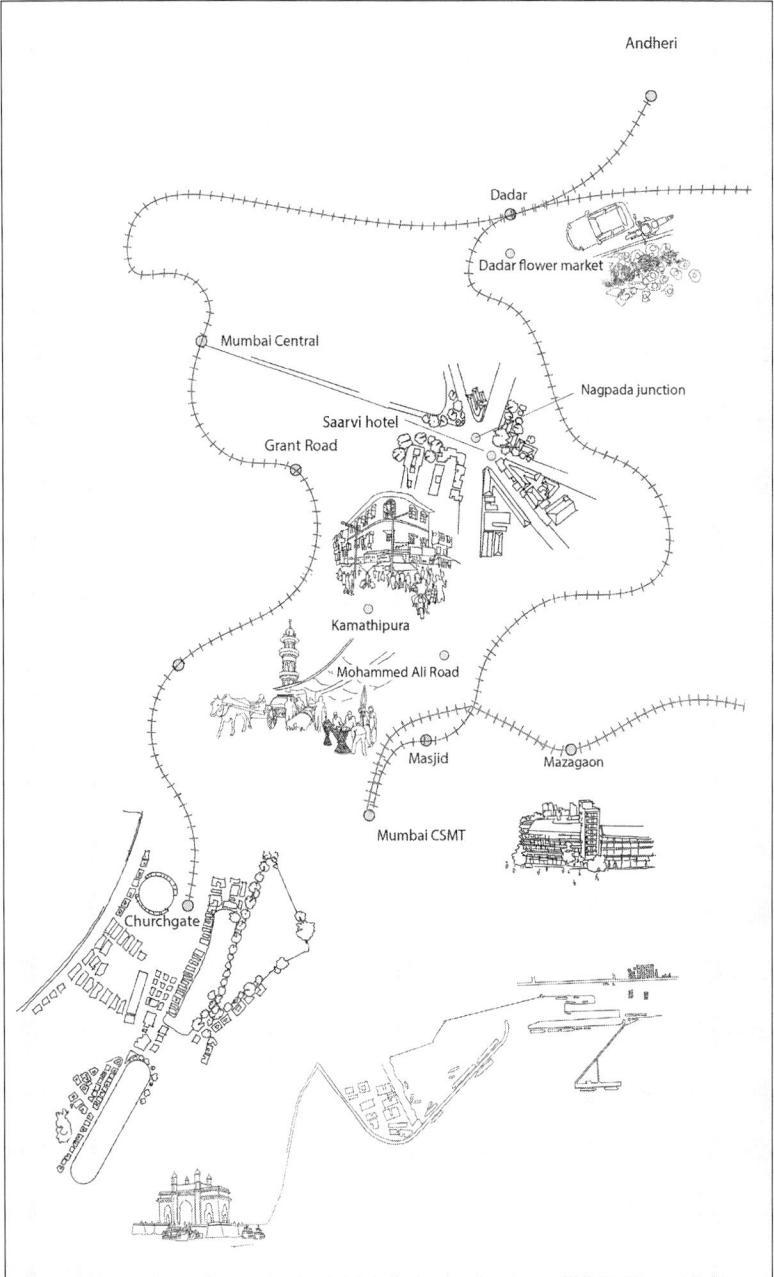

Map 3. Locations of places mentioned in chapters 2 and 3 in relation to proximate railway stations. See Map 1 for location of these stations within the city.

Interlude II

South Bombay

During the 2017 election season I trained research attention on an area of the city very different from the peripheral—so-called "slum"—neighborhood from which Seema had contested in 2012 (the subject of chapter 1). On the suggestion and invitation of the candidate upon whose (ultimately successful) 2017 campaign I focused, a man named Sayeed Rizwan, I headed to an area I'll call Badlapur,[1] situated in the inner-city districts generally known as "South Bombay." I had met Sayeed for the first time in 2012, in the aftermath of his successful electoral bid to the municipal corporation, where he represented a district in the eastern suburbs of Gowandi with which I was intimately familiar from my earlier research about municipal water. Sayeed was elected in 2012 from an area not far from the one from which Seema (whose bid for office was the subject of chapter 1) had been displaced by a change in the gender and caste reservation for that district seat. While I had not followed Sayeed's 2012 bid for office in Seema's former district in the suburban slums (I had spent that election season following Seema's campaign), I had watched Sayeed's political career quite closely over the following years—especially because, during his tenure in Gowandi, Sayeed had taken a keen interest in the area's hydraulic landscape. His tenure as corporator coincided with the implementation of some large-scale infrastructural interventions and water-related projects in the area that I had long been following, and by the time the 2017 election season rolled around he had grown accustomed to my general hanging about and constant questions.[2]

I had mixed feelings about Sayeed's invitation to follow his 2017 election campaign in South Bombay. Anchored by the arterial Mohammed Ali Road stretching eastward from Mumbai Central railway station toward the JJ Flyover, the area encompassing Dongri, Nagpada, Madanpura, Mazagaon, Pydonie, and Bhendi Bazaar is the historic home of Mumbai's Hindu, Muslim, Parsi, and Jewish communities comprising the city's mercantile classes, as well as to the bustling bazaars and wholesale markets comprising the city's erstwhile colonial-era "native town"—situated just north of the fortified area where the British Raj's offices and officers were clustered (see Map 3). Historians have written about the extraordinarily cosmopolitan character of these market districts, which have been the subject of much scholarly attention, both historical and anthropological.[3] And yet notwithstanding the neighborhood's storied cosmopolitanism, in recent decades the neighborhoods in and around present-day Mohammed Ali Road tend to be characterized in both popular and scholarly discourses as an insular space: as a "Muslim ghetto."[4] The area is not infrequently described in an offhand (and often disparaging way) as "mini-Pakistan," even by Mumbaikars professing not to harbor Islamophobic predilections.[5] In this context, political subjectivity in Bombay's "Muslim heartland" is generally presumed to be given by religion and by religious identity.

Although I began the 2017 election season without any previous ethnographic experience in South Bombay, the area felt familiar, not least because so much Hindi cinema (especially that of the gangland genre) is set and filmed in and around the neighborhood. I had long been a regular visitor to the markets and bazaars in and around Mohammed Ali Road, hunting for old film posters, a new bicycle, or a coconut scraper. During the monsoon season of 2015, I had joined a Sunday-morning "Urdu for Hindi Speakers" course at Anjuman-e-Islam's Akbar Peerbhoy College, and spent soggy Sunday afternoons wandering the muddy lanes and savoring paya soup at the storied kebab spot, Sarvi—as famous for its succulent kebabs and perfect paya as for the stories and secrets that infused the atmosphere of the fabled favorite haunt of some of Mumbai's saltier mafia dons of yore. In this context, I wondered whether engaging Badlapur as a research site would risk presuming the categories it professes to research: "Muslim politics," for instance. And yet for these same reasons, researching in Mumbai's "Muslim heartland" seemed to present an important opportunity to probe these same relations—between concepts and concrete, words and worlds, streets and screens.

When the Muslim-identitarian All India Majlis-e-Ittehadul Muslimeen (AIMIM) party announced in 2017 that it would be fielding candidates in the Mumbai elections for the first time (contesting nearly a third of the 227 races), Shahid Latiq, editor of the Urdu daily *Inquilaab,* wrote (echoing a common refrain) that "there is lot of confusion among the Muslim voters with all secular parties contesting against each other."[6] Latiq's diagnosis of "confusion" pointed to the widely held presumption in Mumbai that the political lives of Muslim Mumbaikars are determined by religion—a puzzling presumption which research (my own included) readily reveals as unsubstantiated. For instance, the eastern suburbs where Seema had sought election five years earlier was also a Muslim-majority area. And yet, as demonstrated in chapter 1, while religious leaders and associational ties certainly played prominent roles in that electoral campaign, the relational work that the authority of religious leaders accomplished (or sought to accomplish) was of a piece with that of myriad other, equally prominent election-season actors: caste association leaders, chit fund managers, neighborhood plumbers, prominent businesspeople, schoolteachers, building contractors, and so on. In this context, the interesting question is not whether religious institutions and individual leaders play a role in election campaigning (obviously they did); rather, the question concerned precisely what role religious authority did (and didn't) play.

Following a change in the gender and caste reservation of Sayeed's incumbent district in Gowandi (a low-income neighborhood not far from Seema's), the Samajwadi Party had offered Sayeed the party ticket to contest from Badlapur—the neighborhood where he was born and brought up but where he was largely unknown as a politician. And yet, while Sayeed may have been a political newcomer to the area, South Bombay politics were not at all unknown to him; he had lived in the neighborhood his entire life. Sayeed's personal history provides insight not only into his own political trajectory but into that of Muslim Mumbai more generally.

While both Sayeed's parents are Muslims from Maharashtra, their caste, class, and linguistic backgrounds could not have been more different. His mother hails from the Dakhni-speaking region of Sawantwadi, some five hundred kilometers south of Badlapur, near the Goan border. They're "Goan Maharashtrian," Sayeed told me over breakfast in January 2017.[7] His mother's mother (his Nani) grew up "in the village," where she married twice: her first husband was a wealthy merchant of the Barelvi community—a Sunni revivalist sect of South Asian origin that marries Sufi devotionalism with adherence to Sharia. Nani's husband was "educated," Sayeed tells me, both formally as well as "culturally." He too had Sawantwadi roots, but his businesses were based in Bombay, which is where Nani moved after marriage. Sayeed's mother was one of two daughters from that first marriage, and in line with the family's commitment to education, his mother was sent to Bombay's highly reputed Urdu-medium Anjuman-e-Islam school (not far from where I studied Urdu during the 2015 rains). Sayeed never met Nani's first husband (Sayeed's Nana), because he died young. But more importantly—insofar as Sayeed's trajectory was concerned—Nana died without any sons, leaving Sayeed's Nani to manage the family business and assets together with her daughters. In this context, Nani's husband's family (her in-laws), who were not as successful as Nani's husband had been (and perhaps always a little jealous of their brother's business acumen), grew ambitious, wanting to inherit their late brother's assets—especially the pottery shop in Null Bazaar. For this reason, Sayeed tells me, Nani's late husband's brother fabricated an allegation against her, accusing her of having had an affair with a local doctor. So, Sayeed tells me, Nani "approached a relative of her husband and had a quick marriage, overnight. She didn't tell anyone. She became the fourth wife."

Nani managed the pottery shop in Null Bazaar on her own, "in a burkha," Sayeed tells me, adding that "she was a very strong woman." Nani began searching for a husband for Sayeed's mother, "a boy who they could bring into their own household. There were no men in the house," Sayeed explained, so they needed an inmarriage. They found a suitable boy whose family was willing to settle him in his wife's household, but he was from a "different community," from the region of Mahabaleshwar, in the Western Ghats. Nani knew the boy's uncle, who had a vegetable vending shop nearby her pottery shop in Null Bazaar; she had met the boy once when he was visiting from the village. "He was a village boy," Sayeed tells me, "poor, but educated." And the man who would become Sayeed's father was Maharashtrian; he spoke not Urdu but Marathi.

The marriage was arranged, and the Marathi-speaking village boy moved to Bombay, taking up residence in Nani's household. His new family changed his Maharashtrian-sounding name to something more "identifiably Muslim"—which from his Urdu-speaking family's perspective, as Sayeed explained, meant Muslim of the North Indian, Urdu-speaking variety. "They forced my father to change his name and his language as well; they forced him to speak Urdu." Sayeed would eventually become one of six brothers, and when it came time for their marriages, Sayeed's father wanted his sons to marry girls from Mahabaleshwar, "so that they could speak Marathi." But Nani prohibited it (Nani was "very dominating," he repeats). "She was cultivating a North Indian Muslim identity," Sayeed explains, "so she insisted, 'Urdu Urdu Urdu.'"

In Sayeed's early childhood, his mother gave private Urdu lessons from their home in Badlapur. When Sayeed was six, his mother fell ill and spent the next decade in and out of the hospital. "She stopped cooking" Sayeed remembers, "so I was virtually adopted by my neighbors." These neighbors belonged to North Indian families of Sheikhs and Quereshis— Urdu-speaking Muslims with family businesses in goat butchering. "I was raised in that community," Sayeed tells me, adding that now, here in Badlapur, "they're my biggest supporters." Sayeed himself eventually went on to marry an Urdu-educated Bombay girl. His father paid a fine to their jamaat (religious community) in Mahabaleshwar, Sayeed tells me, because his sons all married outside the community.

Notwithstanding Nani's preoccupation with the refined piety of learned Urdu, Sayeed went to an English-medium school, where he recalls having been powerfully influenced by his English-speaking mentors and teachers as well as by the English-speaking "Khoja lady" who lived above the school and tutored him in English in the afternoons. "The Khojas are philanthropic people," Sayeed tells me, adding that he was "very influenced by them." Only one of the six brothers was sent to an Urdu-medium school: "Nani decided at least one son should be properly Urdu educated," Sayeed explains. But when this Urdu-educated brother enrolled in an English-medium college, "he couldn't keep up because he'd done his maths and sciences in Urdu and was unprepared for the language switch." Sayeed, on the other hand, reached college fluent in English and well prepared. He recalls it was in college that he discovered his real passion: "I love to organize things!" He described for me organizing all sorts of events for his college-going peers, including fashion shows and proms, adding, "I was never the performer; I was the organizer." I ask him to say more, and he pauses, becoming reflective and adding: "I wanted to create. I wanted to give opportunities to people, to create an environment where people could perform." He emphasizes the word *perform*.

Sayeed's interest in politics came much later, in his final year of college, following the 1992–93 Hindu–Muslim riots in Bombay. The immediate impetus of the violence was the destruction on December 6, 1992, of the Babri Masjid in the North Indian town of Ayodhya by a 150,000-strong crowd of kar sevaks (volunteers), affiliated with right-wing Hindu organizations comprising the Sangh Parivar (association of groups comprising the Hindutva "family") who had crashed thorough police barricades and razed the sixteenth-century mosque.[8] The kar sevaks had traveled to Ayodhya from all corners of India to attend a political rally at the contested site, which had been declared by Hindu nationalist outfits to have been the birthplace of the mythical god-king Ram. In the aftermath of the destruction, Muslim Indians all over the country had poured into city streets in protest. In Bombay, those protests became sites of violent clashes with city authorities when police sought to disperse the assembled protesters using lethal force, opening fire on crowds of Muslim demonstrators and arresting people in droves. Within a few days of the demolition of the Babri Masjid, nearly two hundred people (mostly Muslims) had been killed in the Bombay violence. Tensions increased a few days later when Shiv Sena leader Bal Thackeray claimed personal credit for the destruction of the Babri Masjid—claiming (falsely) that the demolition had been led by Shiv Sena "storm troopers" who had been specially trained and dispatched to Ayodhya for that purpose.[9] Over the following weeks, the Shiv Sena, which had recently suffered a humiliating defeat to the Congress Party in the municipal corporation election, seized the opportunity to consolidate their effective control over city space and institutions by channeling the affective energies of the moment—of Hindu assertion and Muslim fear—into public displays of sovereign authority. In his ethnographic account of the Mumbai riots, Thomas Blom Hansen describes what transpired in Bombay that December:

> While the police shot at and arrested Muslim demonstrators, Shiv Sena was allowed to conduct large public celebrations of the demolition, even to

construct a makeshift hutatma (martyrs) column in the Marathi-speaking area of Dadar listing the names of Hindus killed in the December 1992 riots. Shiv Sena also began the so-called maha aartis, mass prayers performed in front of temples as a show of strength against Muslims as well as a way to boost confidence among Hindus. The maha aartis were clearly political demonstrations, as Hinduism has no such tradition of public mass prayer; it was a symbolic response to the Muslims' Friday prayer, regarded by many Hindus as a public show of strength. Accompanied by extensive press coverage, and under the protection of police and army personnel, Shiv Sena leader Pramod Nawalkar led the first maha aarti on December 11, a Friday, at a time coinciding with the Muslims' Friday prayer throughout the city. By the end of December the Shiv Sena leadership decided to launch a regular campaign, and hundreds of maha aartis were performed all over the city well into January 1993.[10]

It was in this general climate that a month after the onset of the December violence, on January 8, 1993, the sporadic violence erupted into a concerted effort led by the Shiv Sena to obliterate Muslim Bombay. Following the gruesome arson-related murder of a working-class Hindu family in the northern suburb of Jogeshwari, groups of men "rampaged the city, systematically looting and burning Muslim shops, houses and businesses" which had been marked for that purpose using electoral data from civic offices.[11] Sayeed recalled how, when he was very young, their family maid—a Hindu Maharashtrian who stayed in the adjacent building—"used to dress me up as Ganesh during festivals." He recalls that his parents were "happy about it; they thought it was cultural." During the riots however, this easy, neighborly coexistence became a source of fear; from the windows of their second-floor home, Sayeed recalled watching police firing bullets into buildings. Amid the violence (which killed an estimated eight hundred people over the month of January), 150,000 Muslims fled the city while another 100,000 huddled in quickly erected refugee camps set up in South Bombay—an area that, due to the Muslim-majority character, was (somewhat inaccurately) hoped to be something of a safe haven.[12]

Unlike earlier episodes of communal violence in Bombay, which had mostly affected lower-income areas of the city (its popular neighborhoods and "slums"), the 1992–93 riots were unprecedented insofar as they implicated the city's upwardly mobile middle classes—systematically targeting

Muslim professionals and business families, and thereby dashing the hopes and dreams of escaping stigmatization through upward mobility that Muslim elites' successes (and social acceptance) had signified to the struggling classes. It was in this context—of terror, humiliation, and rage—that, in March 1993, a group of people with ties to Bombay's underworld (specifically, to Nagpada-born mob boss Dawood Ibrahim, whose character and life history was recently made famous by Netflix's adaptation of Vikram Chandra's novel *Sacred Games*) carried out a series of citywide bombings, targeting transit hubs and other crowded areas, killing scores of civilians. The blasts were widely interpreted by popular media as retributive—a "Don't mess with us" message from Muslim Bombay.[13] As a Nagpada schoolteacher told Hansen in 1993:

> We all felt horrible during those four months . . . all over you would hear these derogatory remarks about Muslims, you felt the hostility all over, in the trains, in shops, in my school. I recall riding on a train when a group of Hindu women spotted me and started talking quietly. One said "We Hindu women should also do something. Look at that Muslim woman there— one should throw her off the train." . . . All this stopped after the bomb blasts—not because they accepted us, but because they feared us.[14]

Before the riots, only one of Sayeed's college friends had been interested in politics—a "political radical," Sayeed explained, "but not radical about religion; he was a leftist." All that changed in 1993, when in the aftermath of the bomb blasts the Bombay police began rounding up prominent Muslim leaders, arresting them under the Terrorist and Disruptive Activities (Prevention) Act (TADA). "They rounded up all the wealthy Muslims in the city after the blasts," Sayeed recalls, people such as Abu Asmi Asmi,[15] a wealthy South Bombay businessman—president of the Maharashtra branch of the Samajwadi Party since 1995—whose travel agency was accused (and eventually cleared) of having helped those responsible for the 1993 bomb blasts to flee the country. "I liked Asmi," Sayeed tells me, "He was philanthropic; he gave money for our college functions, things like that. He wasn't into politics; he was just a businessman." Furious at what seemed an arbitrary, politically motivated targeting of businesspeople like Asmi, Sayeed and his college friends joined their first political protest. "There had been so much violence during the riots," Sayeed recalled, "and they were only rounding up Muslims. We were really angry." After the riots and the blasts, Sayeed channeled his newly awakened political sensibility, volunteering for the newly constituted Ulema Council, a nominally independent body of Muslim theologians formed under the leadership of some of South Bombay's more prominent and respected maulanas (Islamic scholars). The council's mission was to constitute a united body that might represent through "non-political" channels—that is, non-elected channels, and especially non–Congress Party ones.[16]

Now . . . Muslims in Bombay do not (and never have) constituted anything like a monolithic "community"—whatever Islamic fundamentalists, Hindutva organizations, and some political strategists might like to believe (and want others to believe). Like Sayeed, Muslims in Bombay hail from different regions of the Indian subcontinent and the Indian Ocean region and ascribe tremendous value to these regional and linguistic identities. Regional and linguistic groups are further divided by sect and subsect—Deobandis, Barelvis, Wahabis, Bohras, Khojas, Elae Hadis, Ismailis, and Memons—each having its own priesthood committed to the idea that their own sect is the most faithful to the tenets of Islam. Bombay Muslims are also extremely diverse in caste and class, with these differences intersecting in complex ways with already mentioned regional, linguistic, and sectarian identities. Overlaid onto this already staggering complexity is partisan allegiance, with parties and candidates negotiating and forging constantly shifting alliances with local elites (clergy, caste associations, business families), all while voters regularly ignore the advice of local leaders—who anyway rarely agree on who or what to support.[17]

Indeed, notwithstanding the widely held belief—cultivated by parties and fueled by the media—that Muslim Mumbaikars vote their religion as a bloc, this is simply not the case; sociologically and historically speaking, Bombay Muslims have had very little in common outside their shared claim to be adherents of Islam and their geographic concentration in the city. And yet notwithstanding this staggering diversity, during the 1992–93 Bombay riots, Muslims were discursively framed and targeted as a monolith—a framing that was of a piece with national-level "iconography" that surrounded the Sangh Parivar's Ram Janmabhoomi ("birthplace of Ram") campaign to "repossess," in the words of a BJP white

paper published in the aftermath of the demolition, "the birthplace of
Sri Rama."[18] Reflecting on the "perplexing" character of the campaign's
demonization of a relatively poor religious minority, historian Richard
Davis describes how the consolidation of Hindu nationalist political
agenda hinged upon the "mythologization" of a monolithic Islamic adver-
sary: "Framing Muslim identity around a history of medieval conquest
and iconoclasm embodied in the person of Mughal rulers [such as Babar,
the sixteenth-century patron of the Babri Majid], rather than the social
state of contemporary Muslims, rendered the Indian Muslim community much more of a threat."[19] The demonization of contemporary Muslim Indians as an uninterrupted lineage of this "occupying Other," Davis
demonstrates, was a crucial step in consolidating a Hindu nationalist
political agenda.[20]

Back in Bombay, it was in this context of the broader discursive framing and iconography of Indian Islam as a monolithic threat requiring
"forceful subordination"[21] that, in the aftermath of the violence, the Ulema
Council was constituted (where Sayeed cut his political teeth)—an attempt
by some members of Bombay's clergy to establish a common platform
from which to speak on behalf of the city's Muslims. The Ulema Council,
then as now, sought to ground its authority to represent the "Muslim
community" not through the formal institutions of electoral politics but
rather in the varied and conflicting expertise of its myriad religious leaders. The council was of a piece with a broader shift in Muslim Bombay's
political landscape in the aftermath of the riots, which saw the prolifera-
tion of explicitly "non-political" bodies pursuing back channels by which
to advance collective claims; as one prominent journalist describes, Muslim leaders and organizations (such as the Ulema Council or the Bombay
Aman [Peace] Committee) took to "holding press conferences (given scant
attention by the English media), and going in delegations to ministers,"
acting (with somewhat unclear mandate) as "brokers" between Bombay
Muslims and the offices and officers of the state.[22]

Sayeed's background and personal history made him a valuable asset
to the Ulema Council's efforts to knit together a united constituency with
a singular Muslim voice: "I grew up in a really diverse environment,"
Sayeed recalled, had close contacts in a wide variety of social circles, and
"was able to use those connections as part of the Ulema Council." His
ease with difference and general affability landed him a job managing a

prominent and politically connected local eating establishment owned by a relative of Abu Asim Asmi, the travel agent whose arrest following the 1993 riots had prompted the young Sayeed to pay attention to local politics and had jump-started his political career.

In college, Sayeed had focused on computers rather than management. "All my friends went in for management," he told me, "but I didn't want to. I said to myself: 'Where will management take me? What will I learn that I don't already know?'" His real dream was to start an advertising agency, he tells me, but the industry wasn't well developed, which is why he "chose computers." He managed the restaurant for a few years until he had put away enough money to open his own business: a computer training company, which eventually morphed into a design shop. "I was fond of creating logos," he recalls, repeating "I love to create." Eventually, Sayeed's design work outstripped computer training, and by 2002 he finally decided to open a proper public relations firm: "PR came naturally to me," he tells me. By 2007, the young marketing professional's growing reputation earned him his first (and last) "political account," managing the (ultimately unsuccessful) electoral bid of a man named Junaid Khan—a well-known area social worker, educationalist, and passionate advocate of Urdu language and literacy who would become one of my main interlocutors during Sayeed's 2017 electoral campaign. Junaid had fought the 2007 Mumbai municipal election on a ticket of the Samajwadi Party, a party with roots in the North Indian state of Uttar Pradesh, but which had been gaining ground among Mumbai Muslims under the leadership of Abu Asim Asmi. Junaid too grew up in Nagpada, not far from where he currently lives, and where he runs a bustling cosmetics shop that keeps his family comfortable. Junaid is fluent in English but prefers to speak in Urdu; promoting Urdu language, education, and literature is his true calling and life's work. Indeed, while his income comes from cosmetics, he spends most of his time organizing Urdu literature and poetry festivals and liaising with area educational institutions to support Urdu literacy in local schools and colleges. Junaid prefers to stay out of the direct political limelight, but he hails from a politically active family; his father and brother had each, on separate occasions, contested (unsuccessfully) the civic polls. And, as already mentioned, he too had once thrown his hat in the ring, which is how he had met Sayeed.[23] This time around, however, during the 2017 election, the tables were turned, and Junaid would become Sayeed's right-hand man and principal Urdu orator.

Before we end our conversation, I ask what Sayeed what he likes about PR. He pauses, then says: "See, I'm like a film director who enjoys watching his own movies. If there's some person or subject that deserves the limelight but can't get the exposure . . . if I can support that person to achieve their goals . . . I like that. I create the stage," Sayeed smiles, the theatrical language pleasing him: "the stage for worthy ideas and people."[24]

2

Natak

"The Size of the Public Will Be the Size of the Image"

ناٹك नाटक nāṭak, s.m.—dancing; acting; a play, drama, comedy.
ناٹيه नाट्य nāṭya, s.m. The science or art of dancing, or acting; scenic art;
the union of song, pantomime, dance, and instrumental music.

—Platts, *A Dictionary of Urdu, Classical Hindi, and English* (1884)

There is no natya without rasa [juice/flavor/pleasure]. . . . Just as when
various condiments and sauces and herbs and other materials are mixed,
a taste is experienced. . . . Sensitive spectators, after enjoying the various
emotions expressed by the actors through words, gestures, and feelings,
feel pleasure. This feeling by the spectators is here explained as the rasas
of natya.

—Bharatamuni, *The Natyashastra,* ca. 600 B.C.E.

On February 21, 2017, Mumbai voters went back to the polls to elect
the 227 municipal councilors who would preside for the next five
years over the city's annual budget, now around 37,000 crore rupees[1]—by
then the largest budget of any Indian city. On the final day of campaigning, all of the city's major parties organized large-scale rallies, assembling
thousands of flag-bearers to accompany candidates on all-day parades
along city streets. Onlookers gathered in groups along footpaths, assessing the relative size and strength of each party's rally, speculating and
moralizing about the role that cash might have played in producing these
celebratory spectacles. I spoke with a group of men standing outside their
small print shop: "What is it that you are looking for when you watch
these parades?" I asked (in Hindi): "What do the rallies mean?" One man

laughed, waved his hand dismissively: "Koi matlab nahi hai! [There is no meaning at all!].[2] All these people, they're paid to be here. Bas, natak hai," he concluded: It's only theater. I pressed: "Okay . . . but even if people are paid to join the procession and carry the flags, you people are still out here on the street watching the show. So if the rally has no meaning, then what are you looking at?" He paused to consider the question, then answered: "See, it's like an advertisement." Seeming pleased with the word, he continued: "The rally is an advertisement of the size of your public." He was speaking in Hindi but used the English-origin words *advertisement* and *public*. He added: "You need to advertise, see, because no ad, no sale." The man standing next to him bobbed his head in agreement and added: "itna public utna image rahega"—the size of the public will be the size of the image.

This chapter is about natak, and about how theatricality in Mumbai's political life is perceived, discussed, and evaluated. At first, the men at the print shop describe the rally as "meaningless" (koi matlab nahi), telling me that it is "only natak." This evaluation suggests a normative under-standing of a meaningful political rally, that is, not a dramatization but rather a "real" mass gathering—whatever that might be. Yet in the next breath, the same man pulls an about-face and suggests that it is precisely in its theatrical character that the rally is compelling or convincing at all—a sign of the organizer's ability to marshal the myriad resources nec-essary to assemble a "public" and thereby produce a compelling "image" that works (as the man puts it) "like an advertisement." So: when is natak accepted and appreciated as an enjoyable, compelling, indeed necessary ("you need to advertise") aspect of political life, and when is political theater "only natak"—a disdainful dismissal of something as theatrical which ought not to be (or perhaps is pretending not to be)? Moreover, what is to be made of these competing moral evaluations of natak, and of the fact that in this little encounter at the print shop, the very same situation is subject to these two competing moral evaluations of natak simultaneously, and by the very same people?

The Hindi/Urdu/Marathi word natak does not translate easily—notwithstanding its commonplace English gloss as "theater," "drama," or "acting."[3] The word's valences are evident, however, in the theatrical tra-ditions that it is commonly used to describe: natak is used in Mumbai in reference to a wide variety of performance genres. Natak could refer to a play, a comedy routine, or a dance program, as well as to the content of some such performance—to the acting, dancing, or storytelling itself, which is also described as natak. A Mumbaikar wanting to attend a play, for instance, might suggest to a friend in Marathi: Apun sandyakali natkala jauya ka?—Shall we go for a natak this evening?; or in Hindi: Sham ko ek natak dekne jayenge?—shall we go this evening to see a natak? This straightforwardly descriptive sense of natak as a discrete show or performance event carries no moral valence; this is "unmarked natak," which merely calls a play a play. However, when natak is used (as it often is) while talking about "offstage" domains of social and political life (i.e., domains of life that do not explicitly signal themselves as natak), the word tends to take on a distinctly pejorative sense: the man at the print shop tells me that the rally is "only natak"—lest I be deceived and think I was witnessing something else.

An allegation of natak-as-deceit is an assertion that some show (its organizers or participants or both) is seeking to mobilize the emotive power and aesthetic charge of theater (its rasa) while attempting to hide the (literal or figurative) stage.[4] Moralizing talk about who is or isn't "doing natak" pervades political discourse in Mumbai: in Interlude I, for instance, rumors of Seema's virtuosity in "complaint natak" posed a serious enough threat to her electoral viability that a party higher-up requested a character-attesting press statement from me in an effort to counter the negative effects of such allegations. During election season in Mumbai, a great deal of discussion about various candidates and their campaigns is concerned precisely with the delicate work of sorting these different varieties of natak—distinguishing, that is, political theater (overt, unmarked natak that demands no denouncement) from "only natak," which professes or pretends to be otherwise.

"Yeh Public Hai, Public!": "This Is the Public! The Public!"

In order to make sense of this dual register of natak (and before getting into some ethnography), it will be helpful to first attend to the somewhat curious use of the word *public* in Mumbai, where, as the print shop man's words attest ("the size of the public will be the size of the image"), *public* describes crowds of people that gather for political events: things like protest marches, roadblocks, election rallies, and so on. At one level, this man's words seem to echo those of Rakesh at the conclusion of the previous chapter: "People need to see a crowd; they need to see how much public you have." And yet while for Rakesh the embodied crowd itself is the public—assembled in a particular place and space by means of the infrastructural mediations of cash—the print shop man's characterization of the public not only as a materialized crowd itself but more importantly as something that yields an "image" warrants further consideration. What might it mean to evaluate a public as an image?

In considering this notion of public-as-image, it is instructive to turn to another infrastructure of circulation by means of which images and imaginings of the crowd-public are produced and set in motion: Mumbai's world-famous—and world's largest—film industry, Bollywood.

Yeh jo public hai, ye sab jaanti hai; public hai

This public here, it knows everything; it's the public

These are the opening lyrics of film-song superhit "Yeh Jo Public Hai" (This public here), featuring in Manmohan Desai's 1974 Bollywood blockbuster *Roti* (*Bread*). The scene opens with the film's hero (played by silver-screen heartthrob Rajesh Khanna) whispering into the ear of a young woman (played by Bollywood beauty Mumtaz Askari), whose shocked expression gestures toward the urgency in what she has just heard (Figure 6). The scene cuts to the cunning face of the presumed subject of the whisper—the wink-eyed neta (politician)—before Mumtaz dashes across the street and into an open-fronted furniture store where she repeats the whisper into the ear of a seated trader (Figure 7). She pauses by a warehouse-like space to beckon women down from a balcony before reaching the open street, where all the people she has just summoned gather into a crowd—just in time for the arrival onto the scene of our sly-faced neta, who is intercepted at the intersection by our hero, Khanna. Khanna greets the neta with a gently derisive greeting, "Ai babu!" (Hey clerk!), and then gestures toward the assembled crowd, saying: "Yeh public hai, public!" (This is the public! The public!) (Figure 8).

Yeh jo public hai, ye sab jaanti hai, public hai

This public here, it knows everything; it's the public

A man boasting a thick mop of black hair leads a white donkey onto the scene (our neta's would-be steed), only to find himself abruptly de-wigged before the crowd of onlookers by the all-knowing Khanna, who points first to the wig and then gives a condescending pat to the man's naked scalp while singing:

> Aji andar kya hai, aji bahar kya hai
> Ye sab kuchh pehchaanti hai
>
> What's [hidden] underneath, what's [visible] outside
> [The public] recognizes everything

An open-top jeep rolls up carrying a handsome film actor, who is soon swarmed by adoring fans waving rupee notes for signing (Figure 9). A smiling Khanna looks on, cautioning the smug-faced star:

> Ye chaahe to sar pe bitha le chaahe phenk de niche
> Pahale ye pichhe bhaage phir bhaago isake pichhe
>
> If it wants to, it will lift you up [on its head], or will cast you down;
> At first [the public] will run after you, but then you will be running after it

Tired of the crowd, the actor retreats behind a wrought-iron gate. While the star shuts out his adoring, disappointed fans, Khanna cautions:

> Arre dil tute to, arre ye ruthe to . . .
> Tauba kaha phir maanati hai
>
> If you break its heart and if you make them cry
> Then there will be no forgiveness

Cut to Khanna and Mumtaz walking alongside the donkey-mounted neta at the head of the procession as it proceeds over a bridge bearing graffiti enjoining the public to "vote." On the far side of the bridge, the procession encounters an even larger crowd which is revealed to be seated at the foot of a stage from which a hatted man is speaking in front of a poster that reads (in Urdu and English): "Deena Nath Ko Vote Do /

Vote for Deena Nath." Khanna dashes to the foot of the stage, where he addresses the politician (presumably Mr. Nath), singing:

> Kya neta kya abhineta de janata ko jo dhokha
> Pal me shoharat ud jaaye jo ek pavan ka jhonka

> Whether political leader [neta] or an actor [abhineta], whoever will cheat the janata [people][5]
> In a flash their fortune will fly away like a gust of wind

Khanna beats a retreat from the stage, taking along with him the neta's crowd, which he leads toward an open field. In the field, before the eyes of the public and the disgraced neta, Khanna reveals sacks of hoarded grain hidden under piles of hay.

> Bhik na mange, karz na mange
> Yeh apna haq manti hai

> It doesn't ask for alms, it doesn't ask for a loan
> It [the public] knows its rights

Figure 6. Film still from Manmohan Desai's 1974 film *Roti* in which the shocked expression on the face of the heroine (played by Mumtaz) conveys the urgency of what she has just heard.

Figure 7. Film still from Manmohan Desai's 1974 film *Roti* in which the heroine passes on urgent news by whispering it into the ear of a shopkeeper.

Figure 8. Film still from Manmohan Desai's 1974 film *Roti* in which the hero (played by Rajesh Khanna) gestures toward the assembled crowd, saying, "This is the public!"

Figure 9. Film still from Manmohan Desai's 1974 film *Roti* in which an actor is swarmed by adoring fans waving rupee notes for signing.

Figure 10. Film still from Manmohan Desai's 1974 film *Roti* in which the hero and heroine lead a procession as it proceeds over a bridge bearing graffiti enjoining the public to "vote."

Figure 11. Film still from Manmohan Desai's 1974 film *Roti* in which the hero dashes to the foot of the stage to address a politician while the crowd looks on.

Figure 12. Film still from Manmohan Desai's 1974 film *Roti* in which the hero diverts the politician's public away from the stage and leads it toward an open field.

The lyrics and imagery from this wildly popular 1974 film song offer some insights into the valences of "public": the song's opening scene—the whispers and the beckoning—gestures toward a public that is made up of robust and trusted relational networks. Here, the public holds a collective, shared knowing bordering on omniscience (sab jaanti hai), capable of adjudicating "mere surface appearance" (the wig) from underlying (bald-headed) "truths." The public (a singular noun) is shown to love its leaders (netas) as much as its film stars (abhinetas): the song plays this up by emphasizing the shared etymology of neta and abhineta, political leader and film star, hammering home the point with the film-star digression. But if the public's love for society's heroes (political and silver-screen)[6] is not respected and reciprocated, then the abhi/neta's good fortune (which is anyway only on loan from the public) will evaporate; the public will rally behind the hero who enlists the power and authority of his or her position (power and position which are in the first place a gift bestowed by the public) toward the distribution of resources—not as gifts ("it doesn't ask for alms, it doesn't ask for a loan") but for its rightful due ("it knows its rights").

Of Crowds and Publics

It is useful to consider this silver-screen public in light of how contemporary social theory talks about publics—a strand of theorizing profoundly influenced by Jürgen Habermas's classic formulation of the "public sphere" and theory of "communicative action." In his 1962 classic, *The Structural Transformation of the Public Sphere: An Inquiry into a Category of Bourgeois Society*, Habermas outlines the emergence in early modern Europe of a print-mediated discursive space (a "bourgeois public sphere") in which society's literati wrote pamphlets, read one another's writings, and met up in coffeehouses to hash out their opinions—the collective exercise of public reason that worked as a counterbalance to would-be absolutism of state power. Habermas characterizes the public sphere as a discursive space of "social interaction" where "plans of action of different actors are coordinated through an exchange of communicative acts, that is, through a use of language orientated towards reaching understanding."[7] State administration has its own rationality, Habermas argues, and administrative experts use the powers of their offices (say, law) instrumentally toward the state's own ends. However (and this was Habermas's conceptual innovation), state administrators cannot simply do whatever they want, because the administratively employed power of the state acquires legitimacy only and always by means of the communicative power generated in the public sphere. In this context, Habermas maintains, democratic life hinges upon the practices and procedures by means of which administrative power is made to respond to communicatively formed public opinion. Communicatively generated power of the public sphere "make[s] itself felt" indirectly, Habermas argues, "insofar as it assumes responsibility for the pool of reasons from which administrative decisions must draw their rationalizations. With the institutionalization of representative government, legal protections on speech, press, and (especially) rights to assembly, the public sphere—as both an idea and a practice—becomes the legally protected means by which the 'general interest' of society (as opposed to the 'private interests' of profit-maximization in a market economy) would come into being and find expression."[8]

Building upon while also critiquing Habermas's formulations, a second influential strand of contemporary theorizing about "publics"—taking a cue from Benedict Anderson's classic work on "imagined communities"[9]—has explored how mass-mediating technologies (in Anderson's case, print capitalism) enable people who might never actually meet in person—people who may not have very much to do with one another at all—to nonetheless "imagine" themselves as a collective; in Anderson's case, the social collective imagined through the mediations of print media was "the nation." Building on this Andersonian insight—that the mass-mediated circulation of discourse brings social collectives and political subjectivities into being—and following linguistic anthropological work on the circulation of "discourse"[10] more generally, literary scholar Michael Warner outlines a more general notion of "public" as any collective subject that takes shape when "strangers" become aware of their mutual attention to some object of shared interest—a "social space created by the reflexive circulation of discourse."[11] In a similar vein, linguistic anthropologist Susan Gal demonstrates how "publics are created through the circulation of discourses as people hear, see or read a message and then engage it in some way." It is through individuals' "mutual awareness" of their shared participation in some discursive practice, Gal shows, that publics come into being, and act concertedly as such.[12] These formulations are of a piece with a generation of scholarship that has pointed out the exclusionary (and especially gendered) character of the public sphere as formulated by Habermas, pointing instead to a myriad of publics and "counterpublics"[13]—potential and actual—that exist alongside (and in tension with) mainstream, hegemonic forms of bourgeois publicity, and to the wide range of speech genres, objects of interest, participation frameworks and material mediations that comprise "public culture."[14]

At one level, the silver-screen public of "Yeh Jo Public Hai" bears a striking resemblance to notions of a discursively produced collectivity. We watch as exchanges of words and gestures draw individuals out from their private domains—their shops, their homes, their places of employment—and into the town square; this talkative and all-seeing public becomes a collective subject by virtue of its shared focus on an object of attention ("whether neta or abhineta"), and then holds institutionally empowered state actors (our sly-eyed neta) accountable for actions that betray the common interest (say, grain hoarding). Yet even as the discursively produced public of "Yeh Jo Public Hai" seems almost Habermasian in its reasoning and accountability-holding powers, there is something jarring to a liberal sensibility in the song's implicit equating of the "public" as a collective, discursively assembled political subject with the embodied crowd as a throng of adoring fans—a collectivity assembled not by meaningful discourse (whispered words that lead to the holding of a corrupt official to account) but rather by "love" and desire for physical proximity to a fickle film star. The public of "Yeh Jo Public Hai" is conjured, in other words, not only by matters common to the public mind but to the public heart—a heart that is left broken and crying by the callousness of the beloved abhi/neta.

> If you break its heart and if you make them cry
> Then there will be no forgiveness

The ease with which "Yeh Jo Public Hai" moves back and forth between these two collectivities (the discursively produced and the affectively assembled) is jarring to discourse theories of publicity, perhaps because the notion of the public is so often counterposed (either positively or negatively) with the crowd—the reasoned communications of the public sphere juxtaposed with the fleshy, embodied energies of crowds. In this context, attention to our silver-screen public invites a twofold move: first to dispense with the unhelpful binary of discursive reason versus embodied affect;[15] and second, to attend not only to the embodied public (the physical crowd) but also to its image—to the "this" (and accompanying onscreen hand gesture; see Figure 12) of "this is the public!"

> Yeh public hai, public!
> This is the public! The public!

Attending to public as both the embodied crowd as well as the images of that same crowd means asking as well about the "heteroglossic"[16] character of the public—which not only comprises an audience but has its own (actual and potential) addressees.[17] Indeed, as Warner points out, the notion of "public" has multiple valences: it can be an imagined as a "social totality" such as the nation; a "concrete audience" (an embodied crowd); or a collectivity that comes into being through the circulation of texts.[18] What we see in Mumbai is the materially mediated co-articulations among these different but overlapping modes of publicity. When Khanna gestures toward the assembled crowd while saying to the neta "this is the public!" it is not merely the politician who is being addressed but also those of us who are watching the film (and/or looking at screen-captured images on a page). And indeed back in Bombay, we see that the rally-crowd too has multiple and overlapping audience addressees: not only the crowd assembled by virtue of shared attention (or devotion) to a candidate for office, but also people like the print shop man, to whom the demonstrated ability to assemble a large crowd makes the event's object of attention (the abhi/neta) "look powerful"—"itna public utna image rahega," as he put it: "the size of the public will be the size of the image." The public thus comes into focus as a performed image.

After first characterizing the rally as "meaningless," the man at the print shop revises his characterization, describing the communicative work of the gathering: the rally is "an advertisement of the size of your public." He interprets the rally as a show, one that has been intentionally crafted by its organizers to produce a compelling "image" ("the size of the public will be the size of the image") in order to "sell" something to its audiences ("no ad, no sale"). His characterization of the live-action rally-show gestures toward the event's character as a performance—not merely a visual "image" but a multisensory, processual, rasa-infused "encounter."[19] Attending to the rally-show as a performance brings together insights from language-based approaches while also attending to the multisensory encounter that the rally-show affords. "Like written and spoken languages," media anthropologists Margrit Pernau and Imke Rajmani write, "images, sounds, smells, tastes, shapes, and movements are cultivated into meaningful sign systems that form the media through which concepts are communicated, shaped, and changed."[20] Sensory encounters, in other words, are always already "socially framed" by memories that are at once both embodied and conceptual. Reading the crowd in this way thus raises key questions for both audiences and anthropologists: If sensory encounters in the street are the material infrastructures of "meaningful" political communication, then what is it that the rally-crowd might be said to mean, and to whom? Is the assembled crowd an actual public or its representation-image? Or both? If an assembled crowd is read as an indexical sign of a broader public, then who or what comprises the public that the rally-image would signify? How is the relationship between a public and its rally-representation construed by its audiences? Who are the rally-show's audiences anyway—intended and otherwise—and what is the connection between embodied and imaged/imagined publics?

Linguistic anthropology teaches us that making sense of the relationship between signs and what they represent is a "socially contingent" practice of interpretation and speculation enacted by discerning participant-
audiences.[21] Susan Gal and Judith Irvine characterize this process of
meaning-making as one of conjecture: "Participants conjecture—we could
equally say they guess or hypothesize—by turning attention to potential
signs. Existing knowledge suggests what could conceivably be a sign, as
contrasted against its surround. Attention and contrast are presupposed
in conjecturing something as a sign."[22] People make sense of the sudden appearance of a very large number of people in a Mumbai street on
the final day of an election campaign by drawing on their personal and
shared archives—embodied memories and genre repertoires[23]—to make
conjectures: What are we looking at? Is this a show? If so, then what are
we being shown, and by whom? While anything can be studied as a performance (by asking of it "performance questions"), in characterizing the
election rally as natak, I am suggesting something different: not merely
that the rally can be analyzed anthropologically as a performance, but that
the rally-show explicitly signals to its audiences its theatrical character
using collectively archived genre conventions (in Bombay-speak, the rally
is "filmy")—and that indeed the show is thus experienced and engaged
by various audiences as theater.[24]

The accounts that follow train ethnographic attention on the creative
work of assembling and performing the rally-show with which this chapter opened, as well as on the multisensory perceptions and intellections
(yes, intellections) that "audiencehood" entails.[25] The rally's organizers
are rather like film directors—not unlike Manmohan Desai in his direction of "Yeh Jo Public Hai"—borrowing freely from among a myriad of
narrative "frames" and genre conventions.[26] Indeed, the place of the final
campaign rally within the broader sociomaterial and ideational contexts of the election season is like that of the song-and-dance sequence
in Bombay cinema: as Kathryn Hansen writes (drawing on the work of
Hindi film scholar Ravi Vasudevan), "the para-narrative of song and dance
'inserts the film and the spectator into a larger field of coherence,' one that
comprises a complex series of intertextual references to practices that
exist independently of the film."[27] Like a song-and-dance "para-narrative,"
the final campaign rally is a spatially and temporally bound performance
encounter that punctuates the longer-sighted temporal horizon of the

campaign season, gesturing to the "larger field of coherence" similarly to how a song-and-dance number punctuates a film.[28] The rally-show comprises a myriad of intertextual references that ostend to the drama (to recall Umberto Eco's formulation from the introduction) the real-time material city: its streets and markets; its economies and livelihoods; its memories and imaginaries; its registers of language, comportment, and "charisma."[29]

Taaqat: Strength on Display

I was well aware—even before the men at the print shop mentioned it— that many of the rally participants may well have been paid for their participation that day, having spent the previous weeks studying the careful negotiations and forging of relational ties that would be on full display during the final campaign rally. And yet as we saw in chapter 1, since campaigns tend to pay at fairly consistent (if gender-differentiated) rates, the size of a crowd is a sign not merely of ability to pay, but rather signals the size of the public's "belief" (as Rakesh put it at the end of the previous chapter) in the extent and substance of a candidate's established relations with various known and respected area leaders—NGOs, voluntary associations, businesspeople, and religious figures, for instance—people who can then recruit their friends, neighbors, and employees to join this rally rather than another. It is with these people that the campaign team forged and negotiated relations in the weeks and days before the final rally-show.

During the run-up to the 2017 polls, for instance, I followed closely the activities of a self-described social worker named Fareed. Fareed is founder-director of a small, rabble-rousing neighborhood NGO called Taaqat—an Urdu word that means something like capacity, ability, strength, power, energy.[30] (Taaqat is not the actual name of Fareed's NGO, but it is an apt one because the cultivation and display of taaqat is central to the organization's work.) Taaqat's mission, as Fareed described to me, is to create "awareness" about "civic issues" among the mostly Muslim residents of the chawls and tenement buildings among which the tiny Taaqat office is nestled.[31] The weeks before the 2017 election, Fareed's office was abuzz with businesspeople, community leaders, and social workers affiliated with all the major parties—from left-wing Socialists and Muslim identitarians to the regional Marathi chauvinist Shiv Sena party—the sometimes-ally, sometimes-adversary of the Hindu nationalist Bharatiya Janata Party (BJP). When I asked his about his proximity to a party with an on-again, off-again flirtation with Hindutva and antimigrant regional-linguistic chauvinism, Fareed (who is himself an Hindi-speaking migrant from the North Indian state of Uttar Pradesh) shrugged simply: "That's all just for show," he said, using the somewhat disparaging/dismissive Hindi term dikhavat—which conveys a sense of self-aggrandizement or "showing off."[32] "It's all acting," he added, using the English word *acting*. I asked him to elaborate and he continued: "See, the Shiv Sena is practical. They do our work, so I support them." I ask what he means by "they do our work," and he responds with an example: Shiv Sena has set up an NGO in Mumbra, a Muslim-dominated area on the Mumbai periphery. "They're my friends," Fareed tells me, "the people running that NGO; they are all Muslims." The NGO was actually set up by Shiv Sena people, he tells me, but the NGO has a different name, "in order not to alienate their non-Muslim vote base." Fareed says of his friends running the NGO, "They are doing good work."[33] He tells me that, for this reason, the area's (largely North Indian Muslim) voters might take the NGO's advice and support a chauvinistic party candidate in the election. "This is election jadoo," he says with a laugh—election magic. He tells me that earlier that day he had even gotten a call from a local BJP leader asking his support for a candidate contesting from a neighboring constituency, saying that "they need Muslim votes." I ask: "What did you say?" "I didn't reply." Here in Badlapur, though, he explained, he had already decided to support Sayeed, the candidate upon which my research during the 2017 election had focused. Fareed tells me that he himself had been offered a party "ticket" to contest the election in a neighboring district, but had declined, preferring to pursue his work through the "medium" (madhyam) of Taaqat.

Fareed's Taaqat-mediated work primarily involves compiling thick files of papers—documents acquired through official Right to Information (RTI) applications and punctuated with his own photography—of official failures to maintain and repair the built fabric of this low-income neighborhood. Armed with the paper-padded files, Fareed and his small team then organize regular "awareness campaigns": door-to-door visits through the chawls and tenements, for instance, alerting residents to some particular issue, and then mobilizing the newly "aware" to put pressure on area political leaders to resolve the matter. Fareed explains:

Our goal is to create *awareness* about civic issues.[34] If some road isn't being repaired, [residents] should ask: Why isn't it being built? If a *gutter* isn't being cleared/cleaned, they should ask why isn't it being cleaned? The corporator and MLA, the MP [Member of Parliament], they are doing good work! But they are so busy, in so many meetings, that many issues don't reach them . . . [because] there are so many problems. Taaqat foundation has become a *courier boy* for the people [janata] regarding *civic issues*. We see many things and we take photographs, we note the names and numbers of buildings having civic issues. Then we *correspond* [correspondent kar ke] with the corporator and MLA and send our requests; we send the photos and addresses and make our humble entreaty with folded hands and say: "Sahib, please . . ." [Binti kar ke, haath jod ke: "Sahib . . ."].

Fareed characterizes his work at Taaqat as that of communication: a humble "courier boy" shuttling messages back and forth (correspondent kar ke) between elected officials and the people (janata) with Taaqat as the madhyam of that communication.

Courier Boy

Notably, Fareed characterizes the people among whom he seeks to raise awareness and mobilize around some issue not as a public—which would explicitly signal the theatrical register of his communicative work—but rather as janta: "courier boy ban gaya, janta ke lie." Janta (also sometimes spelled and pronounced as "janata"—with three syllables) is a Hindi/Urdu/Marathi word derived from the Sanskrit jan, which means something like "person" or "living being."[35] Janta is a singular noun that casts a wide net, professing to describe a universal collective subject: "the people" or "all of mankind." Commonly used across North India, janta found iconic all-India use following Narendra Modi's announcement of a "Janta Curfew"—a nationwide lockdown announced on March 19, 2020, as part of an effort to halt the spread of Covid-19. Indeed, janta carries a sense of wholeness—"the people" or even "the nation" as a singular totality—which can lend the word a normative valence as those in whose name, in whose interest, and with whose authorization some leader professes to rule. Thus when the National Congress Party's founding leader, Sharad Pawar, famously delivered a public speech in the pouring rain, the party posted the video of the drenched-to-the-skin octogenarian with the heroic caption: "The janta is soaking wet; Delhi [i.e., the central government] only freezes [i.e., remains still, stagnant]."[36] "Janta" thus demands sympathetic attention to the position of that which is described as such.

While Fareed uses the normative term "janta" (rather than the overtly theatrical "public"), the context in which he makes this particular statement is richly suggestive of the dramaturgical frame within which his "courier boy" work is enacted. For starters, Fareed made these statements on camera, to a small-time paid-news operator who had come to Taaqat's office (presumably on the "courier boy's" invitation) in the wake of one such door-to-door "awareness" program. "What was the necessity of this program, taking your team door-to-door to highlight this issue?" the interviewer had asked, "especially when the elected officials in this area were already doing the work, why did you feel the need to take your team from house to house? Is this some sort of preparation for the election?" The interviewer's final question is striking, as this exchange took place a full year prior to the 2017 civic polls. The question gestures toward the fraught interpretive work that attends the theatrical communicative register: Did the door-to-door campaign seek to hail people as a janta, or rather (as the interviewer's question suggests) to perform Taaqat's strength before an audience—a display enacted in the name of the janta? There is no clear answer that Fareed can provide to the question, of course, because in practice the distinction between everyday courier boy conveyances and the drama of prachaar (the Hindi word widely used in reference to election campaigning but which also refers to publicity and advertising; "You need to advertise, see, because 'no ad, no sale'")—collapses.

Gauging from the fawning attention paid to him by the various parties in the run-up to the February 2017 polls, Fareed did indeed seem to be something of an area kingmaker. Keen to understand the underpinnings and extent of Fareed's influence, I took to hanging around Taaqat's office, where—in bits and parts—I asked Fareed to tell me how and why he became active in politics. It all began with the 1992 riots, he began; he was just a kid—in the tenth grade maybe—but he had a "big group of friends" in the area. "We weren't political." He uses the English-origin word *political* (a term of problematization that is the subject of chapter 5). In fact, he and his friends found politics "dirty and corrupt," and worse, "against Islam." Fareed is from a devout Deobandi family, but in the aftermath of the 1992–93 riots, during which Fareed and his group of friends were active in relief work, he recalls that the "political people noticed" and approached him: "The [Congress Party] MLA came to my house with a letter, inviting me to his office to felicitate me. We were very honored to be approached." Besides, he laughs, "we were teenagers, so we began to think maybe this is good thing because if we get into any trouble with the police then it's good to have some political connections." His uncle already had an affiliation with the Congress Party, as a journalist for the Congress-sympathetic Urdu daily *Inquilab*. Fareed recalls how he began to think that "maybe politics is not all bad like it is in films; I began to see that there are good people in politics too." "Good people," by Fareed's reckoning, are those who use their networks and knowledge to help rather than harm.

Fareed rose quickly through the ranks, he tells me, within a few years assuming a position of leadership in the Congress Party's youth wing. But he recalls growing increasingly disillusioned with the local party leadership, who struck him as more interested in doing the work of the area property developers than in helping local residents. "They're all just brokers," he told me with no little disdain, all "political dalals."[37] I ask him for a clarification: "What's a political dalal?" He waves his hand dismissively: "Someone who gets clearances from the SRA [Slum Rehabilitation Authority] or from the BMC for redevelopment projects.[38] Such people don't advocate for the janta; they don't ask questions like 'Why is the area [of rooms in redevelopment buildings] so small?' Because they are on the side of the builders."

Fareed recalls that by the early 2010s he was constantly butting heads with party leaders, particularly in the context of a proposed cluster redevelopment project being promoted by the local MLA that proposed to flatten and rebuild a huge swath of his neighborhood—a working-class locality known as Kamathipura.[39] Widely stigmatized as the historical center of the city's storied red-light district, Kamathipura is home to both an extraordinarily diverse residential population (living in visibly precarious and officially "cessed" nineteenth-century tenement buildings) and a myriad of small-scale manufacturing workshops (suitcases, plastic mannequins, recycled jeans).[40] Fareed recalled how he himself had sought to contest the 2012 Municipal Corporation elections but was refused the ticket because, as he put it, he'd developed a reputation for being "a rabble-rouser on behalf of Muslims," and party higher-ups feared that he would "advocate too strongly" on the behalf of local residents. Fareed explains that he eventually left the party after a falling out with the party higher-ups: "Congress doesn't let people move upwards in the party, particularly Muslims. The Congress Party's support for Muslims is 'all natak'; it's all 'manch pe' [onstage]." He explains: "Muslims are divided in Bombay because our leaders aren't strong enough to stand up to the party higher-ups. Everyone gets scared when the party people come around and say, 'Don't raise this or that issue because then we [Muslims] will be the target of communal backlash.' Even the religious leaders say this! The religious people are the most corrupt. They're paid off by the party higher-ups to say these things." Fareed tells me he left the Congress Party because the sitting MLA was "a lobbyist" for the builders and didn't want anyone "to get in the way" of proposed (and extremely lucrative) area redevelopment projects. It was after being denied the 2012 ticket that Fareed left the Congress Party and formed his NGO. "I'm beyond control of any party," he adds with a laugh, and with no little pride. His commitment and involvement in "political things" haven't changed since abjuring formal party membership, he explains; it's just that now his work is done through the madhyam of his NGO. "There's freedom this way," he explains, "I scare [elected officials] into action by displaying my taaqat [apni taaqat dikha kar]."

Fareed's NGO is at once the medium—madhyam—for pursuing his political goals and the media infrastructure through which he displays virtuosity in those pursuits. Taaqat is thus both site and stage for political action: the madhyam for "doing" as well as for "showing-doing" (to borrow theorist Richard Schechner's phrase).[41] In this context, Fareed's self-characterization and promotional video of Taaqat as a humble "courier boy," entreating political leaders with "folded hands," is clearly tongue-in-cheek: a theatrical diminishment of his media-fueled self-image as the embodiment of nondeference and confrontational assertion. Fareed is (by his own measure) a "rabble-rouser" who does not shy away from the use of strong language—especially when speaking about the "corruption" of others. This disjuncture between Fareed's performed "demeanor" as an assertive (even menacing) Lone Ranger type and his on-camera shift in register characterizing himself as a humble "courier boy" seems to come with a wink, perhaps eliciting a chuckle from an in-the-know public—a public thereby produced through its reflexive recognition of this shared and pleasurable appreciation of Fareed's ironic hand-folding.[42]

Fareed has no qualms about the role that money plays in the forging and affirming of relations. Two days before the final rally in support of Sayeed's campaign, the following exchange took place in Fareed's little office: Fareed's phone rings, and he looks at the screen. Fareed sighs, and before answering the call he shows his screen to the other person in the office, a man he affectionately (and playfully) calls Pappu, who is the proprietor of a well-known neighborhood eating establishment.[43] Pappu looks at the screen and raises an eyebrow—presumably recognizing the name of the incoming caller. "Sayeed Bhai [Brother] should just manage him!," Fareed says, suggesting that perhaps this isn't the first time this particular caller has rung up. Fareed answers the phone, with a long, formal greeting. A few minutes go by, Fareed interjecting periodically "Yes . . . yes . . . yes. Yes . . . yes . . . yes." The yes-ing goes on for a few minutes and I can't quite make out the words on the other end of the line, but I can make out from the tone of voice that the caller is speaking emphatically and with no little frustration. Fareed hangs up, and I ask, "What was that about?" "It was a maulana," Fareed tells me, "a teacher at a nearby Islamic school." I probe: "What did he want?" "He wants to support Sayeed Bhai's election campaign" (Fareed uses the word *support*). I ask, "So why was he calling to complain to you?" "He wasn't calling to complain; he said he wants to offer his support." I must have looked confused, because Fareed explains: "See, the maulana is poor. This is a poor neighborhood, no? He runs a madrasa, and for that reason he knows many people in this area. The maulana said that he wants to support Sayeed Bhai's campaign. So he called to ask me, Why is Sayeed Bhai not supporting him?" I ask Fareed and Pappu's opinion on the maulana's request for "support" (which Fareed clarifies is of the cash variety), and they agree that "Sayeed Bhai should support him. And he will support him also." I ask: "Was the maulana threatening to give his support elsewhere? To talk up some other candidate or to send his students to some other rally?" "No, nothing like that," Fareed explains, waving his hand dismissively. Rather, the maulana asked Fareed to tell Sayeed that the maulana wants to offer his support to his campaign. But unless Sayeed supports the maulana as well—with a cash gift—then any advice the maulana might give to area constituents would fall on deaf ears. Why would anyone believe the maulana's claim that the candidate would help them once he got elected—that he would "support" their school and students—if the candidate didn't even bother to take notice of their "support" during the campaign? It seemed a good point. The money that the maulana requested of Sayeed was meaningful for its semiotic work—in displaying to area voters the strength of the maulana's relations with the candidate.

Like the religious leaders that Fareed earlier castigated for receiving cash in exchange for saying and doing certain things in certain contexts, the maulana too was asking for cash support before throwing his full weight behind Sayeed's candidacy—talking up the candidate and encouraging his students to attend the final rally. But while Fareed makes it clear that the schoolteacher should be compensated for his participation in the campaign prachaar (rally), in the case of the religious leaders mentioned earlier, the acting—saying and doing things manch pe—is characterized by Fareed as "corruption." One kind of natak is celebrated (or at least enjoyed) as a good show, while the other is denounced as "corruption." The difference between political theater and political deception lies in the extent to which the natak explicitly signals itself as such: where the audience of the drama (like the print shop men described at the outset of the chapter) is shown the stage (manch). Indeed, in their enjoyment of the show—standing on the side of the road—the men at the print shop became part of the crowd; the atmosphere of the natak enlists them not merely as audience but also as participants in the drama, while their participation helps in producing the very spectacle whose unfolding they had stepped out to watch.

This matter of participant-audience recalls our earlier discussion, drawing on Warner, of how "publics" come into being through reflexive attention to the circulation of their own discourse: in the film song "Yeh Jo Public Hai" the image of the onscreen "public" whose heart is filled (or broken) by the abhi/neta reflects back to the film-watching audience its own image as a public, conjured by collective attention to the film and shared love of film stars. In a similar way, the election rally-show reflects back to the assembled crowd-audience its own image as a public, assembled by mutual attention to the collective taaqat: a performed image of the scale and strength of the social relations and collective investments in the parade of personalities (business families and teachers; community leaders and candidates) now circulating through the very city streets and spaces both produced and inhabited by that taaqat.

Mahol

In the days following Sayeed's successful 2017 bid for office, I spoke with his "personal assistant," a young man named Wasim, who played a key role in both of Sayeed's successful bids for municipal office, in 2012 and 2017. Wasim lives in Sayeed's incumbent constituency in the eastern sub-urb of Gowandi—a dense, low-rise neighborhood generally referred to as a "slum." Wasim explained to me the ultimate goal of the three-week campaign season was to "mahol create karna"—to create mahol.

The Hindi/Urdu word mahol (sometimes transliterated as mahaul) is generally glossed in English as "atmosphere," "ambiance," or "environment"—in senses both material and social. Mahol is an Arabic word, etymologically related to mahal (place or palace) and mohalla (neighborhood, or "what is around and about") via the Arabic root ahl, meaning "resident" or "denizen."[44] Mahol describes an ambient feeling, both moral and material, whose origins are intangible, almost like weather. Anthropologist Timothy Cooper, reflecting on the meanings of mahol in Lahore, reflects that mahol describes "a sense of immersion" born of the work of navigating the "moral and social qualities of a particular setting." His research in Lahore found two interrelated uses of mahol:

> First, [mahaul] referred to a terrain that possesses the ability to act upon the world. The tactile earthiness of the term is somewhat reminiscent of the concept of terroir in environmental discourses: the habitat, contributing factors, and unique sense of place that can come to be embodied in a crop yield and shape the product from which it is made. . . . Second . . . mahaul describes what might be called a moral atmosphere. Unlike other possible synonyms—context or character, for example—mahaul is an avowedly social formation, referring closely to the cultural dynamics of value stratification, which describes the ways in which tone or mood are shaped by the principles of right and wrong.[45]

Mahol thus shares some conceptual overlap with philosopher Gernot Böhme's notion of atmosphere. "What affects human beings in their environment are not only just natural factors," Böhme points out, "but also aesthetic ones. . . . What mediates objective factors of the environment with aesthetic feelings of a human being is what we call atmosphere. The atmosphere of a certain environment is responsible for the way we feel about ourselves in that environment."[46] In his ethnographic account of Shia Moharram processions in Mumbai, anthropologist Patrick Eisenlohr draws on Böhme's atmosphere formulation in characterizing the "feel" of Shia Mumbai during Moharram as "spatially extended emotion."[47] Cooper's and Eisenlohr's accounts of mahol echo my own sense of the word's valences in Mumbai, where mahol seems to describe an intangible sense or feel of some space or place. For instance, I was once told by residents of a particular neighborhood that (for reasons that were never quite clear to me) I should avoid going over to the neighborhood's far side: "Don't go over there; the mahol isn't good." On another occasion, when a leisurely Mumbai evening chatting with friends grew late, someone observed with a satisfied sleepy smile that "mahol ban gaya" (the atmosphere has been made) which conveyed the sense that the mood of evening felt perfect and complete. Mahol, in other words, seems to describe an ambient effect of myriad factors—moral and material—rather than something actively curated or created.[48] In this context, Wasim's reflection that the goal of the three-week campaign season is to "create mahol" caught my attention because it seems to suggest a dramaturgical sense of intentional stage-setting. "Whoever creates the most mahol," Wasim explained, "that person wins."

In Wasim's rendering, a campaign seeks to convince area voters by means of a multisensory and polyvalent neighborhood feel. Wasim explains: "Everyone's talking and talking, and we want them to talk about Sayeed Bhai. Even kids are important. They don't vote, of course, but you see them wearing hats and waving flags—people see this; it means we are winning!" Wasim recalled how during Sayeed's previous election campaign in Gowandi he "handed out packets of biscuits to kids so they would run around during the days before the election yelling Sayeed Bhai's name. They'd run up and down the lanes just yelling and yelling."

Wasim explained that this competition for aesthetic saturation and semiotic dominance works differently in South Bombay, where people live in "buildings." "Creating mahol is more complicated here because we need contacts with people inside buildings." Indeed (and as the next chapter explores), during the weeks before the election, Sayeed's campaign team found and forged contacts inside each and every building and commercial establishment in the constituency—contacts with "main people" whose established relations enabled them to assemble crowds for chowk sabhaas (street-corner meetings), gatherings in courtyards of residential complexes, or on building rooftops and in basements—people who then (after these meetings) lead the candidate through buildings, knocking on doors and introducing him to friends and neighbors. In the run-up to election day, Wasim explained, this kind of campaigning becomes very personal, especially among the youth of the neighborhood. "Izzat ki bat hai," he explained—"It's a matter of izzat [honor], because if you've been campaigning for someone, you must make sure he wins or else you lose izzat." For this reason, Wasim explained, "main people" [jo main hai—those who are main] will start spending money from their own pockets—especially when it comes to the final rally. "They've been talking about this candidate for weeks so now they need to make sure he looks good! People start running around and expending their own energy and money—to create hawa—or wind."[49]

The primacy of the dramaturgical, scene-setting work of election-season monetary expenditure was particularly poignant during the 2017 campaign season, which came on the heels of India's notebandi (demonetization) initiative. In an atmosphere rife with rumors of notebandi-related cash constriction (and of remonetization-related corruption)—an environment in which no one was quite certain how much cash anyone else might actually have on hand or be able to marshal—the question of whether and how this or that candidate was cash-flush was both a topic of popular speculation and a staple of campaign speeches. Candidates across the ideological spectrum accused India's ruling party of self-interest in the timing and manner of demonetization, while city journalists eagerly reported on rumors of collusion. "How come the BJP is flush with money in times of notebandi?," one English-language daily quoted the Maharashtra Navnirman Sena (MNS) party leader Raj Thackeray, translating from the Marathi-language public speech in which Thackeray accused BJP leaders of flooding candidates' campaign coffers with cash; "What is the source of this money?" It is of course impossible to verify these sorts of implied accusations, and this is hardly the point. What is more interesting is how, under cash constraints of demonetization (whether rumored or real), certain things were interpreted as "signs" of access to cash: "Signs of the city BJP's munificence can be seen everywhere," grumbled a Shiv Sena party worker, citing big-ticket items like oversized billboards and resplendent newspaper ads.[50] The BJP campaign office in one constituency went so far as to employ crowds of party-insignia-bedecked women to mill about in front of the party office for the entire duration of the campaign period—veritable walking-talking rupee notes.[51] Yet notwithstanding the widespread equating of the BJP's oversized ads and other forms of high-profile spending with the machinations of notebandi-related malfeasance, Shiv Sena's own leadership did not distance itself from such ostentatious displays of expenditure but sought instead to keep pace.[52] On one particular day, for instance, each and every one of Mumbai's Hindi, English, and Marathi major dailies arrived with a glossy Shiv Sena pamphlet titled "Mee Mumbaikar" (I am a Mumbaikar) tucked into the pages. If ostentatious ads and hired hands indexed access to cash, then all the city's major parties eagerly sought to perform their virtuosity in this signifying practice. Indeed, in the context of demonetization, candidates from all the city's major parties seemed especially eager to demonstrate that their own networks had enabled them to offset any such cash-constricting effects.

Yet cash itself was undeniably in short supply, even for some major-party candidates. Sayeed's campaign manager explained to me that due to cash shortage there were some campaign expenditures that had been significantly pared down in comparison with his 2012 electoral bid: TV promotions, for instance, had been completely cut, as had billboards, which are expensive both to produce and (even more so) to secure permission to display. Official "permissions" eat a good chunk of campaign budgets, he explained, but some amount of expenditure on permissions was unavoidable: official and unofficial permissions for public meetings and "stage shows" (the subject of the next chapter), for example, and perhaps most crucially for the final rally.

In this cash-strapped context, Sayeed's campaign enlisted other semiotic vehicles—in place of cash—employing creative practices to perform cash-like spectacles, signaling access to the important relations and resources (political, social, material) about which voters were keen to know. To marshal the flag-bearers and marchers, for instance, agreements were forged with area traders and manufacturers to "borrow" groups of laborers for the final rally—a loan that would be repaid not with future repayment in cash but rather with some more-or-less-specified future advocacy of "help": a contact with the municipal corporation in the event of some infrastructural breakdown, for instance, or a problem with industrial or commercial license renewal—a regular and pressing worry in the legal-institutional vagary that characterizes so much of Mumbai's productive and commercial economy.

One group of flag-bearers with whom I spoke in the morning of Sayeed's final rally—while they dressed up in hats and scarves—was composed of around twenty-five teenage boys from the North Indian state of Bihar. I asked them whether they would be paid for their work today. "Maybe our boss gets paid because we're not working for him today," one boy surmises, adding: "The candidate has bought our time." He explains that they work for a monthly wage, including room and board. The rally was on a Sunday, and they generally work a half day on Sundays, ending at 2 p.m. So they would work a little overtime today because the rally would wind up around 5 p.m. But they were happy to "play their role," they explained to me—not only because it was a beautiful breezy Sunday and they were happy to be outdoors rather than in the tiny workshop, and not only because after the rally they would have a proper biryani feast, but because their livelihoods depend on the success of the factory. Their boss's business is their business. "Our boss is from our village," one boy explains. Like them, the owner of the factory where they work is from Bihar—he came to Bombay years ago and found a job manufacturing motorbike parts in a workshop nearby. Then, ten years ago, having learned how to do business in Bombay, he took a small space on rent and started a little factory of his own, manufacturing bags. Then he started recruiting boys from the village to come to Bombay, to live and work in the factory space. These boys have been here a few years, they tell me. "It's not bad; our boss is nice," one boy says. And while they don't make much, because room and board is included they are able to send nearly everything they earn back home. These boys of course wouldn't be voting in the upcoming Mumbai election (either because they're Bihar residents or because they're underage, or both), so clearly this payment is not a cash-for-vote sort of arrangement. And in any case, their labor that day—the labor of rally-going—was being paid for not by the candidate but by their boss, the Bihari bag manufacturer.

I approach a young man who has brought a group of around forty people. He introduces himself as Arvind and explains that he organizes a "friends group" in the nearby "slum area" where they live. I ask him what their group does. He tells me that they intervene to help when there are

problems—water problems, drainage problems, things like that. Arvind
grew up in the slum, he tells me, but since he's educated, people approach
him for help. He works as a cashier at a local hospital, he tells me, so
he's able to help out sometimes; if people need medical help and no beds
are available, sometimes he's able to "help." He and his school friends
formed this "friends group," he explains, because being a group makes
it easier to get the attention of the corporator or the municipal officers
when some work needs to be done. "You're the main?" I ask, trying out
Wasim's term to see if it resonates; he smiles, "Yes, I'm main." In other
words (and this is the key point), even though—and indeed precisely
because—people like the bag laborers or Arvind's forty friends are somewhat like extras on a film set, this doesn't mean that the rally-show is
perceived, either by participants or audience, as natak in the sense of
"fake," "inauthentic," or a "trick." This is because the rally-crowd is not
some anonymous mass of interchangeable bodies (a "rent-a-crowd");
rather, it is spectacular ostentatious enactment of dense relational networks, mediated by help, friendship, and livelihood, by kinship networks
and future business prospects and collective socioeconomic security—
akin to what anthropologist Tarini Bedi's Gujarati-speaking Mumbai
taxi drivers call jaalu: an expansive web of shared relations.[53] The "street
theatre of the 'procession'"[54] is a public display of the wide and intricate
jaalu, rendering sensible (not merely visible) the relational web that is the
infrastructure of everyday Mumbai life: small-scale workshop owners
and their recognizable, fresh-faced young workers; dependable "mains"
like Arvind and his forty friends; trusted teachers and their students;
brokers and deal makers and "big men" of all kinds.[55] Recall from chapter 1 Mastanbhai's initial social worker meeting, the bulk of which was
spent garlanding the various mains—whose public pronouncement of
alliance with Seema's campaign was thereby performed and acknowledged
in a two-way reciprocal bid at promise-making: for the main, openly
announcing support for a candidate by assembling one's public for the
rally-show seeks to demonstrate to the candidate the reach and strength
of the main's relational networks; for the campaign, publicly acknowledging a main's alliance with the candidate seeks to vitiate against a main's
defection (tricky business in a context where "everybody flips"). The
rally-show is a real-time, rasa-coated display of this dense, sticky web of
emplaced relations and reciprocity.[56]

Figure 13. Sayeed and his campaign team during the final campaign rally. Mumbai, February 2017. Photograph by the author.

Flower Power

The final rally was a celebratory maelstrom—a palpable thickening of the air in Badlapur's narrow lanes with the "choke"[57] and thunder of fire-crackers and motorbikes, the forward press of bodies, the torrents of pink-and-white petals, the sweet-acerbic hawa of smoke and sweat, exhaust fumes, and marigold pollen. Amid the sensory assault of Sayeed's 2017 final campaign rally, I was particularly struck by the flowers—not only by the glut of garlands, but also (and especially) by the scattering of small boys armed with plastic bags who drenched the candidate's entourage with blossoms as the chariot made its way through particular sections of the neighborhood.

In her discussion of flowers and garlanding in public processions (religious, matrimonial, political) in South Asia, historian Joanne Waghorne argues that the significance of garlanding and raining flowers on a political figure (in her case, a Tamil king) lies in the "power of imagery" equating a garlanded figure with the divine. Waghorne quotes an old Tamil folk song:

Tondaiman! Tondaiman!
king of our country
He is coming and looking toward us!
covered with a sacred umbrella,
He comes seated in a vehicle fit for a god!
. . . .
It is visible now
the garland on his shoulders!
On his hand, sandal paste and a ring
have come into view.
. . . .
Festooned with pearl garlands,
accompanied by an army on the best horses,
He is coming in that direction,
going now toward the palace![58]

Reflecting on the historical enlisting of religious imagery in political procession, Waghorne notes how, in the poem, "the ring on the raja's hand is a royal sign but garlands and sandal paste are the proper ornamentation of Gods." The effect of this poetic convention—of portraying gods and kings in "identical language"—is that "the hearer cannot distinguish whether a poem describes a king coming toward his palace or a God going in procession back into his temple"; similar ubiquity of garlanding can be observed during Hindu wedding processions, Waghorne notes, when "the bride and the groom are honored as deities."[59] Historian Raminder Kaur traces how, in Bombay, beginning in the 1920s, public processions in celebration of religious festivals (particularly the Hindu festival of Ganapati Utsava and the Shia celebration of Moharram) began to provide "an effective grammar for a broader base of political campaigns . . . [with] ritualistic features of iconic displays, bhajan songs, garlands, incense and celebratory processions [making] their mark on political campaigns."[60] Kaur shows how "the visual, performative, and mediated sites of vernacular culture . . . co-constituted political programmes" in a way that deepened political participation by the urban poor and laboring classes.[61] The ubiquity of flower garlands and petal showers, in other words, is part of a broadly shared festive grammar of public processions in Mumbai. Even while iconically invoking ritual authority, flower garlanding and

showering in the context of the procession appears less as "political deification" in any particular religious tradition than as the creation of mahol
and production of hawa that seeks to draw a proximate public into the
atmospheric ambit of a procession.[62]

Some weeks after the final rally, I asked Wasim (Sayeed's personal assistant) to tell me about how the campaign team had managed to arrange
and orchestrate that flood of flowers. He smiled broadly, proudly:

> Ah, that was an all-day work! That was our biggest work on the day of
> the rally. Sayeed Bhai had us go to Dadar flower market at 5 a.m. and we
> bought an entire truckload of flowers, then we had twenty workers for six
> hours who sat on the roadside dividing up the flowers. Then we put them
> into a hundred carry bags and took them to our main person inside each
> building. Four people had to go to [the wholesale flower market in] Dadar
> to get them! Then we had a hundred garlands made as well—we gave one
> to each building main to garland Sayeed Bhai. The flowers, they had to
> happen the day of the rally itself. Because they're time sensitive; you can't
> buy them the day before!

Wasim explained that, by virtue of the time sensitivity of flowers, such
an outpouring creates an atmosphere of spontaneity—the flood of flowers feels spontaneous. Here we have an apparent paradox: an elaborate,
obviously premeditated coordination effort creates mahol of spontaneity
and authentic outpouring of love and devotion, even while the flower
petals and garlands themselves were obviously and explicitly prearranged.
(Indeed, no effort appears to have been made to disguise the fact that the
flowers—which were of uniform size and color—were orchestrated by
the campaign team itself.) To make sense of this seeming paradox, it is
helpful to recall the print shop man's reflection that the rally "is like an
advertisement." William Mazzarella points out how, when it comes to
advertising, it is not necessary "to believe in it as long as I believe that
someone else believes in it. As such, and like magic, advertising works by
itself; it doesn't require anyone to believe in it directly. Indeed, the condition of its efficacy is my self-determining and autonomous skepticism
toward its claims. My supposedly immunizing critical skepticism allows
me to resonate in good conscience."[63] Like an advertisement, the rally
works on both these levels simultaneously: it explicitly signals its own

theatrical character (allowing for a "disavowal of direct belief"),[64] thereby allowing for an unspoken understanding that this is natak (unspoken except to an anthropologist presumed to be illiterate in such genre conventions). And at the same time, the theatrical register affords the suspension of disbelief that allows the participant-audience to resonate with the pleasure of the rally-show.

The more orchestrated and staged the rally mahol feels, the more compellingly it demonstrates the orchestrators' skills in putting on a good show, as well as their access to resources and networks necessary to pull it off. The persuasiveness of a well-executed show is born of the ever-present dangers of a flop: the cavalcade of flag-bearers and motorcyclists might not turn up; the various mains might ultimately (and unpredictably) decide that they do not want to be seen by their neighbors and friends garlanding (and thereby publicly announcing support) with some particular candidate. Since garlanding two different candidates would reflect badly on the garlander's own trustworthiness (notwithstanding the fact, as we saw in the previous chapter, that everyone knows that "everybody flips"), the final rally is a proclamation by persons of influence of their confidence in one rather than another candidate. The decision of a main to participate in one rather than another final rally is a high-stakes speculation and gamble: publicly announcing a decision to

Figure 14. Influential "main" publicly endorses a candidate by garlanding him as the procession chariot passes through the neighborhood. Mumbai, February 2017. Photograph by the author.

support a candidate works to increase the "size of the public" and thereby "the size of the image"—increasing the hawa of the chosen candidate.

"How Big It Is"

While chatting with a young woman watching the parades from the side of the road out in front of her Badlapur home, I ask her: "Have you decided yet whom you'll vote for?" She shakes her head: "No, not yet. I don't know yet." I ask, "Did you hear any of the campaign speeches?" "No, no," she says. "I stay at home; we ladies stay at home." She explains that she's just stepped out of the house this Sunday afternoon for the rallies in the hope that it may help her decide how to vote. I ask: "But what are you looking for when you watch a rally?" "How big it is," she responds. "That's how we know people are convinced by some candidate. If the public is with him, if there is taaqat in the rally, that means he must have done some good work—that the public is convinced by his work. We vote for the person who has convinced people that he does good work. The rally shows this."

The rally's size and taaqat is a manifestation of public conviction—where what is on display is not (only) the physically present, theatrical crowd of flag-bearers and flower throwers, but rather the broader web of reciprocal relations made materially manifest in the event of the rally-show. And insofar as the woman herself becomes part of the crowd that is at the same time convincing her, she is—in part—convincing herself.[65] Indeed, insofar as a rally's audience becomes part of the crowd by which it seeks to be "convinced," the success (bigness) of a rally is an effect not merely of numbers but of taaqat and hawa—energy and wind—that "convinces" busy Mumbaikars to remain standing on the side of the road and thereby become part of the rally-show. Which is to say: the conviction of which the woman speaks is simultaneously informational and "experiential."[66]

The woman's account of how she assesses the rally ("how big it is") raises comparative questions of the puzzlingly overstated claims to "bigness" that have come to characterize crowd politics in other parts of the world. U.S. president Donald Trump, for instance, has famously overstated the size of his crowds; after a 2018 rally in Houston, Trump tweeted:

The crowds at my Rallies are far bigger than they have ever been before, including the 2016 election. Never an empty seat in these large venues, many thousands of people watching screens outside. Enthusiasm & Spirit is through the roof. SOMETHING BIG IS HAPPENING—WATCH![67]

While Trump claimed to have assembled a fifty-thousand-strong crowd, the *Washington Post* reported that local police put the number of those gathered closer to three thousand.[68] In the American context, such bloated claims have sought to be countered by fact-checking media watchdogs. And what is clear from the American context is that notwithstanding the blatancy (even "absurdity") of Trump's wildly overstated crowd estimates, such revelations do little to destabilize his image in the eyes of his followers.[69] What might our Mumbai rally-show have to say about this sort of thing? If "the size of the public will be the size of the image," then perhaps we need to ask about the public whose image is being signaled: perhaps the public on display at Trump's rally is not simply the crowd of materially present, assembled bodies but rather the broader network of sociomaterial relations, energy, capacity, and taaqat that is being "advertised" by means of the rally-show. Indeed, Trump's tweets about the bigness of his crowd appear more as arousing "solicitations to participation" than descriptions of physical scope or scale of any discrete happening.[70]

This discussion of natak began with a discussion of the concept of public—with the Habermasian notion of the "public sphere" as a communicative space characterized by the "use of language oriented towards reaching understanding." Following our flower-soaked procession as it winds its way through the Mumbai streets, however, leads us away from discourse and toward the image—what Guy Debord famously derided as "mere representation" and the opposite of language-mediated thought (critical or otherwise).[71] And yet the rally-show neither leads to Debord's dystopic "spectacle" society nor beats a hasty retreat to Habermas. People like the print shop men come out on the streets to watch and enjoy and interpret the show, but they do so not by reading "meaning" (matlab) merely from the size of the crowd, but rather by drawing on archived knowledge and embodied memories that yield multiple possible experiences and understandings of the display. The people I spoke to had wildly different readings of the "size of the public" signified by Sayeed's rally: one man told me that the Samajwadi Party rally was "clearly the biggest," while his friend disagreed: Congress's crowd was bigger, but it "had no taaqat." The "size" in question was not quantifiable but rather inhered in the strength, force, intensity, and feeling of the "public" that the embodied crowd images. The distinction between intellection and sensory embodiment collapses.

Audiences

After the election, I met Wasim again in his home in Gowandi to ask more about the boys throwing flowers, which I couldn't get out of mind: Who were those boys throwing flowers? There are always flowers during a rally, of course, but I'd never seen anything quite like what I'd experienced when the rally moved through the butcher's market and boys scampered over awnings and through buildings, drenching the candidate with well-aimed volleys of flowers. Wasim laughed: "See, each area had a responsible person from our campaign team. Everyone wants to make the most dramatic impression on Sayeed Bhai, so that when he passes through some area he gets doused in flowers. Then the candidate will think, 'Wow, my man really did good work here!'" Wasim tells me that the butcher's market was the area for which he himself was personally responsible; the boys with the bags were from his own neighborhood in Gowandi. He'd hired them himself that day to run around in the buildings and throw flowers and set off firecrackers: "mahol create karne ke liey"—to create mahol. For Wasim, in other words, the audience of the natak was the candidate himself.[72]

Wasim's words demonstrate the sense of possibility that inheres in the dramaturgical space of political life, where the occasion of the rally-show presents a ready-made stage for ambitious local leaders (mains) to produce and shore up their own relations of reciprocity—both with their "publics" and with the candidate (and party).[73] They use the rally-show as a stage on which to advertise themselves—to demonstrate to Sayeed their own capacity and taaqat, just as Sayeed is performing his ability to get things done by displaying those same relational networks. Electoral campaigns are moments of possibility and semiotic contingency, providing opportunities for the kind of social and political efficacy (and mobility) whose absence prompted the frustrated Fareed to seek an alternative medium and platform in his NGO.[74] The existence of the myriad of audiences means as well a myriad of potentially conflicting messages sought to be communicated. And deciphering this multiplicity is a key dimension of what people are looking for in a rally-show: What relations of material and symbolic authority are being "advertised" in the rally? What material evidence (signs) is on display, linking the assembled crowd to those relational networks and authorities?

The rally-show, to use Schechner's terms, is both "make-believe" (a performance that overtly signals its own pretense using shared conventions) and "make-belief" (a performance that seeks to "convince" by conjuring into being that which it enacts).[75] On the one hand, the rally signals its own pretense through "conventions": elaborately orchestrated flowers; hordes of hired flag-bearers; a steady stream of garland-wielding known personalities. And at the same time, the rally is a real-time performative enactment of the strength of the reciprocal relationships and networks necessary to pull off a good show. Indeed make-believe and make-belief work together. On the one hand, it is precisely in its explicit forswearing of believability that theater gives its audience permission to indulge in the collective, rasa-soaked enjoyment that might create conviction. And at the same time that it signals its make-believe character, the enactment of the rally-show is fraught with contingencies: the actors could fail to perform as part of the team; they could "flip" and sabotage; the garlanders might choose to participate, or not; the flag-bearers might show up, or not. On the morning of the rally, while the Bihari boys got dressed up, an anxious Sayeed phoned Wasim continuously to ask how many people had turned up; once the rally was underway, Wasim expressed his relief that "the public has come." Thus, while the rally overtly signals its make-believe character, the orchestration of a good show is a compelling sign of the resources and relational networks comprising actual authority. In this way, make-believe produces real belief.

Matlab

While it is common knowledge in Mumbai that the meaning of an election rally inheres in its character as natak, open acknowledgment of this is rare. On the one hand, such open declaration would be absurd (imagine a theatergoer jumping to his feet, pointing toward the stage, and proclaiming: "That man is not really Henry V. . . . He's only an actor!"). The theatricality of the political rally is something so widely known and recognized that it goes unspoken, requiring no explicit marking. The permission to disavow literal belief afforded by the theatrical genre is precisely what lends the rally-show its affective force, persuasiveness, enjoyability and appreciation of its necessity: "You have to advertise!" Watching the rally-show as if those really were flag-bearers, and as if we really are a spontaneous outpouring of love and support—the assembled crowd is swept up by the natak, participating in the drama by playing "audience." The final rally is a temporally and geographically bounded communicative encounter—one that speaks the language of dramaturgy. And yet we see how, even in this spatially and temporally bounded and socially framed performance, the boundaries of the "stage" are porous, constantly shifting, subject to slippage and speculation. Who is acting? Who is playing "audience," and who might be the actual audience or audiences—intended and otherwise? Any clear boundary separating onstage and offstage dissolves, subject to moralizing evaluations by a myriad of potential and actual audiences. As the men at the print shop demonstrate—standing on the side of the road, watching and commenting on the rally's size and taaqat, they too are part of the drama, performing their role as audience; they step out of character only briefly, in order to ensure that the foreign-seeming anthropologist understands that "this is only natak," lest he misunderstand the context and read a literal meaning (matlab) in this performance.

The print shop men's cautioning against looking for matlab in the rally recalls Andy Rotman's discussion of North Indian jute-bag vendors who insist that if the anthropologist thinks that he "grasps the meaning" of the text and images printed on a bag, then he has simply missed the point of the graphics. For instance, when Rotman asks a bag vendor about the "matlab" of an image printed on a jute bag (an image depicting an airplane crashing into buildings that resemble the World Trade Center), he is told in no uncertain terms that "It doesn't have any meaning." If Rotman read any meaning into the image printed on the bag, he was told, "then you didn't understand it." To make sense of this paradoxical situation, Rotman considers Anthony Forge's account of Abelam painters in Lowland New Guinea, who do not distinguish between "figurative and abstract elements" in their art. Even if a figure in a painting resembles something that exists in the world, the painters deny any referential meaning; Abelam painting is a "closed system . . . having no immediate reference outside itself." And yet, as Rotman notes, reflecting on his jute-bag vendors, this doesn't mean that the graphics printed on the bags were "meaningless" to their Indian audiences: "The words and images that they contain were recognizable . . . and they did constitute a system of meaning." As Rotman explains, the graphics were not "texts to be read or images to be decoded; they were icons that testified to a highly affective awareness."[76] In the case of the jute bag depicting the airplane and World Trade Center, they were icons that testified to an awareness of that which is "foreign" and "exotic." Similarly, our rally-show image testifies to affective awareness of the bigness and taaqat—of the social relations and networks of authority on display. Indeed, once my print shop men realized I had understood the event's character as spectacular show, they quickly went back to enjoying the performance, revising their response to my question about the rally's matlab: "It's like an advertisement."

3

Believe
"What's a Show and What's a Lie"

Bombay appreciates a good show . . . but people know what's a show and what's a lie.

—Social media campaign manager, December 2019

سبھا सभा sabhā—Assembly, meeting, company; council; a sitting of the king in council; a judicial court; a levee; hall of audience; a gaming-house; a much-frequented place; place, house

—Platts, *A Dictionary of Urdu, Classical Hindi, and English*

Back in Daulat Nagar in 2012, a few heady February days before polling day, Seema's campaign team organized a sabhaa—also described by her campaign team as a "public meeting"—arranging a few hundred plastic chairs in a local schoolyard and assembling an elevated platform from which the area's state legislative assembly representative (and Seema's copartisan) Mastanbhai was to address an assembled crowd.[1] Seema herself had spent the morning doing prachaar (publicity, advertising, campaigning), parading through the streets trailed by a party-flag-toting entourage composed largely of low-income Daulat Nagar residents.[2] When Seema headed over to the stage her rallygoers followed her, seating themselves in the plastic chairs that had been arranged for the sabhaa. Mastanbhai arrived, mounted the stage, took one look at the audience, surmised (correctly) that this was the very same cash-mediated crowd from Seema's morning prachaar, and stormed off—refusing to address the theatrical public.

A seasoned party worker named Rakesh (the same Rakesh from the conclusion of chapter 1) explained it to me like this: "For prachaar, money is given because it's work. You have to hold a sign. And maybe your friends make fun of you for it. So, for that you get money." But for a sabhaa, people will gather and remain to listen only if the "show" (he used the English word) pleases (pasand) them and holds their attention: "If the speech [taqrir] is boring," Rakesh explained, "then the public won't come." In this context, he asked rhetorically—where the size and energy of the crowd indexes the pleasure and attention-worthiness of the onstage oration—"To pay people to act like they're enjoying . . . ? That looks bad."

While the previous chapter was about publics that are explicitly theatrical (and evaluated as such), this chapter attends to those that are expected not to be: audience-interlocutors for speech-mediated encounters like Mastanbhai's ill-fated sabhaa. Both kinds of Mumbai gatherings—both explicitly theatrical ones like the election rally in the previous chapter, as well as those that assemble for the language-mediated encounters that are the subject of this one—are characterized as publics. So, how are they different, such that one public is expected to be theatrical whereas the other is expected not to be (or at least is meant to do a better job pretending not to be)? At a surface level, the difference might seem to have something to do with language: unlike in a rally, in a sabhaa the public is addressed using words. This chapter demonstrates, however, that it would be mistake to locate the difference between the communicative registers of prachaar and sabhaa merely in the talking, such that the former communicates theatrically while the latter speaks using the "referential and propositional" speech of an idealized public sphere.[3] On the contrary, and as Rakesh's words suggest ("that looks bad"), the sabhaa too is a performance: alongside the public that assembles (and, ideally, remains) as audience for a compelling oration, there is another that performs the evaluative "looking" that Rakesh describes—the audience to whom a paid (theatrical) public might "look bad."

Indeed, the word sabhaa is used interchangeably in Mumbai not only with "public meeting" but also with "stage show"—the latter term notable for its explicit reference to spatialization and emplacement ("staging") of a language-mediated encounter. And this significance of space and place is suggested in the etymology of the word sabhaa itself, which refers at once to a meeting as well as to the site of that same meeting; per Platts's definition (see epigraph), sabhaa describes both a "assembly, meeting, company; council; a sitting of the king in council" as well as the "judicial court; a levee; hall of audience; a gaming-house; a much-frequented place [or] house" where a sabhaa takes place. The difference between the (explicitly theatrical) public of the rally-show and that of the sabhaa (which must not be seen to be theatrical, precisely because it can be) is not merely a question of whether or not the interaction unfolds in the dramaturgical-affective register of natak; both do that. Rather, where the rally-show explicitly signals itself as natak, the language-mediated encounters that comprise the ethnographic heart of this chapter are performances in the Goffmanian dramaturgy of "everyday life" as it is enacted in city streets and spaces.[4] While the final rally described in the previous chapter appears as a spatiotemporally bounded, nonlinguistic communication event, this chapter reveals the broader, language-infused sociomaterial and relational landscape that was on display during the rally-show.

"Full Physical Arena"

Linguistic anthropologists have long noted the inadequacy of the "classic linguistic model of the communicative act: the isolated sentence tossed (like a football) by an anonymous speaker, whose qualifications for play are specified only as 'competence,' to an even more anonymous Hearer who supposedly catches it."[5] As anthropologist Webb Keane notes, "speakers are not unified entities, and their words are not transparent expressions of subjective experience."[6] There is a wide range of "participant roles" that speakers can take up with their words,[7] and within any single utterance there can exist multiple "voices" speaking in a variety of "registers"[8]—a multivocality that Mikhail Bakhtin terms "heteroglossia."[9] Communicative encounters, moreover, are never merely one-directional exchanges between speakers and hearers, but invariably involve another set of heterogeneous "participants" that anthropologist Judith Irvine calls "relevant others": overhearers, neighbors, passersby, implied or hoped-for audiences. In this context, making sense of the "roles" played by these sorts of unofficial, non-"ratified" participants in speech encounters means attending to what Goffman refers to as the broader "social situation" within which any utterance occurs—"the full physical arena in which persons present are in sight and sound of one another."[10]

Reflecting on the difference between the then-recent election of Donald Trump to the American presidency in 2016, for instance, a party worker affiliated with Sayeed's campaign (someone who was not a fan of the Trump presidency) recalled for me what a senior copartisan had recently said in a karyakarta meeting:

> With all the slum redevelopment, how will we do our politics? Campaign-ing is possible in Mumbai because everyone comes out in the streets. As long as there are slums, people are vigilant/awake/alert [jaagta] and there will be politics. But with all the redevelopment, [I fear that] politics in Mumbai will become like in America.

The ability to make sense of the deluge of campaign communications, in other words, depends on attunement to the sensory affordances of everyday street life; so long as "everyone comes out in the streets," the public cannot escape awareness, even if it wanted to. The transformation of the built fabric of the city in a way that precludes sensory encounters of "the streets" (his construal of what it is like "in America") is thus feared to lead to public ignorance by rendering the public imperceptive—unable to decipher the meaning of campaign communications and thus ill-equipped for "politics." Attending to the staging and emplacement of language-mediated, embodied encounters, this chapter demonstrates how the material fabric of the city is also its communicative infrastructure—a built fabric thick with signs whose meanings are rich with interpretive possibility and peril, open to interpretation as well as semiotic slippage as people work out whom and what to "believe."

Understanding language-mediated encounters, in other words, requires attending not just to the literal meaning of words (their "denotational" content) but also to their physical form (what Peircean semiotics calls the "sign vehicle") and to the material infrastructures of their convey-ance, what Goffman calls the "full physical arena" of language-mediated encounter.[11] Indeed, as anthropologists influenced by the American prag-matist Charles Sanders Peirce have pointed out, words are merely one kind of sign and always exist in and among a myriad of other signs in relation to which they take on meaning. Anything can be a sign—a cash note, a dry tap, a flower garland, a sea of empty plastic chairs—if it is interpreted as one.[12] And words—whatever their material form—always co-occur with a myriad of these other sensorily perceptible signs, working together to articulate "semiotic registers": clusters of signs that band together to signify and perform a "category of perceivable personhood."[13] Considering the "full physical arena" therefore requires considering also the role of non-proximate audiences, who may be nonetheless sensorily present through material and technological mediations comprising a broader communicative infrastructure.

In this context—and as Rakesh's words ("that looks bad") suggest—making sense of Mastanbhai's ill-fated sabhaa requires attending to the full communicative landscape within which the "episode of talk"[14] was to take place. The fact that the sabhaa was (rather abruptly) canceled before the speaking part of the event could even transpire demonstrates how the referential meanings and denotational content of words are merely one aspect—and not necessarily the most important one—of the episode. However interesting or compelling Mastanbhai's words might have been (had they actually been spoken), to utter them before either empty chairs or a theatrical crowd would have "looked bad." Rakesh's comment thus prompts us to consider, Who is doing this evaluative "looking"?

As the previous chapter demonstrated, the size and strength of publics are subject to critical evaluation and interest by any number of audiences (known and unknown): a bony crowd could signal weak social networks (or lack of oratory skills) of the onstage speakers; a flop show could make a meeting's organizers "look bad" in the eyes of the party higher-ups—demonstrating to party leaders the poor reputation or organizational "capacity" of area party workers, even perhaps suggesting the strength of rival party workers to "hijack" a show.[15] Meanwhile, the omnipresent news media brings into the "physical arena" any number of potential evaluators—publics that may not have been known (or even to have existed) at the time of some event's planning. This chapter attends to the cacophony of language-mediated encounters over the weeks that preceded (and culminated in) the final campaign rally-show of the previous chapter: the door-to-door campaigns and late-night "mouse meetings"; the formation of WhatsApp groups; the circulation of digital videos and multilingual paper pamphlets; the intimate talk at chowk sabhaas (street-corner meetings) and open oratory at "stage shows."

The accounts that follow demonstrate how people go about making sense of words by attending to their material infrastructures and sociospatial contexts of conveyance and to the social relations that the "full physical arena" of the communicative encounter indexes. We meet the people who enable (and/or block) access to the spaces, places, and technologies (private homes, building rooftops, welfare society meeting halls, WhatsApp groups) where language encounters transpire—work that is necessary precisely because actual audiences invariably outstrip curatorial efforts. What's more (as Irvine points out, making a Bakhtinian point), the meaning of any particular utterance is bound up with a myriad of "implicit links to many dialogues, not only the present one, which together inform its significance, influence its form, and contribute to its performative force."[16] With episodes of talk unconstrained by any imperative of copresence, the ethnographic question concerns the relationship between any particular snippet of speech (a text message, a paper pamphlet, a public oration, a cash note) and the broader semiotic landscape within which some communicative act occurs. Any particular episode of talk is always already bound up with a myriad of other utterances and contexts, and therefore participants in any conversation (speakers, hearers, and relevant others) are always necessarily engaged in the fraught and necessary work of "creative contextualization"[17]—speculating on who might be playing what "role," assessing the relations of power and authority entailed in a speech situation, and trying to work out what some language-mediated encounter might herald:[18] is this "a public performance or a private conversation?" Among those within earshot, who is explicitly or implicitly "drawn into the circle of participation as audience," and who is "excluded"?[19] With the identity and existence of actual and potential parties to language-mediated encounters often unknowable and potentially infinite (and thus subject to much speculation), how is the success or flop of a speech event to be assessed? And to whom or what ought that outcome be credited?

We explored the work of "creative contextualization" already in chapter 1, which focused on communicative work of cash-mediated prachaar within the spatiotemporally broader contextual meanings of money; cash notes were meaningful not merely within the conventional register of commensuration but also and more crucially within an already existing set of relationships among the people among whom cash flows.

Making sense of election-season cash meant attending to its material and affective affordances as a medium of communication—pointing to the geographically wider and temporally longitudinal boundaries of any particular exchange: the meaning of cash was shown to be diachronic, its amassing and distribution signifying and alluding to the histories of its accumulation, while also demonstrating to area voters (and other audiences, intended and otherwise) a candidate's bankable relations with crucial networks of power and authority. By the time the 2017 election rolled around, the media landscape in Mumbai (as worldwide) had been utterly transformed by the ubiquity of social media—especially the communications platform WhatsApp. This chapter thus trains insights from thinking with the material-infrastructural work of money onto the broader landscape of language-mediated encounters—exploring the circulation of words within the broader "mediated sensorium."[20] The accounts show how the meanings of words are bound up with their sensible forms, speech genres, and sociospatial and semiotic contexts, as well as with material infrastructures of conveyance—the written scripts, paper pamphlets, and mobile phone screens; building corridors, neighborhood eateries, and street corners; poetic flourishes, cinematic references, and inside jokes. And what comes into view is a heterogeneous landscape of virtuosi communicators: people whose embodied expertise, perceptual "alertness," and multimodal communicative fluency is at the heart of the high-stakes (and high-octane) work of political communication and representation in Mumbai.

"Social Workers"

In February 2017, two weeks before the final campaign rally of the previous chapter, I attended a "social worker meeting" at one of the four small, street-facing office spaces that Sayeed had rented out for election-season purposes. Sayeed's personal assistant, Wasim, had messaged me earlier that morning to tell me about the meeting, but, having reached the specified office to find the little room empty, I had wandered the neighborhood to see whether perhaps the meeting had been shifted to one of the other party offices. The second office I reached, tucked into a narrow lane, yielded fruit: a small, party-flag-bedecked, warehouse-looking space packed with men. Sayeed sat the back of the room—behind the street-facing table—clean-shaven and bare-headed as always, smartly dressed in a woolen Nehru waistcoat. He was flanked on the left by a fellow whose elegant black hat seemed to identify him as a religious figure of some sort (a whispered question identified him as a priest), and on the right by a large, gray-bearded man with kind eyes, dressed all in white, who I later learned was the municipal councilor (belonging to a different party) from two terms prior. Fifteen or so white plastic chairs were occupied by tidy, professional-looking men, mostly dressed in shirtsleeves and neatly pressed trousers. The walls were lined with a scattering of younger, thinner, jeans-clad, clean-shaven, alert-eyed boys in flashy shirts whose scrappier and more contemporary aesthetic called to mind the karyakartas with whom I had become familiar during Seema's campaign in the popular neighborhoods and "slums" of the eastern suburbs (see chapter 1). When I arrived, a seated man in shirtsleeves was speaking in an educated-sounding (i.e., slang-free) Urdu-inflected Hindi: "We mustn't let people think that Sayeed Rizwan is some outsider trying to come in here, with some personal [zati] interest. We need to make it clear that it is we who have brought him here; we must make it clear that we have invited him to fight from here—because he speaks up at the BMC meetings, because he openly challenges . . . that he'll get us underground parking. That he won't just clean the gutters." One of the younger boys standing along the wall interjects, perhaps a little defensively: "Even in Gowandi," he begins (referring to Sayeed's incumbent district in the eastern suburbs), "Sayeed has done so many things, not just clean gutters like everyone else. He's given us a road," the young man continued. "He's helped with educational things . . . he knows how to do so many things."

"Cleaning the gutters," it must be noted, is a widely understood euphemism—a cynical shorthand for low-cost, highly visible work that disingenuous politicians perform simply to show they're doing something. Because "cleaning gutters" is highly visible (in streets), taking place aboveground and yielding immediate (if short-term) results, it's often described as a favorite and famed way to demonstrate "doing work" while not actually doing anything to redress the deeper structural, infrastructural, and institutional "clogs" that lead to blocked drains in the first place. The euphemistic valence of "gutters" is so common that it has become a trope in satirical film.[21] Back at the social worker meeting, a seated man thus interjects: "Yes! People need to know what's possible to do here . . . not just clean gutters but open schools, sports grounds . . . if we tell what's possible, it will be evident that the previous corporator could have done such things but didn't." Now Sayeed interjects: "This is why the most important thing is the chowk sabhaas. We need to openly announce [bayan karna] the work [kam] that we have done."

Sayeed has been speaking in Hindi, but when he notices me standing in the doorway he switches to English: "Hi, Lisa! Come in," he says, addressing me familiarly, waving me over and proceeding to introduce me: "This is Lisa. She has been writing about my work for many years; she knows each and every water pipe in Gowandi."[22] He turns to me, addressing me directly but speaking at a volume everyone can hear: "Lisa, have you seen how we have resolved the water situation in Gowandi?" Sayeed is aware that I am comfortable in Hindi, but presumably my presence is an opportunity for him to demonstrate his impeccable English to this refined-looking crowd, so I respond in English, saying that I've not visited Gowandi since last year but will certainly make a point to visit as soon as possible. He nods and changes the subject: "This is a social worker meeting," he tells me. "We're preparing for the chowk sabhaas." He switches back to Hindi, turning to Wasim with some instructions regarding teams for the planned chowk sabhaas.

I was struck by the term "social worker meeting." I was familiar with what "social work" meant in neighborhoods like Sayeed's incumbent district in Gowandi (an area similar to Seema's, where, as we saw in chapter 1, "social workers" are experts in managing and mediating everyday life in a built environment shot through with sociomaterial and legal-institutional contradictions). But I wondered what "social work" entailed here in South Bombay, where even the poor lived in residential buildings that, while perhaps ancient and crumbling, were generally not treated for policy purposes as "unauthorized" and which seemed relatively well connected (if only by luck of location) to infrastructural grids and municipal services. When the official-seeming part of the meeting wrapped up, I turned to the man sitting next to me and asked in a low voice: "Sayeed called this a social worker meeting, but what does that mean? What do social workers do around here?" He looks puzzled by the question: "Just . . . general social work." The man introduces himself as Aseem and tells me that he considers himself to be a "social worker." He tells me that he comes from a "political family": his father had been elected as a two-term municipal corporator in the 1970s and then again in 1985–92. Since the 1992–93 riots, however, his family has stayed away from politics. He tells me that he himself had never taken an interest in politics "until Sayeed started coming around." Aseem's family has a shoe-manufacturing business here in Badlapur, he tells me, but most of their karkhana (factory) workers live in Gowandi: "Badlapur and Gowandi are very connected, because South Bombay is where the wholesale markets are located, whereas all the manufacturing happens in Gowandi." He tells me that he'd heard from his Gowandi-based karkhana workers about Sayeed's "good work" there. "We think he could be great," Aseem says, and that is why he's volunteering to "help" with Sayeed's campaign. I ask him what he is doing to "help." "I'm calling my friends. . . . I'm arranging door-to-door meetings with people in buildings." Door-to-door meetings? Aseem explains: "I'm known in the business community, and my family is also known—because of my father. So people trust my judgment. And among the building residents, they trust the building leader's judgment. If I know some important person in some building, I phone that person and tell him about Sayeed, and ask that person to organize a meeting in the building and to accompany Sayeed door-to-door in the building. Because only then will people open their doors to meet the candidate." That's what this "social worker" meeting is for: to prepare for these sorts of local meetings.

I mill about for a while chatting with the others present at the meeting—to get a sense of who they are, what their "social work" entails, what is it is that they might be able to do to "help" Sayeed's campaign, and why they're interested in supporting his candidacy anyway. I meet Kareem Enginwala—a sharply dressed, heavyset, affluent-seeming, tidy-bearded man who looks to be in his fifties. He is wearing a starched, dazzlingly white kurta-pajama[23] and cap that lend him a distinctly pious elegance; his slick iPhone and expensive-looking watch suggest that his marked religiosity goes hand in hand with a business-forward politics. I ask Enginwala about his "social work" activities, and he tells me that he serves on the board of a local educational trust; his "social work" is primarily philanthropic: paying school fees for indigent children and raising money for the trust. His family business is in scrap trading, he tells me, but in recent years he's been dabbling in real estate—trying his hand as a small-scale developer. This is why he's supporting Sayeed. "Sayeed will be good for development," he explains, "and for the area's business environment."

The next person I meet is Yakoob. He lives in the nearby middle-class neighborhood of Mazagaon but owns a shirt factory here in Badlapur. He echoes Enginwala and Aseem: Sayeed's knowledge, vociferousness, and evidenced facility in navigating the ins and outs of the municipal corporation are precisely what Badlapur's business community needs, given the opacity and often-contradictory character of the legal-institutional environment governing local industry and manufacturing in the city. I ask him: "But do you do social work?" Yes, he says, adding that he does "medical social work." Meaning? He tells me (in English) that he's a "philanthropic broker": while he's not wealthy himself, he knows many wealthy people in the community, which allows him to "raise money and direct it to pay hospital bills" on behalf of the area's mostly Muslim poor.

Before I left the social worker meeting that morning, Wasim added me to the campaign-volunteer WhatsApp group so that I could keep up with the daily schedule of campaign events. I had quickly realized that following Sayeed's campaign would require a different kind of informational infrastructure than my 2012 research with Seema had—not only due to the breakneck speed at which social media (especially WhatsApp) became ubiquitous in Mumbai during those intervening years, but also because of key differences between the material morphologies (which are also the communicative infrastructures) of the two neighborhoods more generally. Seema's campaign schedule (as we saw in chapter 1) was constantly in formation: her campaign event schedule was revised continuously, and meetings were convened sometimes with only a few minutes' notice or even on the spot. Rally routes were revised and at times improvisational. And yet the extraordinarily dense built fabric of Seema's ward had made finding and following her campaign activities relatively straightforward; all I had to do was show up in the morning, stop by any of the forty or so neighborhood party offices to ask where she might be, and then wander around until I found her. (At least during the daytime hours; the late-night meetings were by definition more discreet and harder to locate—which of course was precisely the point). The stark difference in the number of party offices in each of the two districts is telling: whereas Seema had forty campaign offices in her 2012 campaign in Daulat Nagar, Sayeed's 2017 campaign in South Bombay had merely four. Wasim later explained to me that this was because "in slums . . .

everything is out in the open." It was in this context that Wasim repeated to me the (half-joking) earlier-mentioned comment by a party leader that, "With all the redevelopment, . . . politics in Mumbai will become like in America." Prachaar is effective in the slums, in other words, because everyone comes out on the streets, whereas in Badlapur (as in "America") people live in buildings and doors open onto building corridors rather than to common spaces like courtyards and streets; "all the redevelopment" therefore poses infrastructural obstacles to "communicating with the public." In this context, a crucial component of election-season communication involves locating and enlisting human intermediaries who can bridge these communicative gaps—who can liaise with the prominent people inside particular buildings who can then arrange for events to be held on rooftops, in basements, and in courtyards of private buildings, and who will then accompany candidates through door-to-door campaigns to connect with potential voters who might not have attended the sabhaa—especially women.

The general invisibility of women in South Bombay's public spaces had struck me immediately when I began frequenting the area for research. In the working-class, also-Muslim-majority popular neighborhoods of the eastern suburbs with which I'd grown familiar, streets are full of women. With employment opportunities for low-income men (as drivers, housing society watchmen, fruit and vegetable hawkers, security guards, janitors, domestic servants, office peons, etc.) generally located in other parts of the city, during daytime hours it is often women who are most visible in the streets—coming going from the market, running small shops, directing NGOs, fetching water, running errands, walking kids to school. In lower-income peripheral areas of Gowandi, I'd grown accustomed to the ubiquity of hijab- and niqab-clad[24] women moving freely through street space: waiting at rickshaw stands, squeezing shoulder-to-shoulder with men into shared autorickshaws, chatting on train platforms from which they too traveled to posher areas of the city—where they might work as maids and cooks and nannies, or (and especially for the younger generation) at call centers, or behind counters at malls, or simply to meet friends in the parks, gardens, and open-air spaces outside the stifling slums.

This out-in-the-open omnipresence of working-class Muslim women was reflected in the gendered composition of the campaign activities I'd witnessed five years earlier in Seema's neighborhood, during the 2012 campaign season. Which is to say, if the visible presence (albeit nothing like predominance) of women in campaign activities in working-class Muslim neighborhoods reflected the gendered character of street space in those neighborhoods more generally, then the same was true in Badlapur: the overwhelmingly male composition of the sabhaa crowds (even those held in "private" spaces on rooftops, courtyards, and basements) that I witnessed in 2017 mirrored the gendering of Badlapur street space. And the reasons for this difference are bound up with neighborhood's economies: as the composition of Sayeed's campaign team suggests (a few bag manufacturers, a shoemaker, a tool importer, a scrap dealer turned developer, etc.), Mumbai's historic market district is largely composed of small, male-headed family firms. Which is to say, the invisibility of a family's women signals the financial prowess of a family's business. In more affluent South Bombay Muslim families, women certainly do move about—not only to visit one another in comfortable homes but also (and notably) in order leave the area precisely in order to be out and about in the city: hopping in a taxi to meet friends for a dosa at a South Indian "Udipi" restaurant; shopping for cheap jewelry in the bustling tourist districts; crossing town to join an aerobics class. With women voters' ears and eyes unreachable, Sayeed's team had to find a way to communicate with them inside their homes. In this context, it was with the men who might be able facilitate access to domestic spaces (and it was indeed largely men) that Sayeed's campaign team sought to forge relations in the run-up to polling—relations forged through networks and introductions made by locally known and influential people such as those I'd met at the initial "social worker" meeting.

Sabhaa

I attended Sayeed's first sabhaa of the season the day after that initial social worker gathering, arriving (per the WhatsApp instructions) in a quiet courtyard behind the Bombay Improvement Trust tenements where Junaid (Urdu scholar and Sayeed's chief orator) had grown up.[25] Indeed, Junaid had organized this particular event (he was "hosting" the sabhaa) because he was well known in the area: he could reach out to important people in nearby buildings, who could then alert their neighbors and friends to come down for the meeting.

I arrived just before 7 p.m. (the sabhaa's official start time) to find around forty people milling about—all men. Campaign workers have propped a cheap loudspeaker atop a taxi, and the terrible sound quality makes it harder to understand what's being said than if there were no sound system at all. There's no stage separating speakers from audience; rather, the divide is marked by a longish table behind which four chairs are arranged. There's a popcorn guy milling about, who I don't think is part of the campaign, but who seems to be a bigger attraction than Sayeed's meeting. People are coming and going, passing through the courtyard from the street to their homes. Aside from the children, everyone in sight is visibly Muslim—men in topis, women in hijabs. Throughout the program, women and children come and go through the courtyard without stopping to listen; they're mostly going for popcorn. A big rat is dashing about merrily. It scampers over the foot of the person nearby, which causes the fellow to gasp and jump with a start, prompting the man to his left to laugh out loud and clap the startled fellow on the shoulder. I'm nervous that the rat might run over my foot too and that I'll scream.

I stand at the back, behind the arranged chairs, waiting for the program to begin. I strike up a conversation with the man standing nearby (who has recovered from his encounter with the rat). I ask him whether he lives here in the building. No, he says, he doesn't live here. He's a butcher, he tells me, and has a shop nearby. He tells me that he came to the meeting today because he had heard that there had recently been a proposal presented in the BMC to move the municipal slaughterhouse—which is located in the eastern suburb of Deonar, just at the edge of Sayeed's incumbent district in Gowandi—outside the city. The butcher tells me that he heard it had been Sayeed who had effectively blocked the slaughterhouse-shifting proposal in the municipal corporation, adding that "this was very helpful for us butchers; there are a lot of us around here and we all source our meat from Deonar." He tells me about how Sayeed had even managed to direct municipal resources to upgrade the existing slaughterhouse facility at Deonar.

Around 7:30 the official part of the meeting begins; the first person to speak from behind the table introduces himself as a retired principal of a nearby Urdu-medium municipal school. He's dressed all in white—kurta, pajama, topi—as are many of the others (including the butcher).

The principal speaks in refined and polite Urdu, poetically equating the municipal corporation to a "trust": "The BMC is the trust that is with us from birth to death: it is from the BMC that we are given our certificates of birth and of death. The BMC registers our marriages and gives us school-leaving certificates. If we want an English-medium school, the BMC can give us one. All these things can be arranged; see how Sayeed got a digital school even in Gowandi. He has done wonderful things [kamal kar diya]. He can do those things here as well. We are Muslims, and with Sayeed we can have our own knowledge without having to learn Marathi. On the twenty-first [polling day], take God's name, say a prayer, and vote for Sayeed."

Next, Junaid takes the stage. The fidgeting crowd falls silent as he begins to speak in a rich, florid Urdu. The audience—whose attention seemed a little half-hearted during the principal's speech—is rapt.

BIT chawls are like little India—all castes are here, all mixed together. There is no communalism in our party. We are secular. We support all— Khojas, Reddys. . . . Communalism is not what we do. Last election, in this very place, I brought to you a Congress candidate. This one is even better! Many corporators see the BMC as an investment: they seek out the ticket—some buy it even—and then the BMC budget is so big that they earn it back. But Sayeed didn't seek out this party ticket. He's from here, he grew up just behind the Arabi Hotel. He's the best Muslim leader in the BMC. He speaks strongly but he keeps good relations with all. Education [talim] is the most important thing that he's been working on. It was he who spoke up against the [proposal requiring] that students perform Suriya Namaskar in municipal schools.[26] He wants to break the South Bombay political culture—which is full of dalals [brokers]: for each and every little repair, permissions and payments are sought. Sayeed Rizwan's system is that all of you will have his office number which you can call directly; he will connect you with the appropriate municipal department.

Junaid wraps up his oration by quickly mentioning a string of proposals that Sayeed plans to pursue: a public garden and sports facility (designed by a well-known Muslim architect) and a municipal hospital for poor laborers (there had been plan and proposal for one a decade ago, he explained, but no one followed it up). After he's finished speaking, Junaid is beckoned over to a long bench where a line of elderly men clad in kurta-pajama suits are sitting in a line. "They're the senior citizens of the area," Junaid tells me in a low voice as we approach the bench, adding, "they're very influential." Junaid stands in front of the bench and converses with the seated men, whose refined, florid Urdu matches the register with which Junaid has just addressed the crowd. After some pleasantries—the purpose of which strikes me more as an opportunity for a speech-mediated encounter in ornate Urdu than to say anything in particular—one of the old men says to him plainly, and without explanation: "Now we won't support anyone else."

What was it that impelled the men on the bench to profess support for Sayeed's candidacy? There was nothing in the content of Junaid's speech that was not already common knowledge. Rather, the conversation between Junaid and the "influential senior citizens" suggests that it was not the referential content but rather the form of the talk—an oration in erudite Urdu—that lent this language-mediated encounter its heft. Indeed, it was Junaid the orator rather than Sayeed the candidate who was summoned by the men on the bench after the meeting for a stylized exchange in high Urdu. By speaking in this refined register, Junaid had skillfully performed a certain kind of "personhood"[27]: genteel and educated, elegantly marrying an explicit avowal of secular principles (and disavowal of cynical identity politics) with a refined and distinctly Islamic sensibility—dignifying Mumbai's often-vilified community of Urdu speakers with promises of Urdu taleem (education). Indeed, and as mentioned earlier, while in recent decades Urdu has come to be popularly associated almost exclusively with religion (as a language associated with South Asian Islam and by extension with Pakistan), this ignores Urdu's subcontinental history as a secular lingua franca of transregional trade, as well as of popular theater and especially cinema.[28]

It's 8:30 by the time the campaign team (Sayeed, Junaid, and a handful of Sayeed's closest friends) leaves for another "chowk sabhaa"—this one on an actual street corner. I chat with Junaid as we walk, turning away from the deafening honking of the main road and heading down a patchily paved lane lined with single-story structures that are built into the footpath along one side. Along the other side are some taller buildings (three or four stories)—structures that are visibly newer than the century-old chawls from where we've just come and whose residents are visibly poorer. We stop at an intersection where some members of Sayeed's campaign team are waiting for us, alongside some people I don't recognize; Junaid identifies them for me as "local people." People are clustered in groups along the sides of the lane—poking heads out of windows, standing in their doorways. Junaid calls the area a "slum." And indeed, the built fabric and space of the neighborhood reminds me of Daulat Nagar, where Seema had contested in 2012. Junaid explains that in areas like this the campaign team obtains police permission (sometimes officially, other times not, depending on location, scale, and duration of the event) to construct a temporary stage at a busy intersections and block traffic for a few hours for the sabhaa. The meeting is being held in the street, in other words, because here there are no courtyards. Or perhaps it's the absence of available courtyards that impels the local police station to grant permission to block the street? Either way, a uniformed police officer approaches us and announces: "You can have an hour."

Junaid doesn't speak at this sabhaa. Instead, a young man in jeans mounts the stage and—speaking not in Urdu but in the informal, everyday Hindustani diction common in Bombay's streets and markets—announces to the gathered crowd that he's not a Badlapur local but rather a resident of Sayeed's incumbent district in Gowandi.[29] He describes how Sayeed has helped them to get new, legal water connections. Both the speaker and the content of the onstage speech differ dramatically from that of the BIT chawl just a few blocks away, and again we see how the form of the words relates to their content. This combined form and content of words takes on significance in relation to the "full physical arena" within which the communicative encounter occurs: in the BIT chawl, Junaid's performance communicated the value of education, Urdu literacy, and community dignity to a highly educated but socially marginalized public; in the "slum" neighborhood a few blocks away, the young Gowandi resident's comportment, clothing, and dialect worked to perform the speaker's personhood (as a "genuine slum resident") and thereby a person whose testimony to the power and efficacy of Sayeed's networks could be trusted.

Relational Chains

The next day, I meet Junaid for tea to fuel up before an afternoon of sabhaas and door-to-door campaigns and to ask some questions about his oration the previous day. (What did he mean by "siaysi [political] culture"?

"Oh, that's when politicians just turn up at weddings rather than actually doing any work.") I'd been hanging around Fareed's NGO, Taqaat,
that afternoon (see chapter 2), but when the squawking crows began to
announce sunset I headed up Mohammed Ali Road toward Sarvi, a well-
known Irani café where Junaid and I had arranged to meet up.[30] We chat
for a while, and after paying the bill (he never lets me pay), Junaid mentions that before the first scheduled event that evening he has to make a
quick stop to visit a family that lived in the flat next door to his while he
was growing up—a Gujarati-speaking, Shia Bohra family (Junaid himself is an Urdu speaker of Sunni lineage). He invites me to join him, adding that he hasn't seen them in over a decade—not since his own family
moved out of the building.

We cross the road and walk a few blocks toward Junaid's childhood
building, in whose courtyard he'd delivered a beautiful Urdu oration the
previous evening. This time, instead of heading around back, we enter
the building from the street-facing side and Junaid stops in front of a
ground-floor door. He rings the bell. The woman who opens the door is
advanced in age but not quite elderly. There's an awkward moment of
silence, and Junaid asks, "Do you recognize me?" The woman pauses a
moment, scanning his face, and then breaks into a smile: "Junaid! Please
come in." Then, over her shoulder, she calls to her husband (in Gujarati),
"Junaid's here!" We follow her into the living room and sit down on the
sofa. Junaid explains (speaking in polite but unflorid Urdu) that he's come
by today because his "good friend is standing for election." She nods,
without seeming very interested in Junaid's "good friend"; she wants to
hear news about his family: Who's married? Who has had kids? Where is
everyone studying? We spend a half hour talking about weddings and
children and university and health—and then Junaid again mentions that
Sayeed is standing for election and that "he's my good friend." The husband dutifully asks, "Which party?" Farid mentions not the party name
but rather the party symbol: "cycle." The husband asks nothing more
about Sayeed—what he's done, what he might do, why Junaid thinks he
might be a good corporator. The husband then changes the subject and
begins talking about their building troubles: "It's been sold, the building, because of the laalach [greed] of the owner." He explains that now
they're afraid they might have to leave their beloved home because of

some kind of "redevelopment nonsense." He speaks in Urdu but uses the English phrase "redevelopment nonsense." By way of response, Junaid mentions Sayeed's work in Gowandi, adding that whatever the problem, Sayeed has demonstrated the "capacity" to help. They aren't interested in hearing any details of Sayeed's work in Gowandi; Junaid's endorsement appears to be enough to convince them. Finally, after all the family news has been shared, Junaid and I get up to go. The Bohra couple seems elated by the visit and sorry to see him leave. They shake his hands warmly, the woman clasping his hand in both of hers. Junaid says: "Please tell the people in the building to vote. Do you remember which party?" "Cycle." "And remember that if Sayeed wins, then I'm here for you." They smile contentedly; they seem to already know this is true—that Junaid will indeed be there to liaise with Sayeed in case of any need. Which is to say: they're not saying they'll vote for Sayeed and spread the word as a personal favor to their erstwhile neighbor, but rather because, by means of this relational work of taking the time to visit the couple's home for tea and to engage in patient talk about matters of mutual concern— marriages and health and education of loved ones; the laalach of landlords and fears for the future—the couple's relations with the would-be representative have just been forged.

This kind of emplaced talk can be understood as an effort to populate the representative relationship—to create a relational chain that reaches from the sitting-room sofa to the municipal corporation. At the initial social worker meeting, Sayeed was praised for "openly challenging" and for "speaking up" regarding matters of common concern. The previous evening, in the courtyard behind the chawl, Junaid performed his personhood as a learned and fluent speaker of high Urdu on behalf of Sayeed, thereby forging a communicative link between Sayeed's campaign and the group of Urdu-speaking elders. Here at the Bohra couple's home, Junaid listened diligently to the couple's concerns, promising to convey their concerns to the corporator in the event Sayeed should win the election, before requesting that the couple please "tell the people in the building" about Sayeed. Much of campaign-season conversation entailed this sort of "talk about talk"[31]—with candidates evaluated by assessing the scope and strength of social networks comprising the relational infrastructure of communication and representation.

Mains

Junaid and I walk over to the campaign office and catch the rest of the team just as they're about to head out for the evening's rounds, the first stop on which is a chawl building at the other end of the neighborhood. Sayeed climbs onto the back of a motorbike; Wasim motions for me to hop on the back of his. In the hustle and bustle of the street I lose sight of Junaid, but presumably he's on the back of some motorbike. We honk and swerve breezily along Mohammed Ali Road, our caravan stopping in a darkish but bustling narrow street, where a smiling fellow is waiting for us.

I climb off the bike and ask Wasim about the smiling man; Wasim tells me he's the building's society chairman. We follow the chairman through an elegant (if crumbling) ornate stone archway into a century-old chawl building, up a florescent-lit wooden stairway. Our team is composed of ten or so people, including an ever-present camera-toting fellow and another lugging armfuls of campaign literature: colorful, image-rich, bullet-pointed "pamphlets" printed in Marathi, Hindi, Urdu, and English. The building is home to people of all sorts of linguistic and religious affiliations: mostly Urdu-speaking Sunni Barelvis, but plenty of English- and Gujarati-speaking Shia Bohras, a scattering of Marathi-speaking Hindus and Konkani Muslims. We stop in front of a door bearing the recognizably Bohra name of the resident family. While our host knocks politely on the Bohra family's door, Sayeed whips his head toward the pamphlet fellow and says urgently, "English! English!"[32] The fellow hands Sayeed an English-language pamphlet just in time for the door to open. Sayeed converses in English with the elderly man who has opened the door, handing him the pamphlet.

We spend an hour or so winding along corridors, up and down the stairs, knocking on doors and handing out pamphlets in the appropriate language. Sayeed and his team demonstrate a social fluency keenly attuned to the building's mind-boggling diversity—switching among languages or changing modes of greeting in skillful, lightning-fast assessments of what "type of person" might live behind which door and what sort of "voice" (vocal or metaphorical) might therefore be most effective in addressing that sort of person.[33] Sayeed hands an Urdu-language pamphlet to an elderly, bearded fellow in a white cap who is later described to me (after I asked a member of the campaign team whether the man's sectarian or regional identity was readily discernible by his attire) as "probably a common Muslim"—most likely a Barelvi variety of Sunni, which is "common" in Bombay—although it's impossible to say for sure, I was told, because "such caps are common among Deobandis and others also." A few doors down, a similarly attired man refuses the Urdu pamphlet that Sayeed hands him, explaining that the candidate doesn't need to worry about convincing them with words: "Is there any doubt in your mind?," he asks rhetorically—then gesturing toward the society chairman while still directing his attention toward Sayeed, he adds: "Wo hamara main aadmi"—"He's our main/trusted man." There was no need to read whatever words might appear inside the pamphlet—in whatever language. Rather, the information that matters most to him is the judgment of the building society chairman—the person whose proven efficacy and responsiveness in attending and resolving matters at stake in the BMC election: liaising with offices and officers of the municipal corporation when taps run dry; finding a hospital bed for an ailing relative.

A little ways up the corridor, a sturdy wooden door is opened by a sari-clad, bare-headed woman, the cross affixed to the inside of the doorway announcing her household as Christian. The pamphlet man—inferring the woman's linguistic preference presumably from some combination of her clothing and cross—thumbs wordlessly through the stack and hands over a Marathi-language version. Sayeed speaks to her warmly in his native Marathi (which I don't speak but follow somewhat). I catch a mention of "digital classrooms," and the woman bobs her head with a smile, responding in Marathi: "Yes, I've heard."

We proceed door-to-door like this, and at some point Sayeed's campaign managers receives a message that Sayeed is due at his next meeting. But Sayeed doesn't alter his pace upon receiving this news; rather, he completes the door-to-door campaign. Having witnessed the confidence inspired by the building society chairman who is hosting the visit, it seems imperative that Sayeed demonstrate, in turn, that he too is reliable. Sayeed is new to area politics, after all, and the credibility of whoever made this introduction for Sayeed to the society chairman—as well as the chairman himself, who is now making the door-by-door introductions and thus presumably commands the trust of building residents—is also at stake. Sayeed takes his time, performing his assiduity as much for the chairman as for the voters.

Back out in the street, Sayeed takes leave of the building chairman and picks up the pace, walking briskly (almost running) toward the wholesale vegetable market, stopping at an open-fronted warehouse space. Above the door hangs a sign announcing "Indian Fruit and Vegetable Suppliers." Inside the space hangs a smaller sign announcing that this is home to a neighborhood Fruits and Vegetable Merchant Welfare Association, giving the name and telephone number of the association president, who is our host this evening. I count around fifty people milling about outside the warehouse, entirely men, most of them visibly Muslim. I ask Junaid about the association: Who are they? What do they do? He tells me that there are at least twenty-five wholesale vegetable shops in this area, "old shops." The shop owners have ancestral and kinship ties to the Hindi- and Urdu-speaking regions of Western Uttar Pradesh. The association doesn't actually do "welfare," Junaid tells me, but rather "does representation" (representation karta hai) for businesspeople in this area; having a registered NGO is important because it allows them to "represent" to the municipal corporation officers or to political leaders—to issue written petitions on association letterhead, for instance.

Inside the narrow space, some chairs have been arranged, but the ones in the back half of the room are quickly restacked to create space for more people to stand. Our host, the association president, makes some brief opening remarks, introducing the candidate: "Sayeed Rizwan will solve the problems of our community! We don't even need to tell him what our problems are because he already knows."

Before Sayeed speaks, Junaid addresses the audience, delivering a few lines in his high-register, poetic Urdu. The speech is short—less than a minute—but appears to have had its desired effect: the room is silent, almost reverential. The soothing sound of the poetic Persian words seems to leave a feeling of genteel respectability hanging in the air by the time Sayeed speaks. Sayeed's direct, unpoetic diction conveys meaning in a register very different from but no less impactful than that of Junaid. Sayeed articulates his insider knowledge and familiarity with particular details of the traders' concerns, telling the assembled men that once elected, he will use his office to construct public toilets for the vegetable hawkers who source from the wholesalers assembled here in the room; in the absence of toilets, the smell of urine has become something of an issue.[34] "The other parties oppose the fariwalas [hawkers]," Sayeed says, "but we'll support them because it's their livelihood and our business." The use of the distancing "they" in reference to the hawkers is a reference to the fact that most of the hawkers are not local residents (or voters) here in Badlapur; by contrast, Sayeed's use of the self-inclusive "our business" articulates himself as a member of the community—suggesting that the issue is personal, that he considers the wholesalers' interests (business) to be of a piece with his own. "No one will take bribes from you because of the fariwalas, and no one will make a living off the toilets either. You can ask in Gowandi, no one makes a living off of toilets. All other parties do bhashanbaazi [merely playing with words], but I have done development." Having asserted that his identity as "one of them" obviates the need for extensive communication—echoing the chairman's introductory remark that "We don't even need to tell him what our problems are, because he already knows"—Sayeed then disparages the "empty talk" of other parties, instead inviting the traders not to be persuaded by mere words, but rather by material signs of his demonstrated accomplishments: "Look at my work, compared with what others have done."

The meeting is short, to the point; the shopkeepers are mostly residents in nearby chawl buildings, and their elderly parents, their wives, sisters, and children are waiting to receive the candidate in their homes— ready to decorate him with garlands, hand him their babies, and in one case revive him with coconut water and a plate of fried chicken (it's dinner hour after all)—thereby extending the relational chain into the gendered spaces of kitchens and sitting rooms.

Sayeed's days are spent parading through buildings and knocking on doors in residential buildings, while the evenings are packed with sabhaas: rooftop meetings and courtyard meetings are often followed by more door-to-door campaigns, where the "main" person in the building who has organized the sabhaa accompanies Sayeed as he knocks on doors—introducing him to women and asking residents to pose questions to the candidate directly. Even though these meetings often featured stages, and even while the apparently one-way direction of speech lent them the ambiance of performance rather than a conversation (which the conversational term "meeting" suggests), sabhaas were distinct from another genre of event (discussed in the next section): the "public meeting" or "stage show." Sabhaa and chowk sabhaa—as well as the English-origin word *meeting*—were the terms generally used to describe gatherings that were not accessible (or even known about) by a broader "public." These meetings—in warehouses and in courtyards and on street corners—were arranged by trusted "mains": business association leaders or housing society chairmen whose knowledgeability about crucial municipal matters has already been established by their demonstrated efficacy in having residents' needs attended to over the years. Sabhaas were attended almost exclusively by men and seemed to serve in part as a point of entry and access to post-meeting encounters with women and elders via door-to-door campaigns. Indeed, the exclusivity of a sabhaa (whether, how, and to whom some meeting is known and accessible) was of central significance during any particular event: meeting attendees were addressed not as a general, anonymous "public" but rather as residents of specific buildings, frequenters of particular markets, stakeholders in particular business and local economies. These sociospatial differences were also intersected by (and also overlaid) other communicative registers such as differences in language (the merchant-class vegetable wholesalers were palpably moved by Junaid's poetic Urdu).

Deciding which registers of speech and comportment might resonate appeared to present less of a challenge to the campaign team in some meetings than in others.[35] In the meeting with the vegetable traders, for instance, the association members shared an occupational position as traders and were all Urdu-speaking Muslims with ancestral ties to North India. In this context, deciding upon a lineup of speakers to deliver pertinent content in a resonant register seemed rather straightforward. In other venues, however, staging a sabhaa clearly entailed a more complex choreography. Three days before the final rally, for instance, I trailed the campaign team to a large, leafy, elite-looking housing society composed of five buildings, located on land held in trust by the Khoja Ismaili Shia community. A largish stage has been erected, and two hundred or so chairs have been arranged in a large open space between the buildings. The chairs are already full by the time we arrive, and another hundred or so people are standing at the back, along the wall, where I also stand. A woman to my left, dressed in an elegant but understated kurta, strikes up a conversation. She introduces herself in native-sounding English, asking where I'm from and what brings me here. I introduce myself (speaking in English) and take her friendly overture as an opportunity to learn a bit more about the neighborhood. She describes the area as a

"Khoja compound," but looking around, it seems the people present are a diverse group. I gesture toward a line of sari-clad women standing just off to one side and ask, "Is the neighborhood mixed?"[36] She tells me that yes, there are some Christians and Hindus living here, but they're all renting tenants. The reason she referred to the area as a "Khoja compound" is because the owners are all Khoja. "If someone sells," she explains, "we sell within the community."

The society chairman opens the meeting, making a short introduction in polite but informal Hindi, noting that "Sayeed Rizwan is the first candidate who has ever come to address our crowd [hamare crowd ko address karna]." I was struck by the inclusive "our crowd," which seemed to refer not merely to Khojas but to everyone present—united by shared residence in the compound and (by extension) socioeconomic class. The chairman continued in Hindi, introducing the first speaker— a faculty member at a local management institute—who stepped to the podium and addressed the crowd in polished English: "I have requested this opportunity to address you because you are the most educated and civilized society. And Sayeed Rizwan is the most educated and experienced leader in the municipal corporation." The professor went on to explain what he means by each of these three terms: *leader, educated,* and *experienced.* Sayeed is a leader insofar as he's "not communal"; for this reason, he can "help the city as a whole to move to the next level." Sayeed is also educated (fluent in English, Hindi, and Marathi), and is experienced insofar as he has learned how to access and channel municipal resources: "Kam kiya hai, karta hai," he says, switching to Hindi: "He has done [good] work, and he continues to do so."

Sayeed takes the stage next, continuing comfortably in flawless English. "You have worms in your water," Sayeed begins, the example working as a colorful and visceral performance of his keen understanding of the embarrassing and infuriating problems faced by this affluent "crowd." After a general murmur acknowledges the truth of this apparent water-worm problem (it was the first I'd heard of it), Sayeed proceeds to narrate the cause of the problem—the technical part of the problem as well as the bureaucratic holdup in redressing it—and is greeted by thunderous applause. After the crowd settles down, a short film is shown on a large screen that's been set up behind the stage. The video is about Sayeed's educational initiatives in his incumbent, low-income district in Gowandi, and the two-minute clip features a series of images of young, hijab-clad girls working at computers. "You've never seen a municipal school," Sayeed says, surmising that this "crowd" would likely have attended (and sent their own children to) private school, "but see what we've done." He goes on to describe the "digital classrooms" and "community participation" initiatives over which he presided during his tenure as elected corporator. The Khojas are a wealthy and philanthropic community, and this part of his speech appears to be directed at them: Sayeed demonstrates the importance he personally ascribes to service—to helping the poor and to increasing educational opportunities for Muslim girls.

After hailing the Khojas, Sayeed performs his secularism by turning his attention—if briefly—to "our crowd's" smattering of Christians. "'Christ Church' is spelled incorrectly on the school's street signboard," he says with an air of hyperbolic exasperation. "Can't your current corporator even get the BMC to spell 'Christ' correctly?" It's a quick address that hits the mark: the current relations representing the society's Christians are so utterly nonexistent that there are errors in the very the written inscription of "Christ Church." The comment earns Sayeed a wave of applause and appreciative laughter.

The last speaker is Abu Asim Asmi—the Samajwadi Party's Maharashtra president.[37] He approaches the microphone and delivers a short, almost brusque-sounding speech in unflorid Hindi: "I'm here for the first time," he begins. "You people have stayed away from politics" (he uses the word *politics*), "but please understand that without a political party no work can be done. Big people [bade log] in this city, they say, 'We're rich, educated, we don't need politics.' But today's politics are dirty because big people like you stay away."

The structure of these sabhaas has become familiar: the "host" speaks first, then a few notables, and finally the candidate. But beyond the surface similarity, the various events differed from one another in profound ways: the referential content of what was said, the spoken language (whether Hindi, Urdu, English, Marathi, or some combination), and the affective register of the words varied from sabhaa to sabhaa, and in some cases (e.g., at the Khoja compound) the lineup of speakers was carefully selected in a fraught, speculative effort to choreograph a speech-mediated encounter that might resonate across a wildly diverse crowd. The orations were sometimes poetic and other times didactic; at other times the speeches were humorous, appearing primarily to function as a way to assemble, entertain the crowd—to assemble a public and keep it from dispersing. Sometimes a single event—and even a single speaker—would tack back and forth among a variety of registers in a way that seemed almost improvisational, keeping pace with a responsive public. And these differences in the content, language, and register of these speech events were bound up with the sociospatial contexts and material infrastructures mediating these episodes of talk.

Jazbaat

Five days before the final rally, Sayeed's campaign organized its first large-scale "public meeting"—scheduled to begin around dusk at the heart of the neighborhood butcher's market. As noted earlier,[38] Sayeed grew up amid Badlapur's community of butchers—it was the khandani dhanda (family business) of his "adopted" family—so it is a locality he knew well and a community from which he hoped for significant support. Before this public meeting, two smaller chowk sabhaas were planned: the first in a small private parking area behind a worn-looking building, home to an elite, English-speaking crowd; the second in a chawl that is home to a mixed-religious crowd of Konkani origin.

We arrive at the first venue, where chairs have been arranged in concentric circles in a way that is designed to yield two-way dialogue. The circular arrangements lends this encounter a more conversational, "meeting"-like feel than others I've attended. The society chairman is speaking. "This is our ward," he says in English; then switches to Hindi: "This time let's give leadership to educated people rather than letting jazbaat [passions; rage] decide.[39] If you want educated people to have a chance to lead, then you have to vote." Then Sayeed takes the microphone, quickly running through his accomplishments in Gowandi (digital schools; water taps) before getting to the point: "Our problems here are different"—he says this in English—the "our" registering an insider positionality. "Parking is a big problem because the fire brigade can't get in. The BMC is the development planning body." He explains his proposal for a designer sports facility with underground parking. "We need attention to dengue," he says, adding that the mosquito-borne disease is more prevalent in elite areas than in his incumbent ward in the Gowandi slums "because there are more trees here." Toward the end of his remarks,

Sayeed pulls out his mobile phone, dials a number and then turns on the speaker function while holding it up to the microphone so that everyone can hear an automated voice telling the caller to "dial one" for water problems. He terminates the call and explains: "Your calls are directed to my office, where we can attend to your problems directly." One of the two society leaders interjects: "A few years ago I went to BMC to get a birth certificate, and I had to run pillar-to-post." As with other meetings, the talking was about talking—the emphasis on Sayeed's potential role as an efficacious link (shortcut even) in a chain of communication. The meeting ends, and Sayeed takes leave of the more prominent-looking men among the all-male crowd. One man clasps Sayeed's hand and says: "We've never gone to the corporator for anything before. But this time we'll go early to vote; we'll get up at seven or eight."

The second meeting is at a road intersection, where the crowd is visibly diverse: equal numbers of women in saris and hijabs; some men in shirtsleeves and trousers, others in Islamic caps and kurtas. The society leader speaks first. His speech is different from others I've heard insofar as he seems to be speaking directly to Sayeed, rather than (as was usually the case) selling Sayeed to his constituency. "We don't need any money," he pleads with the candidate, "we need repairs to our building!" Then Sayeed takes the microphone, and as he begins to speak, someone turns on the sound system's echo effect. Sayeed's voice, audibly irritated, echoes through the speakers: "Turn off the echo!"—the words reverberating in the air for a few seconds before he turns his attention back to the crowd: "You're Konkan people!," he begins. "You remind me of my Nani, who's also from the Konkan region. I'm happy that politics here is changing. Now politics is about development rather than being carried out jazbaat ke nam pe." I ask Junaid what Sayeed means by "jazbaat ke nam pe," and he answers "communal basis"—an all-India euphemism for the age-old trick of stirring up political passions through appeals to identity. This is striking, since Sayeed has just begun his remarks by identifying the crowd—which visibly appears mixed in religion but shares a regional identity as "Konkan people." I wonder: what's the difference between religion-based "jazbaati" politics and identifying a public as "Konkan people"? Sayeed continues: "In Gowandi, I've supported Buddha viharas and [Hindu] mandirs [temples]; I've helped all communities and religions. We need justice for all, not divisiveness." For Sayeed, the inclusivity of

"Konkan people" is counterposed with the divisiveness of religion-based "jazbaati" politics of passion and rage; while both acknowledge identity-based differences, only the latter is accused of intentionally distracting from more pressing work of "justice for all" and "development" of the city as a whole—notwithstanding differences of religion or community identity. Sayeed closes the meeting, telling the crowd: "Please come to the public meeting in the butcher's market this evening and see our strength [taaqat]!"

We reach the butcher's market for Sayeed's "public meeting" at dusk. It's quite impressive: the intersection is blocked off and filled with chairs—hundreds of chairs—and lights and a great big stage. Eight people are onstage, including one woman (who ultimately doesn't speak at all). While there are no women seated in the chairs, there are plenty of women coming and going through the market; the meeting is in the middle of the market's main thoroughfare at prime market hour—just before dinner. It was evident from the outset that this "public meeting" was something quite different from the run-of-the-mill sabhaas, whose form and functioning had by now become familiar. Uncharacteristically, Sayeed was the first to take the microphone and begin speaking . . . and to continue speaking, animatedly and almost without interruption—for a full hour—telling story after attention-grabbing story: "People say that no BMC money is spent in Muslim areas—but that's not true! Look what I've done in Gowandi!" He relates some of the water-related infrastructure projects he has presided over as elected councilor. "Don't listen to people who use this as an excuse for why they aren't doing development in your area. If I can do this in Gowandi then you need to ask them: why haven't you done anything in Badlapur? You've been fooled [dhokha hooa]! I do honest work. Vote for work. Just in the past three months, you can see what work I've done here in Badlapur." He talks about the renovated health dispensary that he has recently inaugurated: "I asked the commissioner, why has the dispensary been closed since 2013? I asked the commissioner for specially sanctioned funds to do work. The funds were approved in the Standing Committee, and now the dispensary is open again. In just three months! Why didn't your corporator do that in the past five years? If I'm elected I can get you not just a dispensary but a hospital." He moves on to talk about schools—"Who says Muslims aren't educated?! I'm fighting for more Urdu schools!"—and about support for religious festivals—"They wanted to close the Deonar slaughterhouse because of the Jain holiday,[40] and the Congress[41] was going along with it. But this is our daily bread! I went to the house and I said, 'If you're going to close the slaughterhouse, then fine, close the fish market as well.' And they all said, 'No, no! How will our Koli people [Marathi-speaking fishing communities] have their daily bread?' I agreed, yes, they shouldn't have that deprived, and neither should our people. So like that the Kolis supported us." The crowd cheers and laughs—they love this story. Sayeed continues on the same theme: "I have no objection to any religion. They should all be supported." He talks about municipal support for events related to Hindu and Christian holidays, adding, "Why not our Bakra Eid?"[42] He recounts how he had presided over the initiative to have exit fees from Deonar slaughterhouse excused on Bakra Eid. "Others are getting support!"

The themes are repetitive but the stories are engaging, and as he's speaking, people continue to gather, stopping, sitting, listening. Kids are running around and trying to get on the stage. Motorbikes buzz past. The team has staged this meeting in a brilliant location, right smack in the middle of the meat market, at the precise moment that people are doing their evening shopping and snacking on keema (spiced minced meat). Over the course of the hour the whole area fills to capacity, and it's the lively, humorous stories and scenarios that people stay to hear, watch, and participate in. By the end of the hour the square is packed— people crowding in, shushing each other, clamoring to see. Kids push one another aside; women crane necks out of windows.

Sayeed invites five teenage-looking boys onstage and garlands them one by one, in a ceremony that recalls the public meeting in Seema's district on the eve of the 2012 election (see chapter 1). I ask a man sitting near me in the audience, "Who are they?" "They're local boys." "But . . . there are thousands of people here, why are they garlanded?" "Because they're main." "Main?" "Meaning, they're the ones who gathered all these people. Behind each of them is a hundred people sitting here."

Junaid steps to the microphone, but instead of his usual Urdu oration he recites a pithy, poignant Urdu couplet, which is greeted by a roar of laughing approval and thunderous applause:

Congress teri haton mei woh lakeer nahi hai;
Badlapur tere baap ki jaagir nahi hai!

Congress Party isn't written into the lines of your hand like destiny
Badlapur isn't your daddy's property!

Junaid tells me later—over WhatsApp—that he had written the couplet the previous night; he writes poetry sometimes. I ask him whether there are particular poets whose work inspires him also to write, and he responds without hesitation: Rahat Indori, a renowned contemporary Urdu poet, well known also for his work as a Bollywood lyricist. Junaid WhatsApps me a couplet:

Sabhi ka khoon hai shaamil yahan ki mitti mein
Kisi ke baap ka Hindustan thodi hai

Everyone's blood is mixed together in this soil
Hindustan doesn't belong to anyone's daddy

I was not familiar at the time with Indori's now-famous couplet—penned three decades earlier but which became wildly popular during the winter of 2019–20 among protesters against the Citizenship Amendment Act and National Register of Citizens (the subject of the next two chapters). As an avid fan of Bombay cinema, I was more familiar with Indori's work in Bollywood, where he is well known for lyrics penned in the Bambaiya dialect of Hindi common to Bombay's street life—songs like "M Bole Toh," the theme song of the gangster-comedy film *Munna Bhai M.B.B.S.*, in which Sanjay Dutt plays a gold-hearted Bombay gangster seeking societal respectability. Indeed, as Bambaiya scholar and documentarian Gautam Pemmaraju writes, "Bambaiya . . . is inextricably linked to the language of cinema. The Hindi film screen in turn draws liberally from the sounds of Bombay street life."[43] The couplet of Indori's that Junaid forwarded to me as an example of the work that inspires Junaid's own creative imagination is immediately recognizable for its striking combination and juxtaposition of voices: the first line in a more formal style of Urdu poetics, the second registering the playfully rough-and-tumble sounds of the Bombay streets. Junaid explains that his poem is similar—and not only in the playfully threatening tone in which some rival party's pretentions to authority are called into question—insofar as each line speaks in "a different voice" and addresses "a different audience."

The first line of his couplet addresses the present crowd, while the second ventriloquizes the voice of the crowd itself, addressing itself in a muscle-flexing tone to Badlapur's Congress Party leadership.

The words emanating from the stage at the butcher's market "public meeting" worked quite differently from how I'd come to understand the meaning and effect of spoken language in the context of sabhaas. Whereas in the latter, selected speakers comported themselves and spoke in registers meant to resonate with particular audiences, to communicate information about the candidate, and thereby to produce and shore up relations of trust. In this "public meeting," by contrast, the repetitive and humorous character of the oratory was suggestive of an idiom of performance—natak—meant to assemble and energize an appreciative crowd on the eve of the election, in one of the most densely trafficked commercial junctions of the neighborhood.

This Mumbai use of the term "public meeting" thus recalls Barnard Bate's rich ethnographic account of Tamil political oratory in South India, in which he notes that "the 'public meeting' . . . occurs more as an appropriation of public space than as an instantiation of a concept of a 'public' space, 'free and open to all.'" Indeed in stark contrast with a liberal, Western inclusive connotations of "public," the "festival"-like events that are the subject of Bate's study amount to a partisan takeover ("appropriation") of urban space by the political party in an "attempt to put a single 'spin,' at least temporarily, onto the cityscape, to ritually construct and impose a single meaning or set of meanings onto a space that is normally multivalenced and polysemic."[44] Sayeed's public meeting at the butcher's market communicates as Bate describes—at the level of aesthetics—a bid at semiotic dominance in which organizers aim to "saturate a particular space with signs of their presence, of their occupation of that space."[45] In this context, the role of oratory at the meeting was the generation of mahol—to create atmosphere—by filling the streets with laughter and stimulating a range of pleasurable feelings: righteousness, humor, optimism.[46] The production of mahol through this onstage drama anticipated the theatrical rally that a few days later would wind its way through this very same junction—accompanied by deafening firecrackers, volleys of flowers, and an intoxicating decibel of enthusiasm. It is through this process of "sensory 'saturation'" that an ordinarily multivalent space such as a street or market is "declared" to properly "belong" to one particular organization.[47] In this context, "public" takes on particularly poignancy; what is ordinarily a space of nonpartisan exchange and encounter (such as the market) is aesthetically resignified as the space of a particular "public."

"The New Door-to-Door"

The day before the final campaign rally, the *Hindustan Times* ran an article in its "Mumbai City" section with a title that caught my attention: "Mumbai Civic Polls: Social Media Is the New Door-to-Door": "Whats-App, Facebook, Instagram, Twitter," the article begins, "it has never been easier to reach out to voters."[48] Having spent the previous weeks out and about, day and night, in streets and on rooftops, in warehouses and corridors, the notion that it has "never been easier to reach out to voters" struck me as somewhat overstated. Undoubtedly, social media, and digital technology more generally, were a crucial part of the communicative infrastructure of Sayeed's campaign over the previous weeks, but the notion that social media was "the new door-to-door"—suggesting the obviating of face-to-face encounters by tiny-screen interfaces—was a far cry from what I'd experienced over the previous weeks. Over the course of the campaign season I'd paid keen attention to the messages circulating on the two WhatsApp groups to which I'd been added by Sayeed's campaign team: the one for campaign volunteers kept me apprised of constantly the changing event schedule; another, much-larger group for general party supporters featured videos—both positive videos and images of Sayeed's campaign—as well as some negative content featuring rival candidates. And yet I'd paid somewhat less attention to the section of Sayeed's campaign team on the production side of the social media campaign: those busy updating the Facebook pages, Twitter account, and most importantly, producing and circulating content to be shared on WhatsApp groups. Having realized this oversight only after the election, I contacted Junaid on a subsequent visit to Mumbai, asking whether he might be able to put me in touch with anyone who had been involved with Sayeed's social media campaign. "No problem," Junaid responded. Sayeed's social media campaign manager was a close friend of Junaid's own college-age son. WhatsApp introductions were made, and within a few days I was sitting at a Café Coffee Day with a smartly dressed young man named Hasan who looked to be in his twenties. Hasan (like Sayeed) is a Konkani Muslim and a native Marathi-speaker, but he's also fluent in Hindi and speaks native-sounding English. Speaking in English, he tells me (echoing Junaid) that he had met Sayeed through Junaid's son. Hasan is in marketing, and while he's not much interested in politics he likes "to help friends"; it was for this reason he took an interest in Sayeed's campaign. And besides, it was a great opportunity for the young marketing professional to gain publicity for his own work.

I ask: so, what did you actually do during the campaign season? He responds: the key to social media is to "attract the right sentiments." Hasan tells me that there are different "sectors" in the neighborhood, which are "attracted" by different "sentiments." The first "sector" is made up of Muslim elites, he explains: "They're not attracted by sentimental issues; they want to know that he's smart and capable. So, for them, we have to explain the future goals and the mission. These people don't use social media very much," he explains—no Facebook, Twitter or Instagram—"for them, we make brochures." I ask how he knows this, and he regards me blankly: "I live here. I'm talking about my parents and their friends. I know this sector." He continues: "Elites only read a WhatsApp message if it's been sent by a friend." I ask why this is the case and he pauses, then answers with a shrug, "Maybe they're just busy; they don't have time." I point out that in my experience, poor people are also quite busy; perhaps more so. He shrugs again, suggesting that for his purposes, the reason doesn't really matter: "Anyway, they'll rarely forward anything onward." For this reason, he explains, the important thing when it comes to marketing a candidate to elites is to carefully curate a WhatsApp group—one with the "right people." Right people? "Known people, only friends and from same area. It has to be people that are known to one another," he explains, "otherwise it becomes a spam group and gets silenced or deleted." He adds: "And all the content has to be in English." He explains that in this area, a significant proportion of the elite sector is made up of Ismailis (with a scattering of Bohras and Konkani Muslims like his own family, as well as a smattering of Christians), "but mostly these people are not religious. They're just professionals, friends."

He explains that the "elite sector" of Mumbai Muslims does not "relate" to Urdu. His own generation studied in English-medium schools where Urdu wasn't part of the curriculum; and while many of his parents' generation learned the Nastaliq script[49] and read the classical

ghazals (devotional poetry) of Ghalib in their own school days, today—
for everyday chitchat and newspaper reading—Urdu has fallen out of
fashion among elites. The language has come to be associated with a
less-educated, non-English-speaking, poorer, and more religious demographic, associated with "Arabized" forms of Islamic piety practiced by
Muslim migrants with ties to North India. Indeed, Mumbai's Muslim
elites sometime treat Urdu as a language almost foreign to the city—
a bizarrely ahistorical idea given that Urdu (and the more colloquial
Hindustani) has long been the lingua franca of Bombay. Urdu was the
language of Parsi theater in the late nineteenth century, notwithstanding the fact that the Parsi community itself was Gujarati-speaking; Urdu
was the language in which secular, humanist intellectuals like Sadaat
Hasaan Manto and Ismat Chughtai penned scathing portrayals of "genteel" pieties of the middle classes and unblinking explorations of female
sexuality; and of course Urdu is ubiquitous in contemporary Bombay
"Bollywood" cinema: while much screenplay is written in the "Urdu lite"
dialect of Hindustani, the songs for which the genre is world famous are
often written in a high-register Urdu that explicitly references the poetic
tradition.

Hasan explains that it is both this long-standing association of Urdu
with learned society, with poetry and knowledge, as well as the language's
more recent association with the authority of local religious leaders
(priests and maulanas), that lends Urdu a particular esteem and credibility in the chawls and working-class areas of Badlapur. "They respect
Urdu," Hasan explains; "for that demographic, content must be in Urdu."
He himself neither reads nor writes Urdu, but since he knows Hindi (and
is conversant in the everyday Hindustani of South Bombay streets and
markets; he grew up there after all), he explains, he just writes social
media content in the Hindi (Nagari) script and then uses a script-changer
app. He pulls out his phone to demonstrate. "I never use Google Translate," he explains, "just the script translator." That way he can curate the
social media content with particular words and phrasing that are specific and have resonance with this particular "sector" in this particular
neighborhood—Badlapur—linguistic peculiarities that Google Translate
would not have taken into consideration. "If it's in familiar, local Urdu,"
he explains, "then people feel that the message is being given by 'one
of ours.'"

Hasan tells me that "hundreds" of WhatsApp groups were created during the campaign season. After the various meetings, "we'd collect people's numbers and form groups; the WhatsApp groups were all initiated by these in-person gatherings." He gives me an example from a more recent campaign that he had managed in the area (the 2019 Maharashtra State Assembly elections had just taken place, so they were fresher in his mind)—a campaign effort that began a full six months prior to polling. He recalls: "We gathered the good crowd [meaning elites] for a good dinner and a proper presentation in English. Maybe seventy people attended that first meeting, and we did a nice talk and presentation." He continues: "I always made sure to give the presentations myself," he explains, because "it must be presented well. Meaning, I have to read the current emotion." He takes out his phone again and pulls up a video that demonstrates with words and images how the candidate had "gotten work done." After these video presentations, Hasan tells me, he would circulate through the room and collect names and phone numbers to create a WhatsApp group: "Internally, the groups need to know one another," he explains; "otherwise it's spam. Maybe sixty or seventy people in a group, max." He recalls how "after a few months, our dinners were overflowing" and the WhatsApp groups were proliferating.

I could recall one such meeting during Sayeed's 2017 campaign which, down with a fever, I had been sorely disappointed to miss. A morning-after WhatsApp recounting of the event had been written in all-caps English:

AN EXCLUSIVE GATHERING OF RESPECTABLE AND PROMINENT PERSONAL-
ITES WAS ORGANISED BY MR. KARIM ENGINWALA AND MR. JUNAID KHAN IN
SUPPORT OF OUR YOUNG AND DYNAMIC CANDIDATE MR. SAYEED RIZWAN
OF WARD NO. —, WHERE AN APPEAL WAS MADE TO AND THROUGH ALL THE
PRESENTERS TO EDUCATE THE PEOPLE OF NAGPADA AND BADLAPUR TO
CHOSE MR. SAYEED RIZWAN, WHO IS AN EDUCATED, HONEST, SINCERE AND
HARDWORKING CANDIDATE.

It went on to mention the names and positions of seventeen prominent people—businesspeople, religious leaders of various sects and subsects, university professors and schoolteachers, philanthropists and a few NGO leaders (including Fareed, whose NGO, Taaqat—discussed in the previous chapter—is geographically situated beyond the borders of the electoral district in which Sayeed was contesting). I learned from Junaid that I had missed "one of the best meetings ever." He had expected only two hundred people, but more than three hundred had turned up. Most of the people who came were "in the education field," he tells me—some doctors and professors. Junaid tells me proudly that "three ladies had addressed the gathering: a professor of Urdu language and literature, a poet, and a housewife." While he didn't mention any forming of WhatsApp groups (it hadn't occurred to me to ask him at the time), it seems reasonable to presume that "internally known" chat groups (as Hasan called them) would have been formed following the evening's presentations, speeches, and supper to which this post-event invitation would have been posted for onward circulation.

Back at Café Coffee Day in 2019, I asked Hasan about the actual content of the WhatsApp posts that he crafts to send to the various groups, recalling for him an incident that had transpired in Badlapur a week or so before the 2017 polls. At the height of campaign season, in the heady days of stage shows and chowk sabhaas and door-to-door campaigns and late-night chooa (mouse) meetings, a little video popped up on all three of the WhatsApp groups affiliated with Sayeed's campaign to which I'd managed to get myself invited. In the three-minute clip, an anonymous speaker narrates a series of photos taken earlier that year depicting Sayeed—flanked by various local social workers comprising his campaign team—at an "inauguration ceremony" for the repair of a local municipal health dispensary which had taken place a few months prior. Discussion of Sayeed's role in the repair and impending reopening of the local dispensary (which had been closed since 2013) had been a staple of Sayeed's recent sabhaa and stage show speeches. The anonymous "negative video" circulating over WhatsApp just before polling accused Sayeed of falsely claiming credit for the reopening of the long-neglected but much-needed area health dispensary (the one he'd spoken about during the earlier-described public meeting)—holding an inauguration ceremony and publicizing it in print and social media.

The video begins with a faceless Urdu voice narrating a series of images —of Sayeed and his team holding a ceremony outside the dispensary:

The municipal davakhana [health dispensary] has been closed for the past few years, but as soon as the election bell rings, the siyasi dangal [political wrestling arena] has begun. Everyone is trying to attach themself to it. Look how the Samajwadi Party candidate, with his saatis [followers] . . . on 29 December 2016 [i.e., two months before the municipal election] got together and put on an act of inauguration of the repairing [repairing shuru karvane ka dhong racha], and through newspaper publicity and via social media, tried to mislead people [logon ko gumrah karne ki koshish ki]. But through an RTI [Right to Information request] from the BMC, what information did we get?

The video then pans in on images of what appears to be an English-language RTI response on BMC letterhead, and the Urdu-speaking voice explains that the proposal for the work had been approved a few years earlier (in 2013), while it was simply sanction for the earlier-approved tender had been given that past fall—a few months before the Sayeed's inauguration function publicized in the newspapers and on social media. "He is trying to take credit," the voice explains (using the English word *credit*), "when the proposal had already passed and the fund had already passed." But "lies are just lies [jhoot to jhoot hi hote hai]," the voice scolds, and "needed to be unveiled [benaqab hona hi tha]." "He should be ashamed for misleading the people [awam ko gumrah kar ke]."

According to Sayeed's version of this story (often recounted in speeches), the crumbling dispensary facility had been languishing without repairs for years—notwithstanding BMC approval for the renovation project. Sayeed characterized this sad state of affairs as evidence that the incumbent party was not predisposed to (or perhaps even capable of) "doing work." In his campaign speeches, Sayeed would emphasize how (by contrast) he had managed to set in motion the wheels of the municipal corporation for this project even while representing a district in the far-off eastern suburbs—writing a letter to the municipal commissioner, seeing the budgetary approvals through, and keeping the pressure on the contractors and engineers until the actual work set in motion.

The "negative video" had caught my attention because the information presented in the video—while professing to be a "public unmasking" (not unlike Khanna's revelatory routine in "Yeh Jo Public Hai" from the previous chapter)—was, on closer consideration, entirely compatible with

Sayeed's own account of the function. Which is to say, there was nothing in the video that suggested jhooth or gumrah—lies or intentional misleading—at all. For instance, the would-be-whistleblowing RTI displayed in the video demonstrated that, notwithstanding approval for the proposed repairs in 2013, the proposal received budgetary approval only in 2016—a few months before the publicized function. Sayeed was, at that point, already an elected councilor (and leader of his party in the corporation) and may very well have been instrumental in moving the project forward by putting pressure on various officers to approve the budget and begin work. Likely his doing so would have been with an eye toward contesting the upcoming election from Badlapur, the approved-but-languishing repair project seen as an opportunity to demonstrate his capacity and willingness to "get work done."

The situation is one with which I was familiar; in my earlier Mumbai research on municipal water I had frequently encountered these sorts of speculations about where credit was due for this or that municipal work.[50] For instance, the video about the health dispensary recalled an incident in 2014 when, following up on a rumor of a similar genre—that is, that a politician (on this particular occasion, the politician in question happened to be Sayeed himself) had claimed credit for a project that I happened to know (since I had been researching and writing about water infrastructure in the neighborhood) had been in the works for many years and had been conceived by the water supply planning engineers themselves. I had therefore asked a senior water engineer about the role that Sayeed had or hadn't played in shepherding the project (the replacement of a section of belowground network of water mains) through to completion. To my surprise (because engineers often had little praise for elected officials), the engineer had dismissed the rumor—not as false but rather as beside the point. Even if some work has already been approved, he explained, "unless there is someone who follows up" (who raises the matter with the corporation, presents a proposal for budget approval, pesters harried and overworked engineers to prioritize the work) then even approved projects can stall indefinitely. In that particular case, while Sayeed was clearly not responsible for conceiving the project, he was credited by the engineer for seeing it through to completion. The "truth" of such matters, in other words, isn't something that can be adjudicated simply by documentary "proof"—documents that, in this case, could easily be said to support either version of the story—that is, either that Sayeed was or wasn't responsible for the repairs. It was with this earlier episode in mind that I interpreted the following 2017 campaign office exchange between a Badlapur social worker and one of Sayeed's campaign team leaders: "What should we do about negative rumors?" the social worker asked, to which the campaign team leader had responded: "Don't dignify rumors with a direct response." And yet the negative video was clearly on the minds of Sayeed's campaign team; a response was necessary, even if not a "direct" one.

Hasan nodded when I recalled for him the 2017 negative video incident; he couldn't recall that particular video but explained that much of the social media content that he produces is actually in response to these sorts of "negative campaigns" by (generally anonymous) others. He explains: "If we're getting attacked, we don't deny it; rather we address the issue by showing the actual problem and the candidate's actual work." He explains that "the real question is: why isn't there water? Or why isn't the dispensary getting repaired? Even if some work had been approved, someone needs to make it happen. So we emphasize that the candidate knows how to actually get it done, whereas work was held up before."

He explains that this sort of "addressing the issue" is always done over WhatsApp: "WhatsApp is where you touch hearts," he tells me. "It's for clearing images." I ask him to say more: What's the difference between, say, WhatsApp and Facebook? He explains: On the official Facebook page you can't put "emotional" things. Facebook content has to be "straight up"—because it is available to unknowable, anonymous audiences. But when addressing and countering something specific—"if someone somewhere said something—then we address it through WhatsApp because that's where you can affect people's emotions." Thinking back to the sabhaas, this made perfect sense: while the material affordances of social media platforms might allow for the anonymous spreading of messages, Hasan's account of how the careful curating of WhatsApp groups during these meetings—something that at the time seemed so banal that I hadn't paid much attention—points to the overlaying and coarticulation of media technologies and infrastructural networks. "No medium is introduced onto an empty stage," writes media anthropologist Ilana Gershon. "Each new medium is instantly enmeshed in a web of media ideologies—old media determine how new media will be perceived. At the same time, every new medium alters how the already existing media are understood to shape communication."[51] Newer digital communicative infrastructures like WhatsApp are "layered" over the face-to-face, "old media" encounters of the sabhaa: the carefully curated conversations mediated by trusted mains, with assembled audiences addressed in resonant registers.[52]

I ask Hasan for an example of how WhatsApp was used during the campaign to speak to "people's emotions." He recalls for me an incident that happened more recently, in the run-up to the 2019 Maharashtra State Assembly Elections. At a "public meeting," Sayeed got angry and uttered some strong words about the sitting MLA—a member of the Hyderabad-based Muslim identitarian party, All India Majlis-e-Ittehadul-Muslimeen (AIMIM, or MIM). "There was some flooding in the neighborhood, and the party of the MLA [i.e., AIMIM] set up a relief camp; the MLA was standing on a corner shaking a bucket to collect money— to draw attention. And Sayeed said, 'Don't do this drama on the street; you're the MLA! Use your government power to fix the problem!'" Sayeed made a video-recorded speech (in Hindi), and the WhatsApp clip was excerpted from that speech. It was a thirty-minute speech, but the bit that was circulated was a thirty-second section in which Sayeed used threatening words. Hasan finds the video on his phone:

> Those people who are roaming around with a bucket, those people think that Badlapur is their personal property, that they're landlords here. But the moment it strikes my fancy [i.e., if I let my instincts take hold], Sayeed Rizwan will drag them to [a well-known public junction in the heart of Badlapur, here identified by the name of a recognized local eating establishment] and thrash them thoroughly.[53]

"This clip was circulated by people saying that Sayeed was threatening people!" Hasan laughs, shaking his head, and explains that "the clip was taken totally out of context; that's not what his speech was about at all. But anyway, the thirty-second clip with those strong words went viral around the neighborhood. It was spread by a 'fake public.'" "Fake public?" He clarifies that it was spread by "party people masquerading as the public, spreading propaganda while pretending to be the public. Because see, on WhatsApp you can spread propaganda and extremism anonymously. Through WhatsApp, a campaign can have people say things that the campaign itself can't say directly on its Facebook page." He explains that this is a strategy commonly deployed by the party in power in the central government—Narendra Modi's BJP. "They do most activities below the belt," Hasan explains; "they use WhatsApp to spread anti-Muslim propaganda—to spread all these photos, images of cap-wearing Muslims and blood. . . . That's all, just caps and blood. Completely unattached to anything. That sort of thing goes around. But people who are awake, they know it's all bullshit, that it's circulated by a fake public."

Fake public. Here it is helpful to recall the previous chapter's account of the Mumbai meaning of "public"—where public refers to a collective subject (at once discursively and affectively assembled) as well as to the public's own mediated/dramatized image. In characterizing the WhatsApp-mediated spread of emotionally charged, decontextualized ("unattached") images and videos as conjuring a "fake public," Hasan asserts that the party workers circulating "propaganda" are mobilizing the affective affordances of imagery ("caps and blood") to intentionally stir up emotion-laden collective attention and strategically deploy it to partisan ends[54]—all the while pretending to be a spontaneous (non-choreographed and certainly non-paid) public.[55] Indeed, when I asked Hasan how he knew that particular video had been circulated by a "fake public," he recounted how those who had forwarded the clip to him did so while saying dismissively, "Look at this natak!"[56] Some people were trying to make an issue out of it, Hasan reflected, "but no one believed it."

I was struck by Hasan's use of the word "believe," which did not refer to whether or not the video was real or fake (indeed, Hasan made no mention of any suspicion that the video was doctored). Junaid later confirmed for me—with a hearty laugh—that yes, Sayeed had said those things. Thinking back to the "negative video" from the 2017 campaign, I realized that Wasim had not questioned the veracity of that video's content either: the documents acquired through RTI were not described to have been doctored; the fact of Sayeed's having claimed credit for the dispensary repairs never called into question. As in that instance, the "belief" to which Hasan here referred was not whether some statement had or hadn't been made; rather, "no one believed" that Sayeed's threat was literal, or that the video somehow revealed Sayeed to be nothing more than a violence-prone goonda (gangster). And this was because the clip was circulated "unattached to anything"—the utterance lifted out of its sociospatial and historical "context" (both the particular situation and setting of Sayeed's full speech that day as well as the long political career characterized by nonviolence). Junaid explained to me afterward, laughing aloud when I recounted Sayeed's strong words, that it was more likely that the clip had bolstered Sayeed's popularity by performing his social fluency—demonstrating his insider knowledge of the neighborhood by naming the precise location of a particularly good site for public humiliation; speaking and comporting himself in a resonant register. "No one took it literally," Junaid told me, because "Sayeed is hardly someone who goes around beating people." It was the interpretation of the words (i.e., as a literal threat) rather than the fact of their utterance, in other words, that was not "believed."

Back at Café Coffee Day, Hasan concluded our conversation with a discussion of the particular fluency with which Bombay city dwellers navigate this terrain of belief: people on the outskirts of the city might be different, but here in Bombay "everyone knows that [the MLA] is just an actor." He pauses, adding pensively, "People here in Bombay don't just believe. Bombay appreciates a good show," he tells me, "but people know what's a show and what's a lie."

"Believe"

Back in 2017, a few days after the "negative video" incident (the one calling into question Sayeed's credit-claiming for the repaired health dispensary), I arrived at Sayeed's central campaign office to find Wasim on the way out the door, accompanied by a half-dozen hijab-clad women as well as a few young men toting video equipment. "They're from Gowandi," Wasim responded when I asked him where he was off to. Presumably seeing my still-puzzled expression, he explained that yet another "negative video" had circulated. In this one, opposition party leaders are shown interviewing women in Gowandi who say that Sayeed hasn't "done any work" there. "So I had an idea," he tells me. "I invited fifteen ladies from Gowandi to come to Lotus Lane [a lower-income area of Badlapur], where they have family, to go door-to-door to visit their cousins and in-laws and to directly describe to them everything that Sayeed has done in Gowandi.

We'll make a video of them talking to their families and circulate it over WhatsApp." He tells me that he's not really so worried about the negative videos because "most people won't be influenced." But he adds that "maybe some might be—people who don't know much, people who sit in some small shop all day and are bored and watch these videos—those people might be influenced." So this way, he explained, "people can hear directly from their rishtedar [relatives]."

We walk in a parade over to Lotus Lane—the women first, Wasim and I trailing behind. The film crew arrives a few minutes after us, on motorbikes loaded with camera equipment. They set up the cameras and sound system in a narrow, bustling lane, blocking half of the road directly in front of the entrance to a cluster of chawl buildings. Passersby gather, stopping to watch and listen—they lean in to hear; they pause on their motorbikes; they peek out of windows to see what's going on. One of the women jokes to me that people are gathering to watch not them but rather me: "You're Sayeed Bhai's star campaigner!" I laugh and point out that she's wrong; all eyes are on the "ladies" and the camera crew. She nods, seemingly pleased.

Once the camera boys are ready, one woman speaks—hijab clad but face uncovered, recognizable to the eyes of any relatives. She begins: "Sayeed Rizwan has helped us so much—whether Hindu or Muslim, he helps us all." After an hour or so—during which they interview four or five women surrounded by a crowd with a constantly changing composition—they head inside to do more shooting. We stop at a small flat on the top floor, home to a round-faced thirty-something man who has been trailing us, keen for the camera crew to make an appearance in his home. Wasim seems to know the man personally, which is confirmed when the man's mother comes out and greets Wasim familiarly; presumably they know one another through some rishtedar in Gowandi, where Wasim also lives. She's laughing a little embarrassedly, but also seems eager to participate in this entertaining diversion. The camera boys pin the mic to her scarf and asks her to say "This time only Sayeed Rizwan," but instead she keeps saying "This time *again* Sayeed Rizwan [ab ki bar phir Sayeed Rizwan]." So they have to take the video over and over again; finally she gets it right and then asks through her laughter: "Is that enough?" The chubby man's daughter gets the mic next: she's in the eighth grade and is very eager. Wasim says to her: "Speak from your heart." She recites in a way that suggests she'd been thinking about what to say, has carefully planned her little speech: "Here everyone is with Sayeed Rizwan—kids, elders, youth," and then she ends with "This time, only Sayeed Rizwan" and gives a thumbs-up. We move on to the flat next door, where a group of school-kids are studying with a private tutor; they pour out into the hall and recite in unison "This time only Sayeed Rizwan!" giving two thumbs up. The whole scene strikes me as a little, well, disingenuous . . . it feels staged. But then I look around and see neighbors peering curiously, amusedly out of doorways and realize that this is precisely the point: to stage an entertaining and festive spectacle that attracts a curious little crowd.

The next day, I ring up Wasim to ask him to forward me the video they made of our adventures in Lotus Lane the day before. He laughs at my question: "Haven't you learned anything at all?" He explains that there's no video; it wasn't necessary to actually make a video. "We had a camera-man there; you saw how the crowd gathered to see what we were doing, to hear the women speak. They came to listen to what the women said because we said we were making a video." In other words, the idea of the "WhatsApp video" that conjures the specter of unknown and anony-mous social media publics was a pretext for gathering an on-the-street, embodied public. But what about the negative video circulating over WhatsApp to which this little drama of "making a video" was staged in response? I ask Wasim: "Was there actually a video?" I'd been asking around about the video, about which everyone seems to know but no one seems to have actually seen. Wasim tells me that even he hadn't actually seen the rumored video. "Maybe there was one, maybe not," he says. But he doesn't seem concerned with figuring out whether the rumored video existed or not; the important thing is that people might have believed that there was a video in which Gowandi women claimed that Sayeed hadn't done any work. It was this possibility of belief that inspired Sayeed's team to assemble a group of women from Gowandi to speak "directly to their rishtedar" in Badlapur and to have a performance of a "video shoot" of the speech-mediated encounter attract the attentions of passersby. It was unclear to me—and probably also to Wasim—whether the possi-bility of actually making a video was ever entertained at all. My sense is that they hadn't given it much thought: the assembling of the video crew was an end in its own right, and they may or may not have decided afterward to use that footage to create something to circulate. The pace and constantly shifting focus of the campaign lent it an improvisational character, and ultimately making an actual video was not a priority (if it ever was).

The breakneck speed and scale at which digital technologies and social media platforms have become ubiquitous in the media landscape (in Mumbai as globally) has led to widespread discussion and speculation about the implications of social media's ubiquity for democracy. On the one hand, the rising availability of cheap smartphones and affordable data plans facilitates access to information and democratizes its production, creating possibilities for increased participation in public life. This is particularly pronounced in low-literacy contexts, since social media allows for communication via images, memes, and video clips rather than only (or primarily) through reading and writing; in a 2019 global ranking of hours spent on video-streaming apps, India rated near the top.[57] And yet in lowering barriers to participation, digital technologies allow for the dissemination of information that has not been subject to the fact-checking protocols of traditional news media, thereby facilitating spread of disinformation as well; across India, more than thirty people were killed in 2017 and 2018 in mob attacks following rumors of child kidnapping that were spread over WhatsApp.[58] The ubiquity of social media means that politicians (elected or aspiring) now communicate with prospective constituencies immediately and with a seeming "directness"—bypassing institutionalized procedures and public debate. French philosopher and digital naysayer Bernard Stiegler identifies in the spread of digital technology the dismantling of democracy's foundation. The functioning of a "social body" as a "democratic society," he writes, requires "pooling" of individual desires and "delegating" them to "representatives" who can act on them through social and political institutions. This "delegation of competence" properly functions within "the time-delayed mode" of the debate proper to the liberal public sphere, Stiegler argues, and it is precisely this "this time-delayed mode" that is "destroyed by the 'real time' of live communications and by the 'just-in-time' adjustment of politics to public opinion." In this context, Stiegler writes, the public has only "become an audience."[59]

Such handwringing about the democracy-destroying powers of digital media, as anthropologist Francis Cody points out, are thus based on the presumption of a "hegemonic space of disembodied liberal debate."[60]

Indeed, as this chapter and the previous one have demonstrated, the distinction between a discursively constituted "public" and a passively consuming "audience" is an ideological one that bears little resemblance to how collectivity and mass political subjectivity are constituted and enacted in Mumbai. This chapter has shown how digitally mediated communications—whether text or image, video or audio—are rendered believable (or not) through "alertness" and "awareness" born of sensory attunement to the sign-saturated city (what Goffman characterizes as the "full physical arena"). This is not to say that there is no difference between an embodied crowd and its digitally circulated image. Or that there is no difference between, say, a paper pamphlet handed out by a candidate who comes to your front door and a WhatsApped image of that same text . . . or for that matter, a WhatsApped image of the candidate handing out the paper pamphlet during a door-to-door campaign. Discussing the emergence of new religious infrastructures (in her case, giant concrete statues) in relation to older technologies (smaller roadside temples and icons), anthropologist Kajri Jain points out that "technologies do not necessarily replace one another in linear succession." Her account demonstrates instead how "new configurations exist in parallel to, link with, reactivate, and remediate existing ones."[61]

The accounts in this chapter have demonstrated how digital technologies are enlisted within already existing networks of relations, layered onto "analogue" emplaced within urban landscapes. How Mumbaikars navigate the constantly changing "configurations" of communications technologies—how they go about making sense (and belief) through this changing material-technological landscape—is not a theoretical question but an ethnographic one. WhatsApp groups are formed among those who are already known to one another, with the digital layered onto the analogue; scripts and diction index on-the-ground geographies and local meanings. The potential dangers of digital technologies (anonymity and decontextualization) are managed and mitigated through everyday practices of "alertness": the embodied encounters by means of which people adeptly evaluate who and what to "believe."

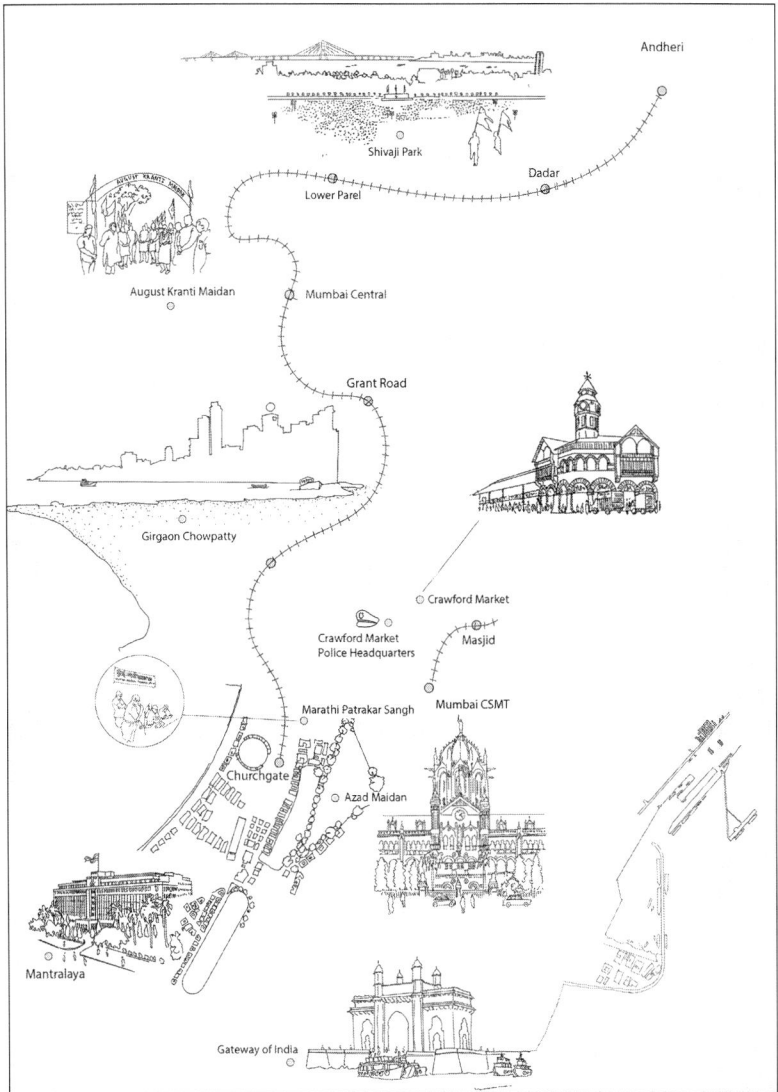

Map 4. Graphic depicting locations of places mentioned in chapters 4 and 5 in relation to proximate railway stations. See Map 1 for location of these stations within the city as a whole.

Interlude III

Places of Protest

In the winter of 2019–20, on the eve of the onset of the Covid-19 pandemic, Indian streets erupted in mass protest against an amendment to national citizenship law that, for the first time in Indian history, made religion a criterion in the granting of citizenship. The 2019 Citizenship Amendment Act (CAA) created a fast track toward Indian citizenship, but on a religiously differentiated basis that excluded Muslims from eligibility. While, formally speaking, the CAA professed to be a mechanism for the extension of citizenship rights—providing a path to national belonging for religious minorities fleeing persecution in neighboring countries[1]—it set off a firestorm not only because the introduction of the religious criterion for citizenship was unprecedented (and possibly unconstitutional) but also because of fears that the new law would be used as part of a constellation of arcane policy tools which together would provide a means to strip Muslim Indians of citizenship. The CAA was passed in conjunction with a move to carry out an exercise to update India's National Population Registry (NPR)—a comprehensive database of every "usual resident"[2] of India (both citizens and noncitizens) compiled by means of a nationwide door-to-door survey.[3] While on the surface the updating of the NPR appeared no cause for concern (survey respondents would be interviewed regarding details of their identity—their place and date of birth, the place and date of birth of their parents, etc.—but would not be required to produce documents), concerns arose about the potential use of the NPR in conjunction with the government's recently announced plans to create, for the very first time, a

National Registry of Citizens (NRC). So while the NPR survey itself would not verify the citizenship status of "usual residents," the information compiled in the NPR would subsequently be used as the basis by which local-level citizenship registry officials would compile the NRC. Using their discretionary power and subjective interpretation of the NPR survey data, local officials would be tasked with compiling lists of "doubtful citizens"—people whose answers to the NPR survey raised "doubts" about their citizenship, and who would then be required to produce documentary proof of their formal citizenship status—paper documents, needless to say, that the Indian state has never made a point of providing to its citizenry. The whole exercise would effectively call into question the citizenship status of every India resident, shifting the burden of proving citizenship to individuals. Those whose verbal testimonials raise unspecified "doubts" would have their suffrage rights immediately revoked and would be required to provide some unspecified paper proof of citizenship; those failing to provide such documentary evidence could face internment and eventual expulsion from India.

Now, given the Indian state's famously patchy, contradictory, and exclusionary regime of documentary practices,[4] the NPR-NRC combination had the potential to raise "doubts" about the citizenship of untold numbers of people—with women, gender minorities, Dalits, Adivasis, and Muslims anticipated to be overrepresented among those facing this prospective stripping of rights: people who were born at home rather than in a hospital, and who thus don't have documentary certification that they exist at all (a common situation in rural communities of Dalits and Adivasis); landless laborers who often have not completed enough education to earn a "school-leaving" certificate; linguistic minorities whose names are regularly misspelled by state officers when transliterated into Marathi, Hindi, or English for documentary purposes;[5] people whose names and places of residence change after marriage (common among women and gender minorities); those who don't own property or hold documentary proof of property ownership; seasonal migrants living on construction sites or other places of employment in cities like Mumbai—and so on. It was in this context that, with untold numbers having their citizenship rights called into question, the new CAA introduced a fast track toward officiality. But it did so on religiously discriminatory basis that excluded Muslims, who (as of 2023) comprised around 14.2 percent (an estimated 197 million people) of India's population.[6] In the weeks and months following the ratifying of the bill into law, people poured into city streets (not only in India but worldwide) to demand the repeal of what came to be known as the kaala kanoon (black law). Protesters took to reading aloud the preamble to the Indian Constitution (of whose protections of Indians' Fundamental Right to equality the CAA was argued to be in violation),[7] pledging noncooperation with the NPR exercise and condemning the police violence being unleashed against university students protesting the new law on campuses in BJP-governed states across North India.

Apart from the staggering scale and energy of the anti-CAA protests, what immediately caught my attention was their apparent disavowal of the forms of political subjectivity to which I had become accustomed, and to which previous chapters of this book have attended: the carefully crafted, relational chains of sociomaterial efficacy and the discerning audience-publics who at once enact and assess them. The protests instead presided over the articulation of a collective political subject—"We the People of India"—whose infrastructures of articulation were both more central and more diffuse. Bursting out of intimate intersections and known neighborhoods, the anti-CAA protests assembled crowds of strangers into the city's vast open spaces, from where image-representations were produced and circulated far beyond the familiar friends' groups and accustomed circuits.

4

Kaaghaz

"We Aren't Hindustani by Paper; We're Hindustani by Blood"

kāgaẓ (kāgad; said to be fr. kāg, "sound or noise" + da, "giving forth").
s.m. Paper; a paper, writing, document, deed . . . a printed or written
sheet, a newspaper

—Platts, *A Dictionary of Urdu, Classical Hindi, and English*

Hum kaaghaz se Hindustani nahi; hum khoon se Hindustani hai

[We aren't Hindustani by paper; we're Hindustani by blood]

—Anonymous placard

On a bright Sunday morning, three days after my arrival in Mumbai in December 2019, my WhatsApp chat groups exploded with forwarded images and videos with which the world would soon become familiar—scenes of police rampaging through Jamia Millia Islamia (hereafter Jamia) and Aligarh Muslim University (AMU) campuses, unleashing violence against unarmed students at two of India's best-known historically Muslim universities who had assembled to protest the new Citizenship Amendment Act (CAA). The viral videos and images depicted police wielding lathis (batons), firing tear gas, and using stun grenades against students.[1] One video showed police tearing through the Jamia library beating students even as they studied; another showed nearly a dozen armed policemen raining a torrent of blows on an unarmed male student until his female classmates intervened—hijab-clad women shielding their bleeding friend from further blows while another waves an enraged, shaming finger at the police (see Figure 16).

Figure 15. Protesters displaying handcrafted placards. Mumbai, December 2019. Photograph by Rohan Shivkumar, shared with the author over WhatsApp.

Figure 16. Still from a video posted on Twitter in which university students shield their friend while another waves a shaming finger at the police. https://x.com/BDUTT/status/1206485512678232064.

The digital images of blood-spattered campuses and hijabi heroism spread fast and furiously, flowing across city lines and national borders. Within hours, an artistic rendering of the caught-on-camera encounter between the helmet-clad police and the hijab-wearing, finger-wagging twenty-two-year-old Jamia student Aysha Renna had become ubiquitous on social media. The image, titled *One-Finger Revolution*, was created by fifty-year-old Tamil filmmaker Ponvannan (see Figure 17), who narrated for the media the inspiration behind his drawing:

> While I was watching visuals of the Delhi Police attacking Jamia Milia Islamia students, I came across a video that made me extremely upset. . . . A young, unarmed girl is seen bravely fending off a group of policemen in full riot gear from hitting a student, and it made me sad and emotional. The way she tells the policemen, who are armed with helmets, shields and sticks, to back off, while wagging her finger—it's very powerful. The image stayed with me.[2]

Figure 17. Artistic rendering of the scene depicted in Figure 16 that went viral on social media. https:// www.pinterest.com/ pin/cartoonist-pon vannan-one-finger -revolution--18535134 0902066183/.

As Ponvannan recalled to *Print* reporter Sonia Agrawal a few months later, "When I saw the emotion on her face, that was a defining moment for me. It felt like that emotion did not need any explanation and a new revolution has begun."[3]

While the country (and world) watched in shock and disbelief the scenes of violence unfolding at one of India's leading universities, furiously forwarding images and issuing categorical condemnations, for residents of the lower-middle-class, Muslim-majority neighborhoods of Shaheen Bagh in and around Jamia, the threat was "local and immediate."[4] As Jamia professor Farah Farooqi explained, "All of Shaheen Bagh's several lakh inhabitants have some links with Jamia. Either they, or their relatives, study there, or they have at least heard of it."[5] Word of the attacks at Jamia spread like wildfire through the neighborhoods adjoining Jamia, and people poured out of their homes in protest. According to media reports, as evening fell a few dozen elderly women had sat down in the middle of the main road connecting Delhi to Noida, holding a candle-light vigil next to the bus stop at Shaheen Bagh. By the next afternoon, the "Shaheen Bagh Dadis" (Shaheen Bagh Grannies) numbered in the hundreds. Images of their stoic, age-worn faces flooded the media, and within a few days nearly fifteen thousand people—from all faiths and

the people of Shaheen Bagh.

Figure 18. Shaheen Bagh "Dadi" Bilkis Bano speaking to the press. Still from *The Quint,* "Symbol of Resistance: How Bilkis Dadi Made It to TIME's Top 100." September 24, 2020, https://www.facebook.com/watch/?v=776654029733986.

from all over India had joined the dadis in what would become a three-month occupation and standoff with the Delhi police (see Figure 18).

As journalist Vaibhav Vats writes in an essay chronicling the heady months of nationwide protests that followed, "It was the unprovoked attack on students there by the Delhi police on 15 December 2019 that converted, what had, until then, been dispersed protests against the new citizenship law into a charged and markedly bigger nationwide resistance."[6] And at the heart of this conversion of dispersed protests into a "nationwide resistance" were the images of the hijab-clad (and thereby visibly Muslim) women: the youthful Jamia students and the Shaheen Bagh Dadis standing up fearlessly and furiously to the weapon-wielding authorities, in a "simultaneous assertion of Muslim and Indian identity."[7]

It was in this image-soaked context that a coalition of Mumbai social activists announced a rally on Mumbai's historic August Kranti Maidan (August Revolution Ground), so named after the occasion of M. K. Gandhi's momentous "Do or Die" speech, delivered at that site on August 1942, inaugurating the Quit India movement for Indian independence.[8] The announcement of the December 19, 2019, rally at August Kranti Maidan explicitly called upon this revolutionary history, summoning Mumbaikars to "join in huge numbers" to oppose the CAA and condemn the December 15 police violence against student protesters at Jamia

Figure 19. Still from a viral video of university students shielding their friend, which was posted on Twitter (@BDUTT). https://x.com/BDUTT/status/120648 5512678232064.

and AMU. Images of the hijab-meets-helmet encounters featured prominently in mobilization efforts in the weeks and months following the
December 15 attacks, appearing on the digital posters advertising protest
events, reemerging in new contexts on handcrafted posters, and in so
doing, taking on what media anthropologist Karen Strassler characterizes
as an "eventist" character: "We might do well to think of images as events
that happen, rather than things that move, agents that act, or signs that
represent."[9] An "image-event," Strassler writes, "is a political process set
in motion when a specific image (or set of images) becomes a focal point
of attention across divergent publics, crystallizing discourses and channeling affects that have been otherwise diffuse and inchoate."[10] Taking
as its ethnographic point of departure the December 19 August Kranti
Maidan protest (and its aftermath), this chapter tracks the "eventfulness" of images, following them as they transform and mutate, becoming
attached to different situations and contexts, conjuring inchoate publics; we see how the circulation of images (especially over social media)
summons crowds into being by activating diffuse desires ("channeling
affects")—desires to "become that image."[11] And yet at the same time, seen

Figure 20. Artistic rendering of Figure 19 that went viral on social media.
December 2019. Author unknown.

People's Alliance against
the Indian Citizenship
Amendment Act!

12 to 2 pm
Friday
December 20

Consulate General of India
365 Bloor Street East, Toronto
(Sherbourne and Bloor)

Figure 21. Digital poster announcing protest demonstrations featuring iconic image of hijab-clad students standing up to state violence. Such depictions of heroism became symbols of the moral authority of Muslim women throughout the winter of anti-CAA protest. Shared over WhatsApp. Collection of the author

from inside the crowd at August Kranti Maidan that day, the analytical divide (and theoretical counterposing) of affective images with representational signs breaks down: while the circulation of images undoubtedly helped conjure the crowd-event, on the ground we encounter people who invariably describe having joined the protest because they themselves had something particular to say—writing up "personal perspectives" on individually handcrafted paper placards, displaying those messages within the sea of mobile phone cameras in the hopes of producing further images.

The anti-CAA protests that unfolded across Mumbai (as across India) over the winter of 2019–20 presided over efforts to articulate and represent a collective political subject: "the People of India." This chapter is about the highly charged, interconnected battles over (on the one hand) the material substance of national belonging and (on the other hand) how such "peoplehood" might be known and represented. Building on insights from chapter 3 regarding how multisensory "alertness" to the materiality of representational infrastructures is the means by which people evaluate words and work out what to "believe," this chapter shows how battles over belonging are fought through moral evaluations of particular substances: kaaghaz (paper) and khoon (blood). The chapter explores the multiple affordances of kaaghaz and tracks the contradictions that kaaghaz—as well as moralizing talk about kaaghaz—mediates. First, we see how kaaghaz is held to be a material substance particularly well suited to the representation and circulation of individually constituted "personal perspectives." And yet the singular subjectivity of the individual awaaz (voice) emerges in the context of the crowd, which comes into focus as a sociotechnical, material infrastructure for the production and circulation of digital renderings of awaaz-images.

Both the affect-laden image-event and the individually reasoned awaaz are mediated by the polyvalence of kaaghaz. With this insight, the chapter follows these contradictory affordances of kaaghaz into other domains of representation, where disputes over the affordances of kaaghaz index conflicts over the substance of citizenship and its representation—culminating in moralizing battles over the extent to which documentary "papers" can (or ought to) represent and adjudicate national belonging and citizenship right. We see how moralizing discourses about the substance of citizenship counterpose kaaghaz with khoon in an assertion of embodiment over representation as the material stuff of membership. And yet the ethnography demonstrates how these conflicts over kaaghaz's contradictory meanings (first as the medium of authenticity and second as "mere representation") is mediated by kaaghaz itself, which enables the production of the collective subjectivity by virtue of the relational encounters that paper's personal-perspective-mediating materiality affords.

"Personal Perspective"

I hopped on a train at Andheri Station around 3 p.m. and headed south toward August Kranti Maidan (see Map 4 in Interlude III). A few stations

short of Grant Road Station, a young woman bounds into the ladies'
compartment and leans against the handrail directly opposite from
where I stand, adjacent to the open train door. She looks to me to be in
her early twenties, and the bulky satchel slung over her shoulder suggests
she's come either from work or university; but wherever she may have
come from, the hand-drawn placard tucked under her arm leaves little
room for doubt about where she's headed. I catch her eye and ask her if
I can click a photo; she smiles brightly and displays her placard so that I
can read it properly: "This is not a political fight; it is war against the
Constitution" (see Figure 22). She tells me proudly (unprompted) that
she's a lawyer—presumably clarifying the significance of the words she's
chosen to write on her placard. She asks me to forward her the photo
I've just clicked so she can post it on Instagram and send it around to her
friends and professional groups. She gives me her WhatsApp number,
which I save in my phone along with her name: Preety.

Figure 22. Woman displaying hand-drawn placard on the train heading to a
protest demonstration. The placard reads: "This is not a political fight; it is war
against the Constitution." Mumbai, December 19, 2019. Photograph by the author.

Preety is keen to talk and has plenty to say during the remainder of our southbound train journey to Grant Road Station. She lives with her parents, she tells me, not far from the protest venue at August Kranti Maidan. Many of her colleagues at the law firm where she works also left the office early today to join the protest. But most of them would join later—after dropping their things at home—whereas she was going to August Kranti directly from the office, which is why she's alone and lugging her bulky bag with her. Her parents "don't approve" of her going to August Kranti today, she tells me, so in order to avoid an argument she didn't stop at home first. "My dad is against the protest," she tells me. "He's saying to avoid the area because there will be so many Muslim people coming in [to this part of the city]." She explains: "See, I'm a Hindu. I'm part of the religious majority here in India. My dad's a businessman, and his whole circle is pro-BJP." Preety's native-sounding English and Marwari surname had already announced her socioeconomic and community background (elite class and dominant-caste Hindu),[12] while her natural-dye kurta suggested something about her social milieu and liberal leanings. "For my dad," she continued, "this protest is totally political, whereas for me, this has nothing to do with politics or with any party. This is strictly a constitutional problem. So as a lawyer," she continues, displaying her placard for me again, "I want to say that this law, and the way that they are creating this divide—to me it's unacceptable."

Preety's carrying a few extra pieces of blank cardboard and also some colored pens. "They're for the others," she explains. "Which others?" I ask. "For anyone!" She explains that there was some extra cardboard lying around the office, so she cut it up into placard-sized squares and is carrying it along. And she had stopped by a stationery shop on the way to the train station to pick up the colored pens. The stationer had given her the pens for free, she recalled with a smile, after she explained what they were for. Then she wrote up her sign, she tells me, "just like that," while waiting on the platform for the train. Now she's carrying the extra cardboard and pens along with her in case she runs into anyone who "also wants to write up a placard."

Preety and I get down from the train at Grant Road Station and start together toward August Kranti Maidan, parting ways after a block or two after making plans to be in touch later that week—to exchange stories about our experiences of protest (more on that in a minute). Our train-crowd tributary soon merges with other streams (and then floods) of people converging from all directions onto the main thoroughfare— a sea of people, many, like Preety, toting handcrafted placards. On the train, Preety's placard, cardboard, and markers had struck me as odd; after all, her placard would be legible only to someone standing within a few feet of her. Anyone within reading distance of her placard would necessarily be part of the crowd, and therefore presumably already in agreement with the anti-CAA message of the event (if not with her particular perspective regarding the act's unconstitutionality). What's the point of a placard, I'd thought to myself, drawing on my understandings from other crowds of which I'd been part, when the whole point is the crowd itself? But as the people pouring in from side streets merged with those along the main road heading toward August Kranti Maidan, and as our purposeful procession thickened into a merry multitude I found myself amid a sea of placards: individual, unique, and many—like Preety's —handcrafted.

Our crowd-parade slowed to a crawl around a hundred meters short of the entryway to the protest venue at August Kranti Maidan. But still, most

Figure 23. Crowd of protesters displaying handcrafted placards. Mumbai, December 19, 2019. Photograph by the author.

people's directional orientation—and that of their placards—remained forward-facing, toward the official venue. This meant that in order to see what was written on the placards, one had to spin around to face the advancing wall of placard-carrying people. I spent a few hours like this (as did those around me), spinning in circles and allowing my eyes to roam, seeking out clever images, interesting critiques, witty remarks, all the while clicking photos of those that caught my attention with my mobile phone camera.

Awaaz

I milled about in the festive throng for a few hours, never reaching anywhere close to the entrance of August Kranti Maidan and its high-profile list of onstage speakers, including nonagenarian freedom fighter and staunch Gandhian, Dr. G G Parkeh—who himself had participated in the Quit India movement launched at this very site in 1942, and in whose name the official "call" for this particular event at August Kranti Maidan had been made over social media. But notwithstanding the rever-berations of actual voices amplified from the stage (presumably the loud-speakers had been positioned to face the road so that those in the streets could hear), from where I stood outside the gates, words themselves were indecipherable. And this was not only because I never reached anywhere near the venue itself, but also because of the chanting and cheering of the placard-waving people assembled in the street, people who had gath-ered not—sabhaa style—as an audience-public for the onstage speeches but rather in order themselves to be "heard." And participants "spoke," moreover, not in a single "voice"—as a crowd—but rather, and as Preety had explained to me, as distinctive voices articulating "personal perspec-tives." The stage-show with its star lineup of speakers seemed somewhat of a formality and an occasion (perhaps even a pretext) for people to artic-ulate their individual critiques and takes—and through the assembled infrastructure of proximate bodies wielding thousands of mobile phone cameras attached to social media accounts, to have their individual voices amplified and circulated.

The digital posters that circulated on social media in advance of the August Kranti gathering had anticipated this. One poster (see Figure 24) features an image of a young woman, lips visibly sealed but holding a placard that reads "Our voice [awaaz/आवाज़] is sharper than your batons [lathi/लाठी]." The poster caught my attention for a few reasons, first for

Figure 24. Digital poster reading "Our voice [आवाज़] is sharper than your batons [लाठी]." Mumbai, December 2019. Shared over WhatsApp. Collection of the author.

its use of awaaz—a word of Persianate origin that finds a place in many South Asian languages (here in Hindi).[13] Awaaz refers to both sound and voice—concepts that, as anthropologist Laura Kunreuther points out, tend in English to be counterposed.[14] The language-centric notion of voice is theorized on the one hand as the site and substance of political subjectivity in a liberal democratic polity: individual citizens "voice" their opinions—whether through expression in a public sphere, over social media, or by casting a vote. Indeed, a second valence of voice for demo-cratic theory lies in the notion that elected representatives "speak" on behalf of their constituents. And yet ironically (and on the other hand), as Kunreuther points out, metaphors of voice are often silent on the material-sonic qualities of political utterance—that is, on what political voice sounds like. And this is because the material-embodied notion of sound tends to be counterposed with the language-centered metaphor of voice: where individually reasoning political subjects have voices, sound is the messy material stuff of unreasoned and irrational masses and crowds. In contrast to this voice/sound binary, as Kunreuther points out in her ethnographic account of "what democracy sounds like" in Kathmandu, the word awaaz (awaaj in Nepali) simultaneously encompasses both dis-cursive and sonic registers. Thinking with awaaz allows for attention to the way that "sound affects us in ways that often exceed words," Kunruther demonstrates, and calls attention to the interconnections between "the rational and the affective," the individual and the collective, rather than their presumed counterposing.[15] This dual register of awaaz is on full dis-play in the August Kranti Maidan invitation poster depicting the placard-carrying woman: the singularity of the figure conjures an individual (if multilingual) discursively reasoning voice, while the poster's inscription "hamari awaaz" (our voice), as a collective (singular) noun, invokes the concerted roar of an assembled crowd—the very crowd that this poster-as-invitation seeks to conjure. Staying with awaaz—rather than, by virtue of translation to English, introducing an unhelpful voice/sound binary—the poster invokes awaaz's affective and collective resonances (as sound) alongside its discursivity (as voice).

But the poster is still puzzling, posing a striking contrast between the text and the image: a lone woman, lips pressed tightly shut while dis-playing a hand-drawn placard reading "Our awaaz is sharper than your batons" (Tumhari lathi se tez hamari awaaz hai). While the girl herself is visibly inaudible (lips sealed), her placard references the sharpness of

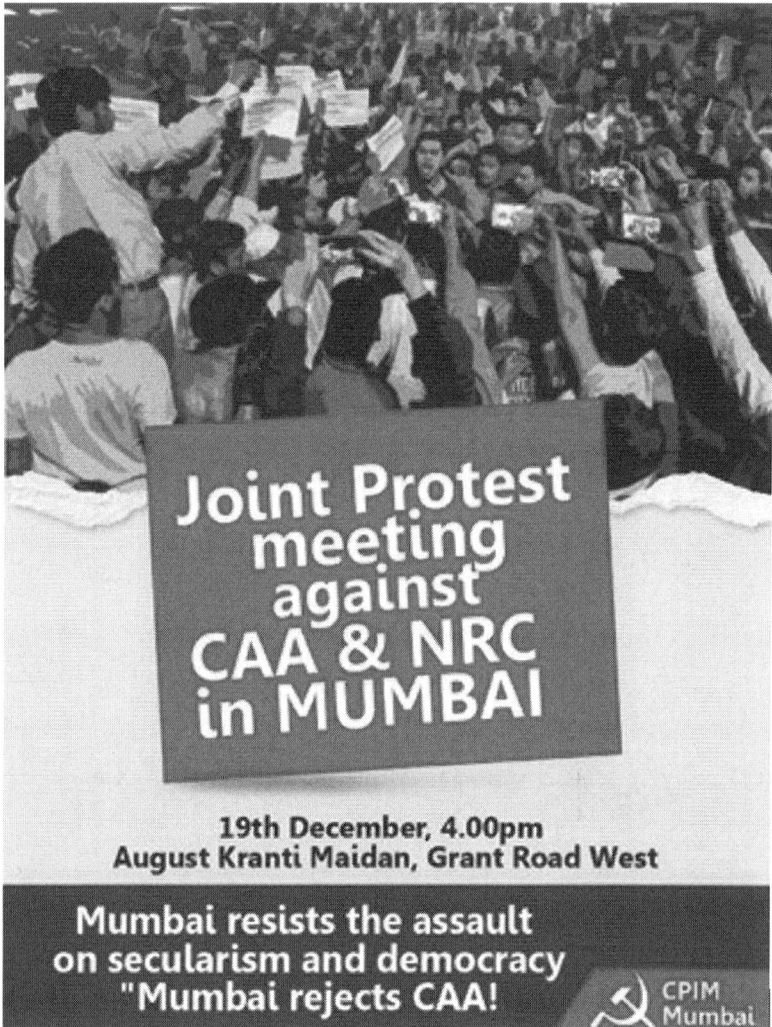

Figure 25. Artistic anticipation of a crowd of protesters displaying handcrafted placards. Mumbai, December 2019. Shared over WhatsApp. Collection of the author.

a collective and yet singular (united) "voice"—"our voice" rather than "our voices." The comparative reference to the sharpness of "batons" identifies this singular/collective awaaz as that of a collectivity called into being by the circulating earlier-described images of lathi-wielding police attacking student demonstrators on university campuses—images whose resonance in this poster reemerge as a "focal point of attention" around which a collectivity might assemble.[16]

Let us consider another digital poster (Figure 25), this one featuring an artistic rendering that seems to anticipate a hoped-for scene:[17] an assembled crowd communicating "personal perspectives" (as Preety put it) by means of one-of-a-kind, hand-drawn placards, all the while enlisting their mobile phones to produce images of one another's "personal perspectives" for circulation and amplification over social media. At the center of the image is an open-mouthed young man, apparently speaking in words. The people around him train their mobile phone cameras on the speaking man, presumably producing images and videos. The artistic rendering of the speaking man appears metaphorical, since the affordances of the assembly's communicative infrastructure—the flesh-and-blood numbers filling city streets, displaying hand-drawn paper placards for mobile phone cameras—was less amenable to audible speech than to written words. This occurred to me only months later, while I was sifting through my photo and video library from that day and came across a video I had shot with my phone—an effort to capture the energetically audible awaaz of the crowd, both in its general din and roar as well as in the sporadic outbreaks of call-and-response chanting. Indeed, notwithstanding the striking primacy of the visual in the sensory landscape that day, the gathering was most certainly audible as well, the general hum punctuated by occasional outbursts of singing and chanting—perhaps most notably (and ubiquitously) the well-known call-and-response chant "Azaadi!" (Freedom!), which was composed in 2016 by Jawaharlal Nehru University's (JNU) former student union president Kanhaiya Kumar, who was among the anti-CAA protest season's most vociferous spokespeople and sought-after orators.

Digression: "Azaadi!"

In accounting for the resonance and ubiquity of the "Azaadi!" chant during the 2019–20 anti-CAA protests, it will be helpful to attend briefly to the chant's lively backstory. A few years earlier, in the spring of 2016, JNU's student union president, Kanhaiya Kumar, gave a speech at an on-campus rally in commemoration of the two-year anniversary of the execution of Kashmiri separatist Afzal Guru[18]—a speech on the basis of which a sedition case against Kumar was registered for raising "anti-national slogans." The charge was dropped when a magisterial investigation appointed by the Delhi government found the charges unfounded, and upon Kumar's release on bail he gave another on-campus speech in which he encouraged his fellow students to "free the nation" from the divisive forces of Hindutva, and during which he sang a call-and-response chant punctuated by the repetition of "Azaadi!":

> Hai haq hamara . . . Aazadi!
> [It's our right . . . Freedom!]
> Hum lekar rahenge . . . Aazadi!
> [We will grab it . . . Freedom!]
> . . . .
> Bhukhmari se . . . Aazadi!
> [Freedom from starvation!]
> Punjivaad se . . . Aazadi!
> [Freedom from capitalism!]
> . . . .
> Brahmanvaad se . . . Aazadi!
> [Freedom from Brahmanism!]
> Hai haq hamara . . . Aazadi!
> [It's our right . . . Freedom!]

When Kumar's "Azaadi!" refrain again stirred up talk of sedition, Kumar explained that in calling for azaadi he was demanding "not freedom from India, but freedom within India";[19] and in any event, as supporters were quick to note, Kumar's "Azaadi!" was an adaptation from a 1991 chant raised during the Women's Studies Conference in Kolkata's Jadavpur University.[20]

Although the "JNU sedition row" eventually died down, the catchy "Azaadi!" chant had a spirited afterlife, most famously making an appearance in the 2019 Bollywood blockbuster *Gully Boy,* which was released just a few months prior to the August Kranti Maidan protest where I recorded the crowd chanting "Azaadi!" (and more on that in a minute). *Gully Boy* is a story about the rise to fame of a young Muslim hip-hop star born and raised in Mumbai's film-famous neighborhood Dharavi—itself renowned for its starring role in Danny Boyle's 2018 award-winning film *Slumdog Millionaire*; the entanglement between the "Azaadi!" chant's on- and off-screen lives are such that *Gully Boy*'s rendering of the chant even references Danny Boyle's film in its lyrics.[21] *Gully Boy*'s storyline is loosely based on the lives of actual Mumbai-born hip-hop star Naezy (born Naved Shaikh), who grew up in a low-income, Muslim-majority Mumbai neighborhood (not Dharavi, but rather Kurla), and of another Mumbai-based hip-hop star, a Christian-born artist named Divine (born Vivian da Silva Fernandes). Not only are the lives of Naezy and Divine the inspiration for the film *Gully Boy,* but the duo actually wrote and recorded many of the songs that were featured in the film, including a wildly popular track titled "Azaadi" that borrows lyrics and phrasing directly from Kumar's controversial 2016 chant. The *Gully Boy* version (written by Naezy and another Mumbai artist, Dub Sharma) is a re-worked and much-toned-down version of Kumar's fiery chant—the primary difference being that all references to Hindutva or of forms of caste-based oppression were removed.[22] As *Gully Boy* writer-director Zoya Akhtar explained to the media in the days before her film's release: "My story is about class, about feeling oppressed by your class. It is about economic disparity, the divide between rich and poor. It represents the point of view of my character and his engagement with the society, his socio-economic space and his anger. My film is not about the caste system or JNU."[23] Azaadi!'s popularity during the anti-CAA protest season is thus bound up both with Kumar's high-profile involvement with the protest demonstrations as well as with the just-released film *Gully Boy* and its wildly popular soundtrack—once again demonstrating the recursivity between onscreen and offscreen worlds. And yet notwithstanding the chant's film-fueled familiarity, the version I heard chanted during the 2019–20 protests was not the *Gully Boy* version but rather the one delivered by Kumar upon his release from jail—with its energetic critique of Hindutva, casteism, and communalism front and center.

In the video I recorded at August Kranti Maidan, the "Azaadi!" chant is audible before the shaky image finds the awaaz's source. The video then zooms in on a sea of placard-wielding people, scanning for moving mouths

Figure 26. Still from my video of the call-and-response chant "Azaadi!" during an anti-CAA protest. The white placard reads: "Hum paper se Hindustani nahi; hum khoon se Hindustani hai" (We aren't Hindustani by virtue of paper; we're Hindustani by blood). Mumbai, December 19, 2019. Video by the author.

from which the audible words might be emanating, and eventually coming to rest on a cluster of people that seems to be the source. The chanting is barely audible over the din, and the quality of the video is deplorable. It was only in stumbling across the video (which I'd forgotten about) that I recalled that there had been chanting that day—or that I thought much about sound at all. Audio or video traces of the event were present neither in traditional nor social media, both of which attended primarily to visual content. It was only upon discovery in my library of the shaky-noisy video of the chant that I became aware of the material affordances of the crowd-as-infrastructure, which is markedly better disposed to the visual than to the audible: inscribed and visualized awaaz (words and drawings) were amenable to imaging, sharing, and posting, whereas audible awaaz (call-and-response collective chanting), while certainly contributing to the event's mahol (atmosphere), did not circulate beyond the time-space of the gathering itself;[24] indeed, of all the reposted images and videos from that day, I searched in vain for a reposted video of any collective chant. Watching the video, I strained to make out what the chanters were saying. Ultimately it was the visual cues—reading a man's lips to make out the word "azaadi"—that enabled me to decipher what was being said.

All of which is to say: notwithstanding high-profile onstage speakers and sporadic outbursts of singing and call-and-response chants during the August Kranti Maidan event, sound was not the primary means
by which awaaz was communicated. While the primacy of the visual at
August Kranti initially took me by surprise, given that protest songs,
sloganeering, and public oratory are staples of political life in India, it
was precisely against this conventional ubiquity of sound that anti-CAA
protesters sought to articulate "personal perspectives." Indeed protest
organizers pointed to potential dangers inhering in the anonymity of the
audible, collective awaaz: in the days preceding the August Kranti event,
messages were posted on Twitter pages and circulated through Whats-
App chat groups (which is where I saw them), warning that "infiltrators"
might try to "disrupt and discredit" the peaceful event by raising "anti-
national and anti-Hindu slogans" all the while hiding in the crowd. One
digital poster read:

> *Important: For tomorrow, Thurs, Dec 19 protest.*
>
> This is contingency planning for a scenario if certain groups or individuals
> try to oppose or disrupt our protest event of Thurs, Dec 19th. When your
> movement grows to mammoth proportions, as ours is, chances are it will
> attract miscreants. If miscreants want to disrupt and discredit our protests,
> here is what they will want to happen
>
> a) Cause mayhem, chaos, panic or violence
> b) Force us into doing things that are unlawful
> c) Get us to say things that are unlawful
>
> How will they do it? One of their ways will be to mingle with you like pro-
> testors and chant unlawful/communal slogans (like anti-national slogans
> and anti-Hindu slogans), which they will later attribute to you.

In this context, where the ineluctable excess and unpredictability of crowd
aesthetics posed a risk not merely of misinterpretation but even of intentional hijack, participants took pains to broadcast their personal perspectives as precisely as possible—not in collective awaaz but rather via
uniquely crafted paper placards. If for Kunreuther, sticking with awaaz
invites us to ask what democracy sounds like, the August Kranti protest
thus prompts us to ask, What does the awaaz of democracy look like? How

is the awaaz of democracy imaged and imagined? What are the material infrastructures by means of which awaaz-images are set in motion and circulated? What are the sensory affordances of the infrastructures mediating these awaaz "image-events": the city spaces, mobile phone screens, paper placards, and proximate bodies?

Instalanguage

While the proximate public was certainly the first audience for the placards, it was not the only or final one. And yet the co-present participant-audience was a crucial component in this communicative infrastructure: those present had to be enjoined to notice a placard, to focus attention on it, to pause long enough to click a photo, and to appreciate it enough to post on their social media platform. Indeed, many placards were explicit in requesting and suggesting that proximate viewers put their social media accounts and networks to work in this way.

Amid the undulating crowd, a young man stood motionless, posing with his prominently displayed placard and locking eyes with a mobile phone camera. His poster dispatched with artistry (even color) altogether, the small-print text—messily scrawled onto torn paper—nearly impossible to decipher in the jostle and bustle of the throng and at any distance greater than a couple of meters; one had to stand directly in front of the placard for long enough to read it, and even then, the handwritten, roman-alphabet transliterated Urdu wasn't easy to decipher. The nine hashtags at the bottom of the placard seem to explicitly enjoin people to enlist their phones—to photograph and post on social media, even suggesting hashtags. Obediently, I clicked a photo (Figure 27), making a mental note to read it later that evening (more on that in a minute).

The hand-drawn hashtags had caught my attention that day, but while scrolling through the thousands of images posted on social media over the following days I noticed that the young poet wasn't alone; many posters sported hand-drawn hashtags. A bit of a social media rookie myself, I shared some of these images with a few of the more media-savvy among my research interlocutors and asked how to interpret the hashtags. To them, the hashtags were read both as literal suggestions for how people posting photographs might tag those images as well as a simple incorporation of "instalanguage" into everyday communication. Whether or not photo-clickers eventually posted images of placards on social media, the

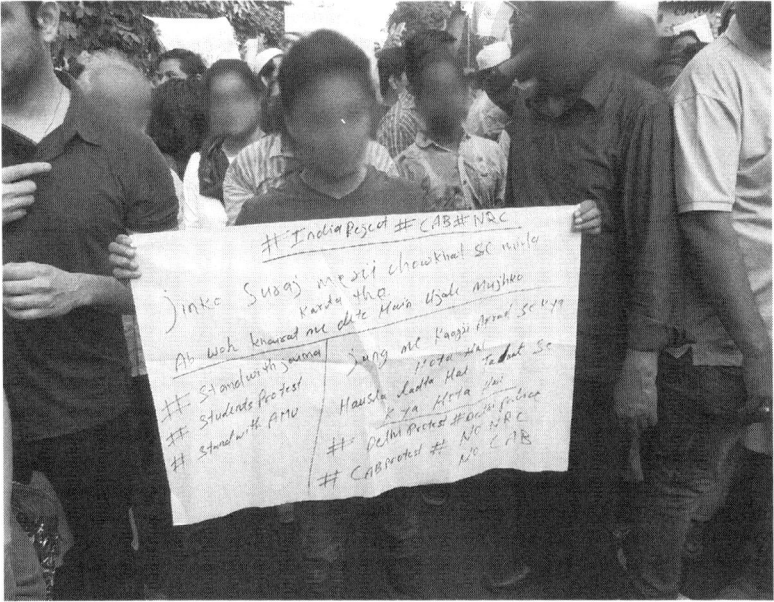

Figure 27. Poster displayed at protest demonstration featuring hand-drawn hashtags. Mumbai, December 19, 2019. Photograph by author.

hashtags worked as an effort to "tag" the meaning in the dual sense that media anthropologists Yarimar Bonilla and Jonathan Rosa describe—where the hashtag "serves as an indexing system in both the clerical and the semiotic sense." In a clerical sense, hashtags "operate in ways similar to library call numbers: They locate texts within a specific conversation, allowing for their quick retrieval, while also marking texts as being 'about' a specific topic." And in a semiotic sense, hashtags have an "intertextual potential to link a broad range of tweets on a given topic or disparate topics as part of an intertextual chain, regardless of whether, from a given perspective, these tweets have anything to do with one another."[25] As "instalanguage," hashtags are efforts to mark a text as being potentially "about" something—efforts (rather than accomplishments) because (unlike the relative stability of library indexing systems) hashtags are much more dynamic than library call numbers, constantly changing and information in relation to perceptions of whatever else is happening.[26]

Preety messaged me a few days after the August Kranti Maidan gathering, asking me to send any interesting photos I might have clicked, and sharing with me her own favorites. Unsurprisingly, the vast majority of the photos that comprised her Instagram "story" were close-up images of placards. Indeed, the days following the initial gathering at Mumbai's August Kranti Maidan witnessed an explosion of imagery in both traditional and social media (as well as traditional media posted on social media) of clever-placard imagery, as people shared and reposted photos of one another's paper posters.

Speaking with Preety by phone, I asked how had she known in advance to make a placard. For that matter, how did anyone know to make placards? Had she discussed it with anyone beforehand? Did her colleagues also make and carry placards? And most importantly, how had she decided what to write on hers? She paused to consider the questions, then told me, "See, going to the protest was an emotional decision." It was "emotion" that impelled her "to take action" and join the protest, she explained,

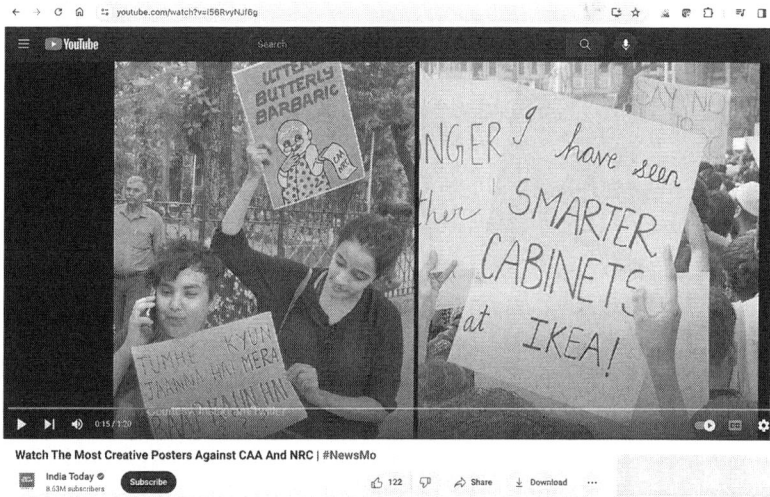

Figure 28. Images of handcrafted posters displayed at protest demonstrations that were later shown on YouTube. One caption (referencing Amul dairy's well-known ad campaign) reads "Utterly, Butterly, Barbaric," another "Tumhe kyun janna hai mera baap kaun hai?" (Why do you need to know who my daddy is?); on the right side of the screen the poster reads "I have seen smarter cabinets at IKEA!" Screenshot taken by the author from *India Today*'s YouTube video feature of "most creative posters." From "Watch the Most Creative Posters against CAA and NRC," *India Today,* December 21, 2019, https://www.youtube.com/watch?v=i56RvyNJf6g. Collection of the author.

but more importantly, "to take a placard to explain the specific reason I was going." I asked her to say more about her "strong emotions," and Preety explained how over the previous months she'd been watching her father's social media consumption with deepening despair:

> He's been watching these YouTube and WhatsApp videos and forwards . . . news which is very biased. Social media basically shows you what you want to see. My dad's WhatsApp and Facebook are filled with pro-BJP content whereas mine . . . mine is not. It's not his fault, he doesn't even realize it's happening to him—that he's being made to believe certain things without questioning . . . because he doesn't know what's authentic and what's not.

She tells me about a heated exchange on her family chat on the morning of the protest. "My family members got on WhatsApp and started saying that 'a dangerous protest by Muslims is going to happen and there could be trouble so everyone should stay away.' I messaged back that 'It's not a protest by Muslims. It is by those Indians who are against CAA.'" She forwards me the screenshot of the chat—which she's overlaid with commentary and (of course) posted on Instagram (Figure 29).

Preety recalled how her family's (especially her father's) social-media-fueled opposition to the protest had "triggered" her. Earlier, she explained, "I could never have imagined myself making a placard and going to a protest, but I was so angry." For Preety, moreover, emotion and reason are inextricably intertwined: it was her anger that impelled her to write up a poster in order to "explain clearly" her "reason" for opposing the CAA. She continued: "I wanted to explain clearly that this has nothing to do with politics, that it's a constitutional matter. I can explain this easily when I sit down with someone to have a conversation," Preety tells me, recalling how she'd "sat down" with her parents to read sections of the Constitution together—again posting images overlaid with commentary on her Instagram (see Figure 30). "But at a protest, how can you make that kind of explanation? So I wanted to condense my perspective. That's why I put it on a placard. It was impromptu. I just tore some cardboard into pieces and made it right there on the train platform. I thought: maybe someone will capture it in a photo and post it somewhere."

As Preety makes clear—and as the hashtags suggest was the case more broadly—her paper placard was crafted with the precise goal that it be

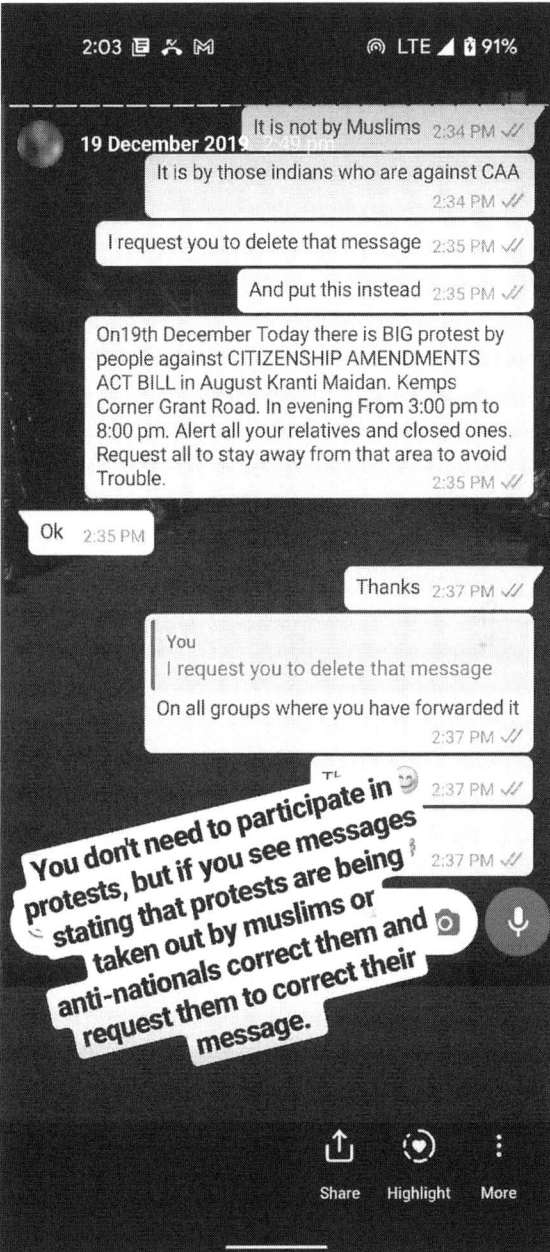

Figure 29. A WhatsApp squabble on her family chat that Preety screenshot, overlaid with commentary, and posted on Instagram before sending it to me by WhatsApp, where I screenshot it myself. Mumbai, December 19, 2019. Collection of the author.

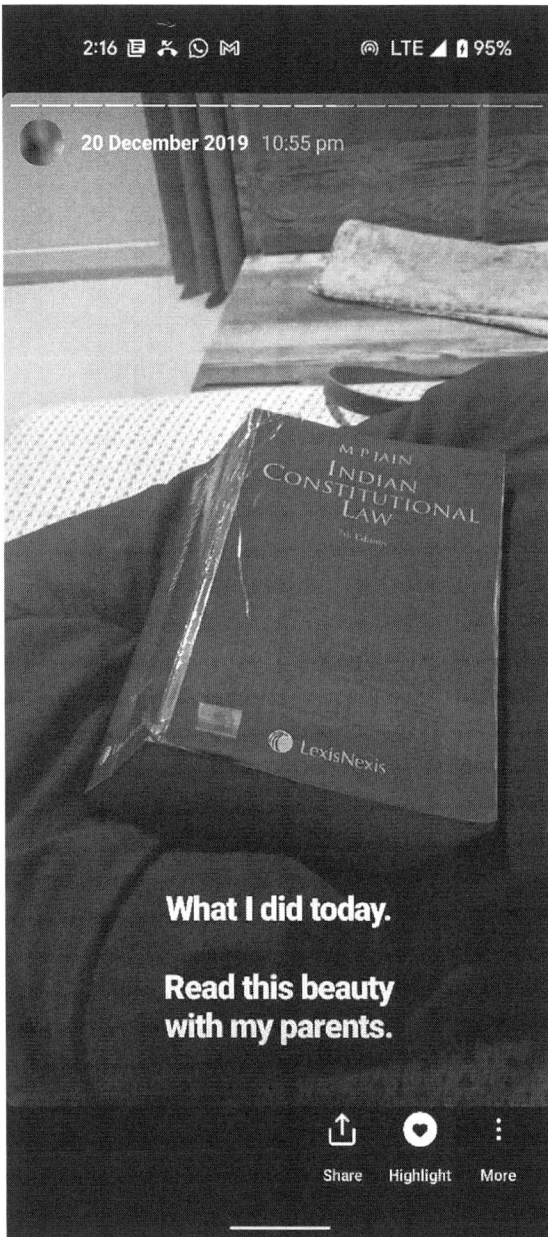

Figure 30. A photograph of the author's copy of the Indian Constitution that Preety posted on Instagram overlaid with commentary, before screenshotting the Instagram page and forwarding it to me by WhatsApp, where I screenshot it myself. Mumbai, December 19, 2019. Collection of the author.

photographed and that those images be circulated over social media by other crowd participants. The infrastructure of the embodied crowd (the streets that afforded material proximity of placard-wielding individuals) and the infrastructures of circulation and amplification of those communicative acts (the photographing and circulating of those images), in other words, were one and the same. The very same people performed both the work of articulating their "personal perspectives" on paper placards and of selecting and amplifying resonant messages.

The emphasis on personal perspectives and emotions at the August Kranti gathering, along with the ubiquity of one-of-a-kind handcrafted posters, is a striking contrast from the visual uniformity characterizing the rally described in chapter 2—where participants dressed up in identical hats and scarves, carried uniform party flags, and participated explicitly in order to contribute to a singular image: the "size and strength of the rally." In contrast with the electoral rally-show, the August Kranti gathering was almost entirely devoid of political party flags, save a smattering of banners bearing the logo of the Communist Party of India (Marxist). The only ubiquitous visual sign was the Indian flag. Indeed, the visual space of the August Kranti gathering was explicitly nonpartisan (a subject I take up in the next chapter)—notwithstanding the fact that almost everyone I spoke to expressed party preferences. Standing on a raised platform at the edge of the crowd, I had been chatting with a man (visibly Muslim, his taqiya[27] and forehead prayer bump announcing Islamic piety) who looked to be in his sixties who introduced himself as an architect and told me that this was first time he joined a morcha (protest demonstration or rally). As we're chatting, some excited hullabaloo becomes evident amid the throngs. The architect points a finger and says: "There's our MLA!" I look up to recognize the face of a seasoned Congress Party politician. The architect calls out to the politician by name; the latter turns his head in our direction, smiles, and waves. And yet notwithstanding such affinities, party identity had no place in the awaaz-image of "the people of India" that the gathering sought to articulate and represent.

Kaaghaz, Khoon, Constitution

It wasn't until I got home that evening and transferred photos from my phone to my computer that I had time to consider the poem that the young man had written out and marked with hashtags (see Figure 27):

Jinko suraj meri chowkhat se mila karta tha
Ab woh khairat me dete hue ujale mujhko;
Jang me kagazi afraad se kya hota hai[?]
Hausla ladta hai tadaad se, kya hota hai

Translated literally, the poem says something like:

Those who got sunlight from my threshold,
Now in charity they are giving light to me;
In war, what's the power of paper?
Courage fights through numbers [tadaad].

Put differently, the poem is saying something like this:

The people themselves are the actual source of the government's power/
authority ("sunlight"), but the government is behaving as if that same
power originates with the government, to be doled out to the people as
charity. But the powerlessness of the government's regime of paper is
nothing when confronted with the courage and strength of our actual
(flesh-and-blood) numbers [taadad].[28]

The poem levels a scathing critique at the government's pretensions
to power—its claim to have a self-proclaimed authority to adjudicate
citizenship and national belonging based on the existence or absence of
some or another bit of paper—kaaghaz—which is counterposed with
flesh-and-blood numbers (tadaad). In counterposing kaaghaz with the
embodied, fleshy strength of human presence, the young poet's use of
kaaghaz reflects long-standing use of the word in Urdu poetry. The recur-
rence of the word kaaghaz during the CAA-NPR-NRC protests in Mumbai (on placards; in poems, written and recited) caught my attention—not
least because kaaghaz isn't a word often used by Mumbaikars (whether
speaking English, Marathi, Hindi, or Urdu) when describing their various identity documents (ration cards, voter IDs, PAN cards, etc.); these
things are generally referred to not as kaaghaz (as is more common in
North India) but rather as "documents," or more colloquially as "proofs."

In the course of my research on regimes of documentation in Mumbai
—on water politics; on slum surveys, on neighborhood upgrading and
popular housing—I'd rarely (if ever) heard anyone say anything like

"The officers are asking for my kaaghaz" or "I have to bring copies of my kaaghaz" over to some or another government office. And yet colleagues working in other Indian cities—Calcutta, Delhi, and Lucknow—maintain that kaaghaz is in fact sometimes used to refer to such documents. Curious about whether perhaps I'd simply overlooked kaaghaz all these years, I WhatsApped the question to colleagues and friends working in Mumbai, starting with a well-known Mumbai artist and housing activist (and longtime friend) named Simpreet, who grew up in North India is thereby attuned to regional differences:

> LISA: Simpreet, can I ask you a quick question? In Gowandi and so on, when people talk about their documents/proofs, do they ever use the word kaaghaz?
>
> SIMPREET: "Proof kya hai" [They'd ask "what is your proof"]
>
> SIMPREET: also "document"
>
> LISA: I've never heard people use "kaaghaz" but colleagues in other cities say that "kaaghaz" is used—in Delhi etc.
>
> SIMPREET: In north
>
> SIMPREET: Not here
>
> LISA: why do you think that's the case?
>
> SIMPREET: Not sure

Curiosity piqued, I posed the same question to three Bombay ethnographers having document-related research projects. The first did a word search in her multilingual fieldnotes, reporting back that "'document' is there everywhere" and "I don't see kaaghaz actually." A second recalled that people refer to "specific papers," adding that "I've never heard the word kaaghaz." A third colleague was the notable exception that seems to prove the rule, reporting that kaaghaz was indeed quite commonly heard in her research—which she carried out among migrants hailing from North India. Wondering whether kaaghaz might be more common among Bombay's native Urdu speakers, I WhatsApped a friend who teaches in a secondary school in the Urdu-speaking South Bombay neighborhood of Nagpada:

> LISA: when people in your area talk about their identity papers (ration cards, pan cards and so on), what word do they use?
>
> N: Documents

LISA: do you ever hear/use "kaaghaz"?

N: No

N: If they hv to show somewhere they always say I hv my documents.

LISA: is "kaaghaz" used only poetically then?

N: Yaa

Indeed, with the ambivalence toward paper documents the crux of the anti-CAA movement, kaaghaz emerged as key problematic, especially in protest poetry. The ubiquity of Urdu poetry during the anti-CAA protest season has been widely noted.[29] In one of the most prominent instances, two days after the December 19 gathering, Bombay-based writer and standup comedian Varun Grover posted a video of himself on his Twitter page, reading his just-penned poem "Hum Kaaghaz Nahi Dikhayenge" (We will not show papers)—a passionate call for mass civil disobedience that begins by declaring: "Dictators will come and go, our kaaghaz [papers] we won't show."

> Raise your batons and shut down the trains all you want;
> We will walk and walk . . . and we won't show kaaghaz
> . . . We will save the constitution before we go;
> and we won't show kaaghaz . . .
> . . . You will try to divide us by caste and religion;
> we will continue to demand only our rights to food
> We won't show kaaghaz
> We won't show kaaghaz

Varun Grover introduces his Twitter-circulated video recitation of the poem with a simple dedication: "Inspired by the spirit of every protestor and India lover. With Hat Tips to Rahat Indori Saab." By the time Grover tweeted his poem, the media sphere was already saturated with images of posters bearing renowned Urdu poet Rahat Indori's pithy, poignant couplet (e.g., see Figure 31)—the very same couplet, notably, that Junaid (our Urdu orator) had shared with me two years earlier as an inspirational example (see chapter 3):

> Sabhi ka khoon hai shaamil yahan ki mitti mein
> Kisi ke baap ka Hindustan thodi hai

Everyone's blood is mixed together in this soil.
Hindustan doesn't belong to anyone's daddy

The resonance of Indori's couplet—which itself became a ubiquitous anti-CAA protest anthem—inheres in the particular way it envisions the relationship of blood (khoon) to soil (mithi) and national belonging (Hindustan), a relationship quite different from that envisioned by Hindutva and institutionalized in the CAA. As anthropologists Dwaipayan Banerjee and Jacob Copeman have explained, the notion of a "shared community of blood" is both "a medium and conceptual resource for Hindutva practice."[30] Tracing how the notion of the "blood community" is entailed in Hindutva, Banerjee and Copeman demonstrate how the CAA is both an iteration and culmination of Hindutva's "hematological geography":

The CAA is a punitive legal manifestation of a long-standing claim . . . that ancient inhabitants of India shared a common blood-tie, only recently

Figure 31. Urdu poet Rahat Indori's couplet featured on a handcrafted placard at a protest demonstration in Mumbai. The couplet reads: "Sabhi ka khoon hai shaamil yahan ki mitti mein. Kisi ke baap ka Hindustan thodi hai" (Everyone's blood is mixed together in this soil. Hindustan doesn't belong to anyone's daddy). Mumbai, December 2019. Photograph by Rohan Shivkumar, shared with the author over WhatsApp.

betrayed and broken by the recent conversion of some to Islam. Because of this shared consanguinity, Muslims could return to the fold, if only they were to give up their allegiance to Mecca. The implications of this Hindutva's knotting together of geography and blood (based on an implicit assumption that Muslim blood had now been recently contaminated by conversion) reveals itself in the logic of the CAA.[31]

Hindutva's ideological equating of blood with national territory, and the insistence on Indian Muslims' primordial "blood tie" to Hinduism, demands they either "reassimilate" to Hindutva or else suffer the inevitable consequences of their betrayal: the delegitimation of their claims to belonging and citizenship. Indori's couplet breezily dismisses this hematological history and geography, supplanting the ideology of primordial blood ties with the actual history of cohabitation and mixing in a territory whose very ground is the substance of that mixing: "Everyone's blood is mixed together in this soil." Meanwhile, the verse's second line meets Hindutva's righteous allegations of "disloyalty" with a gentle, teasing rebuke deserved of a schoolyard bully: "Hindustan doesn't belong to anyone's daddy."

While Indori's couplet comprises the final lines in a ghazal (lyric poem) that the author penned thirty-five years earlier (and in a context that Indori himself could not recall),[32] the salience among anti-CAA protesters of Indori's articulation of khoon-based belonging is clear enough: a historical corrective to the imaginary of khoon in Hindutva's exclusionary articulations of citizenship. As early as the Jamia protest on December 15, 2019, photographs of placards bearing Indori's couplet filled the mediascape. And its resonance was such that not only the couplet but its reconceptualized version of khoon (and also Hindustan) began turning up on placards, where it was often explicitly counterposed with kaaghaz.[33] Rewatching my video of the Azaadi chanters at August Kranti, for instance, my attention fell on a paper placard that inadvertently got caught in the camera frame (see Figure 26):

Hum paper se Hindustani nahi; hum khoon se Hindustani hai

We aren't Hindustani by virtue of paper; we're Hindustani by blood

It was a slogan that, by the time I stumbled upon it in my video still, I had seen a myriad of times—in images of paper placards at protest gatherings

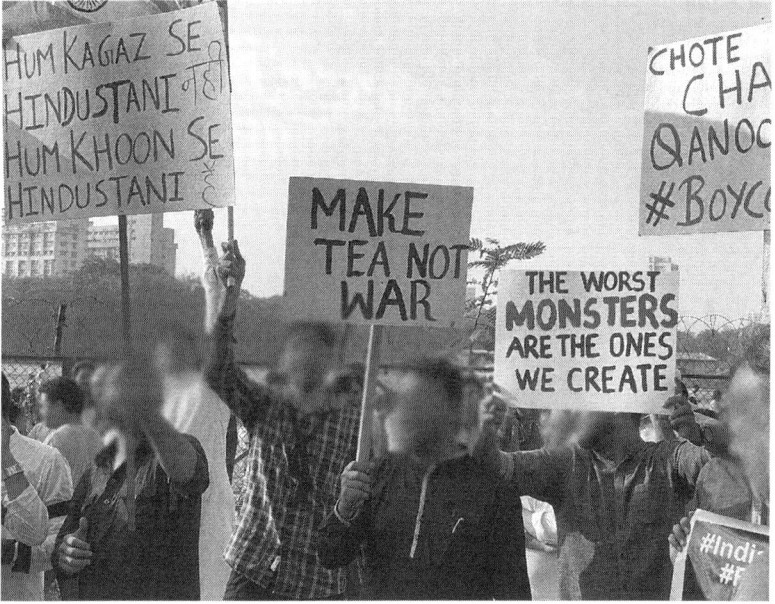

Figure 32. Handcrafted placards displayed at protest demonstration. The placard on the left reads "Hum kagaz se Hindustani nahi; hum khoon se Hindustani hai" (We aren't Hindustani by virtue of paper; we're Hindustani by blood). Mumbai, December 2019. Photograph by Rohan Shivkumar, shared with the author over WhatsApp.

from all corners of India, where they had been photographed, posted, and circulated through social media (see, e.g., Figure 32).

In making sense of the protest valence of kaaghaz, it is thus helpful to consider the uses of the term in the Urdu poetic tradition and to attend to explicit references to Urdu poetics in both the form and substance of anti-CAA poetry, placards, and imagery. In the following verse, for instance, kaaghaz appears (rather straightforwardly) as a way to characterize something as inauthentic or even deceptive:

Kitne hi kushnuma inhen yaaro banaiye
titli kabhi na baithegi kaaghaz ke phool par[34]

No matter how beautiful they appear,
butterflies will never sit on paper flowers[35]

And yet when used to describe written correspondences (especially love letters), kaaghaz changes its normative valence entirely, the papery materiality now idealized as a medium for conveying intimate feelings:

Khat pe khat likhiyega ai shah-savar
ghodi kaaghaz ki bhi daudaiyega.[36]

Oh gallant knight,
How about setting some paper horses [ghodi kaaghaz] in motion as well.[37]

That kaaghaz is up to this task—delivering love, unscathed and intact—is evidenced in the physical and material effects that the absence of kaaghaz-mediated love inflicts on heart and body of the snubbed lover:

Hae lay ana koi qasid-e-dilbar kaaghaz
ho gaya gham se hamara tan-e-laghar kaaghaz[38]

Alas! No messenger has arrived to bring any beloved letters
[dilbar kaaghaz; i.e., letters penned by the beloved]
my body is emaciated from grief, like brittle paper [laghar kaaghaz][39]

In this couplet, kaaghaz appears twice. First, kaaghaz is the material embodiment of love itself: "dilbar kaaghaz" means something like "paper infused with love" or "love incarnated as paper." The second use of kaaghaz then describes the material effects—weakness and pain—of dilbar kaaghaz's absence: the body of the snubbed lover becomes laghar kaaghaz—brittle, fragile paper.

"Please Understand the Chronology"

In her research in the government offices responsible for an employment scheme in the North Indian state of Uttarakhand, anthropologist Nayanika Mathur characterizes India's "government of paper" (kaaghazi sarkar) as the site of a kind of Orwellian double-speak: "Senior officials would scold their juniors for maintaining progress only on paper while simultaneously ordering them to look after the paperwork properly for, after all, what really counted was what was on paper."[40] Mathur observes how, on the one hand, allegations by higher-ups against field officers that some actual work remained only "on paper" (kaaghaz pe) served as a critical evaluation of the sorry state of on-the-ground activity—what Orwell famously described as "doublethink" in *1984*: "To know and not to know, to be conscious of complete truthfulness while telling carefully constructed lies, to hold simultaneously two opinions which cancelled out, knowing them to be contradictory and believing in both of them."[41] And yet, at the same time, Mathur observes how those same higher-ups would instruct lower-level functionaries to "fix" reports such that "on-paper" records remained in order.[42] Indeed as anthropologists John Harriss and Craig Jeffrey point out, the historical and ethnographic record presents "abundant evidence of the significance of caste, class and gender privilege" in patterns of access and exclusion, and reveals the central role of political actors and agents in putting papers to work in reproducing or contesting those entrenched patterns.[43]

And yet, as demonstrated in chapter 1, registering things "on paper" and putting those papers to work in creative ways are also sites at which entrenched hierarchies are regularly obviated (even if this is not the most common outcome). Regimes of documentation present possibilities of resource access as well as the danger of foreclosure of such access; the difference resides not in some characteristic of paper per se (or in any particular paper document itself) but rather in processes and practices by means of which papers are put to work by their handlers.[44] The loss or lack of access to things such as municipal services, housing, education, livelihood, and even suffrage is not ascribed to papers as such (their existence or want; their realness or forgery), nor to the regulatory regimes, policies, or programs within which documents become necessary, but rather to the human-centered processes and agentive practices of putting those regimes to work—notwithstanding the existence, absence, or appraised authenticity of any particular piece of paper. The crucial difference between paper documents that are treated as "genuine" and those treated as "duplicate" inheres neither in some document's origins nor in some material quality of some document in itself, but rather in the real-time work by means of which some documents are rendered efficacious while others are not.[45]

That kaaghaz is simultaneously the site of violent exclusion as well as of potential promise of overcoming those same exclusions yields a great ambivalence in India toward paper documents—which are sign and substance of both possibilities. Indeed, as Varun Grover's powerful poem makes clear, the call for civil disobedience is not tantamount to denying the value of documents per se; Grover's poem does not declare, for instance, that "we will destroy our paper documents because they are meaningless," but rather "we will not show our paper documents in this particular context"—that is, in conjunction with the CAA-NPR-NRC combination. The critique of kaaghaz is thus not of paper documents per se but rather of their enlistment in this particular context and way.

This centering of the intentioned use rather than the material fact of documents as the target of anti-CAA critique is evidenced in the debate that erupted in the media over whether or not the CAA was linked to the creation of a National Registry of Citizens. With protesters pouring into streets in cities across India, the BJP government and its supporters tried to suggest that the CAA and NRC exercises were completely separate. "There is no question of joining CAA with NRC," Union Law Minister Ravi Shankar Prasad stated at a press conference on Tuesday, December 17, 2019—two days after images of police violence against protesting students in Delhi had gone viral.[46] And yet detractors were quick to point out precisely that link been clearly stated on multiple occasions by the BJP home minister. Protesters drew attention to a post made by the home minister earlier that year (on May 2019) in which he lays out the intended sequencing on his Twitter page: "First we will pass the Citizenship Amendment bill and ensure that all the refugees from the neighboring nations get the Indian citizenship. After that, NRC will be made and we will detect and deport every infiltrator from our motherland" (see Figure 33).

Within a week of the act's passage into law, the video from earlier that year (seven months before the CAA was passed into law) in which the home minister enjoins the public to "chronology samajh lijiye"—"please understand the chronology"—went viral on social media. The phrase quickly set off what one media outlet described as a "Hilarious Meme-Fest" on Twitter, mocking the government for downplaying the obvious (and alarming) implications of the CAA as a matter of mere "chronology."[47] And unsurprisingly, "please understand the chronology" quickly became a staple of hand-drawn paper placards.

Given the dual valence of kaaghaz, it was the specification of the government's intended use of paper documents so clearly stated in the home minister's "aap chronology samajh lijiye" speech that rendered kaaghaz a protest-season epithet—a shorthand dismissal of the cynical proposal to treat mere paper documents as if they were the actual embodiment of citizenship.

"The Only Document That Matters"

Amid all the talk of the capriciousness of paper as sign and substance of citizenship, one particular document was held up as the infallible

Figure 33. Still from viral video posted by Home Minister Amit Shah on his Twitter account (@AmitShah). X, May 1, 2019.

substance through which belonging actually could be adjudicated: the Indian Constitution. Preety's handmade placard was part of a genre that grounded critique of the CAA not by questioning the appropriateness of deducing citizenship status from identity documents per se, by rather by citing the constitutional prohibition on differential application of law. "All the articles in our Constitution can be amended, but the Preamble . . . cannot," a Bombay High Court lawyer told the media that had gathered outside the courthouse January 2020 to record seventy lawyers reading aloud the Preamble to the Indian Constitution. Another lawyer explained how the CAA is unconstitutional in two ways: "Firstly, it violates Article 14 of the Constitution, which says nobody should be denied equality before the law. Secondly, it also violates Article 15, which prohibits discrimination on grounds of religion, race, caste, sex or place of birth."[48] The gathering of lawyers in Mumbai was of a piece with similar gatherings across the country; Preamble readings took place in Lucknow, Delhi, and Chennai, leading one reporter to conclude that "in the anti-CAA agitation where 'Kaaghaz Nahin Dikhayenge' is the raging intonation,[49] the

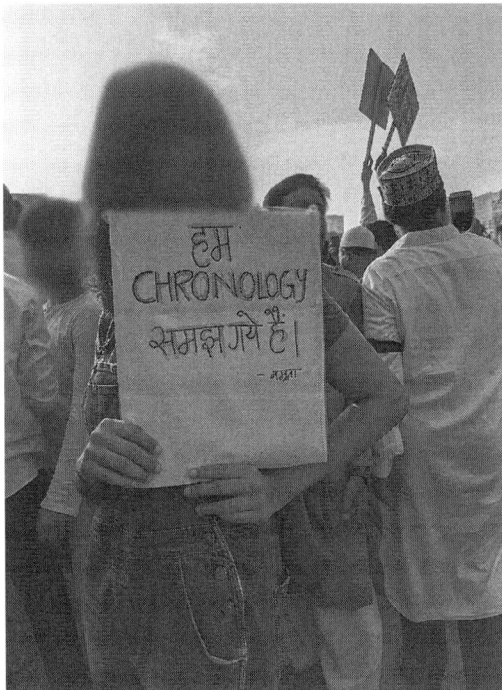

Figure 34. A placard displayed at a protest demonstration reading "Hum chronology samaj gaye hai" (We have understood the chronology). Mumbai, December 27, 2019. Photo by V. Chitra, shared with the author over WhatsApp.

Preamble is the only document that matters, that protesters display like the defining proof of their citizenship."[50] And significantly, protesters did not merely display paper printouts of the Preamble, but read aloud from those paper printouts as well—echoing the dual meaning of awaaz, which conveys audible sound as well as individual voice or "personal perspective."[51] Assembling to read aloud (and in unison) from paper printouts of the Preamble, the gatherings at once asserted the authenticity and individuality of voicing subjects (awaaz as "personal perspective") while emphasizing the crucial importance of subjectivity's material mediations: paper, sound, cameras.

Paper's materiality sits at the heart of both valences of kaaghaz. On the one hand, the Constitution's solid dependability is attributed to its character as dilbar kaaghaz: a material embodiment of equality before law, written down for anyone to consult and cite.[52] And on the other hand, the capricious character of governmental documentary practices is such a truism that it has long been a theme in popular satire. For example, in Hindi satirist Harishankar Parsai's mid-twentieth-century story *Bholaram Ka Jeev* (The soul of Bholaram) the punch line has the missing-in-action

Figure 35. Bombay High Court lawyers reading from paper printouts of the Preamble. Still from video was screened on the *Times of India*'s Twitter account TOI Plus (@TOI+), "In protest of #CAA, #NRC and #NPR, lawyers read the Preamble of the Constitution of India outside Bombay High Court." Twitter, January 20, 2020, https://x.com/TOIPlus/status/1219206773397049352. Author of the video unknown. Author's collection.

soul (jeev) of recently deceased, impoverished former government peon Bholaram eventually found hiding inside his own file folder in the dusty government office—refusing to go to heaven until Bholaram's file is approved. The story is funny, and darkly so, because (so the story goes) the soul properly resides in the earthly body until death sets it free; it does not get waylaid in a dusty government file waiting for approval. The story is darkly funny, in other words, because it plays out the all-too-familiar experience of paper-mediated injustices to an absurd conclusion. Similarly, the CAA-NPR-NRC combine was such a shocking affront because it sought to institutionalize and empower a notion so widely accepted as ludicrous as to be the subject of a satirical literary genre: that paper documents in themselves are the substance of citizenship—an idea that shamelessly treats kaaghaz ke phool (mere paper flowers) as if it were dilbar kaaghaz (paper embodying and conveying authentic love).

Amid the outrage, legal scramble, mass protests, and police violence, the home minister gave a TV interview (widely circulated on social media, which is where I saw it).[53] In the interview, he sought to deflect the conversation from the flood of concerns raised over what the CAA-NPR-NRC combine would mean for the millions of Indians without identity documents, assuring all non-Muslims that "all the Hindu, Sikh, Buddhist, Christians, they will get citizenship. . . . We want to walk up to them and give them citizenship. They wouldn't be asked for any documents [dastavez]."[54] Whatever his intention in giving the speech, the meaning that the home minister's words conveyed was clear enough: the power of documents does not inhere in the paper per se, but unfolds processually and discretionally—in the power-inflected contexts and encounters by means of which papers are produced (or not produced), empowered (or declared doubtful), and declared effective (or deficient).[55] While Shah's words presumably hoped to calm the nerves of the millions of non-Muslims scrambling to get their documents in order, it affirmed suspicions among Muslims that not even their documents could save them from being stripped of citizenship.

"To See and to Do"

Back at August Kranti Maidan, the dual valence of kaaghaz was on full display: just as the whimsical mediations of kaaghaz were discursively counterposed with the embodied realness of khoon (blood) and strength

of tadaad (numbers), the very people comprising the tadaad had inscribed critiques of kaaghaz on kaaghaz itself—writing by hand their
personal critiques of paper on paper placards. This enlisting of paper as
an ideal medium of intimate ideas and "personal perspectives," moreover,
wasn't incidental. Preety, for instance, explicitly contrasted the affordance
of paper placards with that of the digital, explaining to me how with
digital media "you don't know what's authentic and what's not. But when
I write on a placard, you can't alter that."[56] Preety thus characterizes the
material affordances of paper precisely as that of authenticity. It wouldn't
have sufficed to sit at home and make digital posters; they had to be written on paper—handwritten on paper even—in order to faithfully convey
personal perspective. At the same time, the digital (while perhaps unreliable in itself) has its own role to play in the conveyance of authenticity. "If
my placard is captured in a photo and someone captures and shares it,"
Preety explained, "then I've shared my personal perspective and point of
view." While paper mediates authenticity, the sociomaterial infrastructure

Figure 36. A placard displayed at a protest demonstration reads "Kaaghaz ke
Fools" (Paper fools), a play on the title of well-known Hindi film *Kaaghaz ke
Phool* (Paper flowers). Mumbai, December 27, 2019. Photograph by Rohan
Shivkumar.

by means of which that authenticity is "captured and shared" encompasses the digital as well.

How did protest-goers make sense of this apparent contradiction between kaaghaz as medium and message? I posed the question to my friend Rohit, who'd carried a paper placard explicitly critiquing the duplicitousness of kaaghaz at a protest a week later on Azad Maidan (see Figure 36). While I wasn't present at the Azad Maidan event, I had seen an image of his paper placard on a mutual friend's Instagram page, recognized Rohit, and rang him up. I asked if he found it ironic that he wrote his critique of paper on paper. He found the question silly: "Oh the material could have been anything. It didn't make a difference that it was paper. It could have been written on anything." He explained that it wasn't even important to him to carry a placard at all; to him, the important thing was to actually go: "That motion of going for something . . . to take time out to actually do something." He recounted to me how he had seen the images of the young women at Jamia—sheltering their bleeding friend and scolding the lathi-wielding police—as well as the images of the elderly women of Shaheen Bagh braving the bitter cold and hostile Delhi authorities to block traffic in peaceful protest. "Those old Muslim women, they've paralyzed the government! Because see, the government can't have the visual of physically removing these old women. That was so inspiring. I thought, 'Sure, I can just go on with my own life,' but I thought, 'Like them, you too should disrupt your own life! Get involved with what's around you. Take time out, to see and to do.'" That's why it was important, he explained, to "actually be there." This importance of embodied presence is why it was so necessary to physically assemble—both in flesh and with hand-inscribed placards—rather than, say, simply tweet from home, or (as in the next chapter) draw up petitions, gather lawyers, and go on delegations to elected officials and government ministers and so on.

If the ultimate audience for the placard-mediated content—amplified by the camera-wielding participant-public—was the one scrolling through the bazillion digital images of the paper placards circulated over social media during and after the event, then what was the point of traveling all the way downtown to gather at August Kranti Maidan? That is, if the final goal was to have one's "personal perspective" communicated over digital platforms, why not just stay at home, design a cool poster, and then post it on social media? The question, at first glance, seems ridiculous, because obviously—intuitively—there's a difference between sweating it out under the midday sun to wave a placard and chant "Azaadi!" amid the jostle and bustle of the crowd, on the one hand, and, on the other, sitting at home under the ceiling fan designing a poster while listening to the Bollywood remake of Kanhaiya Kumar's no-longer-"seditious" chanting of "Azaadi!" on Spotify. Something important happens between the act of crafting a paper placard and the digitally mediated encounter with some placard's images by an appreciative (or unappreciative) public. What, then, are the communicative affordances of the crowd itself?

Notwithstanding the urge "to see and to do," Rohit explained to me that he hadn't gone to the August Kranti Maidan anti-CAA protest the previous week, because he "didn't agree" with the premise whereby "space is demarcated by the state to 'protest.'" He explained: "The whole point of a protest is to disrupt! Where you are permitted to protest, it isn't a space of disruption. A protest is supposed to shut down the road." That's what made the women of Shaheen Bagh so powerful, he explained: they had disrupted the capital, had shut down a public road without permission. "What's the point of a protest if it's in a garden? The government gives us the permission and then says 'go and play your role'—that's not a protest!"

In Rohit's reading, the "organized" and "permitted" character of the August Kranti protest turned it into a piece of theater—not a real protest but a dramatization of one: a "protest" (in scare quotes) in which participants were simply invited to "play their roles." Identifying the protest gathering as theater had turned Rohit off to the demonstration, but not because the theatricality made it somehow deceptive—"only natak" in a disparaging sense.[57] Indeed, the conveners had taken care not only to secure all the proper permissions but also to make sure that it was public knowledge that they had done so. For Rohit, the problem with the event's theatricality was simply that, to his mind, this wasn't the time for "protest" but rather for (unvirgolated) protest—protest that is not "allowed" and which thereby "disrupts."[58]

Like many young people I spoke to, Rohit was somewhat new to protest politics; he recalled having participated in demonstrations on only "a couple" of occasions prior to December 2019. In this context, Rohit recounted how he had initially been shocked by what he saw on social media in the days following the August Kranti gathering—by how many people had turned up (unofficial police estimates put the turnout around 100,000, although the officially reported number was 25,000) and by the visuals: "there was such a cross section of society . . . office-goers next to Muslims wearing caps and hijabs, and the mix of students and liberals—it was the first time I saw that." He was moved as well by the wave of popular mobilizations across India: "This was the first time I could remember that there were so many protests cropping up all over the country." Rohit recalled that he realized he'd initially misunderstood the point of the protest: "It wasn't about disruption or breaking anything, but something else." Inspired by the "mood of the moment," as he put it, he revised his earlier judgment—that the "organized" character of the protest rendered it meaningless ("what's the point?")—and headed downtown to the Azad Maidan protest a few days later.

Rohit had joined a group of his artist friends for a placard-painting session before hopping the train toward Azad Maidan, but he hadn't written up a poster at his friend's house in the western suburbs. "I would have said something in that form—on a placard—if I had thought of something clever. See," he explains, "the thing about placards is that they have to say something smart, something that stands out. A point that can catch attention in the midst of a whole group. I'm always looking for a poster that stands out. You have to make your point quickly—jump in and jump out! But nothing came to mind."

But it didn't matter to him that he hadn't thought up anything satisfying enough to write up a placard; unlike Preety, he wasn't going because he had something particular that he wanted to say with words. To him, the most important thing (as he put it) was "to move with people who don't move in same circles as me; to stand there together." Rohit explained that he while regularly interacts with Muslim Mumbaikars through his work, "they still look at me as different because I'm not Muslim." To Rohit, it was important to physically go to the Azad Maidan so that other people there would see him—so that "people from the Muslim community would see that there are people who don't look them but who are also against CAA-NRC and who are there to support." For Rohit, his body was its own "placard" that conveyed a distinctive message: that Muslim Indians were not alone in their opposition to CAA.

Rohit had gotten on the train empty-handed, but somewhere along the hour-long ride downtown inspiration struck: "Kaaghaz ke Fools" (Paper

fools)—a reference to the 1959 Guru Dutt film *Kaaghaz ke Phool* (Paper
flowers). "See, the whole CAA-NRC thing was about kaaghaz," Rohit says,
recalling that Varun Grover had been listed among the speakers for the
Azad Maidan event, and that he had been looking forward to hearing
Grover recite "Hum Kaaghaz Nahi Dikhayenge," which Rohit had seen
the poet recite on Twitter. "I liked the poem," Rohit explained; "I liked
how he had recited it very plainly. Because of the poem, everyone started
reading up on this CAA thing, asking, 'What is this kaaghaz?'" And yet
even while Rohit recalled his excitement about hearing the onstage speakers, they weren't the reason he was going. After all, he reflected, "I could
just have listened to the speeches later on YouTube." Rather, for Rohit, the
point of actually going was "to see and to do." And drawing up his paper
placard over the course of the hour-long train journey from the western
suburbs was part of the doing.[59]

Rohit's "Kaaghaz ke Fool" poster was a hit. "There I was," he recalled,
"sitting next to scores of Muslim men—men dressed in Pathan suits[60]
or wearing the cap and with surma [charcoal] in the eyes, identifiably
Muslim men. Here they were wanting to take photos of me and of my
placard! Some people even posed for photos with me. I was really happy."
Indeed, while Rohit's intended audience—both that of his visibly non-
Muslim self as well as that of his clever placard—was first and foremost
the other protest participants and their mobile phone cameras. While
the materiality of the digital and of embodied presence are once again
revealed to be parts of a shared communicative infrastructure, for Rohit
the digitally mediated encounter is secondary, even instrumentalized as
the mere pretext for the flesh-and-blood embodied experience. The most
important thing was the "moving together" with "those who don't look
like you." It is in this moving together that "we the people of India" sought
to constitute itself as a mass political subject, and to render sensible its
collective awaaz.

5

Politics

"The Protests Were Becoming Politicized"

The August Kranti gathering was the first and also the last protest demonstration Preety attended that winter; she didn't go to the one at Azad Maidan a week later where Rohit and his "Kaaghaz ke Fools" placard posed with Muslim-looking strangers for selfies while Varun Grover recited his Twitter-famous poem "Hum Kaaghaz Nahi Dikhayenge" for the crowd. Preety told me that she had already "said what she had to say" at August Kranti the week before, and then paused before continuing—a trace of frustration in her voice—"and I also felt that the protests were becoming politicized. But see, this has nothing to do with politics or supporting any party."

Preety's critique of the protests against the Citizenship Amendment Act as overly bound up with the churnings of party politics is curious. How could opposition to a constitutional amendment, proposed and backed by the ruling party, not be a partisan issue? And why should political opposition not be construed as such? Even more striking, however, was Preety's characterization of the protests as *increasingly* politicized in the aftermath of the August Kranti gathering—striking because Mumbai's political leadership had played such an overt role in the anti-CAA mobilizations from the very outset. The front-and-center role of Mumbai's party leadership in the anti-CAA protests (both as organizers and addressees) presented a sharp contrast to the mass mobilizations that had attended the nationwide India Against Corruption movement in 2011 and 2012, when institutions of party politics were themselves the object of critique.[1] It is true that the December 19, 2019, August Kranti gathering was largely devoid of visible party insignia; the only party flags on display were those of the Communist Party of India—which due to its small size was treated by the event's organizers as more a leftist social organization than a political party.[2] And yet the stage at August Kranti had hosted a lineup of speakers that included a healthy contingent of major-party leaders. Indeed, not only had elected politicians featured among August Kranti's onstage orators, but Mumbai's political leadership was actively and openly involved in organizing the gathering from the outset. The event's official hosts—a newly convened national platform calling itself Hum Bharat ke Log—"We the People of India" (the first four words of the Indian Constitution's Preamble)—had worked closely with Mumbai's political leadership and city police in coordinating logistics for the demonstration, even outlining the official "agenda."

The involvement of parties, moreover, was not done in secret; the event's convenors spoke readily about party involvement with the press. The popular English-language daily *Indian Express,* for instance, detailed the collaboration and its agenda:

> In meetings with Congress' Balasaheb Thorat, NCP's Nawab Malik and Samajwadi Party leaders, a clear agenda was conveyed that the protest would only be opposed to Citizenship Amendment Act and National Register of Citizens. The committee also met Chief Minister Uddhav Thackeray to push the Maharashtra government to follow the footsteps of West Bengal, Kerela and Odisha in rejecting the citizenship law.[3]

Front and center of the "agenda" was that the BJP-controlled Indian Parliament repeal the offensive law. As the winter progressed, the opposition-controlled Maharashtra state government became an additional addressee of demonstrations in Mumbai, with conveners and participants demanding of the chief minister—Shiv Sena's president, Uddhav Thackeray—an official resolution not to carry out the proposed NRC exercise, in conjunction with which the new citizenship law was said to pose a threat to the rights of so many. The Mumbai articulation of "We the People of India" as a collective political subject, in other words, was not a claim to autonomy from the machinations of electoral democracy and party-mediated representation, but rather an explicit assertion of the central and necessary role of the parties in advancing a particular political "agenda." In this context, what might it mean to disparage the protest demonstrations as "politicized"?

While the characterization of that first August Kranti Protest as somehow not "political" sits puzzlingly alongside the front-and-center roles played by party politicians as organizers, orators, and audiences, Preety's characterization was also understandable, given the studied absence of party insignia both from pre-circulated digital posters as well as from physical signage at the various gatherings themselves. Given the obvious and explicit party involvement in organizing and facilitating the protest demonstrations, why did Mumbai's party leadership refrain from overtly signaling as much? The deliberate curation in Mumbai of a nonpartisan appearance for the protests presents a striking contrast with India's other opposition-controlled states, where party leaders were at the helm of anti-CAA protest mobilizations, their organizing role and partisanship front-and-center. On December 17, 2019, for instance (two days before Mumbai's first large-scale gathering at August Kranti) leader of West Bengal's ruling All India Trinamool Congress, Mamata Banerjee, spearheaded an anti-CAA protest in the state, which a few weeks later (on January 27), became the fourth opposition-controlled state—following Kerala, Punjab and Rajasthan—whose legislative assembly passed an official resolution demanding that the CAA be repealed. With the claiming of credit a staple of political communication,[4] why did political parties stay out of the limelight during Mumbai's anti-CAA protests (even while taking a central role in their coordination) rather than claim credit for the impressive and energetic crowds like their counterparts in other opposition-controlled states? What frictions and contradictions does this moralizing discourse about "party politics" index in Mumbai, and what analytical purchase might be gleaned by attending to it?

This chapter attends to this two-part puzzle posed by moralizing talk about "politics." The first part of the chapter explores the shared concern of Mumbai's Muslim leaders, secular activists, and political parties that the anti-CAA mobilizations not be construed as merely "a Muslim issue" and tracks the collaborative efforts to curate "cosmopolitan" (rather than "Muslim-looking") crowds of anti-CAA demonstrators. And yet with the CAA widely understood (by Muslims and non-Muslims alike) to pose a threat primarily to Muslims, the protests attracted a disproportionate number of Muslim Mumbaikars, whose visible markers of religious identity (hijabs and caps and so on) inadvertently lent the demonstrations a "Muslim" appearance. In this context, the city's Islamic leaders found themselves ambivalently (if not unwillingly) involved, due to their long-standing role mediating everyday life by facilitating ties with political parties, government offices, and the city police.[5] While newly established secular activist and student organizations were keen to obviate Muslim Mumbai's entrenched networks of local religious authority—and to instead articulate a different sort of collective political subject ("We the People of India")—those same activists inexorably found themselves in the awkward position of cooperation with (and even occasional dependence upon) religiously inflected relations of trust, local authority, and partisanship. Given Shiv Sena's identity as a "sons of the soil" movement, Maharashtra's Sena-led coalition government strained to manage the optics of its odd-bedfellows alliance with Muslim Mumbai's political leadership and to obviate central government allegations that the CAA protests were a sign that Maharashtra's governing parties and local community leaders were merely "playing politics,"[6] that is, mobilizing religious sentiments and whipping up Muslims' fears merely in order to deploy those passions strategically, for narrowly interested, "political" advantage.

While Maharashtra's governing parties thus sought to stay out of the spotlight, the energy and scale of the protests was nonetheless widely interpreted as a sign of the supportive stance of the state government. In this context—and lest Mumbai's tolerance for Muslim-looking crowds be interpreted (as the BJP was keen to suggest) that the Shiv Sena had abandoned its traditional (Marathi–Hindu) voters—Chief Minister Uddhav Thackeray beseeched coalition and religious leaders to stop organizing mass protests, and instead offered back-room verbal promises on the matter of Muslim Mumbaikars' safety in a Shiv Sena–led Maharashtra. For their part, activist-organizers—keenly aware of the political imperative facing the Maharashtra chief minister's party to maintain an image of peace and tolerance in contradistinction to the images of state-sanctioned violence emanating from BJP-governed states—wielded Uddhav Thackeray's crowd-image predicament to advantage. Crafting placards "thanking" the Mumbai police and the Thackeray-led government for their continued support, activists sought to discipline the chief minister into continuing to allow the protest gatherings by assigning an explicit meaning to the crowd-image—namely, that supporting the protests is what differentiated Mumbai's leadership from that of blood-soaked BJP-governed cities in North India. The accounts reveal, moreover, that protest organizers were not alone in seeking to assign meanings to the crowd: anti-CAA demonstrations became a narrative, pretext, and stage for all manner of political reputation- and relation-crafting—some of which had an oblique relation to the issue at hand (i.e., the CAA). The chapter follows these high-stakes struggles to manage the metapragmatics and thereby "control the narrative": the anxious efforts to curate unruly crowd-images and to assign them significance; to anticipate and manage potential and actual audiences (intended and otherwise); and to obviate inevitable misconstruals (or hijackings) by unintended audiences—an ever-present possibility given the ineluctable risks of semiotic slippage that the public-as-image affords. Attended by ambivalent talk about "politics," these tensions eventually erupt, revealing the contradictions at the heart of such battles to represent.

"A Nonpartisan Critique"

Curious about the hide-and-seek role played by Mumbai's political leadership in the December 19, 2019, August Kranti demonstration (on the one hand explicitly involved; on the other hand uncharacteristically avoiding the limelight), I tracked down the person identified by Mumbai's news media as the chief organizer of the event: Feroze Mithiborewala.[7] I rang him up, introduced myself as a research scholar, and asked whether he might have time to tell me the backstory of the gathering. Feroze happily obliged, and we met the next morning at the home he shares with his mother in the western suburbs.

The third-floor flat is bright and breezy, sparsely furnished but with a healthy smattering of family photos adorning the walls. Feroze and I sit near the window, where we avail ourselves of a breeze carrying morning freshness along with the honking and "choke" of rush-hour traffic, which deposits a fine film of dust on my notebook.[8] Feroze looks to be in his mid-fifties, with a thick mustache, a mop of jet-black hair, and a ready smile that, by Feroze's own reckoning, lends him an uncanny resemblance to Bombay film actor Anil Kapoor. Feroze starts midsentence—as, I soon learn, is his way—telling me about the planning meeting yesterday among the members of his newly convened group Hum Bharat ke Log. He rattles off the series of programs Hum Bharat ke Log has planned for the coming weeks: for instance, January 14 is Sankrant—the beloved all-India kite-flying festival announcing the end of winter with the north-ward movement of the sun in the Hindu calendar—and Hum Bharat ke Log will be holding an anti-CAA kite fight on Juhu beach.

I ask him to please back up and to tell me a bit more about the origins of Hum Bharat ke Log. "It's a national-level platform," he tells me, con-vened during the heady days when the Citizenship Amendment Bill was being discussed in the Indian Parliament—which was only a few weeks ago but feels like longer. It was a Sunday, Feroze recalled, and he had been listening to a rousing speech posted on Facebook by activist-academic Yogendra Yadav. "For the first time in Indian history," Yadav had pointed out, "citizenship will be linked to religion." Moved by the scholar's speech—both its liberal-secularist sentiments and its erudition—Feroze had rung up Yadav. "He took my call," Feroze tells me with a smile, "and he told me about a protest demonstration they were planning in Delhi on the nineteenth [of December]. So, I said let's make it a national call."

Later that same day, a "National Appeal" written in English—India's lingua franca of the aspirational and educated—was circulated through activist networks all over India under the banner "Hum Sab Nagrik [We All Citizens]: National Campaign for United Citizenship." While invit-ing people to "come together under a common banner," it was asserted that the campaign would maintain "a fluid existence," without any for-mal organizational structure. "We shall not invite any community based organisations or major political parties to endorse this call," the notice read, "though any citizen would be free to join." The message called for "a coordinated nation-wide protest on 19th December across many cit-ies,"[9] and that "in each of these [demonstrations] we should take an oath (to be drafted) and give a memorandum (to be drafted) addressed to the President of India and ask the state legislature to pass a resolution against CAB." In Mumbai, the circulated call was accompanied by an invitation to attend a "preparatory meeting" to plan the event, which was initially envisioned to be held not on August Kranti (that would come later) but rather on the public beach at Girgaum Chowpatty (see Map 4 in Interlude III). The message concludes with details of the planning meet-ing as well as contact information for the core conveners of the national platform.

Feroze explained that the demonstration's objective was to register "a nonpartisan critique" of the bill while it was being debated in the Parliament. He explained that because the Parliament had a large BJP majority, it was of paramount importance that popular apprehensions be represented as the concerns of citizens rather than of partisans—allowing for the possibility (however remote) that some BJP legislators might rethink the wisdom of supporting such a controversial and troubling bill, but without risking allegations of partisan disloyalty. But the lightning speed with which the bill made its way through both houses of Parliament (the day of the planning meeting turned out to be the very day that the bill was passed by the upper house), meant that by the time the December 11 planning meeting came around, the bill had already become law. Feroze explained to me that this development transformed the demonstration's audience and thus their demands: alongside the injunction to repeal the just-enacted Citizenship Amendment Act (the audience of that demand being the BJP-controlled Parliament), they added an additional request that the opposition-controlled Maharashtra government forswear the plan to create a National Citizen Registry and pass a government resolution to that effect. This reconfiguration and expansion of the demonstration's addressee is reflected in the minutes from the event's planning meeting, which—in contravention to the earlier idea of a "nonpartisan critique"—now emphasized the front-and-center role to be played by party politics:

- Organisations and Political Parties can carry their flags as well
- A memorandum will be given to the Governor, the State Govt and the President of India
- . . . the programme will include both social organisations and political parties.

In a scramble to get all the requisite permissions before the planned gathering on the nineteenth (which was just a week away), Feroze and his HBKL co-conveners organized themselves into "teams" according to their competencies and existing networks of contacts: some were tasked with reaching out to party leaders, others to the police, to the media, and to various activist and social organizations. But three days before the planned event—on December 16—the organizers had yet to secure official permissions to convene at their proposed location on the public beach downtown. This was because getting the necessary permissions to gather on the beach was turning out to be more complicated than they'd expected, since (as it turns out) it isn't possible for the municipal authorities to give official permission to use a stage or sound system on a public beach. In an effort to sort out the pressing matter of venue, an "all-party meeting" was quickly convened at the Maharashtra Pradesh Congress Committee office in South Mumbai. "We were planning to have a lakh people," Feroze explained to me, "so we needed to have a sound system."[10] The police commissioner had offered Hum Bharat ke Log permission to hold their event on Azad Maidan—the cordoned-off, hidden-from-public-view location near the municipal corporation headquarters that had been designated by a 1997 Bombay High Court ruling as Mumbai's "designated space" for protest gatherings.[11] Feroze explained that with violence unfolding across the country, the Mumbai police were a bit skittish about people gathering in large numbers on the streets. "But we said no; Azad Maidan is too small."

Having reached an impasse, they left the police headquarters without having secured official permission for their gathering, scheduled for just two days later. "We didn't have permission," Feroze recalled, "but we were thinking, 'Let's just do it anyway, on the beach.'" Later that same evening, however, he got a call from a friend—another member of the Hum Bharat ke Log "core team"—informing him that the police had just granted permission to hold their protest gathering, but not on the beach, rather at the fenced-in garden grounds at August Kranti Maidan. Police permission to hold the event at August Kranti had been "brokered," Feroze explained to me, by someone who wasn't even a member of the core team: the president of the Bombay Aman Committee (Bombay Peace Committee), the South Bombay organization whose mission and expertise inheres in liaising with city police with the goal of maintaining aman (peace) in Mumbai's Muslim-majority localities.[12]

In light of the Bombay Aman Committee's (BAC) long-standing and hard-earned relations of trust with city police, one of Feroze's longtime activist friends had (unbeknownst to Feroze) approached the committee's leadership with a request that the organization reach out (through police contacts) to reassure the skittish authorities that the planned gathering posed no threat to public safety—an overture by means of which the BAC's leadership effectively took responsibility for any potential "breach of peace"—and to thereby secure the necessary permissions for the planned event. Feroze described his anger upon learning that his trusted friend had gone "behind his back" to approach the committee's leadership for "help." Confused, I asked, "What was wrong with asking for help?" Feroze regarded me blankly, then responded, "Because we were organizing it! So we should have been told." I probed: "Okay, but then why didn't anyone tell you?" Feroze sighed and explained that, see, his friend who'd reached out to the BAC was well aware that Feroze was loath to collaborate with "those religious people"; the committee, he explains, "is totally dominated by the clergy." Feroze qualifies his remark: "The leadership is not actually clergy itself, but they're all part of that same group."

"Those Religious People"

Feroze's characterization of the Bombay Aman Committee as dominated by "religious people" caught my attention, because it was quite different from how others have described the committee and its activities. Independent journalist Jyoti Punwani—longtime chronicler of Muslim Mumbai who has written extensively on the BAC—notes that historically the organization has not had an especially religious composition or orientation. Rather, it was an initiative of South Bombay business elites who—in the aftermath of the 1984 Hindi–Muslim violence in Mumbai's industrial suburbs—sought to curb the impact that creeping religiously inflected tensions might have on the economic fabric of South Bombay's famously cosmopolitan commercial districts—convening interfaith outreach and mediating conflicts among communities of traders. BAC founder Wahid Ali Khan (the current president's late brother) was the owner of a travel agency as well as two of the city's largest imported goods markets and was for many years was the primary agent for the neighborhood's many Hindu importers. When violence eventually did break out in South Bombay in 1992–93, Punwani reported indefatigably on the relief work carried out by Khan and other BAC volunteers. And in the aftermath of the violence she followed BAC volunteers as they worked tirelessly to bring witnesses to testify before the Srikrishna Inquiry Commission, to secure through court action the release of the commission's report (which indicted Mumbai policemen for their role in the riots), and to advocate for the implementation of the commission report's recommendations (which are still pending). Punwani, who knew Khan so well that she'd walked in his funeral procession after he was killed by an unidentified gunman in 1999—emphasizes that while the BAC founder himself, "with his trademark beard, could be recognized as a Muslim anywhere," the committee's work was not religious per se. Rather, its purpose was to "negotiate with the establishment in times of crisis."[13]

Given the extraordinary heterogeneity of Muslim Mumbai, which is differentiated not only in sectarian terms but in a myriad of ways along lines of class, caste, gender, occupation, family structure, language grouping, place of origin, political orientation, and so on (discussed in Interlude II), the BAC's aspiration was not religious but rather pragmatic: to "negotiate with the establishment." And yet as memories of the riots faded and the city got back to the business of surviving and (sometimes) thriving through millennial Mumbai's liberalization-era trials and transformations, Feroze recalled how Mumbai's myriad Muslim-led organizations and leaders turned inward and "stopped calling people like us"—meaning "liberals" and "reformists"—with whom they tended to disagree on religious matters. More recently however, with Hindutva on the rise (and for which a monolithic "Muslim community" is conjured as its other), the impetus to imagine the diverse and richly textured social fabric of Muslim Mumbai as if it were in fact a monolithic "community" in order to "negotiate with the establishment" has returned: "They're starting to call us again," Feroze tells me.

Feroze narrated for me two recent issues on which he and his "liberal reformist" friends had locked horns with Muslim Mumbai's "community leaders"—both of which notably involved the fraught terrain of women's rights and Islamic feminism. First, in 2016, Feroze—a nonpracticing Bohra (Shia) Muslim—clashed with Muslim Mumbai's religious and political establishment when, together with liberal human rights activists affiliated with Bombay-based Indian Muslims for Secular Democracy (IMSD), he joined hands with the Bharatiya Muslim Mahila Andolan (Indian Muslim Women's Movement) to challenge a recent ban on women's access to the inner sanctum of the Haji Ali Dargah, the fifteenth-century shrine and dargah (mosque) of Sufi saint Pir Haji Ali Shah Bukhari, which is situated on a small islet off of Mumbai's western coast. Women had enjoyed unrestricted access to the inner sanctum for over five hundred years, until sometime in 2011 when the charitable trust governing the dargah declared that permitting women into the inner sanctum was un-Islamic and decided unilaterally to prohibit women from entering. After efforts to dialogue with the trustees failed, the Bharatiya Muslim Mahila Andolan approached first the state's minister for minority affairs and then the chairman of the Maharashtra Minorities' Commission—neither effort yielding fruit.

I met one of the conveners of the Bharatiya Muslim Mahila Andolan, a woman in her late forties named Neema, who recalled that when she approached the minister for minority affairs he told her there was nothing he could do to intervene because it was "a religious matter." Neema laughed dryly: "How can this be religious matter when it's not codified anywhere? And this was from an elected representative." The minister directed Neema and her colleagues to instead approach the Maharashtra Minorities' Commission. When the chairman of the commission sent them right back to the minority affairs minister, Neema recalled, "We realized we were alone." Neema told me that in Mumbai, it was only Feroze and his activist friends with Indian Muslims for Secular Democracy who supported them in their (ultimately successful) petition to the Bombay High Court, where they contested the legality of the ban on women's entry to Haji Ali Dargah on the constitutional grounds that it violated gender-based rights to equal access to public spaces. Feroze recalled how after the petition was filed, he got a phone call from the Bombay Aman Committee: "They were saying, 'Come, on bhai [brother], don't do this.' But of course, I didn't listen."

Feroze sparred with Muslim Mumbai's would-be "community leadership" again a few years later when he and his Indian Muslims for Secular Democracy activist friends came out in support of a highly controversial proposed national law that sought to criminalize "triple talaq"—a practice with contested standing in Islamic law (there is no mention of the practice in the Quran), whereby a marriage is unilaterally and instantaneously dissolved when the word talaq (divorce) is pronounced three times in succession.[14] The proposed law came on the heels of a 2017 Indian Supreme Court ruling that triple talaq was unconstitutional and therefore invalid. The new bill went a step further, proposing to criminalize the pronouncement of triple talaq, with those found guilty punishable with up to three years' imprisonment. The political debates around the proposed law criminalizing triple talaq were fierce and complex—bringing human rights activists and some Islamic feminist groups into an unlikely coalition with the Hindu nationalist outfits who had proposed the bill. Meanwhile, national-level mobilization against the bill was spearheaded by the conservative Islamic All India Muslim Personal Law Board, for whom the proposed criminalization of triple talaq was said to chip away Muslim Indians' long-established rights to govern Muslim family affairs (which in India are governed by the 1937 Muslim Personal Law [Shariat] Application Act—commonly known as Muslim Personal Law).[15] Opposition parties, with the Congress Party at the helm, challenged the proposed bill in the Parliament, criticizing it as a cynical use of Muslim women as pawns in an effort to chip away at Muslim Personal Law and community autonomy. And yet widespread opposition to the bill criminalizing triple talaq should not be interpreted to indicate support for the practice; as Hyderabad-based feminist activist A. Suneetha has pointed out, "The current opposition to the state regulation of arbitrary talaq is perhaps not indicative of either the communities' understanding of this practice or concern about women victimized by such a practice."[16] Since triple talaq's lack of legal standing had already been established in 2017, criminalizing the practice, it was argued, was unnecessary and would merely introduce a ready way to harass Muslim men with the new law.

In Mumbai, the All India Muslim Personal Law Board worked together with religious, political, and neighborhood leaders in an unprecedented mobilization in advance of the Supreme Court ruling on triple talaq—assembling an estimated fifty thousand Muslim women at Azad Maidan to register their opposition to the bill. Thus, in using his secular activist platforms and networks to register support for the bill, Feroze broke ranks not only with Mumbai's Muslim leadership but also with human rights activists concerned about the likely misuse of the law. Against this backdrop of recent and bitter fallouts over his support for the BJP's bill criminalizing triple talaq (the bill became law in 2018), Feroze was surprised when South Bombay's Muslim leaders "started to call again." The previous month, in advance of the November 2019 Supreme Court's anticipated judgment regarding the future of the contested site of the demolished Babri Masjid at Ayodhya, Feroze had been pleasantly surprised to be invited for a meeting at the Islam Gymkhana, where religious people, community leaders, and party politicians put their differences aside to discuss the more immediately pressing matter of how to respond to the impending ruling, which was not expected to go in their favor: "We all wanted to keep the peace," Feroze recalled.[17]

By 2019, with the CAA-NPR-NRC combine threatening to call into question the citizenship of Muslim Indians, the "Muslim community" was once again conjured into being. In this context, the point of contention concerned how "Muslim Mumbai" as a collective subject ought (and ought not) to be represented, how relations with political parties ought (and ought not) to be construed, and who had the capacity to mediate representations by controlling and curating the image of the protesting crowd. For their part, as already mentioned, the Mumbai conveners of Hum Bharat Ke Log were intent on keeping all signs of religion—Islamic or otherwise—far away from the protest.

And yet predictably, Hum Bharat Ke Log was not the only activist network and platform that emerged to register protest against the CAA that winter; another national-level group formed around the same time under the banner National Alliance Against CAA, NRC, and NPR—the Alliance for short—whose leadership held very different ideas about how "community" identity ought to be represented. While the Maharashtra branch of the Alliance took shape under the leadership of retired Bombay High Court judge Khosle Patil—a non-Muslim social activist known for his postretirement advocacy in rural Maharashtra on behalf of landless and lower-caste (Bahujan) agricultural workers[18]—the Alliance's primary convener in the city of Mumbai was the acting president of the Mumbai branch of Jamaat-e-Islami Hind, Abdul Haseeb Bhatkar.

Keen to understand these struggles over how religious identity should or could be construed in curating crowd images during the anti-CAA protests, I met Bhatkar a few weeks after the August Kranti gathering in his small office in Mumbai's eastern suburb of Kurla, where he recalled for me how the Alliance had "made a resolution to let students and leftists take the lead." He explained: "Everyone was in agreement" that opposition to the CAA could not be allowed to be seen as "a Muslim issue," because to allow that to happen would be to "fall into the BJP trap" of further isolating Muslim Indians in a what ought to be treated as a constitutional matter. But from Bhatkar's perspective (and unlike for Feroze and his activist friends), letting "students and leftists" take the lead didn't necessarily mean that religious people had no role to play whatsoever.

"We wanted a Muslim scholar to speak at August Kranti," Bhatkar recalled; "there were so many leaders who were speaking, so we said: why not an Islamic one?"

It was in the midst of this heated standoff between the Alliance and Hum Bharat Ke Log over whether or not a religious leader ought to be included among the lineup of speakers invited to address the gathering at August Kranti Maidan on December 19 that a social activist who was on good terms with both groups had approached the Bombay Aman Committee president with a request to put the organization's good relations with the authorities to work in the service of securing permissions for the fast-approaching protest gathering. What had initially struck me as a petty (even ungrateful) response to the eleventh-hour intervention by the Bombay Aman Committee became clear: Feroze was concerned that the overt involvement of religious leaders in the protest movement risked casting the CAA as a "Muslim issue"—and thereby politically isolating Muslims.

Initially furious that "those religious people" had hijacked their event and "corralled" the demonstration "into a garden," Feroze soon warmed to the August Kranti venue as "blessing in disguise," since after all, it is the site from which Mahatma Gandhi launched the Quit India movement in 1942: "August Kranti is where freedom marches." The next morning— the day before the protest—Feroze went for an "all-party meeting" at the Congress office to "tell them the new plan," to prepare a press release, and to "run around" securing all of the other necessary permissions: from the state government's Archeology Directorate ("usually this kind of thing would take weeks"), the BMC's Garden Department, the central government's Heritage Office and Archaeological Survey, and finally the local Gamdevy police station, whose final approval was contingent on all the others'. A letter was quickly typed out and dispatched from the Congress Party office, but was just as quickly returned unsigned because a Congress staffer had titled the rally for which permission was sought "BJP Hatao!"—"Stop the BJP!" Eyes rolled and a new letter was drafted, this time describing the event as a "Peaceful Protest against the CAA-NRC." Then, Feroze tells me, there was a phone volley: they sent "a boy" to bring the letter around for all the necessary signatures—from the Heritage Office and the Archaeological Survey, and to the local police at Gamdevy—while the additional commissioner of police (happy to help after the Bombay Aman Committee stepped in to broker) made path-clearing phone calls from his office at the police headquarters at Crawford Market (see Map 4 in Interlude III). When "the boy" tasked with running around to gather signatures called up Feroze to report that a junior officer at the local Gamdevy police station was refusing to give permission without the approval of his superior—who happened to be in Nagpur that day—Feroze simply rang up the additional commissioner. "The additional commissioner called over to Nagpur and the Nagpur officer called back to Gamdevy to give his permission, and just like that it all got done." Feroze animatedly recalled the breathlessness of this last-minute frenzy: "This all happened between 12 and 5 p.m. on the eighteenth."

On the morning of nineteenth—the day of the protest—only one thing was still pending: Where would they find the money to pay the fee for use of the public garden? Feroze rang up a senior Congress Party leader—someone who had been helpful in getting them this far—"but he said he'd been paying for so many things recently and suggested that we should call someone else." The person he suggested, however—also a party politician—was someone with whom Feroze had recently locked horns in the triple talaq and Haji Ali Dargah court battles. So instead of reaching out directly, Feroze asked a mutual friend to ring up the politician, who immediately agreed to put up the money. And not a moment too soon: "The gates opened at 12:00."

The "Muslim-Looking" Crowd

Back at August Kranti Maidan on December 19, 2019, I had approached three men standing together at the edge of the crowd, each with a stethoscope draped over his shoulders. They were smartly dressed—their starched collars and neat trousers suggesting perhaps they had come directly from the office. While their uniformly bearded faces signaled that they may well have been Muslims, the prominently displayed stethoscopes asserted that it was their professional identity as doctors rather than any religious identity as Muslims that they wished to display today. I introduced myself and asked about the stethoscopes. Yes, they are doctors, one of them told me in polite Hindi. I asked if they'd come together from the clinic and was told that no, they didn't work together; rather, they have joined the protest today as a "friends group." One of them introduced himself as Dr. Siddiqui—an identifiably Muslim name—and I ask the others whether they are Muslim as well. "Yes," Dr. Siddiqui responded, then quickly adding: "But we're here as Indians, not as Muslims. And anyway, what difference does it make that we're Muslim?"

Whether or not the CAA was a "Muslim issue," whether or not the anti-CAA gatherings were "Muslim spaces," and whether and how Muslim imagery should or would inform the anti-CAA narrative was a fraught question—for participants, for organizers, and (not least) for Mumbai's political class. Much energy was spent that heady winter on efforts to (as it was often said) "control the narrative" regarding the "Muslim" character of the protests. In Mumbai, all the various groups and factions organizing in opposition to the CAA were in general agreement that the CAA was simply the most recent iteration of the ruling party's broader political logic and longer-sighted strategy of divisiveness—a cynical attempt to politically isolate Muslim Indians. One interlocutor suggested that announcing a national NPR-NRC exercise could only be read as "natak," since a simple calculation of the time and monetary expenditure that it would require rendered the whole affair practically untenable. In this context, it was argued, to let opposition to the CAA be represented as "Muslim" would be to fall lazily into this divisiveness trap. Preety's insistent, furious refrain that opposition to the CAA was "a constitutional matter and not a Muslim issue" thus met with widespread agreement among protest-goers; for Rohit, this was precisely why it was so important to stand—and to be seen standing—"with Muslims."

But of course, the reason that the opposition to the CAA risked being seen as "a Muslim issue" was precisely because it so clearly targeted Muslims. Which is to say: even if many agreed the CAA was technically a constitutional matter and something that theoretically had the potential to affect all Indians, the context in which the CAA was passed (the move to create a National Registry of Citizens and the home minister's enjoinder to "understand the chronology")[19] left little doubt in many minds as to the CAA's anti-Muslim intentions. Evidence of this was cited in the fact that it had been students assembled in protest at historically Muslim universities of Aligarh Muslim University and Jamia Millia Islamia who had been on the receiving end of police violence that Sunday following the passing of the bill into law—notwithstanding the fact that simultaneous protests had taken place in and around (non-historically Muslim) university campuses in Kolkata, Mumbai, Chennai, and Hyderabad.[20]

The crowds that filled the streets of Indian cities and on campuses across India (and the world) in the days following the brutal violence against the student protestors at Jamia and JNU were—by all accounts—animated by outrage at images of violence circulating on both traditional and social media. Foremost among these images was that of the furious, hijab-wearing Jamia students who shielded their classmate from the blows of police batons, and whose palpable rage was caught on camera and circulated on social media. At the August Kranti protest I had spoken with a group of visibly Muslim (hijab-wearing) women—a couple of lawyers and a psychologist. The psychologist introduced herself as Nada and told me that this was the first time she'd ever gone to a public protest. "We had been asleep," she said, "and Jamia woke us up. The image of those girls," she continued, "those brave young girls." She tells me she was profoundly shaken by the image. "Those two twenty-two-year-old girls, they changed everything for me."

The day after the August Kranti event, news media reported that "it was like Mohammed Ali Road had been transported to Gowalia Tank."[21]

Figure 37. Placards with secular messages displayed by visibly Muslim women at a protest demonstration. The placard to the far right reads "Dalits, queers, and women will destroy the Hindu Rashtra." Mumbai, December 27, 2019. Photograph by Rohan Shivkumar.

Images of this Muslim-looking anger was circulated, rendered as art and subsequently as placards. Indeed, visibly "Muslim" appearance of the demonstrations was unavoidable, even as placard-mediated perspectives were studiously cosmopolitan: "Dalits, queers, and women will destroy the Hindu Rashtra [nation]," read one of the four secular placards held by a cluster of niqab- and hijab-wearing women (see Figure 37). The visibility of Muslims in public space (outside of central Mumbai areas like Mohammed Ali Road) was striking and attention-grabbing, because in the years since the 1992–93 Bombay riots the city's Muslim community and political leadership had maintained an unofficial policy (working closely with the police) to prevent mass political gatherings, instead organizing broker-mediated "delegations" to various politicians and ministers. In the three decades since the riots, there had been only two instances of large-scale, visibly Muslim mass political gatherings (a 2012 gathering on Azad Maidan was an exception that proved the rule when the crowd turned violent, and the media gushed with praise at the police for their restraint). "Irony of ironies," Punwani wrote in the aftermath of the August Kranti gathering, "the sense of safety Muslims in Mumbai obviously felt now was thanks to the very forces that had rendered them vulnerable during 92–93."[22]

"Thank You Uddhav"

With reports of police violence pouring in from all corners of the country, no one seemed to know quite what to expect of the August Kranti Maidan gathering on December 19. The organizers had taken all the necessary permissions (from the BMC, from the police), and that morning's *Indian Express* quoted the joint commissioner of police saying that "adequate police presence will ensure that the protests pass off without any problem. We are in touch with the organisers of the protest and both sides are on the same page. We are confident that the event will pass off peacefully." Another officer told the reporter that since the protest at August Kranti Maidan "is all over social media, we do not have an estimate of how many people will be attending the rally." A crime branch officer explained that they fear that "protest may be infiltrated by some motivated elements who may try to incite the crowd and foment violence." For this reason, two thousand "security personnel" (as they were described) would be deployed.[23] While I was not quite sure what the afternoon might have in store, I was confident that the Mumbai police would avoid violence at all cost. After all, this crowd was gathering not only in opposition to the CAA but also (and with official permission) in condemnation of police violence against student protesters, especially in Delhi. It was clear that, in enabling this mass gathering, Maharashtra's Shiv Sena–led coalition government was of a mind to enable and facilitate an image and spectacle quite different from those emerging from Delhi. And as our merry crowd-parade crossed a narrow lane on the walk from Grant Road Station toward August Kranti Maidan, I spotted a handful of policemen relaxing in plastic chairs, sipping chai as if it were absolutely ordinary for a hundred thousand people to block Nana Chowk on a Thursday afternoon. The police seemed not the least bit worried; the whole city would become a stage that day for Shiv Sena's display: a peaceful and celebratory gathering of staggering scale.

That the behind-the-scenes hand of the government in facilitating such a smooth and festive event was widely understood was evident in the posters thanking both the police and the chief minister. An image of a hand-scrawled placard reading "Thank You Mumbai Police" appeared in Preety's Instagram "story" the day after the August Kranti gathering (Figure 38). While social activists and conveners of the anti-CAA protests were in agreement with religious leaders that the demonstrations ought to avoid taking on a "Muslim face," Mumbai's political leadership was equally resolute in curating a nonpartisan image of the protests: while maulanas (Islamic scholars) feared the community isolation that would result if the CAA-NRC combine were to be seen as primarily a "Muslim issue," party leaders were keen to obviate suspicions that genuine outrage over the CAA was being harnessed for mere political gain. And as Preety's account of having avoided subsequent protests because they were "getting politicized" indicates, these concerns were not unfounded.

"The Interests of Certain Political Parties"

On December 27, 2019, the same day Rohit displayed his "Kaaghaz ke Fools" placard at the anti-CAA protest gathering at Azad Maidan, the BJP convened its own rally in support of the new citizenship law—just a few kilometers away at August Kranti Maidan (see Map 4 in Interlude III). Indeed, amid the flurry of anti-CAA protest demonstrations in Mumbai during the winter of 2019–20, a scattering of pro-CAA gatherings in

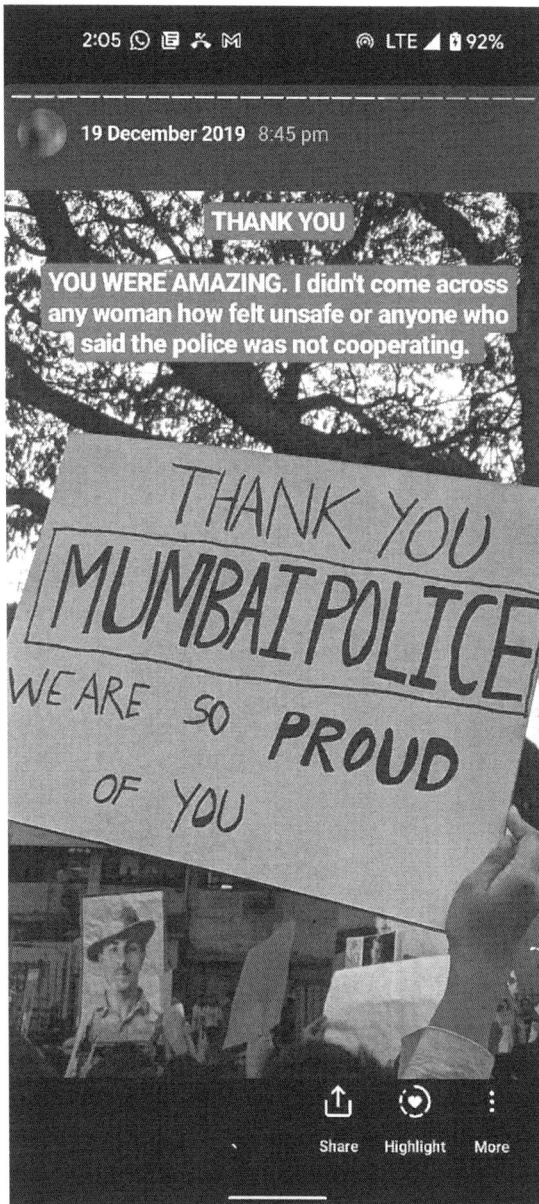

Figure 38. Image of handcrafted placard displayed at protest demonstration reposted on Instagram. The comment on the image reads "THANK YOU. YOU WERE AMAZING. I didn't come across any woman how [*sic*] felt unsafe or anyone who said the police was not cooperating." Mumbai, December 19, 2019. Shared with the author through WhatsApp.

Mumbai also took place. These events, while few in number, were notable for the moralizing discourses present in the media coverage that circulated in their wake. At a small pro-CAA gathering (estimated at between fifty and seventy people)[24] that had taken place simultaneously with the 100,000-strong December 19 anti-CAA demonstration on August Kranti, a journalist reported that participants had disagreed over what to even call their gathering: while some called the event a "people's protest," the reporter was later corrected by a participant when she used that term; this was not protest but rather a samarthan—an endorsement—the purpose of which was to "counter the environment of doubt and negativity" of the protest demonstrations. The anti-CAA crowds ought not be taken seriously, the reporter was told, as it was only because of "the interests of certain political parties" that the CAA was being opposed.[25] The goal of this pro-CAA samarthan was to demonstrate that "Mumbai was in support of the CAA"—whatever the throngs a few kilometers away might suggest.

The BJP's pro-CAA demonstrations sought to frame the anti-CAA protest gatherings as evidence of politically motivated manipulation—a refrain echoed in the ruling party's critiques of the opposition-controlled Maharashtra government more generally: "Is the State government in its right mind?," the Marathi daily *Maharashtra Times* headline quoted former BJP chief minister Devendra Fadnavis the day following the tit-for-tat large-scale rallies on December 27. The article focuses primarily on the logistics of the event itself (rather than debates over the law),[26] noting that the Maharashtra police had denied permission for the BJP to hold a procession "rally" and that they were therefore limited to holding a mere "sabhaa" at the August Kranti Maidan ground.[27] "Some people are spreading anarchy only for the sake of their chair," Fadnavis is quoted as saying—where "chair" here is metonymic with holding political power in Maharashtra and therefore a jibe directed at former party ally, chief minister and Shiv Sena leader Uddhav Thackeray. The disproportionately large number of visibly Muslim protestors at anti-CAA demonstrations was cited as evidence of cynical efforts by opposition parties to whip up Muslim fears merely for political gain. And indeed, this very notion that the Muslim appearance of the crowd might render anti-CAA gatherings vulnerable to allegations by the ruling party that opposition to the CAA was being fueled by religious leaders and their party bosses for mere political gain was of course the very same concern over which anti-CAA protest organizers (both Feroze's outfit and the Alliance) had been wringing their hands. It was for precisely this reason that religious figures and party leaders were studiously avoiding the spotlight at anti-CAA protest events and, as Bhatkar had explained to me, had decided to "let the students and leftists lead."

And yet notably, just as anti-CAA organizers sought to obviate allegations or suspicions that the protests were "politically motivated," moralizing talk about the pro-CAA gatherings was framed in precisely those same terms: the demonstrations "endorsing" the CAA were disparaged by anti-CAA protesters for being BJP-organized events and therefore as "not genuine." In the hours before the simultaneous pro- and anti-CAA rallies on December 27, elected corporator Sayeed Rizwan (whose successful campaign was the subject of chapters 2 and 3) posted two video clips on his Twitter page. The first, under the tagline "Came across this Video on WhatsApp where BJP has set up a team to give Flags so that the protest looks genuine," depicts a street scene in which Indian flags are being handed out from the back of two tempos[28] parked just outside the pro-CAA rally venue. The second, posted a few minutes later, is shot from behind one of the tempos and depicts one man wrapping another's head in a saffron-colored turban, presumably in preparation for the latter's participation in the pro-CAA rally.[29] "Koi Baap Apne Beti Ke Shaadi Mein Itna Show off Nahi Karta, Jitna Modi ji Aur Amit Shah Rally Mein Karte Hai" [Even a father at his daughter's wedding doesn't show off as much as Modi and Amit Shah do in a rally], reads the tagline.

The videos and their taglines claim that pro-CAA gatherings are not "genuine" (but rather mere "show") because tying of turbans and handing out of national flags is allegedly performed by party workers.[30] Amid the comments posted below the turban-tying clip, one reads "Bhai, yeh log nautaki [sic] karne me he toh famous hai"—"Brother, these people are famous for their nautanki": their drama. These disparaging characterizations of the pro-CAA rallies as not genuine, as mere show off, as only nautanki (which is another word for natak),[31] are notable: in contrast to the election-season rallies described in chapter 2—where, as we saw, theatricality (nautanki/natak) was appreciated and valued as a legitimate, desirable, even necessary component of an election campaign—a rally that disingenuously professes not to be party-organized is disparaged as mere "show."

A few days later, at lunch with a journalist friend, I pulled out my phone and showed him the video, curious to hear his take on the disparaging dismissal of the rally as "only nautanki." By way of answer, he pulled out his own phone and scrolled through photos he'd taken at the anti-CAA protest at August Kranti on December 19. Pointing at the nautanki video on my phone, he surmised that the pro-CAA event had probably been the subject of popular derision because "it looked just like a political rally." I asked him to explain. "Just like at a political rally, the flags and all that—they're all pre-made. And everyone knows that [the organizers] can just hire all those people." The critique, in other words, was not of the involvement of party politics in staging a spectacle per se, but rather in the genre of the show: the BJP was staging a natak while characterizing it as a sabhaa.

Ultimately however, whatever the assessments of crowd size and party involvement, of money and flags, the big news of the day was the confusion and hilarity that ensued when Fadnavis tweeted his arrival at the wrong venue (Figure 39). The outsized attention paid to Fadnavis's (understandable) mistake is noteworthy insofar as it gestures to the metapragmatics of collective assembly. Throughout the winter of 2019–20, the language of "crowd" was at once both a performative bid at semiotic dominance through the staging of a "media event"[32] and also (and more quietly) a real-time performance of the behind-the-scenes political networks that made some crowd event possible in the first place. As the ubiquity of "Thank You Uddhav" signage at anti-CAA events suggests, there was no doubt about the behind-the-scenes role of party leaders in facilitating or obviating the anti-CAA demonstrations. And yet this inevitability landed the Shiv Sena chief minister in a pickle: whatever the "personal perspectives"[33] written on the placards might have been, the loudest message conveyed was the fact of the chief minister's tacit support for (or at least toleration of) the gatherings. Whatever did or didn't happen in Mumbai throughout the protest season was fodder for speculative interpretation and a sign of the contradictions and internal frictions: a Shiv Sena–led coalition government presiding over massive Muslim-looking crowds in Mumbai, protesting a measure that the Shiv Sena—erstwhile party of ethnolinguistic chauvinism and antimigrant Islamophobia—had itself supported in the Parliament only a few months earlier.

Azad Maidan? Isn't that where the anti-CAA protests are happening? And the pro-CAA is at August Kranti? Make sure you go to the right rallies folks! 😅

> **Devendra Fadnavis** ✅ @Dev_Fadnavis · 10m
> Reached Azad Maidan in Mumbai and joined the massive gathering of citizens to support the #CitizenshipAmendmentAct !
>
> #MumbaiSupportsCAA
> #IndiaSupportsCAA

Figure 39. Viral Twitter post poking fun at a prominent Maharashtra politician for mistakenly citing the location of the opposition party's rally instead of his own. The post reads "Make Sure you go to the Right Rallies Folks! 😅" The original tweet was deleted—but not before being retweeted and circulated by other people, which is how I accessed it. Twitter, December 27, 2019. Author's collection.

The anti-CAA protests posed a predicament for the chief minister and his party. A former ally of the BJP, the Shiv Sena had initially voted in the Lok Sabha (lower house of Parliament) in favor of the Citizenship Amendment Bill, but then withdrew its support after forming an alliance government with former political adversaries, the Congress and National Congress Party—an odd-bedfellows coalition formed primarily with the goal of keeping the BJP out of power in Maharashtra. After becoming chief minister of this fragile coalition, Uddhav Thackeray withdrew his support for the controversial bill, staging a walkout (and thereby abstaining) ahead of voting in the Rajya Sabha (upper house). And while senior politicians from the other parties to Maharashtra's coalition government were actively involved in the December 19 protest (helping to organize and fund the event, as well as featuring among the lineup of onstage speakers), the demonstration was conspicuously devoid of any overt signs of the Shiv Sena—the party of the chief minister—even as the supportive police (noticeably absent riot gear, and in some areas reportedly passing out water and bananas) ensured that the chief minister's support was understood, as suggested in the many posters "thanking" the chief minister.

Over the following weeks and months, increasingly unsatisfied with mere tacit tolerance, anti-CAA protest organizers (including some Congress and National Congress Party leaders) began to put pressure on the chief minister to follow the example of West Bengal, Rajasthan, Punjab, and Kerala in passing some sort of an official resolution stating that the Registry of Citizenship exercise would not be carried out in Maharashtra, and/or demanding that the CAA be repealed. Yet in the face of repeated efforts to convey this demand, the chief minister remained silent, his attention resolutely elsewhere: the morning of the tit-for-tat December 27 demonstrations—while Fadnavis lambasted Uddhav from the stage at August Kranti and protest demonstrators thanked the chief minister at Azad Maidan—the BMC tweeted photos of poker-faced Uddhav Thackeray in attendance at an urban design exhibition just a few blocks from the protest venue at Azad Maidan, where he was calmly "appreciating" the creative efforts of an international NGO's architectural proposals for public street space—an initiative supported the Maharashtra government in the hopes of "developing the vision of safe, inclusive & accessible streets."[34]

"Delegation" and "Dialogue"

First thing Monday morning—on the heels of the Friday-afternoon anti-CAA protest gathering on August Kranti Maidan on December 19—Uddhav Thackeray met a "delegation" (vafad) of Muslim Mumbai's political, religious, and community representatives, under the leadership of the Samajwadi Party's Maharashtra president and elected MLA Abu Asim Azmi. Mumbai's popular Urdu daily *Mumbai Urdu News* reported that the delegation had been convened following the "vigorous protest" (zabardast ehtijaj) at August Kranti Maidan a few days earlier, and emphasized that the delegation leadership sought to impress upon the chief minister that—whatever anyone might say to the contrary—it was in fact

Muslim Indians who would be most vulnerable to be stripped of citizen-ship rights by the CAA-NPR-NRC combine.[35]

The delegation was composed of senior members of Muslim Mum-bai's various community organizations: the Ulema Council (where the young Sayeed Rizwan had cut his political teeth in the aftermath of the 1992 riots; see Interlude II), the Bombay Aman Committee; a few dozen Islamic scholars and clerics; and—last but not least—a significant con-tingent of Mumbai's political class of Muslim MLAs, MPs, municipal cor-porators, and political party workers. That the chief minister so promptly received Asmi's delegation in the wake of the protest suggests something of the urgency with which Asmi sought to capitalize not only on the highly visible manifestation of mass support for Mumbai Muslims evi-denced at August Kranti, but also that with which the ever-busy Uddhav sought to assuage the concerns of Muslim Mumbaikars in the wake of the demonstration—the scale and energy of which appeared to have taken everyone (even the organizers) by surprise.

While details of Uddhav's meeting with the delegation were given prominence only in the city's Urdu media (journalists taking care to name individual members of the delegation),[36] color photographs of the event featured in all major Mumbai newspapers—English, Marathi, Hindi, and Urdu. The ubiquitous images suggested that the delegation had been received graciously at the chief minister's Mumbai home—known as Varsha—where, in the presence of Mumbai's chief of police, Uddhav sought to "instill confidence" in Mumbai Muslims.[37] "The government will not allow anyone to seize the rights of citizens of any particular com-munity or religion in the state," the chief minister told the assembled lead-ers.[38] Muslim Mumbaikars had nothing to be afraid of, the *Mumbai Urdu News* report went on, because the CAA and NRC would "never be imple-mented" in the state of Maharashtra. And as for the detention camps, wor-ried talk about which had been making lively rounds on social media, they were being built not for "Indians" but rather for "foreign nationals who have served their sentence for the cases related to drugs or other [offenses]."[39] Having sought to clear up any "misunderstanding," the chief minister rounded off his assurances to the Muslim delegation with a plea: "I request that you please not organize any further demonstrations in the state."[40]

The colorful images of Uddhav Thackeray's meeting with Mumbai's Islamic leadership splashed all over the Mumbai media was a jarring juxtaposition with the carefully curated, secular one that anti-CAA protest organizers had been working so hard to create. Keen to understand the impetus behind this high-profile media spectacle (whose closed-door facade was readily belied by the open-door invitation to the press), I asked Feroze for his thoughts on the matter. Wasn't this precisely the image that not only secular activists like him but also Muslim Mumbai's religious leadership and political class had all been trying so hard to obviate? Feroze explained that while it was true that all were in agreement that this must not be allowed to be portrayed as a "Muslim issue" ("because then we'll fall into the BJP trap"), it was also true the CAA-NPR-NRC combine obviously targeted Muslims. Muslim Mumbaikars were understandably worried, which is why they kept turning up in such large numbers at the demonstrations. And besides, he added, religious leaders have grown accustomed to being "involved in political matters" through these sorts of officially private yet highly mediatized "delegations."[41]

Feroze puts me in touch with a longtime activist friend who had been part of the delegation, a Samajwadi Party office-bearer named Siraj Malik. I ring up Mr. Malik and we meet up a few days later outside the Press Club in South Bombay. It was an unseasonably warm afternoon, so we headed to the municipal canteen around the corner to find some shade and a soda. Once seated, I ask Malik about the impetus behind the delegation of Islamic leaders to meet Uddhav. Echoing Feroze, he begins: "See, the BJP is trying to make this a communal issue, and we won't let that happen. But at the same time, the public is afraid." He explained that local Urdu newspapers had been full of talk about detention camps—whether, why, and for whom such camps are being constructed. With everything circulating over WhatsApp, "people don't know what to believe." It was in this context that the delegation to Uddhav was convened. "Most of these religious people," Malik explained, "they're honest and people trust them. So, it's important that these maulanas are well informed—that they make public statements and tell people not to be afraid because the chief minister is with us."

The day after the delegation, the media reported on the chief minister's verbal promise that no National Population Registry exercise would be carried out in Maharashtra. And yet by all accounts, this outcome was dissatisfying. Uddhav had not mentioned any formal resolution to that effect, nor had he directly denounced the CAA itself. His official position was that the Maharashtra government would wait for the Supreme Court verdict on new citizenship law, whose constitutionality had been legally challenged in the courts. While the Shiv Sena's post-riot détente with Muslim Mumbai had been sustained over the decades by these sorts of informal, backroom assurances, this time around it appeared that the politics of "delegation" did little to dispel the atmosphere of fear.

A week after the delegation to the chief minister, I woke to a *Times of India* article posted in one of my Mumbai-based WhatsApp chat groups that had a headline so unlikely that I had to read it twice: Sanjay Raut, Shiv Sena MP and official party spokesperson (executive editor of the Shiv Sena mouthpiece *Saamna*), had accepted an invitation to speak at an event scheduled for the following day, organized by Jamaat-e-Islami Hind (JIH) and the Mumbai-based Association for Protection of Civil Rights.[42] The event was described as a "meet," the purpose of which (as a JIH spokesperson told the *Times* reporter) was to "debate" the relationship between the CAA and the NRC in order to "understand their constitutional implications." Clarifying why Raut was being invited to address the JIH-hosted gathering, the article recalled the Shiv Sena's unclear position on the CAA, explaining that the Shiv Sena had first supported in the Lok Sabha before abstaining in the Rajya Sabha and was now "waiting" for a Supreme Court verdict on the CAA before considering any official resolution.

The "debate"—or "dialogue" (vaartaalap), as *Saamna* described it in Marathi—was to take place the next day at the Marathi Patrakar Sangh (Marathi Journalists Association), a striking choice of venue (since the conveners themselves are largely Urdu-speakers) that seemed to identify the event as a variety of press conference. Among the participants who would dialogue/debate with Raut was senior advocate and president of the Association for Protection of Civil Rights, Yusuf Muchhala—the Mumbai lawyer who had represented Mumbai Muslims at the Srikrishna Commission in the aftermath of the 1992–93 riots. Muchhala is a household name among Muslim Mumbaikars (at least among the generation that remembers the riots), because his cross-examination of senior Shiv Sena leaders in the aftermath of the violence had played a key role in the commission's eventual indictment of the Shiv Sena for its role in the riots.

Muchhala worked tirelessly in the years following release of the Srikrishna report (through the Association for Protection of Civil Rights) to advocate for implementation and legal action on the commission's findings, and action on the report is still pending. Needless to say, the idea that the Shiv Sena's spokesperson was going to engage Muchhala (among others) in a public debate hosted by the Jamaat-e-Islami Hind at the Marathi Patrakar Sangh struck me as a show I would do well not to miss. Would Raut really turn up? If so, in what language would he address a crowd of Urdu-speaking Muslims? I read the article again, but the *Times of India* didn't give any details regarding the timing of the planned event. I googled around, but the handful of articles I found seemed more interested in the incongruous fact of Raut's speaking at a JIH event than in details about when and how to attend it.[43]

I forwarded the article to a few contacts, asking if anyone knew anything about it. A few minutes later, I received a WhatsApp response from Junaid (the Urdu scholar I'd met during Sayeed's election campaign a few years earlier): a digital poster advertising the event, which (curiously) did not mention any of the names of the speakers listed in the *Times of India* announcement (Muchhala, for instance) but instead included a long list of the twenty community organizations and NGOs whose charitable contributions had made the meeting possible. While most of the sponsoring groups were Islamic organizations, there was a motley crew of others as well, including a Catholic charity, a police reform advocacy group, an association of human rights lawyers, and a Sai Baba devotional association. In contrast to the "you're-not-going-to-believe-this" tone and substance of the *Times of India's* announcement, the WhatsApp poster advertising the program seemed to have different goals: not to sell newspapers (or earn "clicks") but rather to fill a room. As earlier chapters have demonstrated, people tend to turn up at some or another event when the event has been endorsed or supported by a known and trusted organization or "main," and when an invitation has been extended personally, over WhatsApp—rather than broadcast over Facebook or advertised in the media. The event's organizers appeared to be assembling a media-facing event in which the Shiv Sena spokesperson would address a distinctly Muslim crowd.

At first blush, the event's goals appeared identical to those of the previous week's delegation to the chief minster: "to clear misconceptions

floating around on social media," as JIH spokesperson Salim Khan explained to reporters.[44] But although these sorts of meetings with delegations of Muslim leaders to hear petitions or "community concerns" had
become a staple of Shiv Sena politics in post-riot Mumbai, this was something different: this time, a Shiv Sena spokesperson would be meeting
Muslim Mumbaikars on their own turf, as an invited guest to a "debate"—
rather than as a host receiving a petitioning supplicant.

I arrive at the Marathi Patrakar Sangh at 5:45—fifteen minutes before
the advertised start time—and a friendly fellow seated at a card table
downstairs asks me to sign my name in a register before he directs me
to the third floor. The room is freezing—the air-conditioning turned up
high in anticipation of the rush of warm bodies. Media people are futz-
ing with cameras at the back of the room, but most of the three hundred
or so stage-facing chairs are still empty. I head back outside, where I wait
in the warm evening breeze as watch as people arrive and mill about
excitedly, greeting one another. Junaid arrives around 6:30, flanked by
Kareem Enginwala—the scrap-dealer-turned-real estate-investor I'd met
during Sayeed's election campaign—and by that time the room is packed.
It strikes me that, for a Bombay crowd, this one is remarkably punctual,
presumably because Sanjay Raut is coming. A section at the back has been
designated for "ladies," and forty (or so) hijab-clad women are seated
there. The rest of the crowd is mostly men, less than half of whom display any visible signs of Muslim identity (caps and so on). I sit down next
to Junaid (himself a practicing Muslim but not visibly so), eager to avail
myself of the poet-scholar's boundless "who's who" knowledge of Muslim Mumbai—and also to be within earshot of his incisive and witty
commentary. "Who are all these people?," I ask Junaid. "Are they mostly
Muslims?" "Mostly," he says, looking around; "Maybe two-thirds." Behind
the stage is an enormous printed poster that reads (in English):

> Relationship between CAA, NPR and NRC
> A dialogue to understand constitutional implications and line of action

At the right side of the poster are listed the names of three "Guests of
Honor": Shiv Sena spokesperson Sanjay Raut, Peoples Union of Civil Liberties president Mihir Desai, and Yusuf Muchhala, whose contribution to
the evening's events is labeled "Presidential Speech." Beneath Muchhala's

name appears the long list of sponsors that I'd seen on the digital poster. A podium has been arranged at the right side of the stage, and at the center of the stage is a long table covered with a white satin cloth. Behind the table is a line of eight red, audience-facing chairs and behind the chairs, men mill about chatting amicably, clasping hands. The first two rows are reserved for media people, and in the row just in front of us is a cast of characters that changes continuously throughout the introductory remarks and first few speakers. Raut is nowhere to be seen, and indeed, it is not until he arrives (midway through the third speaker) that the crowd settles down.

A slim man in a brown cap takes the podium, and Junaid identifies him for me as JIH Mumbai president, Abdul Haseeb Bhatkar (this was a few weeks before my earlier-recounted meeting with him). Bhatkar speaks in measured, polite Urdu, rehearsing the purpose and agenda of tonight's gathering: "People are pareshaan [troubled, disturbed]," he begins, because they don't understand the relationship between these things—the CAA, NRC, NPR. "Is this a policy of inclusion or exclusion?" The thrust of his speech is that—contrary to so much speculation—the combination of policies and procedures will affect all Indians, not only Muslims.

The next person to take the dais is advocate Mihir Desai,[45] who speaks fast, in a Bombay-style mix of Hindi and English, and cuts to the chase —listing the "three questions that is in each of our minds": What is this CAA, and whom will it affect? What's this National Population Registry exercise that's slated to begin in April, and what's the connection to the National Citizenship Registry? And third, what is the purpose of this National Citizenship Registry anyway? He begins on a philosophical note: "What is citizenship? It's the right to have rights. The right to speak, the right to vote." He explains to the crowd that all the other rights depend on this one thing, citizenship. He gives a breakneck-speed history of India's changing citizenship laws over time. The Indian Constitution outlines various paths to citizenship: until 1987 it was only through birthright; then in 1987 it was birth plus one parent had to be citizen; then in 2004 it was that the other parent couldn't be illegally in India— where "illegally" means overstaying a visa or having crossed illegally, without proper documents. But see, Desai explains, this is where things get tricky, because it's not possible to prove that someone crossed illegally if they don't have documents; so the NRC is a way of shifting the burden of proof to everyone individually. "In a country where 70 percent of people don't have birth certificates, this is a big deal." And of course this is no surprise; since migrant laborers can't prove their residence, where on earth would they get birth proof? So who will be excluded? Not just Muslims, of course; the poor don't have documents more generally. He ends on the same note as Bhatkar: this is not merely a "Muslim issue."

I'm rapt by Desai's take-it-to-the-mat outline of the scope and scale of the matter, and glance over at Junaid to gauge his response. But Junaid doesn't appear to be listening. Rather, he's tapping away at his phone: he's clicked a photo of the stage and is posting it to a WhatsApp group along with a message about the lineup of speakers and Raut's anticipated arrival. For Junaid, the import of the evening appears to inhere less in what's said (after all, what Desai was saying was hardly news) but rather in the fact of the event itself. I look around to see that nearly everyone is texting. I steal a glance at Enginwala's phone screen (he's seated to my right) to find he's scrolling through an article about high-end wristwatches.

The next speaker, a black-hatted fellow with a long white beard that matches his bright white button-down, is introduced as Maulana Daryabadi.[46] I whisper to Junaid: "Who's he?" "He stays in Bhendi Bazaar," says Junaid, suggesting that in this context, the geographic location of Daryabadi's life and work in South Bombay's Bhendi Bazaar market district is the maulana's most notable and identifying characteristic. (A quick Google search identifies Daryabadi as general secretary of the All India Ulema Council, Mumbai, the organization where the young Sayeed had volunteered after the riots awakened his political consciousness; see Interlude II). Daryabadi begins, and at this point the speeches are becoming repetitive—"They're trying to divide our country with this unconstitutional and discriminatory citizenship law, but anyway it's a misunderstanding that this only impacts Muslims." I glance down at my phone and see that Jyoti Punwani has responded to my message asking whether she's coming. "Only to listen to Raut," she writes.

A tall, bespectacled fellow in a smart woolen waistcoat and a furry black cap boisterously breezes in while Daryabadi is speaking—smiling and greeting people loudly, seemingly oblivious to Daryabadi's in-progress oration. An usher directs him to a seat in the press section, directly in front of us. I throw Junaid a puzzled glance, and he rolls his eyes, chuckles, and whispers that he'll tell me about this fellow later on. Then suddenly

everyone is on their feet and the room is filled with camera flashes. Amid
a handful of large bodyguard-looking men is Raut. Dressed smartly in a
gray waistcoat and white button-down (with ready-for-business rolled-
up sleeves), Raut is confident and compact in stature, with a thick mop
of jet-black hair and an extraordinary, impressive mustache. The furry-
hatted fellow who arrived just a few moments earlier leaps to his feet and
strides past the bodyguards to wrap Raut in a high-profile bear hug; Raut
seems to recognize the man and reciprocates the embrace while cameras
flash. Unable to contain my curiosity, I turn this time to Enginwala: "Who
is he?" Enginwala, seemingly as unimpressed by the fellow as Junaid, tells
me the man's name is Hashmi, and—with a dismissive handwave—adds
that "he edits a magazine." I make a mental note to follow up and turn my
attention back to Raut, who is receiving a rock star's welcome—as much
by the giddy-on-its-feet audience as by the camera-happy media—as he
makes his way up onto the stage.

Raut is introduced by retired justice Khosle Patil—the Alliance's
Maharashtra convener—who opens his remarks by attributing credit to
Raut for orchestrating the Shiv Sena's bold split from its erstwhile ally,
the BJP. After Patil's short, rambling speech to an increasingly impatient
audience, Raut takes the podium. The room falls silent. He begins with a
laugh and a smile, asking—in Marathi—the question that was at the forefront of my mind as well: "In which language should I speak?" The audience responds with nervous laughter and responds with a mix of shouted
responses—"Hindi!" "Marathi!" Raut, visibly enjoying himself, begins in
Marathi: "This program is in Mumbai, at the Marathi Patrakar Sangh,"
he says slowly, speaking over the sound of the murmuring audience, "so
I will have to at least start in Marathi." The crowd erupts into relieved
laughter. Raut—a master showman—waits until they are quiet before
continuing. "You're all Mumbai residents," he says, his poignantly cheeky
reference to the darker context of this meeting—which is animated precisely by concerns about proving residence—elicits a wave of affirmative
murmurs and applause from the audience, "which means that you all
know Marathi. You all understand Marathi and can speak it also. I know
this because whenever you come to [the Shiv Sena offices]—when you
come to Saamna or to meet Uddhav—then you all speak in Marathi." The
audience is rapt, responding with laughter and shouts of "Yes! We know
Marathi! We can speak in Marathi!" Raut pauses before adding that "today,

circumstances are such that I am happy that you have welcomed me," this last phrase powerfully reframing what could be taken as an act of concession (the Marathi chauvinist party spokesperson addressing a Hindi/Urdu-speaking audience in their own language) not as an act of deference but rather of reciprocity: when the Hindi speakers come to the Sena offices they speak in Marathi; thus, as an invited guest at a Jamaat-e-Islami Hind–hosted meeting, he will speak in Hindi.

Raut continues, switching to Hindi: "Khosle Patil has said—rightly said—'Don't be afraid' [Daro mat]. I have also come to say this—that the one who gets scared is dead [jo dar gaya mar gaya]." Raut pauses to wait for the roar of applause to subside, before adding: "Being scared is not permitted [darna mana hai]." This is the overarching theme of Raut's twenty-minute speech, whose breathtaking irony was noted by Punwani in the next day's paper: "Here was the spokesman of a party which had terrorized Muslims for the better part of its existence, asking them not to be afraid."[47] "Stand up!," Raut told the mostly Muslim audience, "but don't just stand for your own religion. We are all citizens of this country, and wherever there is injustice on each other then we must stand for each other. They [i.e., BJP leaders] are afraid of this—that if we stand up for each other, then what will happen to them? And in any event," Raut added in a remark so audacious that it took my breath away, "the Shiv Sena's relationship with the law is different. You all know this. We don't think much about the law. The law is only on paper [kaaghaz pe]. Our laws are different." The significance of Raut's words—judging by the gasps of surprise and outburst of shocked laughter—was not lost on this crowd of mostly Muslim Mumbaikars, who had so often been on the receiving end of the Shiv Sena's disregard for the law. "We're not afraid of any law," Raut continued, "and you shouldn't be either. Nothing is going to happen. Nothing is going to happen. So remove the fear from your hearts!" He hammered home the point that, as long as the Shiv Sena was in power in Maharashtra, Muslims had nothing to fear from any law: "On behalf of Uddhav Thackeray, I say that there is no reason to be scared. We are with you. Bhiyu naka! [Do not fear!]," Raut concluded, speaking the final words in Marathi—bringing the crowd to its feet with cheers and applause.

Raut steps away from the dais and back toward his place at the table next to Muchhala, where—whether on the inspiration of Justice Patil or that of the media people (in the excited commotion it was hard to tell)

—the seven men lift their arms high into the air, posing for a victory photo. It's a baffling image: Shiv Sena spokesperson Sanjay Raut sharing a victory pose with Yusuf Muchhala—the advocate who had worked for decades to bring to justice Shiv Sena leaders deemed responsible for the 1992–93 violence—at a JIH-hosted function. After the photo, Raut and his entourage of bodyguards and camera-toting others make their way up the aisle and out of the room, glad-handing along the way. Hashmi dives in for another hug. Most of the media people follow Raut out of the room, along with a significant portion of the audience. I follow too, completely forgetting—in the heady commotion—that Muchhala is scheduled to deliver the "Presidential Speech" next. Standing outside, I message Junaid, who tells me Muchhala has just finished his speech—which only then do I realize I've missed. Kicking myself, I wait outside for Junaid, hoping he might tell me what Muchhala has said—and also perhaps tell me about this Raut-hugging Hashmi.

Junaid and I chat as we walk toward the train station. He tells me that Muchhala's speech was, predictably, a little critical, pointing out that while Raut had said "Daro mat" ("Don't be afraid"), he had been silent on the matter of an official resolution against implementing the CAA-NCR in Maharashtra; and of course Muchhala had also pointed out (as if this audience needed to be reminded) that the Shiv Sena hadn't been terribly helpful as far as implementing the Srikrishna Commission report was concerned. Overall, however, the tone of Muchhala's speech was that the Shiv Sena seems to be open and willing to be helpful now. It was hardly a ringing endorsement, but coming from Muchhala, it was remarkable.

I cut to the question that's burning in my mind: What's the story with this hatted fellow Hashmi and his apparent desire to be seen at a public gathering hugging Sanjay Raut? Junaid laughs and waves his hand dismissively: "He's a chamcha." Literally meaning "spoon," chamcha is an epithet used to suggest that someone is shallow and lacking in substance, whose words and comportment are just for show—like the shininess of a spoon. Hashmi has a "glossy Urdu magazine," Junaid explains (the characterization of the magazine as glossy echoing his characterization of the man; Junaid is a poet, after all), which is why he was sitting in the press section. The magazine is vacuous in terms of content, Junaid tells me, but Hashmi gets "political people" like Raut to pay for advertisements. "It's good PR for Raut and his ilk," Junaid continues, "because they like to show that they're good friends with a maulana-type person. But Hashmi's not actually a maulana or even a devout person. He's a businessman. But people like Raut can't tell the difference," Junaid says dryly, "because he dresses like a religious type. Hat and all." I ask Junaid about Hashmi's business, and he tells me that Hashmi has recently returned from Saudi Arabia—from Mecca, where he had a tailoring business. Earlier he had been a ladies' tailor here in Bombay, where he worked in the film industry. He also had a shop in South Bombay that grew popular among visitors from the Gulf; so eventually he moved his business to Mecca. He returned a few years ago, after learning Arabic, cultivating a Gulf aesthetic in dress and comportment. He runs a travel business now, processing visas and making arrangements for Mecca-bound pilgrims. He needs government contacts for his travel business—visa processing and so on—so that's why he's always trying to please these political people. "He's a dalal," Junaid tells me—a "broker"[48]—disdainfully summing up his critique of the man as two-faced: on the one hand, he is described as cultivating an impression of himself as a "devout person" in order to forge contacts with people like Raut (recently Hashmi had organized an Urdu cultural program, inviting BJP and Rashtriya Swayamsevak Sangh [RSS][49] leaders as guests of honor); on the other he uses those contacts in his private business, making a profit of others' actual religiosity (i.e., Hajj pilgrims). Junaid surmised that all the Raut-hugging was to show off his cozy relations with Raut—a performance for this "who's who" audience of Muslim Mumbaikars of his connections with powerful people.

While Junaid's assessment of Hashmi is his personal assessment, the significance of the explication is less in its accuracy per se than in the broader relational landscape to which it gestures and to the moral evaluation it yields.[50] Indeed, while the event at the Marathi Patrakar Sangh initially seemed to bear the trappings of a media-addressing affair (perhaps even a variety of press conference)—Mumbai news reporting on the event (and its unlikely guest speaker) the following morning was limited. While at least one Marathi paper had found the event itself noteworthy enough to announce in advance, the only post-event Marathi reporting was in Raut's own paper, *Saamna*, which ran an article made up entirely of excerpts from Raut's own speech and accompanied by the post-speech victory photo.[51]

The English-language press was little better. Except for Punwani's substantive article,[52] reporting mostly rehearsed the "get-a-load-of-this" fact
that Raut had accepted an invitation to speak at a JIH function at all: *Indian
Express* devoted significant space in its brief write-up to Raut's laugh-line
statement that "There was a question among people whether I will come to
the event or not when this organization invited me." The *Mumbai Mirror's*
post-event coverage merely printed the victory photo, accompanied by a
caption and a three-sentence text box.[53] Coverage by the Urdu media, by
contrast, thoroughly detailed what had been said and by whom: "Jamaat-e-
Islami Mumbai made a wonderful effort to bring all sects and groups onto
one platform," a *Mumbai Urdu News* reporter wrote;[54] *Inquilab* devoted
most of its long article to direct quotations from the various speakers,
giving equal space to Raut, Patil, Muchhwala, Daryabadi, and Desai.[55] And
while the Urdu papers published images of the onstage speakers, selected
images were not of the victory shot but rather of Raut addressing the gathering (and his co-panelists) from the podium.

Judging from the media coverage the event appears to have been the
site of multiple agendas and took on different meanings for its myriad
audiences. On the one hand, the Shiv Sena's (and Raut's) erstwhile animosity toward Muslim Mumbai meant that some old-timers might need to be
"convinced" that they could trust this professedly "secular" coalition government led by their not-so-long-ago-after-all antagonists.[56] In this spirit,
by inviting Raut to engage in a friendly "dialogue," JIH leaders (who were at
the forefront of the anti-CAA campaign in Bombay) sought to demonstrate to Muslim Mumbaikars that they were now batting for the same
team. Inviting Raut to share the stage on Muslim Mumbai's own turf—at a
JIH function chockabloc with prominent Mumbai Muslim personalities
—afforded an opportunity for a performative enactment of this new relationship that worked in both directions. That this event was not taking
place on the Shiv Sena's "home turf" was acknowledged by Raut himself
when he conceded to speak in Hindi as an act not of necessity but of reciprocity. Just as Muslim delegations to Shiv Sena offices make their petitions
and requests in Marathi, Raut explains, he would extend the same linguistic courtesy to his Hindustani-speaking hosts. The JIH-hosted "dialogue"
with Raut sought to enact this new relationship between the Shiv Sena
and Muslim Mumbai—a staging (quite literally) of these reconfigured

relations of representation. Raut's concluding onstage pronouncement (uttered in Hindi, no less) that "there is no reason to be scared. We are with you"[57] was less an effort to persuade the audience than to describe what his preceding twenty-minute onstage performance had sought to accomplish, with the victory photo (which was prompted by Raut's own media team) seeking to testify to the success of Raut's performance when it appeared the following morning on the front page of Saamna.

I was initially puzzled by the dearth of media coverage—puzzlement that brought to my attention (and called into question) my own latent, wrongheaded presumption that mediated communication with non-present publics was the point of the gathering (which, after all, was hosted by a journalists association). Closer consideration suggests that, while I hadn't been entirely mistaken, the material infrastructures of mediation in question were not merely (or even primarily) the cameras and head-lines, but rather (and also) the social-communicative relations embodied by the people in the room: the association leaders, religious scholars, businesspeople, and other trusted "mains" whose words were quoted in the Urdu news and who—it was hoped—might go on to reassure their friends and neighbors and clients and students that, with the Shiv Sena in power, Muslim Mumbai had nothing to fear and that there was no need to demonstrate the strength of their numbers by gathering in the street. "Stop counting your numbers," Raut had said (echoing Uddhav's appeal to the Muslim delegation the previous week to stop gathering for demon-strations), "because if you are 20 crore [200 million], we too are 110 crore [1.1 billion]. Instead of counting our respective numbers, we must fight together for the country, all 130 crore [1.3 billion] of us."[58] In some ways, and notwithstanding the disparaging valences of the words, Junaid's characterization of Hashmi as a "chamcha" and a "broker" (for using con-tacts with powerful people born of a cultivated public performance of "Islamic credentials" for private purposes) seems to describe the ambiva-lent valence of this entire event. On the one hand, posing for the victory shot with Raut, Muslim Mumbai played its part as "onstage extras" to Raut's performance of his relations with this political constituency. And at the same time, Muchhala's conclusion that the Shiv Sena "seems to be open and willing to be helpful now" suggests that this just-reaffirmed relation-ship can (and by Muchhala's reckoning ought) to be put to instrumental use in advancing the interests of Mumbai Muslims.

"To Silence Protests"

Notwithstanding the feel-good photos and what appeared to be a mutual willingness to be "helpful," the Shiv Sena's continued evasive stance regarding any Maharashtra resolution against the CAA-NRC combine was a reminder of the precarity of such verbal promises in a context where the survival of the governing coalition in Maharashtra hinged on the Shiv Sena's not alienating its Hindutva-sympathetic cadre.[59] What was more, just as Shiv Sena leaders vociferously condemned police antagonism toward protesters in BJP-controlled states, the Mumbai police's own relationship with protesters began to show signs of strain. Just as Raut uttered strong words in support of anti-CAA protesters at the Jamaat-e-Islami Hind event—proclaiming that while the BJP was "trying to silence protests, . . . the youth of the country knows what is right and what is wrong"—only the previous day the Mumbai police had refused a request by feminist groups, LBGTQ+ activists, and Mumbai students for permission to hold a "Stand against CAA, NRC and NPR" rally on the occasion of the nineteenth-century feminist reformer Savitribai Phule's birthday. The permission request letter had stated that the organizers expected up to a thousand people and therefore requested permission to use a microphone and loudspeaker. The police's written response (in Marathi) not only denied the requested permission—citing concerns that a "problem of law and order [is] very likely to happen"—but issued a notification (and thinly veiled threat) under Section 149 of the Indian Penal Code: if the protesters were to gather anyway, in spite the event's being denied permission, then anyone present at the gathering could be held liable for any "cognizable or indictable offense arising out of an anti-national act or statement" that might occur. The rally's organizing committee (which included at least one young activist lawyer among its ranks), not to be intimidated by police threats that they could be charged with "anti-national" activity (and certainly not to be outmaneuvered), drafted a letter in response. "We have perused the contents of your letter/notice dated 1st Jan 2020 under section 149 of CRPC 1973, in response to our subject letter," their (English-language) letter began, continuing:

> In light of the contents of your letter, which do not deny permission to hold the peaceful protest as intimated by us, we presume that there is no

objection to us going ahead with the protest. This is to clarify that there is no question that any anti-national, communal or unlawful content will be used in this peaceful protest by us which we are holding in accordance with our constitutional rights. However, if any outsiders or troublemakers try to create problems, the same is not our responsibility. Needless to state, that if any unlawful activity takes place at the hands of such outsiders or troublemakers, police are required to take any appropriate action against them as per law. We trust you will cooperate with us in this regard.

Having thus challenged the police's attempt to preemptively place upon the protesters the burden of responsibility for any potential "unlawful activity" that might transpire—rhetorically tossing that burden like a hot potato right back onto the police before circulating the letter through social media, where it was published online[60]—the organizers proceeded with their rally, strategically changing the venue to a location where permission had not been officially denied, and dispensing with the permission-requiring sound system.

While the evening passed without incident, the next day's media reporting (both traditional and digital) was full of raised eyebrows: while some wondered whether the permission-denial episode signaled a souring of relations between protesters and the police, others were focused the behind-the-scenes dynamics of permission-brokering, because another request for permission from the Mumbai police to demonstrate (against police brutality against anti-CAA demonstrators in the North Indian state of Uttar Pradesh) had been granted on the very same day. The latter gathering was convened by known personalities from South Bombay's political class, including (notably and unsurprisingly) Muslim Mumbai's go-to police whisperer, the Bombay Aman Committee. While transgender and feminist activists scrambled for a new location for their rally, the BAC-mediated gathering convened theirs directly outside the offices of the state government, (the Mantralaya) where they chanted "Mumbai Police Zindabad" (Long live the Mumbai police) and "UP Police Murdabad" (Down with the Uttar Pradesh police), praising the former for "restor[ing] people's faith in democracy."[61] The *Indian Express* published articles side by side on the two gatherings, effectively inviting the reader to speculate over the meaning of the Mumbai police's inconsistent position toward anti-CAA protests.

The more inscrutable and inconsistent police behavior became, the more vociferously protesters sought to attribute responsibility for the behavior of the police directly to the Shiv Sena—and even to Uddhav himself. Which is to say, protesters seemed less interested or concerned with figuring out what was really going on or what the police behavior was a sign of than in "controlling the narrative" regarding how police behavior should be widely interpreted, that is, as the hand of Uddhav. Whether or not Uddhav or the Shiv Sena government was actually behind the police's behavior was anyone's guess; after all, the acting Mumbai police commissioner had been appointed by the previous, BJP-led administration. But the unwavering assignment of responsibility for police behavior to the Shiv Sena landed Uddhav in a pickle.

Uddhav's Pickle

Uddhav's pickle erupted into a full-blown crisis a few days later when, following violent attacks by masked assailants on university students in Delhi, Mumbai students convened a late-night, unauthorized sit-in protest at Gateway of India—bang in the heart of Mumbai's tourist district, right across from the iconic Taj Hotel. I woke on the morning of January 6 to find my WhatsApp chat groups flooded: dozens had been injured in the violence the previous evening on the JNU campus in Delhi—a traditional site of leftist activist politics and whose student leaders had been at the forefront of anti-CAA protests in that city. While all political parties condemned the violence (Congress blamed "fascists," while the BJP pointed to leftist "forces of anarchy"),[62] what was clear enough was that notwithstanding the university administration's having alerted the Delhi police, the authorities stood by for hours while masked assailants roamed the campus with clubs and hockey sticks—characterized by opposition party leaders as deliberate government inaction. "What we are seeing on live TV is shocking and horrifying," the *Indian Express* quoted Congress Party senior politician and former home minister P. Chidambaram; "Masked men enter JNU hostels and attack students. What is the Police doing? Where is the Police Commissioner? If it is happening on live TV, it is an act of impunity and can only happen with the support of the government."[63]

At the time of the attacks, fifty or so of Mumbai's more active anti-CAA activist-organizers had been gathered outside the Grand Hyatt Hotel in the western suburb of Santa Cruz, holding signs, singing protest songs, and handing out flowers as a preemptive token of gratitude to the "co-operative" Mumbai police officers standing guard outside the hotel[64] where BJP minister Piyush Goyal was holding a "Dialogue over CAA" with Bombay-based film personalities (a notice of which had been leaked to the media).[65] Viral images and videos of the violence at JNU flooded social media, and by 10:00 p.m., Mumbai student activists had circulated a social media "call for Occupying Gateway":

Call for OCCUPYING GATEWAY

Appeal to all the Students/student groups

    We the students of TISS [Tata Institute of Social Science], IIT [Bombay], University of Mumbai etc. have actively and successfully occupied the heart of the city at Gateway until we don't know when! We need more represen-tation across student groups/collectives/fronts. Please come and join in large numbers with your banners. We need food, warm clothes, newspapers and a lot of you here.

By 11:28, an IIT Bombay (Indian Institute of Technology Bombay) stu-dent activist group tweeted a video posting in which hundreds of stu-dent protesters were gathered; by 2:30 a.m., South Bombay hoteliers had sent food, water, and other provisions. Around 11:00 the next morning I called Feroze, who had spent the night at Gateway. "At 2:00 a.m. cops came to talk to us," he told me. "They said, 'We'll give you another loca-tion. You can go to Azad maidan.' But we said, 'We're not shifting,' and they backed off."

    I reach Gateway of India around noon. Police are everywhere, milling about, smiling and laughing, and generally having fun, like it's party. I wade into the crowd to get a feel for the energy, a sense of who is there, and (as there's no sound system, only some megaphones floating around) to get closer to where I might hear the songs being sung, the poems being recited. In the crowd, I bump into a friend—a university professor who's there with some of her students. We chat for a while, but before long, one of the squawking crows in the tree above us relieves itself on my head and I leave to search for paper towels. Making my way to the back of the crowd—between the people and the water—I come upon an open space where a group of students is painting signs: "TISS stands with JNU"; "Stop violence against students"; "Delhi police down down"; "Don't turn universities into war zones."

I take a few pictures before skirting along the edge of the crowd. The space where the crowd meets the road is thick with media people interviewing some or another politician or film personality. I click a photo of a young man who's holding in the air a hand-drawn placard that reads "MUMBAI POLICE THANK YOU; DELHI POLICE SHAME ON YOU" (Figure 40). He has positioned himself so that his placard might be captured by media cameras trained on a person being interviewed (someone I don't recognize). The young man is not in the crowd of protesters but rather in the media crowd (indeed, he is the sole placard carrier in the vicinity), signaling that the intended audience of his placard-mediated message—either the police allow us to stay here, or Mumbai is no different from Delhi—was perhaps not actually the explicit addressee of the message (i.e., the present police) but rather the Maharashtra government, whose orders any police action would ultimately be interpreted to reflect.

Figure 40. Image of man holding handcrafted poster at Gateway of India protest demonstration. The poster reads "MUMBAI POLICE THANK YOU; DELHI POLICE SHAME ON YOU." Mumbai, January 6, 2020. Photograph by the author

The placard gestured toward the delicate dance of images that was being played out at Gateway. In his press statement on the JNU attacks—made earlier that morning and immediately reported by the Mumbai media[66]—Uddhav had stated that "students are safe in Maharashtra" and that "nothing will happen to them." When asked about the students gathered in protest at Gateway, he had responded: "I understand their rage . . . Shiv Sena is with young people, so they need not worry." The "Mumbai Police Thank You; Delhi Police Shame On You" placard appeared as a holding-to-account on this promise that Mumbai was a safe space for student protest as well as a warning that police action toward student protesters would be the measure by which the government of Mumbai would be differentiated from that of Delhi. And indeed, the next morning, the Marathi daily *Loksatta* printed the chief minister's statement that "students are safe in Maharashtra" snugly alongside an image of the "Mumbai Police Thank You; Delhi Police Shame On You" placard.[67]

I spent the evening following along on social media from home—the energetic singing and poetry, the dancing and speeches that continued through the night. For the most part the evening's events were festive and celebratory (notwithstanding what Feroze later described as the "chaos" that broke out after the megaphones died). But things heated up after a young woman had held aloft a placard that read "FREE KASHMIR" and the image exploded on social media. When I woke on Tuesday morning, that poster seemed to be all anyone wanted to talk about. A Twitter spat had erupted after the BJP's Devendra Fadnavis shot off a tweet in the wee hours: "How can we tolerate such separatist elements in Mumbai? 'Free Kashmir' slogan by Azadi gang at 2 kms from the [chief minister's office]? Uddhavji are you going to tolerate this 'Free Kashmir' anti-India campaign right under your nose???"[68] Fadnavis's challenge drew a sharply chastising response from NCP's Jayant Patil, who tweeted back (at 6:36 a.m.): "Devendraji, it's 'free Kashmir' from all discriminations, bans on cellular networks and central control. I can't believe that a responsible leader like you trying to confuse people by decoding words in such a hatred way. Is it losing power or losing self-control?"[69]

The woman holding the "Free Kashmir" sign—a Maharashtrian woman named Mehak Mirza Prabhu (the media was quick to note that Mehak is not Kashmiri)—was charged with posing a threat to "national integration" under Section 153B of the Indian Penal Code. In a tearful apology posted on Facebook, Mehak—a self-described "storyteller" by profession—explained that the separatist construal of the placard had been a misunderstanding; she had picked up the placard (which she claimed she hadn't made herself), taking it to be a reference to freedom of speech for people in Kashmir in the context of the ongoing internet lockdown. "They should also have freedom to express themselves. So keeping this thing in mind, I picked up the placard," she said. For its part, the Shiv Sena too came out in blazing support of Mehak's self-accounting, Sanjay Raut claiming in a widely cited editorial in *Saamna* that "a Mumbaikar Marathi woman could understand the pain of Kashmiris. . . . If the Opposition [i.e., the BJP] and its supporters feel expressing yourself fearlessly is sedition, it is not good for them and the country."[70]

By the time the "Free Kashmir" poster hullabaloo broke out, the image wars at Gateway were already heating up. By Monday evening, right-wing organizations had applied for police permission to hold their own event—not far from Gateway of India—in a protest demonstration against what was described as "left-wing violence" at JNU. "Allowing permission to some and denying others would not have sent the right signal," a senior officer told the *Indian Express*, adding that "There was also a threat that there could be law and order problems if other protests were allowed." The *Indian Express* further reported that at some point on "late Monday" evening—whether before or after Mehak picked up the "Free Kashmir" placard is anyone's guess—"the top police brass, in consultation with the state government . . . decided to move the protesters from the [Gateway of India] site."[71]

At 10:40 the following morning, the Mumbai police tweeted: "Dear Mumbaikars, Azad Maidan is the designated place for all agitations in South Mumbai. . . . However some agitators gathered at an important South Mumbai location for a long duration without any permission . . . thereby causing immense inconvenience to office going Mumbaikars, local residents, tourists & also caused major traffic congestion in the area. Despite repeated sincere endeavors from local police to convince them to relocate to Azad Maidan, they remained unreasonably adamant. Consequently, in the interest of the general public, they were relocated to Azad Maidan in a peaceful & professional manner." After a few hours of WhatsApp posts reporting on the confusion inside Azad Maidan and debating about what do to next, at 3:02 that afternoon a Whats-App post announced: "Just in—Protestors detained in Azad Maidan have been released." A few minutes later, a student leader circulated a message announcing the time and place to convene that evening for a "debrief" meeting and to decide how and whether to reconvene the protest.

"We Need the Parties"

Around sixty people have turned up—mostly young people, as well as a handful of lawyers and activists like Feroze. The student leader who had called the meeting, a PhD student at TISS named Farid, announces that we should begin. We're seated in a large hall, with chairs arranged in a large circle around the edges of the room. A young activist-lawyer named Leena opens the meeting with a recap of what happened earlier that day. They rounded up five hundred people and transported them to Azad Maidan, but overall it was nonviolent and the police behaved themselves. Students were detained inside Azad Maidan for a few hours to collect personal information before releasing them all a few hours ago. This wasn't a violation of the students' rights; the police are allowed to detain them for up to twenty-four hours. Since morning, there had been a lively debate on WhatsApp about what to do now. Should they reoccupy Gateway? Reconvene the protest at Azad Maidan? Something else? So that's the agenda of the meeting. I'd seen the WhatsApp debate, and most seemed to agree that convening on Azad Maidan was pointless: "It could go on for months without anyone seeing or taking notice."

Leena opens the floor, asking for reflections and thoughts. A young man raises his hand, introduces himself as Sameer, and tells us the name of his college. "I was there for twenty out of the thirty hours of the occupation," he begins. "All was very good. Only problem was with coordination. People broke off into their own groups and factions; everyone was doing whatever they wanted [apni marzi]. There were so many conflicting messages—was it called off? The communication gap was a problem." Next a young woman speaks, a recent college graduate named Paromita. She says, "I have three points," and turns to the notebook where she's written them down. "First, we need legal knowledge. We need to know who are our experts—who to ask when we have doubts. Second, we need do self-censorship, because one unconstitutional word and we're done." The crowd hums a bit at talk of censorship. Paromita continues: "Third, if media is pressing you for a byte, just give some vague statement."

One of the HBKL organizers chimes in next, a young man named Arun. "People want to contribute, and that's good," he says, "but people need to know who to listen to. If someone wants to use this or that slogan—'Free Kashmir' or whatever—we need to figure out how to deal with this. Because see, I approached one person to say I thought her poster was inappropriate and she got angry, told me that she was expressing herself. . . . We need to have a team of volunteers [with legal knowledge]," he concludes. A young man raises his hand and recalls how he had been instructed by someone he didn't know but who claimed to be an organizer, telling him that a "media blackout" had been declared and instructing him not to speak to any media people whatsoever. "But it's not good to have a media blackout!," he exclaimed with no little frustration, "because then the media can just give whatever bad press they want; but we need to control the narrative."

Leena nods vigorously: "We need to coordinate, to curate the message. But how do we do that when the whole thing was unplanned? There was no coordination because we weren't prepared for such a long duration. We didn't know how long we'd stay. People just came spontaneously. But we need to make all decisions collectively because there are possible legal implications for all of us. If someone says something off-script and it goes viral? . . . Everything goes viral now. So we need to have leadership." Feroze has been sitting quietly but now speaks up: "Speaking of leadership, I think we also made a mistake by not doing more to involve party people. We need the parties. If the parties had been involved, then things might have gone differently. We could have given each party some number of minutes to speak something. The netas [politicians], they all came to Gateway to support us but we didn't let them speak! If we had let them speak then the cops wouldn't have chased us off so quickly. It damages the movement to exclude the parties." A young man pipes up: "But the netas will politicize it! They'll make it a party thing!" A student leader quips: "And what's so wrong with that?" He laughs and adds—presumably referring to Raut's editorial—"Besides, the Shiv Sena's messaging on the Kashmir thing was awesome." Feroze nods his agreement: "Everyone has their role to play, even the parties. For instance, I could never have thought up Gateway of India as the right spot. That could only have come from a student." Leena interjects with a laugh: "Actually, it wasn't a student who thought of Gateway; it was an IT person, a marketing professional." Everyone laughs. It's getting late and people seem tired. Someone I don't recognize chimes in: "Look, whatever happened at the end, Gateway went really well. And we can build on this, because now mahol ban gaya"—the atmosphere has been created, the scene set.[72]

Conclusion

Drama of Democracy

On January 22, 2024, Prime Minister Narendra Modi presided over the long-awaited inauguration of the new Ram Mandir on the banks of the Sarayu River in Ayodhya—a gigantic temple constructed at the spot where the sixteenth-century Babri Masjid was razed by a mob of Hindu nationalist kar sevaks (volunteers) in December 1992, unleashing sectarian violence across the country.[1] The land had remained tied up in legal battles until 2019, when a supreme court judgment handed the disputed site over to a Hindu temple trust, clearing the path for the construction of the new Ram Mandir where the Babri Masjid had stood.[2] Speaking at the January 2024 event, Modi described the inauguration as "the day India gained independence," thus invoking Hindu nationalism's version of Indian history as one of Hindu subjugation by Muslim rulers and foreign invaders.[3] The "thousand years of foreign rule" trope—which made international news in 2023 when Modi rehearsed the line for a joint session of the U.S. Congress[4]—is the ideological heart of the century-old Hindutva movement, which holds that India's colonization ("slavery") began not in the eighteenth century, with the consolidation of the British empire, but rather a millennium earlier, with Muslim conquests in the region.[5]

Hindutva's periodization of Indian history (where an earlier epoch of rule by Hindu kings is said to have been superseded by an age of Muslim domination, which was in turn swept aside by European imperialism) has been interrogated and discarded by professional historians (Indian and otherwise), who have found the notion that religion (and religious conflict) is the primary driver of South Asian history to be untenable.[6] And yet notwithstanding evidence unearthed by professional historians, nonhistorian purveyors of Hindutva ideology nevertheless insist on a version of history in which the arrival of Muslims in India heralded the destruction of Hindu civilization: the forcible conversion and "enslavement" of Hindus, and the wholesale demolition of temples and building of mosques in their place.[7] In this context, for Hindutva ideologues the restitution of Hindu civilizational glory hinges upon on things like architectural "restorations" such as the temple at Ayodhya, as well on the general purging of Muslim cultural influences (which are by definition characterized as "foreign") from Indian arts, music, and language. Observers across the political spectrum thus characterized the January 2024 inauguration of the Ram Mandir in Ayodhya as the culmination of the Hindu nationalist movement over which Modi's political career has presided. More than just "another biggish ribbon-cutting event," the inauguration was celebrated by India's broadcast media as "'the moment' when India experienced a 'civilisational reawakening' and when it exited its 'colonial mindset.'"[8] The laser-lit festivities in Ayodhya were attended in person by a parade of prominent personalities—film stars, business tycoons, politicians and ministers—whose dancing and merry-making was captured by national television channels and live-streamed into the furthest-flung corners of globe.

While some celebrated, others raised alarms. In conjunction with other high-profile Hindutva legislative agenda items over which Modi has presided (the Citizenship Amendment Act, for example), and in step with escalating and increasingly unchecked vigilante violence ("bulldozer justice")[9] against people suspected of Hindutva-transgressing practices (trading or consuming beef, for instance, or entering into interfaith marriages), the Ram Mandir movement's realization is characterized by scholars of Indian politics as the culmination of a categorical shift in Indian democracy "towards a de jure Hindu majoritarian state."[10]

The inauguration of the Ram Mandir comes at a moment when the popularity of the party of Hindutva has indeed reached an all-time high: a December 2023 survey by the Delhi-based Centre for Policy Research (CPR) reported that 47 percent of urban Indians explicitly identify with the party—a full 8 percentage points higher than only a few months earlier.[11] And yet, drawing on insights from Mumbai, I will conclude this book by suggesting that perhaps this is not the whole story. *Drama of Democracy* opened by pointing out that contemporary diagnostics of democracy's ailments tend to hinge on normative presumptions of liberalism—premises that simply do not hold much water in Mumbai. While the city is site of no little political passion (even upheaval), Mumbai's energetic churnings diverge from the diagnostics by means of which democracy the world over tends to be narrated: the rise of "populism" wherein charismatic authority and the figure of a leader obviates representative institutions and procedures; the forestalling of substantive citizenship and political accountability by the influx of money into elections; a "post-truth" epistemological crisis in which people can't work out who or what to believe; irrational mobilizations of "identity" that fuel passionate political divisiveness; a "crisis of representation" in which the masses pour into the streets to assert that elected politicians do not actually represent them. While Mumbai's political life is undoubtedly cash-flush, charisma- and affect-animated, concerned with belief, punctuated by crowds, and shot through with passionate attachments to linguistic, regional, ethnic and religious identifications, the precise ways in which these phenomena are (and are not) problematized by Mumbaikars are illegible to these framings, pointing to very different material-practical terrain and conceptual vocabulary of representation—which have been the subject of this book.

Drama of Democracy has offered an ethnographically grounded account of representative democracy, one in which *representation* is not the opposite of the *real*, but rather is where reality is enacted, encountered, and evaluated. Rather than counterpose representational sign with embodied action, this book has asked: How are performative bids to represent enacted and assessed? Notably, the 2023 CPR surveyors asked their respondents this very question. With the Ram Mandir temple inauguration in Ayodhya taking place on the eve of India's general elections (scheduled for April–May 2024), respondents were asked for their perceptions of the event: Did the temple inauguration *really* "correct historical wrongs done to Hindus," as the government claimed? Or was it an electoral stunt in the run-up to polling, enacted "merely to win Hindu votes"? The response was striking: among those explicitly identifying with the BJP, more than a third (35 percent) described the inauguration as a pre-poll stunt—an assessment that was shared by approximately half of all respondents. And

yet even more remarkably, notwithstanding this widespread characterization of the temple inauguration as a polling stunt, when asked about
their "satisfaction" with the Modi government's construction of the Ram
temple complex in Ayodhya, only 17 percent of all survey respondents
expressed any discontent. Put another way: while half of surveyed Indians (including a full third of those who personally identify as BJP partisans) characterized the temple inauguration *not* as the actual rectification
of "historical wrongs" at all but rather as an election-season gimmick
intended "to win Hindu votes," a full two-thirds of those describing it as
such did not find this grounds for disapproval of the event. What is to
be made of this extraordinary empirical finding, whereby a spectacular
event explicitly professing to "rectify a historical injustice" is widely recognized not to be doing that at all, and yet still does not garner commen-
surate disapproval?

The overwhelming approval (or at least not explicit disapproval) of
the temple inauguration event, combined with widespread acknowledgment that its claim to be "righting wrongs" ought not to be taken literally, suggests that a great many people evaluated the event as a variety
of performance. This was political theater, but not of the disparaged "only
natak" variety (outlined in chapter 2), where theatricality is denounced
as deceptive when (and only when) it professes to be otherwise. While
India's secular political leadership, progressive intellectuals, professional
historians, and legal experts sought (and fought) for decades to counter
the Ram Mandir movement's claims to be "righting historical wrongs"—
gathering a deluge of archival, archaeological, and legal evidence to the
contrary[12]—the accounts in this book demonstrate that communication
in a performance register is not readily amenable to disputation by a
"setting-the-record-straight" variety of truth claim. In chapter 3 we saw
how a sensational and disparaging video that circulated over WhatsApp
was countered by the targeted candidate's campaign team not by disput-
ing the video's specific allegations but rather by staging a correspond-
ing spectacle: a live "making-a-counter-video" performance that sought
not to counter inaccuracies with "facts" but rather to *upstage*—and to
thereby to redirect the election-season hawa (wind) so that it might blow
in the candidate's favor. In light of this, the 2023 CPR survey suggests that
the premise upon which the marshaling of scientific evidence to counter
political support for the Ram Mandir movement was based may have

been similarly mistaken: appreciation and support for the Ram Mandir movement (as perhaps for Hindutva more generally) simply does not require literal "belief" in its storyline (i.e., that constructing the new temple corrects "historical wrongs done to Hindus"). One can appreciate and resonate with a good show *as such* without being "deceived" by literalist interpretations of its storyline; to recall the words of the social media campaign manager in chapter 3, people can tell a show from a lie.

Drama of Democracy's conceptual toolbox would pose of the Ram Mandir inauguration a very different set of questions: If the event was evaluated as a show, then what exactly was on display? What were people turning up (or tuning in) to watch? With significant numbers of people abjuring the literal significance that the government ascribed to the event ("rectifying wrongs"), what *did* the event enjoin people to "believe"? Images from news reporting as well as social media commentary circulating during and after the event suggest that the inauguration-show was being assessed using the very criteria according to which Mumbaikars appreciate and evaluate a pre-poll rally-show: for starters, a who's-who lineup of the personalities on parade. Journalists covering the Ram Mandir inauguration reported feverishly on who turned up and who did not: photographs of Indian business mogul and Asia's wealthiest person, Mukesh Ambani (who declared January 22 a holiday for its India offices), posing with cricket legend Sachin Tendulkar were splashed across the pages of India's mainstream media undoubtedly increased "the size of the image" (to recall a formulation from chapter 2), thereby contributing to the Modi campaign's mahol and hawa—its atmosphere and directional momentum. Meanwhile, India's four Shankaracharya (Hinduism's top spiritual leaders) were conspicuous in their pre-announced absence, and video clips of their explanations swirled over social media (punctuated by opposition-leader commentary seeking to ascribe political significance to their absence).[13] Research on how these sorts of appearances and absences were evaluated —and by whom—would certainly make for interesting reading.

Drama of Democracy's conceptual toolbox suggests that perhaps India's tryst with majoritarianism ought not to be taken quite so literally "at its word"—at least not entirely. Indeed, scholars of Indian politics have long noted that Indian voters are by and large not ideological but rather eminently pragmatic in their electoral behavior.[14] In a recent large-scale study carried out in the medium-size cities of Jaipur and Bhopal, for instance, political scientists Adam Auerbach and Tariq Thachill marshal large-n survey data to demonstrate the remarkable savviness of the voting poor in selecting and forging relations of political representation that render their material claims effective. In contrast to any presumption that ethnic, religious, or even partisan identity would predict political trust or confidence in the context of gloves-off majoritarianism that characterizes political discourse in India (especially at the national level), Auerbach and Thachill's account establishes that voters are looking for something very different in their representatives: education, practical expertise, and demonstrated efficacy in everyday, practical problem solving.

The non-ideological character of concrete authority (especially at the local level) sits awkwardly alongside the undeniable salience of ideology and identity in popular political discourse—an awkwardness that joins an array of puzzles for which scholars of contemporary Indian politics do not have clear answers. Why, for instance, has Modi's brand of majoritarianism garnered so much more support in India's northern regions than in (no-less-Hindu) southern states such as Tamil Nadu, where Dravidian ideology, anti-Brahmanism, and regional language identity remains unmoved by the Rashtriya Swayamsevak Sangh's Sanskritic version of Hindu nationalism? Or perhaps even more awkwardly for literalist readings of Hindutva's ideological discourse, how can we account for what seems to be a growing popularity of the BJP among Indian Muslims?

Drama of Democracy invites a consideration of political communication beyond face-value readings. Consider, for example, the continuing deluge of defections in Maharashtra to parties allied with the BJP-affiliated ruling bloc. In one high-profile instance, in March 2024 Maharashtra state legislator Ravindra Waikar[15] said goodbye to Uddhav Thackeray's party after a half-century affiliation, during which Waikar represented Mumbaikars four times as a corporator and three times as MLA. Cynical readings of Waikar's defection to the breakaway faction of the Sena led by Eknath Shinde cited familiar explanations: some speculated that, under the pressure of an Enforcement Directorate probe into irregularities in his real estate dealings, Waikar had buckled and sought protection from the ruling bloc (a situation that recalls the allegations of "complaint natak" that damaged Seema's reputation in chapter 1); others suspected that Waikar had simply been incentivized with cash to join the ruling coalition. To speculate on the veracity of such allegations would be to miss the point; more interesting is Waikar's own recounting of his reasons for the move: he explained to the media that, after his repeated requests to the state government to fund infrastructure projects in his constituency went ignored, "I realized that in order to do development I had to be part of the government." Now, of course this is not the way that representative democracy is meant to work; and the denial of urban development funding to opposition-affiliated politicians was subsequently (and rightly) the subject of high-profile exposé by Mumbai's fearless and tireless news media.[16] Yet at the same time, Waikar's explanation recalls accounts from this book demonstrating that the gift-mediated forging and reconfiguration of alliances and trust is what the crafting of relations of representation practically entails, especially in the run-up to polling.[17] To recall the words of a veteran karyakarta in chapter 1: "everybody flips."

Indeed, as chapter 1 demonstrated, the role of cash gifting and exchange in forging and reconfiguring sociopolitical networks of power and authority in Mumbai is hardly news—and certainly not unique to this particular historical conjuncture (even while the size of the alleged sums are somewhat unprecedented). Pushing past facile assumptions that cash transfers signal mere market-like exchange, chapter 1 attended to money's multiple meanings, demonstrating how election-season cash animates intricate, contingent, highly speculative relational and informational networks by means of which representation is actually produced and instantiated—and political contestations and substantive citizenship claims articulated. On the one hand, we saw that gifts of cash work much like any other gifted good in producing relations of trust mediated by debt and obligation. On the other, cash gifts perform semiotic work, indexing access to powerful networks of knowledge, resources, and authority. In light of these findings, perhaps the more pressing question with regard to Waikar's joining the BJP-allied faction of the Sena is not whether or not money was given but rather what Waikar's new relationship with the ruling bloc might mean for his capacity (his taaqat, to recall a formulation from chapter 2) to access municipal resources and funding for local developmental work and to wield the practical authority necessary to get the work done. Waikar's wager is that the allegations of disloyalty necessarily attending his defection will be outstripped by his renewed and revitalized taaqat: his strengthened capacity to represent.

Thinking with Waikar's wager, moreover, leads us straight to the paradoxical co-articulation in Mumbai (as in India) of non-ideological voting with spectacular majoritarianism: just as Waikar speculated that perhaps his stagnating political career would shift back into gear if he were to become "part of the government," the ruling coalition was eager to court the seasoned politician in the run-up to the parliamentary elections precisely because of Waikar's enduring relations with area voters, social workers, and "mains" of all sorts. Beginning with the mass defection that toppled the Uddhav Thackeray–led government in Maharashtra, the BJP-affiliated ruling bloc in Maharashtra has been keenly courting corporators and local-level influence brokers—those who have spent much of their lives cultivating relations of trust with local residents.

Take, for example, Waikar's constituency, known as Jogeshwari East, which was one of the Mumbai areas worst affected by the 1992–93 riots that wracked the city in the aftermath of the destruction of the Babri Masjid in Ayodhya,[18] and where contemporary residents express no interest in revisiting the road which led to that dark episode. An in-depth report marking the twenty-fifth anniversary of the violence notes that for Mumbai's post-riot generation, the "divide" between Hindu and Muslim residents of Mumbai's popular neighborhoods and "slums" has been "bridged by three factors."[19] First (and recalling Sayeed Rizwan's family history recounted earlier), unlike earlier generations of working-class Mumbai children who attended Marathi- or Urdu-medium schools (depending on their religion), in contemporary Mumbai, children of all communities often study together in English-medium schools. Second (and as this book also demonstrates), the post-riot generation of working-class Mumbaikars is extraordinarily active in neighborhood-based voluntary associational life and "social work" organizations. And third, local leaders from Mumbai's myriad Muslim communities have taken a proactive interest in liaising with the Mumbai police, especially at times of heightened tension—a dynamic we saw especially in chapter 5. The Jogeshwari building where one of the worst episodes of violence unfolded during the 1992–93 riots—where six Hindus were burned alive in their home—has since been converted into a women's welfare center by a nongovernmental youth organization. Speaking with a media reporter after the 2019 Supreme Court ruling (which handed the Ayodhya site to the Ram Mandir trust), the coordinator for that NGO (also a Jogeshwari resident) explained that "on Friday, after the verdict was announced, we met several residents to ensure there was peace and communal harmony in the area. Things have changed for the better here."[20]

Mumbai has indeed changed in the three decades since a mob of Hindu nationalist kar sevaks tore through barricades of the Babri Majid and destroyed it with iron rods, igniting sectarian violence across the country. In this context, what are we to make of a Mumbai legislator representing a constituency where community leaders of all faiths espouse "peace and communal harmony" suddenly forming an alliance with a political coalition espousing exclusionary majoritarianism and "bulldozer justice"? Our Mumbai toolbox suggests that perhaps Waikar's wager has a second dimension: beyond the bet that "flipping" will increase his own taaqat, perhaps he is also wagering that Hindutva's muscular swagger ought not to be taken entirely at its word. Undoubtedly there is a core constituency for Hindutva, one that has been prevalent on the subcontinent's political landscape for a hundred years and whose violent vigilantism has been given carte blanche in recent years.[21] And yet it is entirely possible that the spate of defections to the BJP and its alliance partners does not indicate a concomitant expansion of true-believer majoritarian sentiment, support for the vigilante violence that attends it, or approval of the tightening authoritarian chokehold on media freedoms and public expression. Let's be honest: this is a bleak moment for democratic freedoms. At the time of writing, some demonstrators and activists arrested during the 2019–20 anti-CAA protests are still being held without bail. And yet while India's shrinking spaces for free expression are read by some commentators as a sign that India is embracing autocracy, the outrageous attempts to intimidate and muzzle might also be read as an anxious attempt to keep pace with rising discontent.[22] While there is obviously a core constituency for divisiveness, violence, and authoritarianism, it is increasingly apparent that support for with parties allied with Hindutva does not necessarily indicate unbridled support for these things. Tellingly, when Maharashtra Congress Party veteran and former chief minister Ashok Chavan[23] defected to the BJP in February 2024, the Mumbai media

reported "murmurs of discontent" among long-standing party workers—
especially the core cadre associated with the party's ideological body, the
Rashtriya Swayamsevak Sangh.[24]

Indeed, notwithstanding the continuing spate of defections to the
Hindutva-affiliated bloc (a full quarter of the BJP's candidates for the
2024 parliamentary elections were themselves defectors), contemporary
Mumbai appears unmoved by incitements to divisiveness. When Islamist
terrorists bombed the local train during rush hour in July 2006, killing
two hundred and injuring four times that number, Mumbaikars responded
not with retaliatory rage but with exasperated anguish; the next morning, when the trains restarted, Mumbaikars of all faiths squeezed right
back into the overcrowded train compartments, standing shoulder-to-
shoulder just as before.[25] The response was similar two years later, in
November 2008, when Mumbaikars watched in horror and grief as mili-
tants unleashed another series of gruesome attacks on the city.[26] Contemporary Mumbai appears impressed not by spectacular destruction (the
bulldozing of buildings or bodies) but rather by development, increased
educational opportunities, and the promises of participation in global
modernity. In this context, returns on the ruling coalition's investment
in someone like Waikar—with the hopes of drinking from the seasoned
politician's relational reservoirs of trust during an upcoming election—
may ultimately hinge on the extent to which Mumbai voters engage discourses of divisiveness not literally but rather with the remarkable everyday fluency with which Mumbaikars adeptly navigate and assess political
signs and representations more generally.

This book's introduction posed the question of whether there exists
some natural affinity between political style and substance, whether
democracy's defenders speak the language of rationality and sincerity
while political emotion, imagery, and embodiment properly belong to
the authoritarian right. Indeed, this is a question many were asking during a year when—amid resurgent Trumpism—sixty countries (representing half the world's population) headed to the polls. In this context, it is
notable that one of this book's key findings is that virtuosity in the performance arts of political communication is not the unique purview of
any particular political orientation; in Mumbai, all parties speak the affective language of theater. To point this out is not to underplay the very real
violence that performance itself can entail; on the contrary, spectacular

violence can itself be a macabre variety of theater, as it was during the 1992–93 riots.[27] The fact that performance of violence results in actual death does not make it any less of a show; quite the opposite.[28] Three decades ago, power and authority were enacted in Mumbai through discourses of divisiveness and dramatic displays of violence with impunity. And yet in the contemporary city, interreligious animosity and acrimony appear no longer to capture the public imagination as a compelling storyline. A pragmatic public may indeed be enthralled by its own pageant of power. This is the constitutive contradiction of representation, playing out in the theater of political life and the drama of democracy.

Acknowledgments

The research for this book began over a decade ago and has benefited enormously from the insights and exertions of a great many people and institutions. In 2011, I joined a research group under the leadership of Peter van der Veer at the Max Plank Institute for the Study of Religious and Ethnic Diversity in Göttingen, and over the three years that I spent on the Urban Aspirations in Global Cities project some the key ideas animating this book took shape. For their insights and engagements, I am grateful to Nate Roberts, Ajay Gandhi, Radhika Gupta, Shireen Mirza, Ishani Dasgupta, Leilah Vevaina, Jayeel Cornelio, Jin-Heon Jung, Angie Heo, Neena Mahadev, Tam Ngo, Shaheed Tayob, Yuqin Huang, Roshanack Shaery-Yazdi, Jinyang Yu, Rumin Luo, Uday Chandra, Sajide Tursun, Anderson Blanton, and Peter van der Veer. Also in Göttingen, I was fortunate to have the opportunity to workshop early iterations of some ideas in this book with scholars at University of Göttingen's Center for Modern Indian Studies (CeMIS), where I was affiliated in 2014–15. Thanks especially to Patrick Eisenlohr, Nellie Chu, Rupa Vishwinath, Srirupa Roy, Lalit Vachani, and Sumeet Mhaskar. Ideas in chapter 1 benefitted as well from discussions during a 2016 symposium on "Money and Politics in India" hosted by the Center for the Advanced Study of India (CASI) at the University of Pennsylvania. Thanks to Milan Vaishnav, Adam Auerbach, Michael Collins, Jennifer Bussell, Jeffrey Witsoe, Simon Chauchard, Neelanjan Sircar, Tariq Thachill, and Devesh Kapur for their insights.

In Louisville, I am grateful to Karl Swinehart, Simona Bertacco, and Srimati Basu for their feedback, especially on ideas in chapter 2. Chapter 2 (in some ways the heart of the book) benefitted as well from discussions with seminar participants at University Illinois at Chicago (2019), University of Pennsylvania's Center for Modern India Studies (2019), University of Pennsylvania's South Asia Center (2019), University of Leipzig (2019), Indiana University Bloomington (2019), Stockholm University (2020), and The Max Planck Institute for Social Anthropology (2022), and Università degli Studi di Napoli L'Orientale (2022). I am especially grateful to my coresearchers on the European Research Council (ERC) project "India's politics in its vernaculars," led by Anastasia Piliavsky at King's College London. With the generous support of the European Research Council, I was able to enlist the expertise of the brilliant Sharvari Shastri in tracking and translating Marathi-language media coverage of the events in chapters 4 and 5, and the formidable Capucine Tournilhac, who helped me tighten my arguments and prepare the manuscript for submission. For their engagements during workshops in Cambridge in 2021 and 2023, I am grateful to Ram Rawat, Lisa Mitchell, Uday Chandra, Francesca Orsini, Lipika Kamra, Dilip Menon, Piers Vibetsky, Tomasso Sbriccoli, A. R. Venkatachalapathy, Milinda Banerjee, Edward Moon-Little, Dale Luis Menezes, Ajay Skaria, S. V. Srinivas, and, above all, Anastasia Piliavsky.

The book's overall framing benefitted tremendously from the lively conversations that took place over the course of a wonderful week in Sintra during a Wenner Grenn workshop on Anthropology of Global Populisms in March 2023; the energy and ideas that emerged from our conversations in Sintra inspired me to engage more directly with the concept of "populism." I wish to thank Danilyn Rutherford, Gary Wilder, Leticia Cesarino, Luciana Chamorro, Karem Ussakli, Jason Frank, Kabir Tambar, Kristóf Szombati, Nitzan Shoshan, Nusrat Chowdhury, Robert Samet, Naomi Schiller, Donna Auston, Banu Bargu, and especially William Mazzarella.

I spent much of the Covid-19 pandemic working remotely from Sweden, where dark winter days were brightened by my little writing group's bimonthly Zoom meetings. For their brilliant interventions and suggestions on many of the book's chapters, I am grateful to Rachel Sturman, Lisa Mitchell, Ursula Rao, Nikhil Rao, Ravinder Kaur, Srimati Basu, Tarini Bedi, and especially Llerena Guiu Searle, who provided invaluable guidance and feedback on way too many drafts of chapter 3. Also during those long pandemic months, I had the tremendous fortune to participate remotely in the American Institute of Indian Studies Lucknow-based Urdu program, where under the sagacious tutelage of AIIS's Lucknow faculty, I learned to read and write the Nastaliq script. For her endless patience and good humor, I am especially grateful to our poetry teacher Sheeba Iftikhar—particularly for her help in translating the couplets in chapter 4—and to AIIS's Urdu program director Ahtesham Khan for welcoming me into the program. And thank you as well to my Urdu reading group members Swarnim Khare and Rabea Murtaza for cozy afternoons spent together on Zoom, working our way through Saadat Hasan Manto's Bombay stories. I am also tremendously grateful to AIIS for fellowship support from 2018 to 2020.

In 2021–23, I spent two delightful years writing up the latter chapters of this book while affiliated to the Max Planck Institute for Social Anthropology in Halle (Saale), with generous support from the Alexander von Humboldt Foundation. In Halle, my thinking was deepened through ongoing conversations with the wonderful group of researchers affiliated to the Anthropology of Politics and Governance department under the leadership of Ursula Rao. I am grateful to Samiksha Bhan, Claudia Lang, Jovan Maud, Hanna Nieber, Julia Vorhölter, Desirée Kumpf, Mascha Schultz, Tyler Zoanni, Michiel Baas, and especially to Ursula Rao. During the summer of 2022 in Halle, I had the opportunity to workshop ideas in this book during regular meetings and seminars with a remarkable group of visiting scholars; thank you to Carol Upadhya, Anindita Chakravarty, Jason Cons, Bidisha Chaudhuri, Srimati Basu, Robert Desjarlais, William Mazzarella, and Amy McLachlan. I am especially grateful to Viola Stanisch and Viktoria Giehler-Zeng for their kindness and constant support during my time at the MPI in Halle.

At the University of Minnesota Press, I wish to thank Editorial Director Jason Weidemann, Managing Editor Mike Stoffel, Production Editor Carla Valadez, Marketing and Engagement Specialist Shelby Connelly, and especially Zenyse Miller, who made everything smooth and easy. Thank you as well to Douglas Easton, who prepared the index, and to Rohit Kudale who drew the maps.

I have the tremendous good fortune to have colleagues and friends who have been willing to read so many chapter drafts and to think together through ideas. For believing in the book—and in my ability to write it—

I am deeply grateful to Lisa Mitchell, Adam Auerbach, Rachel Sturman, Tarini Bedi, Llerena Searle, and especially to Jonathan Spencer and Laura Kunreuther, who read the manuscript in its entirety.

My greatest thanks is owed to the city of Mumbai, and to the people whose energy and creativity and unflappable good humor bring that brilliant city to life day after day.

Notes

Introduction

1. Bombay's name was officially changed to Mumbai in 1995 when (following a blood-soaked season of politically orchestrated rioting) the linguistic- and regional-chauvinist Shiv Sena assumed control over the Maharashtra state government (for an illuminating discussion of the city's renaming, see Hansen, *Wages of Violence*). However, this "before-and-after" story elides the nomenclatural complexities of the contemporary city. Many people continue to use "Bombay," especially (but not always or exclusively) Urdu-speaking Muslims, portions of the political left, and the city's intelligentsia. Many people will use both names—sometimes alternating according to the language (or accent) in which they are speaking: "Mumbai" when speaking Marathi, "Bombay" when speaking Urdu, Hindi, or English. What's more, because *Bombay, Bambai, Bumbai,* and *Mumbai* exist along multiple spectra of vowel and consonantal sounds, it is not always clear (and perhaps intentionally so) exactly which name is being used.

2. Shivaji Park is the largest public park in the Island City; the twenty-eight-acre open space is beloved by cricketers, morning walkers, and evening friends' groups.

3. On June 29, 2022, after a heady week of tortuous legal maneuvering that reached the Supreme Court, Thackeray resigned from his post as Maharashtra chief minister.

4. Khoka comes from Marathi—the official language of the state of Maharashtra and the native language of around 40 percent of Mumbaikars—but has made its way into the everyday "Bambaiya" Hindi that is Bombay's lingua franca. For a discussion of Bambaiya see Pemmaraju, "Dalvi."

5. That is, 500 million rupees, equivalent to around $6 million US at that time.

6. Deshpande, "Mumbai Dasara Rallies."

7. The Black Lives Matter movement was spurred by the unchecked police violence against Black Americans, and expressed outrage at this police violence

and at the apathy and inaction of the country's political classes on both sides of the ideological spectrum.

8. Elam, "Hong Kong."

9. Nikas, "Pro-Bolsonaro Riots."

10. See Chowdhury, "Figurative Publics." For a discussion of the "crisis" thesis, see Tormey, "Contemporary Crisis."

11. Anthony, "Occupy Wall Street."

12. Quoted in Giridharadas "The Real Battleground."

13. Giridharadas.

14. The unseated president declared that the recent election had been "so corrupt that in the history of this country we've never seen anything like it," that "your leadership has led you down the tubes," and that it was up to them—"the real people"—to "save our democracy." For the full text of Trump's January 6, 2021, speech see Naylor, "Read Trump's Jan. 6 Speech."

15. In 2008, UNESCO inscribed Ramlila on the Representative List of the Intangible Cultural Heritage of Humanity. See UNESCO, "Ramlila."

16. Except for 2020 and 2021, due to the Covid-19 pandemic.

17. On Maharashtra's party system, see Palshikar and Deshpande, *The Last Fortress.*

18. The election is still pending at the time of writing.

19. Khapre, "Why BJP Only a Spectator."

20. S. Banerjee, "Sena versus Sena."

21. The *Indian Express* described the Dusshera rallies as "mega battle of optics between the two Shiv Senas," with the BJP "a spectator in the grand Sena shows." Khapre, "Why BJP Only a Spectator"; Banerjee, "Sena versus Sena."

22. Eshwar and Palod, "Gaddar vs Khuddar."

23. The quote is taken from news media NTDV's YouTube video feature "Team Thackeray vs Team Shinde at Big Dussehra Rallies."

24. I follow Talal Asad's notion of "embodied practices" as those that facilitate "the acquisition of aptitudes, sensibilities, and propensities through repetition until such time as the language guiding practice becomes redundant. Through such practices, one can change oneself—one's physical being, one's emotions, one's language, one's predispositions, as well as one's environment." Asad, "Thinking about Tradition," 166.

25. Dalton, *Democratic Challenges;* Hay, *Why We Hate Politics.* See also Chandhoke, "Revisiting the Crisis of Representation Thesis."

26. By "fundamental rights" the Freedom House report means the right of a sovereign people to choose its leaders through free and fair elections, to express themselves and engage in free exchange of information and ideas, and to be protected by fair and equal protections of the rule of law. India's Freedom House status remains at "partly free" at the time of writing. Freedom House, "India."

27. Vaishnav, "Indian Women"; "India Sees Six-Fold Jump in Voters"; M. Banerjee, *Why India Votes;* Mitchell, *Hailing the State;* Auerbach et al., "Rethinking the Study of Electoral Politics."

28. For a wonderfully succinct review of these debates and of new interventions, see Auerbach et al., "Rethinking the Study of Electoral Politics."

29. I borrow this representation/re-presentation formulation from Friedland, *Political Actors.*

30. Pitkin, *The Concept of Representation,* 9.

31. Laclau, "Power and Representation," 97–99.

32. Disch, van de Sande, and Urbinati, *The Constructivist Turn.*

33. Michael Saward, *The Representative Claim,* 4, quoted in Tawa Lama-Rewal, "Political Representation in India," 163.

34. Plotke, "Representation Is Democracy." Joseph Schumpeter's minimalist notion defined democracy as "that institutional arrangement for arriving at political decisions in which individuals acquire the power to decide by means of a competitive struggle for the people's vote." Schumpeter, *Capitalism, Socialism, and Democracy,* 269.

35. Scholars have challenged the conceptual distinctions among representation, participation, and deliberation, noting how representation necessarily figures also in deliberative and participatory settings. Young, *Inclusion and Democracy;* Urbinati and Warren, "The Concept of Representation"; Mansbridge, "Clarifying the Concept of Representation." See discussion in Tawa Lama-Rewal, "Political Representation in India."

36. Frank, "The Living Image."

37. Lefort, *Political Forms of Modern Society,* 279, quoted in Frank, "The Living Image."

38. Friedland, *Political Actors,* 20, 32.

39. Friedland, 55.

40. Friedland, 6.

41. Frank, "The Living Image." Elsewhere, Frank argues that "populism" is insufficient to the task of "thinking through the particularity of popular assembly as a form of democratic representation," because political crowds are not "direct expressions of such sovereignty" but rather are themselves representations. See Frank "Beyond Democracy's Imaginary Investments." And yet Frank's formulation hinges upon the same counterposing of presence with representation that the material in this book will destabilize.

42. Friedland notes how the eighteenth-century shift from incarnation to absence was in step with contemporaneous religious churnings: "Re-presentation is essentially analogous to the Catholic conception of transubstantiation in which the body and the blood of Christ are materially re-presented, or incarnated, within the bread and the wine of the Eucharist. I use the nonhyphenated form, representation, to refer to the process by which an intangible body is abstractly represented in spirit rather than in substance; this form is analogous to the various

Protestant conceptions of the Eucharist in which the body and blood of Christ are symbolically referred to by the bread and the wine." Friedland, *Political Actors,* 8–9.

43. Friedland, 21.

44. See Mazzarella, "The Anthropology of Populism," 47; see also Jonsson, "Populism without Borders," for a discussion of the normative valence of "populism."

45. Mazzarella, "The Anthropology of Populism," 47.

46. The chapters that follow have much to say about the "public sphere" and the notion of "public" more broadly; for now, suffice it to note that while a generation of critical scholarship (particularly feminist scholarship) has highlighted the gendered and exclusionary character of the public sphere as formulated by Jürgen Habermas—calling for the pluralization of the concept of publicity through attention to various "counterpublics"—embodied crowds tend to be characterized somewhat uncritically as an emergent, unmediated phenomenon born of collective affect. Habermas, *Structural Transformation.* For discussions of "counterpublics" see Fraser, "Rethinking the Public Sphere"; Hirschkind, *The Ethical Soundscape*; Warner, "Publics and Counterpublics."

47. German and French conceptual history, also playing past the anglophone preoccupation with procedures of authorization and accountability that stem from presumptions of representation as absence, has a rich conceptual tradition theorizing the "symbolic" and "embodied" quality of political representation. For a discussion see Tawa Lama-Rewal, "Political Representation in India."

48. Freitag, *Collective Action and Community,* xii, 6, 19. It was in this context, Freitag argues, that Indian nationalism struggled to incorporate community identities that had flourished independently from the British colonial state in the "public arena."

49. Anderson, *Imagined Communities.*

50. Mitchell, *Hailing the State,* 21, 208.

51. Mitchell, 7.

52. Mitchell, 2.

53. Spencer, "Post-colonialism and the Political Imagination."

54. Geertz, *Negara;* Turner, *The Anthropology of Performance,* 181.

55. Radcliffe-Brown, "On the Concept of Function."

56. Geertz, *Negara,* 123.

57. Geertz's characterization of spectacular performances of the theater state as "ritual" echoes developments in religious studies inspired by Austin's notion of the performative. Before Austin, scholars of religion used the term "performance" to characterize ritual as the "execution of a preexisting script." The idea of performativity invited scholars of religion to focus on ritual as action. Performativity offered scholarship on ritual some key conceptual innovations, most importantly by asking how "performative actions produce a culturally meaningful environment." Bell, "Performance," 208.

58. Cameron and Kulick, *Language and Sexuality*.

59. "Could a performative utterance succeed," Derrida asks, "if its formulation did not repeat a 'coded' or iterable utterance, or in other words, if the formula I pronounce in order to open a meeting, launch a ship, or a marriage were not identifiable as conforming with an iterable model, if it were not then identifiable as some way as a 'citation'?" Derrida, "Signature Event Context," 18.

60. Butler, *Bodies That Matter*, 2; Wedeen, *Peripheral Visions*, 16. See also Butler's *Notes Toward a Performative Theory of Assembly* for an extended discussion of "performative assembly."

61. Wedeen. *Ambiguities of Domination*, 14.

62. T. B. Hansen, "Politics as Permanent Performance," 25.

63. T. B. Hansen, *Wages of Violence*, 54–56.

64. Morris, *Foundations of the Theory of Signs*, 4, quoted in Eco, "Semiotics of Theatrical Performance," 112.

65. Goffman further specifies that by "performance" he means "all the activity of an individual which occurs during a period marked by his continuous presence before a particular set of observers, and which has some influence on the observers." Goffman, *The Presentation of Self*, 22. See also Clough, introduction, for an account of performativity that is attentive to audience—where the "performative efficacy" of discourse inheres in how it affects its interlocutors.

66. Llerena Searle, personal correspondence with the author, 2024.

67. In his critique of what he calls "media talk," Asif Agha points out that "any social process of communication involves relationships between acts of communication and their uptake." Much as political performativity seems to presume its own efficacy by virtue of methodological oversight to uptake, much contemporary talk about the totalizing power of commercial media (mediatization) problematically "narrows the gaze of social actors to a small sample of their own activities, [resulting in] a curious kind of performative enclosure made largely of media talk." Like political performativity, "media talk" takes commercial media's pretentions to power at its word by overlooking questions of uptake. Agha, "Meet Mediatization," 164. See also Cody, *The News Event*.

68. Schechner, *Performance Studies*, 12.

69. Eco, "Semiotics of Theatrical Performance," 109.

70. Eco, 110.

71. See Björkman, "The Ostentatious Crowd," for a discussion of "ostentatious display"—a concept I develop drawing on Eco's formulation of "ostention."

72. Mediation of course is not a realm of activity unique to politics; rather, as Mazzarella explains, mediation comprises the "ambiguous foundation of all social life": "Mediation involves the conceptual, technical, and linguistic practices by which the actually irreducible particularities of our experience are, apparently, reduced: in other words, rendered provisionally commensurable and thus recognizable and communicable in general terms." Mazzarella, "Internet X-Ray," 476.

73. See Björkman, *Pipe Politics, Waiting Town,* and *Bombay Brokers.*

74. Eco, "Semiotics of Theatrical Performance," 113.

75. Pernau and Rajamani, "Emotional Translations," 54.

76. The work of Brian Massumi would be an example of a "strong" version of affect theory.

77. Mazzarella, "Affect"; Berlant, *Cruel Optimism,* 53; Clough, introduction; Schaefer, "The Promise of Affect," 3; Chumley, "Qualia and Ontology." See also Keane, "Semiotics and the Social Analysis of Material Things," "Signs Are Not the Garb of Meaning," and "On Semiotic Ideology." Indeed, while scholars of affect and multisensory anthropology sometimes position embodied-sensory approaches explicitly against language-based approaches to meaning-making (dismissed as "bloodless"), linguistic anthropology inspired by the work of semiotician Charles Sanders Peirce, in attending to the materiality of signs, has come (from the other direction) to much the same conclusion. Lily Chumley describes how "sensory and somatic experiences" are semiotic processes—mediated by "qualisigns" that are imbued with value through processes that are both social and historical.

78. Chumley, "Qualia and Ontology."

79. Taking discursive practices of problematization as a point of methodological and analytical departure builds on the insight of anthropologist Biao Xiang on the agentive quality of "the will and capacity to problematize the present." As Xiang notes, "formal theories . . . often explain away rather than within problems" and in so doing "fall short in capturing how people feel, calculate, and struggle inside the practices" (Introduction). Here I share Piliavsky and Scheele's call for anthropological attention to "ethnographically derived political concepts." See Piliavsky and Scheele. "Towards a Critical Ethnography."

80. Williams, *Keywords.*

81. This dual valence—at once performance and performative—is evident in the etymology of the word natak, which is derived from the Sanskrit natya, which Platts's 1884 *Dictionary of Urdu, Classical Hindi, and English* defines as both "the science or art of dancing, or acting" and the "scenic art; the union of song, pantomime, dance, and instrumental music" itself (1112).

82. Drawing on Charles Sanders Peirce, *pragmatics* here refers to meanings of speech that are "inferred from context and paralinguistic features, including intonation contours and voice qualities." Urban, "Metasemiosis and Metapragmatics," 90.

83. *Metapragmatics* refers to the codes and conventions by means of which people go about interpreting non-semantic meanings of speech; for discussion see Urban.

Interlude I

1. All names of people and places are changed unless otherwise indicated.

2. The gender reservation for women was replaced by a reservation for candidates holding Other Backward Class certificates. Seema does not hold this

certificate, and in any event the 50 percent reservation for women in the Mumbai Municipal Corporation means that parties were likely to allocate to men any tickets for seats not explicitly reserved for women. For a discussion of the history of caste reservations in government jobs and electoral politics, see Yadav "Electoral Politics"; and Corbridge and Harriss, *Reinventing India.*

3. Björkman, *Pipe Politics.*

4. Björkman, 232–33.

5. The Bombay Municipal Corporation officially changed its name to Brihanmumbai Municipal Corporation in 1996 as part of a broader renaming initiative, while preserving the widely used acronym "BMC." In line with popular usage in Mumbai, this book uses "BMC" and "the municipal corporation" interchangeably.

6. See chapter 2 for a discussion of natak.

7. Needless to say, I declined the request.

8. Quoted in Björkman, *Pipe Politics* and "Becoming a Slum."

9. On June 25, 1975, Prime Minister Indira Gandhi declared a national emergency. During the twenty-one-month period of "the Emergency," political and civil rights were suspended.

10. For an account of how these dynamics have played out in Delhi, whereby a "multiplicity of tenure regimes" have been obviated by an "aesthetic governmentality," see Ghertner's *Rule by Aesthetics* and "India's Urban Revolution."

11. In conjunction with country-level Liberalizing reforms, in March 1991 the government of Maharashtra launched a new set of development control rules (DCRs) granting private-sector developers of tenement-style slum-redevelopment housing incentive-development rights as a kind of housing cross-subsidy. By compensating builders of slum-rehabilitation tenements with development rights, it was imagined, the urban poor could be rehoused at little or no cost to the state government. The basic idea behind the 1995 Slum Rehabilitation Scheme (an amped-up, more market-reliant version of the nonstarter 1991 Slum Redevelopment Scheme) was to use exclusively market incentives to demolish all of the city's slums and to rehouse eligible residents in mid-rise tenement buildings—now as title-holding property owners. Political leaders in Mumbai sought to legitimize this highly peculiar policy framework (which anti-migrant detractors denounced as "rewarding squatters" and encouraging migration) through a two-part strategy: first by excluding from Slum Rehabilitation Scheme eligibility any household that could not provide documentary proof of residence in a structure as of a January 1, 1995, cutoff date; and second through a government circular passed in 1996 on the heels of the new scheme, which disallowed even the provision of civic amenities and other permissions to houses and households whose structures (and whose residence in those structures) could not be proven to meet the cutoff date of eligibility for some hypothetical slum-rehabilitation scheme.

12. Elite Mumbaikars, incidentally, also rely on mediators for such things, albeit in somewhat different ways; see Björkman, *Bombay Brokers.*

13. Tenants make up an estimated 60 percent of so-called slumdwellers, who themselves are estimated at more than 60 percent of Mumbai's official population.

14. This is demonstrated in chapter 1.

15. Scholars of Indian politics have used terms such as "broker," "middleman," and "agent." See also J. S. Anjaria, "Ordinary States"; and Hansen and Verkaaik, "Introduction." I have characterized such various activities as "brokering"—a conjunctural formulation that attends to the contradictions that are mediated through such practices, and to the particular people who cultivate and trade in the expertise necessary to do so. See Björkman, *Bombay Brokers.*

16. For an account of similar dynamics in the mid-sized North Indian cities of Jaipur and Bhopal, see Auerbach and Thachill, *Migrants and Machine Politics.*

1. Cash

1. See Srivastava, "Is Your 'Bai' on Long Leave?" Echoing this sentiment, another English daily announced on its front page a few days later that "rates for buying the votes of slum dwellers [were] Rs1000 to Rs1500." Makne, "BMC Polls."

2. The candidate on whose campaign I focused my research during the 2012 election season spent nearly four times as much on her 2012 bid as she did on her successful 2007 campaign; estimates from other wards are similar. Campaign expenditures in 2012 were reported to range from 20 lakh (about $40,000 in 2012) to a crore (Rs 10 million, or about $200,000 in 2012) for "prominent candidates." See Mankikar, "Cashing In on the Election Fever."

3. Michelutti, "The Vernacularization of Democracy." See also Piliavsky, introduction.

4. See, e.g., Scott, "Corruption"; Wit, *Poverty, Policy, and Politics;* Kitschelt and Wilkinson, *Patrons, Clients, and Policies;* Schaffer, Introduction.

5. This discussion recalls the classic distinction between "parochial" and "market" corruption. See Scott, *Comparative Political Corruption,* 88.

6. Scott, "Corruption." More recently, Auerbach and Thachill have argued that "machine politics" in urban India can have potentially democratizing tendencies as well. See Auerbach and Thachill, *Migrants and Machine Politics.*

7. Mauss, *The Gift.*

8. See Scott, *Comparative Political Corruption,* for discussion of "market corruption"; see Sahlins, *Stone Age Economics,* for discussion of "generalized reciprocity." My analysis here draws on Keane's theorizations of marriage exchange negotiations in Indonesia. See Keane, *Signs of Recognition.*

9. Parry and Bloch, Introduction, 12.

10. Bohannan, "The Impact of Money," 500.

11. Maurer, "The Anthropology of Money," 20. Maurer provides a detailed review of the anthropological literature on money.

12. Maurer, 20.

13. Simmel quoted in Maurer, 23.

14. Gregory, *Gifts and Commodities,* 41.

15. Mauss, *The Gift.*

16. Appadurai, *The Social Life of Things.*

17. The reliance of vote-buying literature upon classic money theory is not overtly stated but rather is implicit in the framing of research agendas narrowly around the question of how cash-for-vote exchanges are enforced. The possibility that flows of cash might be doing some other kind of work altogether is foreclosed at the outset.

18. Jaffe, "Indexicality, Stance, and Fields."

19. Parmentier, "Money Walks, People Talk."

20. Parmentier, 52.

21. Keane, "Money Is No Object."

22. In an effort to avoid splitting the so-called secular vote, the Congress Party joined forces with the National Congress Party (NCP). After weeks of high-profile horse-trading, the senior leadership of each party settled on a formula that gave 169 seats to the Congress Party and the remaining 58 to NCP. Meanwhile, the "saffron" alliance between Shiv Sena and the Bharatiya Janata Party joined forces with Dalit leader Ramdas Athavale's Republican Party of India, settling on a formula allowing each party to contest 135, 63, and 29 seats, respectively.

23. In a constituency of 40,000 people, this means that social workers comprise 5 percent of the population. While this number may seem like an exaggerated estimate, the notion that one out of every twenty people (or five households) engages—at least on occasion—in some form of "social work" does not seem far-fetched.

24. This rumor was given credence a few weeks after the election when, sitting in Mastanbhai's office one afternoon, I witnessed an exchange between the MLA and some young social workers from his constituency who were involved in organizing local residents for a Slum Rehabilitation Project. One of the boys explained that of the twelve hundred houses in the project area, around eight hundred were without the proper combination of documents. The boys explained that the builder's men were trying to put "their own people" on the list in place of those local undocumented residents—that is, to sell off the allotments and pocket the money. The boys had gotten into an "argument" (lafda) with the "builder's men" and seemed shaken. Mastanbhai responded firmly: "No, no, everyone who was in your survey will get a room; all the people there will get rooms. Bring me the list of the undocumented people." When the boys still seemed nervous, the MLA added encouragingly "I'm goonde ke bap [godfather of the rascals]; who's going to tear down a house in my area without my permission? Tell them you're from my village; they won't touch you." This exchange suggests that the boys were concerned that the builder would try to assert the superiority of his own networks of power and authority either by having the boys' own homes demolished or else through threats of physical violence. The MLA's statement reveals the slippage between the threat of actual physical violence ("they won't

touch you") and the danger that the builder might use his network of connections to unleash destructive violence on their homes.

25. See chapter 2 for an extended discussion of the Mumbai use of the English-origin word *public*.

26. Here Seema is referring to the practice of accepting money in exchange for dropping an official complaint—a practice for which Hasina had become infamous during her tenure two terms prior. Seema's rhetorical question ("Have I ever accepted your money?") is an effort to distance herself from any demolitions that may have occurred in the past.

27. This conversation was conducted mostly in Tamil between Seema's husband and the Trust leaders. The translation was provided to me in Hindi by Seema's sister-in-law. Seema (who is Maharashtrian) understands Tamil but does not speak readily; direct exchanges between Seema and the Trust leaders took place in Hindi.

28. Recall that the Congress Party had forged a pre-poll alliance with the NCP for the 2012 BMC election.

29. The significance of prachaar as advertising is taken up in chapter 2.

30. A chit fund is a rotating savings and credit association system that is common in India.

31. Mauss, *The Gift,* 1.

32. For accounts in which relations constituted through exchange are shown clearly to be contingent and susceptible to failure, see also Geschiere, *Witchcraft, Intimacy, and Trust;* Herzfeld, *Cultural Intimacy;* and Roberts, *To Be Cared For.* These, in different ways, reverse the received picture in which the terms of exchange follow unproblematically from degree of social proximity; see Sahlins, *Stone Age Economics.*

33. Keane, *Signs of Recognition,* 144

34. Keane, 144.

35. Keane, 87.

36. See chapter 2 for discussions of hawa and mains.

37. As this particular exchange happened in Tamil, it was unclear whether offers of cash were made by Seema and her team. However, judging from other meetings in which cash was discussed, it is quite likely that a cash transfer was at least implicit in this conversation.

38. Keane, "Money Is No Object," 69.

39. Keane, 69.

40. Notably, Furqan no longer resides in this neighborhood; he built the house around the same time that he moved to Navi Mumbai (to minimize commute times to his office), suggesting the importance of the house as a spectacle of wealth.

41. Mauss, *The Gift,* 37–38.

42. Bohannan, "The Impact of Money."

43. Parry and Bloch, Introduction, 12.

44. Parry and Bloch, 22.

45. Parry and Bloch, 24.

46. Parmentier, "Money Walks, People Talk," 52.

47. Parmentier, 66.

48. Parmentier, 65.

49. Here, "everyone" refers to social workers.

50. The aftermath of the election—not only in Daulat Nagar but across Mumbai—was notable for the absence of any retribution against neighborhoods that booth-wise polling data showed to have voted the "wrong" way.

51. Furqan explained to me that he regretted having disappointed his constituents, but he had been called away by his duty to care for his mother.

52. The suffix "-wala" means something like "the one who." So "election-wala Santosh" would mean something like "the Santosh who contested the election."

53. The option, Karim tells me, is that "once the ground floor is complete and I'm about to start on the first floor [which is where the building becomes vulnerable to complaint] I go to the BMC and pay money to the officials for a 'stop-work notice.'" He shows me one on his phone. "This way, see," he goes on, "if someone asks the BMC 'why haven't you stopped that work?' then the officials can say 'we did stop the work.' So, like that, they're safe and I'm also safe."

54. Many construction materials are sourced beyond the territorial boundaries and administrative jurisdiction of the city.

55. The role of "trust" in Karim's work as a "point man" recalls Mattison Mines's account in *Public Faces, Private Voices* of "big men" in Tamil Nadu, for whom "the degree of trust" someone commands is given by "the reliability of a relationship in terms of the knowledge of the other party or parties in that relationship." Which is to say, a person's trustworthiness and reliability is bound up with their socio-relational networks. "A person who can claim good connections with influential people finds it easier to accomplish social objectives and to influence others" (Mines, *Public Faces, Private Voices*, 58). The reliability of these broader relational webs that comprise the basis of an individual's "reputation"—a "public sense" established over time—that he or she will behave in "predictable and reliable ways" (32).

56. Carse, "Keyword," 27.

57. Carse, 31.

58. Carse, 34.

59. To be clear: this is not a normative argument in defense of the influx of cash into elections, but an upending of elitist discourses of "vote buying." For discussion of the many perverse effects of money's influx into Indian elections, see Kapur and Vaishnav, *Costs of Democracy.*

Interlude II

1. Badla is a Hindi-Urdu word that means "compensation" or "exchange"; Badlapur therefore means something like "place of exchange."

2. For an in-depth account of those hydraulic interventions, see Björkman, "The Engineer and the Plumber."

3. For a thorough account, see Kidambi, *Making of an Indian Metropolis*.

4. See Gayer and Jaffrelot, "Muslims of the Indian City," 21. Anthropologist Radhika Gupta thus makes a powerful argument for the need to reconceptualize urban areas in Indian cities that are discursively marked as Muslim "ghettos"—areas like South Bombay, for instance, which is the ethnographic basis of her own intervention. The "ghetto," Gupta argues, ought not to be conceptualized as "material space or territory" where some population is segregated (whether by force or volition); rather, she calls attention to the myriad sites and situations where "processes and relationships of power and hegemony in society that led to the creation of the ghetto, whether forced or voluntary, are manifest." Gupta enjoins ethnographers to consider the diverse processes by means of which what she calls "the ghetto effect" is produced and reproduced, not least by the anthropologist's own engagements. In a profoundly reflexive analysis, Gupta interrogates her own reproduction of this "ghetto effect" in her inadvertent selection of Mumbai's inner-city areas as the site for her own field research on Mumbai's Ismaili Muslims—a selection made unthinkingly, based merely on the area's "outward markers of 'Muslimness'" and its popular association with "the Muslim underworld." Gupta adds that "such processes of othering lead to the homogenization of sectarian and sub-sectarian diversity among Muslims, particularly characteristic of Mumbai." Gupta, "There Must Be Some Way," 353–60.

5. Gupta, "There Must Be Some Way," 353–60.

6. Sarkar, "BMC Polls."

7. Sayeed narrated his biography for me over the course of two breakfast conversations.

8. While initial media reports described the demolition as spontaneous, an official inquiry commission later revealed that the events of December 6 were "neither spontaneous nor unplanned," and held top leaders of the Hindu Nationalist Sangh Parivar—the Rashtriya Swayamansevak Sangh, Vishwa Hindu Parishad (the World Hindu Council), Shiv Sena, Bajarang Dal, and Bharatiya Janata Party—directly responsible for the illegal demolition. See "Babri Masjid Demolition." For an overview of the broader historical context, see Davis, "The Iconography of Rama's Chariot."

9. As Hansen points out, "This claim was untrue; indeed, a group of high-ranking Shiv Sena leaders actually arrived in Ayodhya too late even to witness the demolition." T. B. Hansen, *Wages of Violence,* 121.

10. T. B. Hansen, 121.

11. T. B. Hansen, 122.

12. Notwithstanding the hoped-for security in numbers, witnesses reported widespread violence and arson even in these Muslim-majority areas, evidence of which was later confirmed in the official government Srikrishna Commission inquiry report.

13. T. B. Hansen, *Wages of Violence,* 125.

14. T. B. Hansen, 125.

15. Real name.

16. As one Ulema Council spokesman told Hansen in 1993, "Our greatest contribution has been to wean people away from Congress and to ensure their defeat now in two elections"; Kashmiri himself had earlier been an active member of the Muslim League and represented South Bombay in the Maharashtra State Assembly. T. B. Hansen, *Wages of Violence,* 172.

17. Engineer, "Politics of Muslim Vote Bank."

18. Rama is another name for the Hindu god Ram; see Davis, "The Iconography of Rama's Chariot," 31.

19. Davis, 49. "Muslims constitute a minority of about 12 percent of the Indian population, and for the most part form a poor, dispersed, politically insignificant, and unthreatening religious minority. What could cause such a hysterical reaction toward these people?" (49–51).

20. Davis, 49–51.

21. Davis, 47.

22. See Punwani, "Mumbai's Muslims and 'Friends,'" 16. This shift toward back-channel "broker" politics, Engineer writes, took place in conjunction with a sharp decline in Muslim support for the Congress Party, whose discredited local leadership had stood by as "helpless spectators" during the riots and the post-blast arrests. Support for the Congress Party had already been on the decline over the previous decade among Mumbai Muslims, who had grown impatient with its "soft Hindutva" stance especially on the Ramjanmabhoomi-Babri Masjid issue. See Engineer, "Politics of Muslim Vote Bank," 199.

23. I met Junaid for the first time during the run-up to the 2017 polls—but not through Sayeed. Rather, I was introduced to Junaid by a university colleague who knew him through literary circles. Bombay is in many ways a very small city.

24. Sayeed explained that he had never sought the limelight himself and that it was with some hesitation that he had decided to accept a party ticket for his first election, in 2012.

2. Natak

1. At that time, around $5 billion US.

2. Platts translates the Arabic word matlab (مطلب) as "question, demand, request, petition; proposition; wish, desire; object, intention, aim, purpose, pursuit, motive." Platts, *Dictionary,* 1044.

3. See epigraph for Platts's translation of natak.

4. The existence of a proscenium stage (the audience-facing, invisible "fourth wall" separating the audience from the action) to visually and architecturally frame the onstage drama is perhaps the most obvious contemporary architectural convention signaling that something is a performance, but as the rally-show indicates, it is neither necessary nor sufficient. While this chapter shows that

natak can be clearly signaled without a stage, the following chapter, on political oratory, features stages that don't signal theater.

5. I discuss janata (also transliterated as janta) later in this chapter.

6. For an account of the myriad meanings of love in a South Asian context, see Orsini, *Love in South Asia.*

7. Habermas, *The Theory of Communicative Action,* 44.

8. Habermas, "Popular Sovereignty as Procedure," 484. In this context, the Habermasian story goes, the procedures of representative democracy "should produce rational outcomes insofar as opinion-formation inside parliamentary bodies remains sensitive to the results of surrounding informal opinion-formation in autonomous public spheres" (488).

9. Anderson, *Imagined Communities.*

10. Here, "discourse" refers not merely to spoken or written words but rather to all of the material stuff—the media—that comes to count as a sign in any communicative encounter or event. See Gal and Irvine, *Signs of Difference;* see also Wortham and Reyes, *Discourse Analysis.*

11. Warner, "Publics and Counterpublics," 90.

12. Gal, "Contradictions of Standard Language," 173.

13. See, e.g., Fraser, "Rethinking the Public Sphere"; Hirschkind, *The Ethical Soundscape.*

14. Ajun Appadurai and Carol Breckenridge propose the term "public culture" as that "space between domestic life and the projects of the nation state—where different social groups . . . constitute their identities by their experience of mass-mediated forms in relation to the practices of everyday life." And yet where they characterize "public culture" as a "zone of contestation," Christopher Pinney draws on Mbembe's reflections on "The Banality of Power and the Aesthetics of Vulgarity in the Postcolony" to note that this same space is "a zone where consumers appear to share in a common language of cultural agency, a zone in which as Achille Mbembe has observed, diverse positions are inscribed in 'the same epistemological space.'" The Mumbai public—which is a noun rather than an adjective—lends support to this Pinney's notion of a "common language" and "epistemological space." Appadurai and Breckenridge, "Public Modernity in India," 4–5; Pinney, "Introduction," 14.

15. Here we can take a cue from William Mazzarella's (re)formulation of "affect" which pushes past the persistent mind-body dualisms inherent in "strong" versions of neo-Spinozian affect theory posited by scholars such as Brian Massumi and Gilles Deleuze. Mazzarella demonstrates instead how "affect points us toward a terrain that is presubjective without being presocial. As such it implies a way of apprehending social life that does not start with the bounded, intentional subject while at the same time foregrounding embodiment and sensuous life." Mazzarella, "Affect."

16. The term *heteroglossia*, coined by M. M. Bakhtin in *The Dialogic Imagination,* refers to "the simultaneous use of different kinds of speech or other signs,

the tension between them, and their conflicting relationship within one text." See Ivanov, "Heteroglossia," 100.

17. Anthropologist Ursula Rao demonstrates the interconnections among these multiple valences of public, showing ethnographically that the print-mediated public is also a materialized entity—a concrete collectivity that is actualized through material-practical engagements with print media. Rao, *News as Culture.*

18. Warner, "Publics and Counterpublics"

19. Here I follow Mazzarella in his injunction to an "analytic of encounter"—where "encounter" is understood as a "resonant occasion and trigger for everything social theory understands as 'identity,' 'culture,' 'desire,' and so on; encounter as a moment of mimetic yielding that at the same time actualizes the intelligible differences that people then proceed to inhabit as 'me' and 'you,' 'ours' and 'theirs.'" Mazzarella, *The Mana of Mass Society,* 6.

20. Pernau and Rajamani, "Emotional Translations," 54.

21. Jaffe, "Indexicality, Stance, and Fields." Drawing on the Peircean distinction between "indexical" and "iconic" signs, Alexandra Jaffe describes how through the process of "iconization," historical and social relationships can become naturalized, such that the actual associations are formalized as "styles" or "registers."

22. Gal and Irvine, *Signs of Difference,* 88.

23. Mazzarella characterizes this sort of remembered sensory experience as an embodied "archive": "the residue embedded not only in the explicitly articulated forms (linguistic categories) commonly recognized as cultural discourses, but also in built environments and material forms, in the concrete history of the senses, and in the habits of our shared embodiment." Mazzarella, *The Mana of Mass Society,* 8.

24. By contrast, in his account of the Rath Yatra that preceded the demolition of the Babri Masjid in Ayodhya, Richard Davis shows how the orchestrators "sought to deny the religious lineage" of the procession's iconography, even while acknowledging and encouraging "the devotional character of the response to the procession." The imagery of the Rath Yatra was "more performative than representational," Davis argues, seeking, through the mobilization of mass affect (the procession was strategically routed through "centers of Sangh strength"), to "displace ruling authority symbolically away from elected officials onto the leaders of the yatra." Davis, "The Iconography of Rama's Chariot," 46.

25. Moores, *Interpreting Audiences.*

26. Goffman writes that "definitions of a situation are built up in accordance with principles of organization which govern events—at least social ones—and our subjective involvement in them; frame is the word I use to refer to such of these basic elements as I am able to identify. That is my definition of frame." Goffman, *Frame Analysis,* 10–11.

27. Hansen, "The Indar Sabha Phenomenon," 109n32; here Hansen is quoting Vasudevan's "The Melodramatic Mode."

28. For a discussion, see Ulka Anjaria, *Understanding Bollywood.*

29. T. B. Hansen and Verkaaik, "Introduction."

30. The word taaqat is derived from the Arabic ṭauq (طوق), meaning "to be able to do, or to bear." Taaqat (طاقت) translates as "Ability to accomplish, capability; ability, power, energy, force, strength; ability to endure, power of endurance, endurance, patience." Platts, *Dictionary,* 450–54.

31. Fareed speaks in Urdu-inflected Hindi (aka Hindustani) but uses the English terms *awareness* and *civic issues.*

32. Rekhta.org translates dikhavat as "exhibition, display, pomp, ostentation, show-off."

33. Tarini Bedi's account of "dashing as performance" shows how Shiv Sena provides a platform upon which people can perform their talents, leadership, organizational skills, and personality characteristics ("dashing and daring"). She demonstrates how Shiv Sena provides an opportunity for self-fashioning, social aspiration, and mobility that is unmatched by other parties (regional or national). This theatrical idiom of political communication—natak in the unmarked sense—is the hallmark of Shiv Sena's political style. Bedi, *Dashing Ladies,* 40.

34. Fareed spoke in Hindi, but the terms in italics were spoken in English.

35. See Chowdhury's *Paradoxes of the Popular* for a discussion of the meaning of janata in the context of "popular politics" in Bangladesh.

36. Janta chimb bhijli, Dillli maatr thijli.

37. In contemporary Bombay the words dalal and dalali are generally used disparagingly to mean "pimp" (and the act of pimping), either literally or figuratively. In Chowdhury's work on Bangladesh, dalal has the disparaging meaning of "collaborator"—that is, someone who collaborated with India against the national liberation of Bangladesh in 1971. Chowdhury, *Paradoxes of the Popular;* for in-depth discussion, see Björkman, "Introduction," 26–28.

38. Established in 1995 by the newly elected Shiv Sena government, the SRA is a planning authority under Maharashtra's Department of Housing. Its mandate is to serve as planning authority for "slum areas" within the jurisdictional boundaries of the BMC. In 2014 the jurisdictional boundaries of the SRA were expanded to include areas within the Mumbai-adjacent Thane Municipal Corporation.

39. For a brilliant digital exhibition of Kamathipura and its redevelopment travails curated by a Bombay-based research team at the Tata Institute of Social Sciences, see the MakeBreak website, https://makebreak.tiss.edu/kamathipura.

40. Maharashtra Housing and Area Development Act, 1976 (MHADA) outlines provisions for reconstruction and repairs of buildings that pay a "cess tax" ("cessed building" tax). In short, in contemporary Bombay, "cessed building" is development-speak for a crumbling tenement building located in the Island City of South Bombay (generally but not exclusively pre-Independence buildings, although MHADA includes provisions for buildings constructed as recently as 1959) whose owners pay this cess tax (or at least are supposed to be paying this

tax) and are therefore potentially available to be brought under a market-driven cluster redevelopment scheme.

41. Schechner, *Performance Studies*, 12.

42. Goffman defines "demeanor" as "that element of the individual's ceremonial behavior typically conveyed through deportment, dress, and bearing, which serves to express to those in his immediate presences that he is a person of certain desirable or undesirable qualities." Goffman "The Nature of Deference and Demeanor," 489. Here I follow Asif Agha's use of "register" to refer to "cultural models of speech that link speech repertoires to typifications of actor, relationship, and conduct." Agha "Registers of Language," 23.

43. In the words of Abhijit Avasthi, a group creative director for the advertising agency Ogilvy & Mather: "Pappu is an underdog, a lovable character who is not smart enough. In fact, all of us have met some or the other Pappus at some point in our life." Avasthi is credited with introducing "Pappu" to the advertisement world. Rajiv Singh, "'Pappu' Connects with Consumers."

44. Platts provides a number of definitions. He defines maḥall (محل) as "place (in general; but orig. 'place of alighting, or of abiding'), position, situation; abode, residence, house, building, mansion, palace; hall, or chamber (of a grandee's residence)." He translates maḥalla (محله) as a "district, division, quarter (of a city or town), ward, parish;—a camp." And he defines ahālī as "people (of a house, village, etc.), denizens, inhabitants; persons, individuals, members; dependents, followers," and ahālī-mawālī, ahālī o mawālī as "people at large, poor and rich; courtiers; retainers, train, retinue, followers, dependents." Platts, *Dictionary*, 1010. Timothy Cooper characterizes mohalla as "what is around or about." See Cooper, "'Live Has an Atmosphere,'" 655. In an ethnographic account of mahol's Mumbai meanings, Sumanya Velamur writes that "māhaul is a concept that includes within its ambit a spatial culture, physical surroundings, and a spatial habitus." Velamur, "Religion-Marked Spaces," 165.

45. Cooper, "'Live Has an Atmosphere,'" 652.

46. Böhme, *The Aesthetics of Atmospheres*, 1.

47. Eisenlohr, "Latency."

48. As Böhme points out in *The Aesthetics of Atmospheres*, however, "atmosphere" can be deliberately created.

49. To a certain extent, the work of "mains" in Mumbai electoral campaigns recalls Sara Dickey's account of the role of film-star fan-club leaders in political campaigns in the South Indian city of Madurai. And yet there is a crucial difference: where Dickey's club leaders seek to produce and develop their own "personal political power" by means of a "politics of adulation" that bolsters the reputations of their chosen stars ("the initial goal is primarily to promote not oneself but the image of the hero"), in Mumbai the reputational flow works in both directions, with the reputation and image of the abhi/neta produced by means of performed association with area mains. See Dickey, "The Politics of Adulation," 361–62.

50. "Despite Note Ban, Cash Is King."

51. Simon Chauchard, WhatsApp correspondence with the author, February 2017.

52. See the introduction for a discussion of "ostentatious display."

53. Bedi, *Mumbai Taximen.*

54. The rally-show recalls Shuddhabrata Sengupta's description of wedding processions in status-conscious New Delhi, where the procession through public streets is captured on video, whereby the procession-as-image not only "sends out a series of messages to the world" regarding a family's social status but also produces the social importance of those participating in the festivities: "People can display themselves and be seen for the display that they offer." Sengupta, "Vision Mixing," 296.

55. This discussion of relations on display recalls Mattison Mines's discussion of temple processions in Tamil Nadu, in his book *Public Faces, Private Voices.* With a "big man's" trustworthiness bound up with the reputations of those comprising his associational networks (Mines, 39), these relations are periodically put on display through such public performances and ritual processions: spectacular events whose organizers go to great lengths to assemble eminent personalities representing a "galaxy of institutions" (68) to be displayed along strategically chosen procession routes where "sponsors have clientele . . . among whom the leaders wish to publicize who they are" (67), and before crowds of onlookers who turn up precisely to watch who has turned up to display themselves alongside whom. A key difference between Mines's account of such dynamics of display in 1980s Madras and this account of contemporary Mumbai inheres in the source of reputational authority. In Mines's account—even while he points out that inherited forms of "social capital" do not automatically translate into reputation, and that "even hereditary leaders have few followers when they lack charisma and skill" (57)—reputation appears to be an affordance of inherited caste and class position. In Mumbai, on the other hand, what Bedi calls "jaalu" in *Mumbai Taximen* is comprised by more horizontal and unpredictable forms of social value and urban expertise. For discussion of "publicity brokers" in Mumbai, see also Björkman, "Introduction"; and Björkman and Collins, "Publics."

56. This anticipates the discussion in chapter 4, where the ruling party's rallies were disparaged as "only natak" because the flag-bearers were bused in from outside Bombay. Which is to say, the problem with theatrical crowd inheres not in the fact of its being cash-mediated but rather in its being nonlocal while professing to be otherwise.

57. See Bedi, *Mumbai Taximen,* on the meaning of "choke" in Bombay parlance.

58. Waghorne, *The Raja's Magic Clothes,* 166.

59. Waghorne, 166. "The combination of garlands and dancing girls properly belong[s] only in the retinue of a royal personage, in a wedding procession, or in the house of a God" (Waghorne, 46).

60. R. Kaur, *Performative Politics,* 75. Ganapati—literally, "father/leader of the people (gana)"—is a commonly used name in Mumbai for the elephant-headed Hindu deity Ganesh. Kaur demonstrates how, in the context of colonial prohibitions on political assembly, the religious festival of Ganapati Utsava was a forum for articulation of social critiques (including critiques of colonial rule).

61. Kaur, xv. Kaur further describes how "colonial prohibitions on political gatherings was circumvented with the use of a religious festival to publicly disseminate views against the ills of society, including the excesses of colonial governance. Such events signaled the rise of an indigenous populace conscious of its force as a 'people' with particular rights and claims to democratic participation" (3).

62. Recent years have seen a rising concern in both popular and scholarly writings in India about the "danger" posed by a "culture of political veneration" whereby political leaders are "treated like Hindu deities"—a phenomenon that Sen and Nielsen characterize as "political deification." Outlook, "Danger of Deification," cited in Sen and Nielsen, "Gods in the Public Sphere." While flower garlanding has obvious origins in Hindu religious and ritual practice, the ubiquity of flower garlanding as part of political processions in Muslim-majority localities in Mumbai calls into question any clear "political deification" formulation that would read the transposing of religious iconography onto political ritual as "the inseparability of aspects of religious and political life." See Sen, "Between Religion and Politics," 631. The festooning by pious Muslims of political leaders (of any religious persuasion) is a common and religiously unproblematic practice in Mumbai (and in India more generally) destabilizing a facile reading of religiosity into such practices and gesturing instead to the ritual, theatrical, and festive dimensions of political life. In contemporary Pakistan, by contrast, where the semiotic dominance of Hindu festival life is less pronounced, flower garlanding appears less common (although anthropologist Timothy Cooper suggested in a personal conversation that the festooning of political leaders in Pakistan is probably still done in "rural areas of Punjab and Sindh where the residual influence of Hinduism is still strong").

63. Mazzarella, *The Mana of Mass Society,* 119. Mazzarella draws on Žižek in this formulation.

64. Mazzarella, 5.

65. Thanks to William Mazzarella for pointing this out.

66. As James Ferguson point out, "sociality (and especially the sociality of ritual solidarity) is not fundamentally a matter of transmitting information, but of sharing a distinctive kind of experience." Ferguson, *Presence and Social Obligation,* ii.

67. Quoted in Rizzo, "President Trump's Crowd-Size Estimates."

68. Rizzo.

69. Rizzo writes in the *Washington Post:* "It's a bit absurd to imagine 30,000 people or so squinting at a Jumbotron while the president addressed a much smaller crowd of 5,000 to 6,000 inside the venue."

70. William Mazzarella, personal correspondence with the author.

71. Critical theory—borrowing the concept of "critique" both from a Kantian conception of criticism as probing the limits of knowledge as well as from Marx's effort in *Capital* to provide a "critique of political economy" that reveals the knowledge structures underpinning and perpetuating relations of capitalism—entails the effort to use reason to interrogate seemingly natural forms of knowledge. By revealing how oppressive social relations are disguised by the naturalization of historically specific ideas or concepts (like reason itself), early critical theory was conceived as a project that aspired toward social transformation and emancipation from structures of domination. See, e.g., Horkheimer, "Traditional and Critical Theory." In Adorno and Horkheimer's later joint work, *Dialectic of Enlightenment,* however, what was earlier conceptualized as a self-reflexive attempt to use reason to probe the limits of knowledge is radicalized as a critique of reason as a totalizing force.

72. Bedi describes a similar situation wherein Mumbai Shiv Sena party workers would "invok[e] the performative act of 'giving' *darshan* [visibility or appearance]" to party leader Bal Thackeray: "[M]ost Shiv Sena women were not as interested in 'taking' his blessings in the form of darshan as they were in making themselves known to him, thereby allowing *darshan* to become a relationship that creates visibility not for the deity, but for the devotee." Bedi, *Dashing Ladies,* 50.

73. This recalls Mines's discussion in *Public Faces, Private Voices* of the role of public procession in the production of public authority among "institutional big men."

74. Thanks to Lisa Mitchell for helping me think through this point.

75. Schechner, *Performance Studies,* 42.

76. Rotman, "Baba's Got a Brand New Bag," 39.

3. Believe

1. See chapter 1 for an account of Seema's 2012 bid for municipal office in Daulat Nagar.

2. See chapter 1 for elaboration of the term prachaar.

3. As Richard Bauman and Charles Briggs explain, "Locke's theory of language . . . stands as a cornerstone of 'scientific' conceptions of language that rest upon the conventionality of the linguistic sign, the cognitivist linking of the linguistic sign to ideas, the privileging of the referential and propositional functions of language in the service of rational, philosophically rigorous thought and expression as against everyday 'civil' discourse, and the suppression of indexicality (including prominently intertextuality) as inimical to pure reference." Bauman and Briggs, *Voices of Modernity,* 190.

4. As Goffman points out, conversation is "not the only context of talk." Drawing attention to speech that "comes from a podium" ("political addresses, stand-up comedy routines, lectures, dramatic recitations and poetry readings"), Goffman

calls attention to episodes of talk in which "hearers" are not "a set of fellow conversationalists" but rather an audience. In this context, the role of the audience "is to appreciate remarks made, not to reply in any direct way." Goffman, "Footing," 12.

5. Irvine, "Shadow Conversations," 131. The problems with the model are multiple: what counts a communicative act (or "utterance")? What's the relationship between some specified snippet of speech and the broader "discourse" of which some utterance comprises a part? What role is played by the broader social and material context within which some "speech event" occurs?

6. Keane "Voice," 271.

7. An entity or person that "physically transmits" words is the animator of words; the author of an utterance is whoever has "selected the sentiments that are being expressed and the words in which they are encoded"; and the principal is "the person whose beliefs have been told, who is committed to what the words say." Goffman "Footing," 144.

8. Asif Agha cites Irvine's 1990 chapter on "Registering Affect" to define speech registers as the "voices a speaker takes on in different social situations." Registers are made up of both linguistic and nonlinguistic signs, which come to be associated (through a process Agha calls "enregisterment") with a stereotyped "population of users." Agha, "Voice, Footing, Enregisterment."

9. Bakhtin, *The Dialogic Imagination.*

10. Goffman "Footing," 144.

11. Goffman, 136.

12. Peirce wrote to Philip E. B. Jourdain in 1908 that it is "anything which is on the one hand so determined (or specialized) by an object and on the other hand so determines the mind of an interpreter of it that the latter is thereby determined mediately, or indirectly, by that real object that determines the sign." Quoted in Fisch, *Peirce, Semeiotic, and Pragmatism*, 342.

13. Agha, "Voice, Footing, Enregisterment," 76. People can often recognize many more semiotic registers than they themselves are capable of speaking, Agha points out, and the "range of registers" that one speaks enables access to a range of social situations, with some registers being more highly socially esteemed than others. Agha, *Language and Social Relations*, 167.

14. Irvine, "Shadow Conversations," 131.

15. See Björkman, "The Ostentatious Crowd," for an ethnographic account of a theatrical rally that was widely described as having been "hijacked."

16. Irvine, "Shadow Conversations," 140.

17. Irvine, "Shadow Conversations," 141.

18. What Goffman calls the "participation framework." Goffman, "Footing," 11.

19. Irvine, "Shadow Conversations," 141.

20. The expression is developed in Caroline Jones's article "The Mediated Sensorium" and cited in sensory anthropologist David Howes's review on "Multisensory Anthropology." In that article, as in most of his work, Howes has made

a case (theoretically and ethnographically) for approaching "the senses" not as distinct from one another but rather for exploring the "variable boundaries, differential elaboration, and many different ways of combining the senses across (and within) cultures" (20).

21. The 1983 Hindi cult classic *Jaane Bhi do Yaaro* (Just let it go, friends), uses the trope of "gutters" to highly comedic effect during the funeral elegy for a recently bumped-off municipal commissioner who has—just a few frames earlier—been shown accepting large sums of money from a shady builder in exchange for official permissions to overbuild shoddily constructed buildings. Speaking from atop a just-inaugurated new bridge (whose sand-heavy composition will soon result in its spectacular collapse), the new commissioner gets choked up while recalling his dead predecessor: "Mr. De'Mello used to say: the progress of a nation, if it can be recognized by anything, it is by this: gutter [Desh ki unnati ki pehchaan, agar kisi cheez se hoti hai; toh woh hai gutter]. He lived for gutter [chokes back a sob] . . . and he died for gutter. And while he was dying [breaks into sobs], his last word was: 'gutter' [applause]."

22. I met Sayeed while conducting research in Gowandi for my book *Pipe Politics*.

23. A kurta-pajama is traditional South Asian men's attire consisting of two pieces: a kurta and pajama. A kurta is a long, loose-fitting tunic that typically falls to the mid-thigh; the pajama is a pair of loose-fitting trousers that tapers at the ankle. Like the jacket and trousers of a Western pantsuit, the pieces can be worn separately, but like the pantsuit, the kurta-pajama is intended to be worn as an outfit.

24. A hijab is a head covering; a niqab is a face covering.

25. For a history of the Bombay Improvement Trust see Kidambi, "Housing the Poor."

26. The Suriya Namaskar, or yogic Sun Salutation, had been proposed as a required daily practice for all children in municipal schools. Mumbai's Muslim clergy and political leadership vehemently opposed the initiative as heretical.

27. For a discussion of "personhood" see Agha, "Voice, Footing, Enregisterment."

28. This Urdu-mediated encounter about Urdu-medium taleem recalls Bakhtin's notion of "multivocality," which point to aspects of discourse that are not attributed solely to the individual speaker but rather point to the existence of another party—a "relevant other," in Irvine's terms—whose "utterances are invoked by the one at hand because they are partly imitated, quoted or argued against." As Irvine points out, any episode of talk "has implicit links to many dialogues, not only the present one, which together inform its significance, influence its form, and contribute to its performative force." Irvine, "Shadow Conversations," 140.

29. For a discussion of the relations between Hindi, Urdu, and Hindustani see Kachru, "Hindi–Urdu–Hindustani."

30. Sarvi is introduced in Interlude II.

31. Thanks to Lisa Mitchell for this phrasing.

32. Bohras are known for their high level of education, which in Mumbai is equated with literacy in English.

33. As Agha writes, "The term voice is based on a corporeal metaphor of phonation—the friction of air over vocal chords—even though the phenomenon it names is not restricted to, and hence has no necessary connection to, oral speech" (39).

34. Five years later the toilets remain unconstructed; apparently the shop owners hadn't been so bothered by the smell after all.

35. See Mazzarella, *The Mana of Mass Society,* for a discussion of "resonant encounter" as a "moment of mimetic yielding that activates differences that people then inhabit" (289). The skills in "activating resonance" that the campaign team displays recalls Mazzarella's discussion of what Marcel Mauss calls "the collective forces of society" that "activate attention and harness commitment." Mauss quoted in Mazzarella, 16.

36. Muslim women rarely wear saris in Mumbai.

37. As mentioned earlier, Asmi's name is unchanged, since his position renders him easily identifiable.

38. See Interlude II.

39. Jazbaat is the plural form of the Persian word jazba (جذبه), which is defined in Platts as "Passion, rage, fury; violent desire." Platts, *Dictionary,* 378.

40. Since Jains are vegetarians, there had been a proposal to close the slaughterhouse in order not to offend their sentiments.

41. The Indian National Congress Party.

42. Bakra Eid, also known as Eid al-Adha (the Festival of Sacrifice), is one of the most important Islamic festivals celebrated by Muslims worldwide. The word bakra refers to the goats that are ritually slaughtered in conjunction with the festivities.

43. Pemmaraju, "Dalvi," 286.

44. Bate, *Tamil Oratory,* 79–80.

45. Bate, 80.

46. See chapter 2 for a discussion of mahol.

47. Bate, *Tamil Oratory,* 80.

48. "Mumbai Civic Polls."

49. Nastaliq is the script common to Persian and Urdu.

50. See Björkman, "The Engineer and the Plumber" and *Pipe Politics.*

51. Gershon, "Media Ideologies."

52. "Placing post-1980s media technologies on a continuum with these older forms of the bazaar," Jain writes, "makes the changes wrought by liberalization appear more as an intensification and layered expansion than a fundamental transformation." Jain, *Gods in the Time of Democracy,* 23.

53. "Kuch log yeh dabba ley kar ghum rahe hain, ye log samajte hai key Badlapur in ki milkiyat [propriety/property] hai, ye yahan ke zameendar hain. Jis din Sayeed Rizwan apni pe aa gaya to [restaurant] par la kar itna marunga na."

54. Hasan's account of "propaganda" recalls Sayeed's disdainful dismissal of jazbaati politics.

55. In Mazzarella's terms, this means "activat[ing] attention and harness[ing] commitment" (*The Mana of Mass Society*, 138). For a rich account of the "cyber volunteers" comprising the BJP's social media "digital army," see Chaturvedi, *I Am a Troll*. Chaturvedi's account reveals the fraught role of money inside this work: while her interlocutors adamantly deny they are paid for their digital labor ("we are true bhakts [devotees], and do the work for our ideology"), the accounts are littered with suggestive and oblique references to questions of employment: "But how does he manage to make a living? He looks around, lowers his voice and says, 'See, I am committed. . . . But others I have heard are looking for payments per tweet and even forming companies to get digital and social media campaigns of ministries'" (Chaturvedi, 84). For an account of the BJP's pioneering use of social media campaigns intentionally professing to be "nonpolitical," see Jaffrelot and Verniers, "The BJP's 2019 Election Campaign."

56. Hasan's words recall the previous chapter's discussion of natak in the deceptive sense.

57. K. Kaur, "Review of the Fake News Ecosystem," 23.

58. Saldanha, Rajput, and Hazare, "Child-Lifting Rumours."

59. Stiegler "Telecracy against Democracy," 172; emphasis in original.

60. Cody, "Metamorphoses of Popular Sovereignty," 62.

61. Jain, *Gods in the Time of Democracy*, 16. "Little withers in the age of mass reproduction," Jain astutely notes; "There's just more of everything" (178).

Interlude III

1. The new law pertains to Christian, Buddhist, Hindu, Sikh, and Parsi refugees from Pakistan, Bangladesh, and Afghanistan.

2. According to the "Citizenship (Registration of Citizens and issue of National Identity Cards) Rules, 2003," published in the *Gazette of India* on December 10, 2003, a "usual resident" is someone who has resided in a locality for at least six months and who plans to remain for another six months.

3. India's first NPR was created in 2010 and was updated in 2015 in conjunction with the rolling out of a national drive to issue biometric identity cards (the Aadhaar program). For discussion, see Rao and Nair, "Aadhaar."

4. The literature on India's patchy documentary regimes is vast. See, e.g., Akhil Gupta, *Red Tape;* Mathur, *Paper Tiger;* Björkman, *Waiting Town.*

5. This is especially prominent among Muslim speakers of Urdu, which is written in the Nastaliq (Persian) script. While the use of Nastaliq was, until very

recently, common across North India, the association of Urdu with Pakistan has led to widespread Urdu illiteracy among non-Muslims.

6. Pandit, "Muslim Population in 2023."

7. Articles 12 to 35 in Part III of the Constitution of India deal with Fundamental Rights.

4. Kaaghaz

1. S. Gupta, Khan, and Khan, "Protests Spread across India."

2. Quoted in Dutta, "Face of the Jamia Protests."

3. Agrawal, "Shaheen Bagh."

4. Vats, "Liberation Square."

5. Quoted in Vats. One lakh = 100,000.

6. Vats.

7. Vats.

8. "Do or die," Gandhi announced to a crowd of unprecedented scale (estimated between 40,000 and 100,000) assembled for the oration. Demanding British withdrawal, Gandhi announced that "We shall either free India or die in the attempt." See Gandhi, "The 'Quit India' Speech." For location, see South Bombay map in Interlude II.

9. Strassler, *Demanding Images*, 243. Considering the "eventfulness" of images, Strassler suggests, means attending to how "specific images police and disrupt the public 'space of appearance'" (243). She borrows the phrase "space of appearance" from Arendt, who characterizes the "public realm" as a space where (as Strassler puts it) "people are, ideally, enabled to see and be seen, recognizing each other's perspectives on matters of common concern" (16). Her formulation also draws on Rancière's argument in *The Emancipated Spectator* that an image "is always an alteration that occurs in a chain of images which alter it in turn" (quoted in Strassler, 250).

10. Strassler, 137–38.

11. Mazzarella, "Political Incarnation as Living Archive," 5.

12. Preety's surname identifies her as belonging to a relatively elite "Baniya" caste background—known as a community of businesspeople, merchants, and traders.

13. Platts translates the Persian word awaaz (آواز) as "Sound, noise; voice; tone; whisper; echo; shout, call, cry; report, sentence." Platts, *Dictionary*, 101.

14. Kunreuther, *Voicing Subjects*, 2.

15. Kunreuther, 3.

16. Strassler, *Demanding Images*, 137.

17. This poster was clearly produced by someone affiliated with Communist Party of India (Marxist), which, due to its small size, tends to be characterized in Mumbai more as a social organization than as a political party. For a discussion of the role of Mumbai's political parties in relation to the protests, see the next chapter.

18. Afzal had been found guilty of involvement with a 2001 attack on the Indian Parliament.

19. Part of the speech is accessible and commented on the YouTube page of the *Hindustan Times*. See "Kanhaiya Kumar Speech at JNU."

20. Dutt, "'Hum Kya Chahte? Azaadi!'"

21. "Aa nahi ban'na mujhe Slumdog Millionaire; yeh slumdog hai mission pe"; "I'm not doing this to get rich [to become a 'Slumdog Millionaire']; this slumdog has a different mission."

22. Manuvaad (caste discrimination) and brahmanvaad (rule by dominant castes) were replaced by bhed bhaav—which translates roughly as "discrimination" without specifying the basis.

23. "There's No Mainstream Voice."

24. See chapter 2 for a discussion of mahol.

25. Bonilla and Rosa, "#Ferguson," 5.

26. Papailias, "Witnessing."

27. Taqiya is a type of cap worn by many Muslim men.

28. "ta'dād, s.f. Numbering; enumeration, computation, number; amount, sum; measure, extent, length." Platts, *Dictionary*, 326.

29. The ubiquity of Urdu poetry in the anti-CAA movement was perhaps most famously noted with regard to Pakistani poet Faiz Ahmad Faiz's Urdu nazm (versed poem) "Hum Dekhenge" ("We Shall See"), which was originally penned in 1979, in protest to Zia Ul Haq's regime, before being widely embraced as an anti-CAA anthem; see "Who's Afraid of a Song?"

30. D. Banerjee and Copeman, "Hindutva's Blood," 1.

31. Banerjee and Copeman, 24. Banerjee and Copeman further explain how, in the writings of Hindutva's founding father, Vinayak Damodar Savarkar, "blood operates . . . as evidence of an original Hindu-Muslim consanguinity, at the same time as it portends violence and death if Muslims do not give themselves over for incorporation into a Hindu body politic" (4).

32. "I don't remember the exact year or the context in which it was written," Indori told *Indian Express* reporter Sana Fazili in 2019, who had asked for his thoughts on why the couplet had found such contemporary resonance among anti-CAA protesters; "I have recited this ghazal at many mushaiaras [symposia] and had even forgotten about it, but I don't know what's happened in the last three to four years that like a crop rises again, these words have risen again." Fazili, "'Kisi Ke Baap Ka Hindustan Thodi Hai.'"

33. For a discussion of "Hindustan" in the context of CAA protests, see Taneja, "'Hindustan Is a Dream.'"

34. کتنے ہی خوش نما انہیں یارو بنائی
تتلی کبھی نہ بیٹھے گی کاغذ کے پھول پ

35. Translations are by the unpoetic author. This couplet is by the nineteenth-century Lucknow poet Manzoor Ali Aaqib, "Hansti hai kaenat bhi insan ki bhul par."

36. خط پہ خط لکھیے گا اے شاہ سوار
گھوڑی کاغذ کی بھی دوڑائیے گا

37. In other words: "I know you're busy and all, but send some letters [paper horses] my way, would you?" From "Sar miraa kaat ke pachhtaaiyegaa" by Khwaja Mohammad Wazir.

38. ہائے لایا نہ کوئی قاصد دلبر کاغذ
ہو گیا غم سے ہمارا تن لاغر کاغذ

39. Couplet from classical Lucknow poet (and contemporary of Mirza Ghalib) Imam Bakhsh Nasikh, "Hae laya na koi qasid-e-dilbar kaaghaz."

40. Mathur, *Paper Tiger,* 131,

41. Orwell quoted in Mathur, 131.

42. Mathur, 130–31.

43. Harriss and Jeffrey, "Depoliticizing Injustice," 508. Harriss and Jeffrey's gloves-off critique is responding to Akhil Gupta's portrayal in *Red Tape* of the structural violence wrought by everyday bureaucratic action in India government offices as authorless.

44. My own writings on Mumbai's popular neighborhoods describe how even when people furiously recount histories of (say) taps drying up at the hands of documentary regimes, those critiques are directed not at documents themselves—and only rarely toward the institutions and offices by means of whose procedures these personal histories of loss might have transpired—but rather toward particular people (social workers, government officers, elected politicians) who had turned out to be either incompetent or duplicitous in putting papers to work. See Björkman, "The Engineer and the Plumber" and *Pipe Politics,* for accounts of creativity and agility in the official use of paper documents to facilitate rather than occlude water distribution.

45. For an extended ethnographic explication of this point—i.e., that the power of papers is processual rather than intrinsic to the document—see Björkman, *Waiting Town.*

46. Ravi Shankar Prasad is quoted in "No Question of Linking CAA to NRC."

47. For instance, "Brown parents explaining to their kids that, in an arranged marriage, the wedding happens first and then the love happens afterwards, on its own." Ritu Singh, "Amit Shah's Epic."

48. Gajara, "Bombay HC Lawyers."

49. "Kaaghaz Nahi Dikhayenge" is a reference to Varun Grover's poem "Hum Kaaghaz Nahi Dikhayenge," discussed earlier.

50. Harikrishnan, "Anti-CAA Protests." That same week, the Maharashtra government issued a circular making it compulsory for primary school children to recite the Preamble in school beginning January 26, 2020. The circular sought to implement a General Rule (GR), passed by the Maharashtra Legislative Assembly seven years earlier, by a Congress-controlled government, but never implemented; the enforcement of the 2013 GR in the midst of the anti-CAA protests

sought to emphasize what Congress leaders insisted was the unconstitutionality of the CAA. See "Maharashtra: Reciting Preamble Mandatory in Schools."

51. As noted in the epigraph to this chapter, the Persian term kaaghaz is derived from kaagh (sound or noise) and da (giving forth): the giving forth of sound.

52. While Mumbaikars busied themselves making paper placards and reading aloud from paper printouts of the Preamble, the fraught relationship between the identity documents and the Constitution played out in a Bombay courtroom, making headlines when a local magistrate acquitted a Bengali-speaking Muslim couple falsely accused of "living illegally in India" by citing the couple's election card as "proof of citizenship." "Even the election card can be said to be sufficient proof of citizenship as while applying for the election card or a voting card, a person has to file a declaration with the authority in view of Form 6 of Peoples Representation Act to the authority that he is a citizen of India and if the declaration is found false, he is liable for punishment." The magistrate concluded—echoing Preety's sentiments—that while "a person may lie, the documents will never." And yet while documents may or may not "lie," there is certainly plenty of disagreement about how to "read" the "paper truths" that they speak. See Samervel, "Election Card Is Proof."

53. This interview was given to APB News and first uploaded on October 4, 2019. Details can be found in Venkataramakrishnan, "Who Is linking Citizenship Act to NRC?"

54. As Ashok Bharti, chairman of the National Confederation of Dalit Organisations, remarked: "When the government of India did not give any citizenship documents to Indians ever, how can they ask for it?" Quoted in "Newly-Convened Alliance Underscores Potential Impact."

55. In this context, the home minister's use of the Hindi word dastavez is supremely (if unintentionally) apt: derived from the Persian word dast, which means "hand," dastavez as "document" explicitly references centrality of the human hand in authorizing documents. The final part of Platts's comprehensive unpacking of the term thus equates dastavez with a favor-seeking gift or bribe: "what a man takes with him as a means of promoting his suit; what one gets into his hand and depends on; a signature; a note of hand, bond, deed, title-deed, voucher, certificate, instrument, charter, etc.;—a small present to be given into the hands of a person whose favour is sought" (*Dictionary*, 516).

56. This faith in paper and suspicion of the digital of course flies in the face of commonplace notions proffered by anticorruption champions of "e-governance" that digital technology affords "immediation" and "transparency." For discussion, see Mazzarella, "Internet X-Ray."

57. See chapter 2 for discussion of natak.

58. In counterposing of the theatrical with the real, of course, Rohit rehearses the common contemporary counterposing (discussed in the introduction) of representation with embodiment—of representation with re-presentation.

59. Rohit's train-mediated flash of creative inspiration was of a piece with a recurrent theme of train-mediated encounters that emerged in my conversations with anti-CAA protest participants (recall that I had met Preety on the train). For a historical account of the Indian railways as an infrastructure of political communication and claims-making, see Mitchell, "'To Stop Train Pull Chain.'" The role of the Bombay local train in the city's social life has been the subject of popular and scholarly writings. Annelies Kusters writes about how Deaf Mumbaikars traveling in the less-crowded handicapped compartments enlist the train compartment as "space to communicate." Kusters, "Deaf on the Lifeline of Mumbai." The role of the Bombay Local as not merely a means of transport but as social-communicative (and gustatory) infrastructure rose to silver-screen fame in Ritesh Bhatta's award-winning 2013 film *The Lunchbox*, in which the train-mediated deliveries of homemade food to office working menfolk become an accidental vehicle for the transmission of lunchbox-tucked exchange of handwritten notes between two strangers, who are thereby drawn into an emotionally cathartic (and romance-tinged) correspondence. For an ethnographic account of the role of the Bombay local trains in producing and shoring up food-mediated kinship relations, see also Kuroda, "Shankar."

60. A Pathan suit is a long shirt (kurta) worn with baggy trousers. It is commonly worn by men across the South Asian subcontinent but is often associated with Muslims because of the garment's origins in the Muslim-majority areas in present-day Afghanistan and Pakistan.

5. Politics

1. In the summer of 2011, anticorruption activists launched a national campaign and mass mobilization demanding the creation an independent ombudsman office that would have the power to prosecute government officials accused of corruption. See Nigam, "Staging the 'People,'" for a discussion of the differences between the two mass mobilizations.

2. "We decided to let the leftists and students lead," I was told by one major-party leader who had been instrumental in organizing the gathering. The Azad Maidan event that Preety skipped, by contrast, was devoid of any explicit signs of political party involvement. That event was convened by the Joint Action Committee (JAC) of Maharashtra, a student-led organization that came into being in January 2016 in the wake of the suicide of Rohith Vemula, a Dalit university student whose suicide following months of caste-based harassment was the JAC characterized as "institutional murder."

3. Barnagarwala, "10 Days, 20,000 Participants."

4. We saw this in especially in chapter 3; see Auerbach and Thachill, *Migrants and Machine Politics*, for a discussion of credit claiming in the medium-size North Indian cities of Bhopal and Jaipur.

5. See chapters 2 and 3.

6. On March 14, 2020, the *Business Standard* reported that Devendra Fadnavis had "alleged [that] the Maha Vikas Aghadi government was playing politics on CAA, NPR and NRC" issues. See "Fadnavis Attacks Maha Govt."

7. Name unchanged.

8. Bedi, *Mumbai Taximen,* 59.

9. Here, the appeal further reads: "This is a special day for two reasons: this is the day (in 1927) of martyrdom of Ramprasad Bismil and Ashfakullah Khan; this is also the day (1947) when Mahatma Gandhi visited Ghaseda village in Mewat (now Haryana) to appeal to Meo Muslims not to leave for Pakistan (70,000 Muslims walked back from Pakistan border responding to this call)."

10. One lakh = 100,000.

11. Longtime Mumbai journalist Joyti Punwani describes the pernicious effects this has had on public protest as means of political communication in Mumbai: "Interaction between the protesters and the public was the life blood of the protests. It was essential that Mumbaikars knew why a section of them were so worked up that they were marching down the roads in the blazing sun." Indeed, Punwani recalls one Marathi slogan that stood out, "baghta kai / shaamil wha," meaning "why are you watching? / Join us." The slogan would be directed "at bystanders on the footpaths and people who crowded the windows of the buildings . . . drawn out from the insides of their offices by the din of slogans." This all "died" in 1997, with the creation of the sequestered "designated space" for protest on Azad Maidan. See Punwani, "Remembering City's Exuberant Morchas."

12. The Bombay Aman Committee (discussed in Interlude II) played a key role during the 1992–93 riots and in the Srikrishna Committee report on the riots (discussed below).

13. Punwani's accounts, drawn from her reporting work during and in the aftermath of the riots, appear in a short book, *Justice Denied—Why? The Srikrishna Report and the Maharashtra Government's Responce,* compiled on the request of the Bombay Action Committee and published in 1998; Punwani, "'My Area, Your Area,'" 237. Punwani personally recounted to me having walked in Khan's funeral procession.

14. Aloud, in writing, or electronically, via email or messaging.

15. In India, marriages among Muslims are considered "private" matters, internal to the community, and therefore are not required to be registered with civil authorities (unless the couple decides to do so, under the Special Marriage Act of 1954). See Esposito and DeLong-Bas, *Women in Muslim Family Law.*

16. Suneetha, "The Real Debate."

17. As expected, the Supreme Court ruled that the land on which the Babri Masjid had stood would be handed over to a government trust for the building of a Hindu temple. The court also ordered the government to hand over five acres of land to the Uttar Pradesh Sunni Central Waqf Board to build a mosque, as compensation for the demolished Babri Masjid. See "Ram Mandir-Babri Masjid Case Verdict."

18. The term "Bahujan"—meaning "the many" or "the majority," or sometimes "plebeian"—is used in politics in reference to people belonging to Scheduled Castes (i.e., formerly "untouchable" castes, also known as Dalits), Adivasis (indigenous people, also known in India as Scheduled Tribes), so-called Other Backward Classes (a mix of lower but non-Dalit castes), and (sometimes) lower-caste (Pasmanda) Muslims. For discussion, see Corbridge and Harriss, *Reinventing India,* especially chapter 9.

19. See discussion in chapter 4.

20. CNN reports that the Jamia and AMU protests were of a piece with simultaneous protests that occurred in at least nine Indian states. S. Gupta, Khan, and Khan, "Protests Spread across India."

21. Punwani, "'Thank You, Uddhavji.'" Gowalia Tank was the original (and still in use) name for August Kranti Maidan, which was renamed sometime after Independence in remembrance of the site's significance as the place from which Gandhi launched the "Quit India" movement. The term "Gowalia"—from the Gujarati and Marathi words for "cow" (gao) and "keeper" (wala)—was a reference to the public water tank where cattle owners would come to bathe their cows. While cowsheds were moved out of the downtown area in the 1950s, the term "Gowalia Tank" is still commonly used.

22. Punwani.

23. The police officer quotations are taken from "Mumbai Anti-CAA Protest."

24. The reporter notes that it took her over a half hour just to find the event, which was "squeezed between food stalls and an underground walkway." Deodhar, "What Happens at a Pro-CAA Rally in Mumbai."

25. Deodhar.

26. "For and Against." To the latter effect, the article merely quotes Fadnavis saying that all the Bangladeshi infiltrators (घुसखोर) need to be expelled from India.

27. See chapter 3 for an extended discussion of sabhaa.

28. A tempo is a three-wheeled delivery vehicle (a small truck).

29. The color saffron is widely recognized as a signal of support for Hindu nationalism, or Hindutva.

30. When I watched the video, however, it was unclear to me how the trucks and volunteers were being identified as party-affiliated.

31. See discussion of natak from chapter 2.

32. "Media events," Yarimar Bonilla writes (drawing on Dayan and Katz's formulation), are distinguished from mere "news events" both by their effective monopolization of media platforms and by their real-time character: "The fact that the events are unfolding in real time means that they are unpredictable," Bonilla explains, thus creating a particular kind of narrative tension—viewers are not just watching history being documented, but rather history unfolding unpredictably before their eyes. In addition, the immediacy of the broadcast creates

a sense of community and participation in the event. Bonilla, *Non-sovereign Futures,* 159. See also Dayan and Katz, *Media Events.*

33. See chapter 4.

34. From the official Twitter handle of the BMC (@mymbc).

35. Ahmed, "In Maharashtra."

36. This echoes Ursula Rao's account of how Hindi newspapers in Lucknow practice a "policy of naming" by means of which editors seek to meet "the desire of urban citizens for publicity," thereby enabling ambitious citizens "to create an advantage in face-to-face negotiations." Rao, *News as Culture,* 47–48.

37. Ahmed, "In Maharashtra."

38. "Uddhav, Jagan Rule Out NRC Exercise in Their States."

39. "Maharashtra: No Detention Centre Will Be Set Up." The article goes on to state that "these foreign nationals are kept in detention camps during the time till they complete their documentation process for deportation. So, there is no need [to fear detention camps]."

40. Ahmed, "In Maharashtra."

41. Here Feroze echoes Punwani's account of how, in the aftermath of the 1992–93 riots, mass mobilization of Muslim Mumbaikars was increasingly obviated by broker-mediated channels of communication. Punwani, "Mumbai's Muslims and 'Friends.'"

42. Wajihudin, "Sanjay Raut to Speak." JIH is the Indian offshoot (post-Independence) of Jamaat-e-Islami, an Islamist organization whose stated objective is "Iqaamat-e-Deen": establishing and maintaining an Islamic way of life. JIH's primary activities are religious and social, involving evangelical outreach, interfaith dialogue, and social welfare activism. While JIH does have a small party (the Welfare Party of India), the organization pursues political goals ("democracy in politics is possible," its website states, "only when justice and equality in social life") primarily through social welfare voluntarism and activities. JIH has an extraordinarily active and well-organized students wing, the Students Islamic Organisation (SIO), whose influence is described by John Esposito as "out of proportion to its numbers" due to its "disciplined organisation, welfare work, its reputation for honesty and street power." SIO volunteers were extremely active in organizing anti-CAA protests in Mumbai, where—as I later learned—young professionals enlisted a variety of skills in orchestrating and coordinating some of the larger events, playing a largely behind-the-scenes role in things like event management (lighting, sound, stage setup), transportation logistics, advertising, and social media campaigning. "Secularism, Democracy, and Fascism"; Esposito, "Jamaat-i Islami of India," 156.

43. "Both the Jamaat's decision to invite Raut, and his presence at a meeting organized by the conservative Muslim religious body has raised eyebrows," notes Jyoti Punwani in her *Mumbai Mirror* article about Raut's upcoming address. "Raut is known for his hard-hitting editorials . . . in the Sena mouthpiece, *Saamna,*

which have on occasion been stridently anti-Muslim." Punwani, "'Sena Is Now Part of Secular Coalition Govt.'"

44. Punwani.

45. Name unchanged.

46. Name unchanged.

47. Punwani, "What Was Sanjay Raut Doing?"

48. For a discussion of the ambivalent valence of dalal in Bombay, see Björkman, "Introduction."

49. The RSS is a right-wing volunteer organization and paramilitary group promoting Hindu nationalist ideology. Founded in 1925, the RSS is today closely associated with India's ruling Bharatiya Janata Party.

50. As anthropologist Lee Ann Fujii points out, rumors are often less interesting for their veracity than for what they can reveal about available and relevant categories of meaning as people use preexisting concepts to make sense of the world. Rumors can thus be illuminating insofar as they render visible and intelligible the available ideas through which experience is made meaningful. Fujii, "Shades of Truth and Lies."

51. "Don't Put Labels of Caste and Creed on Nationalism."

52. Punwani, "What Was Sanjay Raut Doing?"

53. "Sena MP Sanjay Raut Assures Muslims of Safety." NDTV also printed a story on the meeting, under the Raut-quotation heading: "Daro Mat . . ." See "Maharashtra's Lesson Is 'Daro Mat.'"

54. "He Who Is Afraid Is Already Dead."

55. Khan, "Government Accused of Continuously Lying."

56. For an informative perspective, see Punwani, "'Sena Is Now Part of Secular Coalition Govt.'"

57. कोई डरने की जरूरत नहीं, हम है आपके साथ (koi dharne ki zaroorat nahi, hum hai aapke sath).

58. A crore is equal to 10 million.

59. Indeed, two years later the coalition foundered on these very grounds; see conclusion.

60. "Mumbai Police Clamping Down on Anti-CAA Protests?"

61. Acharya, "Protesters Cry Out Appreciation."

62. See "Parties Condemn Violence at JNU." Media investigators later reported that the attack had been coordinated by WhatsApp groups with ties to the RSS-backed student organization Akhil Bharatiya Vidyarthi Parishad. See Parth MN, "JNU Violence."

63. "Parties Condemn Violence at JNU."

64. Since the organizers hadn't had time to seek permission for their gathering, they were relying on the goodwill of the police, who (as it was announced in the pre-gathering WhatsApp "call") had so far been largely cooperative.

65. The meeting had been brokered by Bollywood film producer Mahavir Jain, often described as "Modi's man in Bollywood," and who had also orchestrated

the infamous "Bollywood Selfie" just before the 2019 general election. See Pathak and Sethi, "The Real Story."

66. *Asian News International* posted its video of Uddhav's statement on its Twitter page immediately, at 9:43 a.m. on Monday, January 6. See Asian News International (@ANI), "#WATCH Maharashtra Chief Minister Uddhav Thackeray on JNU violence." By 3:11 that afternoon the *Mumbai Mirror* had posted an article (with an embedded link to ANI's video) which included the statement that Maharashtra students are safe and that he "understood" the rage of those gathered at Gateway.

67. See "A Wildfire of Student Discontent across the Country."

68. Tweet from Devendra Fadnavis's Twitter handle, @Dev_Fadnavis, https://x.com/Dev_Fadnavis/status/1214209648238055426

69. Tweet from Jayant Patil's Twitter handle, @Jayant_R_Patil, https://x.com/Jayant_R_Patil/status/1214420467504816128.

70. The Sanjay Raut quote was, for instance, cited by *Nagpur Today*; see "Saamana Stands by Girl with Free Kashmir Poster."

71. Z. Shaikh, "Protest against Violence at JNU."

72. See chapter 2 for a discussion of mahol. The onset of the Covid-19 pandemic and the announcement of a national lockdown in March 2020 put an abrupt end to the mass mobilizations in India against the CAA-NPR-NRC combine.

Conclusion

1. Discussed in Interlude II.

2. In the decision, the Supreme Court declared that the destruction of the Babri Masjid had been illegal and offered an alternate plot of land some miles away for the reconstruction of the destroyed mosque.

3. The prime minister is reported to have made this comment at the temple inauguration. See Kidangoor, "India's Narendra Modi Broke Ground."

4. *Asian News International* reported on Modi's remarks to the U.S. Congress.

5. "Almost for 1000 to 1200 years we were slaves," Modi told a crowd of Indian Americans in his 2014 address at New York City's Madison Square Garden. Text of Prime Minister Shri Narendra Modi's September 28, 2014, address to the Indian community at Madison Square Garden, New York, is available at https://pib.gov.in/newsite/PrintRelease.aspx?relid=136737.

6. Eminent Indian historian Romila Thapar summarized the historical evidence in a January 14, 2023, lecture at the India International Centre in New Delhi, aptly titled "What History Really Tells Us about Hindu-Muslim Relations."

7. Professional historians have pointed out that the idea has origins in British colonial historiography—first articulated by James Mill in his 1817 *The History of British India*. Dispensing with Mill's "two nations" theory that religious conflict between Hindu and Muslim "nations" has been the perennial driver of Indian history, a generation of historians working with subcontinental archival

sources have instead detailed a "nuanced interface and intermingling of cultures." Thapar, *Our History*, 44.

8. Cited in Khanna, "Modi, Ambani and 'Entitlement.'"

9. Bhatia "Demolitions."

10. Jaffrelot and Verniers, "A New Party System."

11. Verma and Kunjumon, "Support for BJP."

12. For a summary of the historical and legal evidence, see Anupam Gupta, "Dissecting the Ayodhya Judgment."

13. "'Are We Supposed to Just Sit Outside.'"

14. Auerbach and Thachill, *Migrants and Machine Politics;* T. Hansen and Jaffrelot, "Introduction."

15. Name unchanged.

16. Acharya, "'Open Loot of BMC Funds.'"

17. See accounts in chapters 1 and 3.

18. As discussed in Interlude II.

19. Punwani, "25 Years On."

20. Sadadekar, "For Residents of Jogeshwari Chawl."

21. Hindutva's cultural and ideological organization the Rashtriya Swayamsevak Sangh (RSS) was founded in 1925.

22. The continued detention without bail of anti-CAA activists and protestors, four years after arrest during the anti-CAA protests, is regularly the subject of mainstream media outrage.

23. Name unchanged.

24. "Maharashtra: Murmurs of Discontent."

25. I was on the Bombay local train when the bombings occurred (and narrowly missed the blasts at Dadar station) and was also among the throngs that hopped back on the train the next morning.

26. I was in Mumbai during the 2008 attacks as well.

27. Thomas Blom Hansen's account of 1992–93 Bombay riots powerfully demonstrates this. Hansen argues that during the riots, "'Ritualized violence' [was] driven by the imperative of public assertion and performance" (*Wages of Violence,* 65).

28. That even those on the receiving end of the deadly violence may have evaluated the carnage as "public assertion and performance" rather than literally as a desire to eliminate Muslims is evident in chapter 5. Mumbai Muslim leaders hosted Shiv Sena spokesperson Sanjay Raut in a "dialogue" in order to explore the possibility that the very party (perhaps the very people) who presided over the carnage thirty years ago might now be potentially trustworthy and "helpful" allies.

Bibliography

Aaqib, Manzoor Ali. "Hansti hai kaenat bhi insan ki bhul par." In *Ata-e-Yazdan.* Bhopal: Noor Press, 1982. Rekhta.org. https://www.rekhta.org/ghazals/hanstii -hai-kaaenaat-bhii-insaan-kii-bhuul-par-manzoor-ali-aaqib-ghazals?lang=ur.

ABPLIVE. "Amit Shah ने NRC और Citizenship Amendment Bill 2016 को लेकर दिया बड़ा बयान | Exclusive Interview." YouTube video, October 2, 2019. https:// www.youtube.com/watch?v=i33V2Fj_X9U.

Acharya, Pratip. "'Open Loot of BMC Funds': Citing Express Report, Opposition Leaders Slam Maharashtra Govt, Civic Body." *Indian Express,* updated February 1, 2024. https://indianexpress.com/article/cities/mumbai/bmc-maharash tra-govt-civic-body-9136523/.

Acharya, Pratip. "Protesters Cry Out Appreciation for Mumbai Police at Rally." *The Free Press Journal,* January 4, 2020. https://www.freepressjournal.in/mum bai/protesters-cry-out-appreciation-for-mumbai-police-at-rally.

Adorno, Theodor W., and Max Horkheimer. *Dialectic of Enlightenment.* Translated by Edmund Jephcott. Stanford: Stanford University Press, 2002.

Agha, Asif. *Language and Social Relations.* Cambridge: Cambridge University Press, 2006.

Agha, Asif. "Meet Mediatization." *Language & Communication* 31, no. 3 (2011): 163–70.

Agha, Asif. "Registers of Language." In *A Companion to Linguistic Anthropology,* edited by Alessandro Duranti, 23–45. Malden, Mass.: Blackwell, 2004.

Agha, Asif. "Voice, Footing, Enregisterment." *Journal of Linguistic Anthropology* 15, no. 1 (2005): 38–59.

Agrawal, Soniya. "Shaheen Bagh and the New Wave of Protest Art That's Sweeping across India." *The Print,* February 16, 2020. https://theprint.in/features/ shaheen-bagh-and-the-new-wave-of-protest-art-thats-sweeping-across-india/ 364944/.

Ahmed, Rais. "In Maharashtra, the Citizenship Law Will Not Be Implemented." *Mumbai Urdu News,* December 23, 2019.

Anderson, Benedict. *Imagined Communities: Reflections on the Origin and Spread of Nationalism.* London: Verso, 1991.

Anjaria, Jonathan Shapiro. "Ordinary States: Everyday Corruption and the Politics of Space in Mumbai." *American Ethnologist* 38, no. 1 (2011): 58–72.

Anjaria, Ulka. *Understanding Bollywood: The Grammar of Hindi Cinema.* London: Routledge, 2021.

Anthony, Andrew. "'We Showed It Was Possible to Create a Movement from Almost Nothing': Occupy Wall Street 10 Years On." *The Guardian,* September 12, 2021. https://www.theguardian.com/us-news/2021/sep/12/occupy-wall -street-10-years-on.

Appadurai, Arjun, ed. *The Social Life of Things: Commodities in Cultural Perspective.* Cambridge: Cambridge University Press, 1986.

Appadurai, Arjun, and Carol A. Breckenridge. "Public Modernity in India." In *Consuming Modernity: Public Culture in a South Asian World,* edited by Carol A. Breckenridge, 1–20. Minneapolis: University of Minnesota Press, 1995.

"'Are We Supposed to Just Sit Outside and Applaud while PM Modi Does Puja?' Puri Shankaracharya on Ram Mandir Event." *Economic Times,* January 17, 2024.

"Around 20,000 Join Anti-CAA Protest March at August Kranti Maidan, No Untoward Incident Reported: Mumbai Police." *Mumbai Mirror,* December 20, 2019. https://mumbaimirror.indiatimes.com/mumbai/other/around-20000 -join-anti-caa-protest-march-at-august-kranti-maidan-no-untoward-inci dent-reported-mumbai-police/articleshow/72891443.cms.

Asad, Talal. "Thinking about Tradition, Religion, and Politics in Egypt Today." *Critical Inquiry* 42, no. 1 (2015): 166–214.

Asian News International (@ANI). #WATCH | "Last year India celebrated 75 years of independence." X, June 22, 2023. https://x.com/ANI/status/16719785 57407633410.

Asian News International (@ANI). "#WATCH | Maharashtra: Shiv Sena (Uddhav Thackeray faction) performs 'Ravan Dahan' at Shivaji Park in Mumbai, on the occasion of #Dussehra." X, October 5, 2022. https://x.com/ANI/status/157768 4110516318209.

Asian News International (@ANI). "#WATCH Maharashtra Chief Minister Uddhav Thackeray on JNU violence." X, January 6, 2020. https://x.com/ANI/ status/1214105276401373184.

Auerbach, Adam Michael, Jennifer Bussell, Simon Chauchard, Francesca R. Jensenius, Gareth Nellis, Mark Schneider, Neelanjan Sircar, et al. "Rethinking the Study of Electoral Politics in the Developing World: Reflections on the Indian Case." *Perspectives on Politics* 20, no. 1 (2022): 250–64.

Auerbach, Adam, and Tariq Thachill. *Migrants and Machine Politics: How India's Urban Poor Seek Representation and Responsiveness.* Princeton: Princeton University Press, 2023.

"Babri Masjid Demolition Neither Spontaneous nor Unplanned: Liberhan." *Hindustan Times,* November 24, 2009. https://www.hindustantimes.com/india/babri-masjid-demolition-neither-spontaneous-nor-unplanned-liberhan/story-iioNvexOdUdMlhqco6VWSK.html.

Bakhtin, Mikhail M. *The Dialogic Imagination: Four Essays.* Edited by Michael Holmquist. Translated by Caryl Emerson and Michael Holmquist. Austin: University of Texas Press, 1982.

Banerjee, Dwaipayan, and Jacob Copeman. "Hindutva's Blood." *South Asia Multidisciplinary Academic Journal,* nos. 24/25 (December 2020). https://hdl.handle.net/1721.1/134399.

Banerjee, Mukulika. *Why India Votes?* Delhi: Routledge India, 2014.

Banerjee, Shoumojit. "A Sena versus Sena Show of Strength." *The Hindu,* October 3, 2022. https://www.thehindu.com/opinion/op-ed/a-sena-versus-sena-show-of-strength/article65966729.ece.

Barnagarwala, Tabassum. "10 Days, 20,000 Participants: How the Mumbai's August Kranti Maidan Protest Was Brought Together." *Indian Express,* December 20, 2019. https://indianexpress.com/article/cities/mumbai/10-days-20000-participants-how-the-mumbais-august-kranti-maidan-protest-was-brought-together-6175802/.

Bate, Bernard. *Tamil Oratory and the Dravidian Aesthetic: Democratic Practice in South India.* New York: Columbia University Press, 2009.

Bauman, Richard, and Charles L. Briggs. *Voices of Modernity: Language Ideologies and the Politics of Inequality.* Cambridge: Cambridge University Press, 2003.

Bedi, Tarini. *The Dashing Ladies of Shiv Sena: Political Matronage in Urbanizing India.* New York: SUNY Press, 2016.

Bedi, Tarini. *Mumbai Taximen: Autobiographies and Automobilities in India.* Seattle: University of Washington Press, 2022.

Bell, Catherine. "Performance." In *Critical Terms for Religious Studies,* edited by Mark C. Taylor, 208. Chicago: University of Chicago Press, 1998.

Berlant, Lauren. *Cruel Optimism.* Durham: Duke University Press, 2011.

Bhatia, Gautam. "Demolitions as State-Sanctioned Collective Punishment." *The Hindu,* August 10, 2023, sec. Lead. https://www.thehindu.com/opinion/lead/demolitions-as-state-sanctioned-collective-punishment/article67180107.ece.

Björkman, Lisa. "Becoming a Slum: From Municipal Colony to Illegal Settlement in Liberalization-Era Mumbai." *International Journal of Urban and Regional Research* 38, no. 1 (2014): 36–59.

Björkman, Lisa, ed. *Bombay Brokers.* Durham: Duke University Press, 2021.

Björkman, Lisa. "The Engineer and the Plumber: Mediating Mumbai's Conflicting Infrastructural Imaginaries." *International Journal of Urban and Regional Research* 42, no. 2 (2018): 276–94.

Björkman, Lisa. "Introduction: Urban Ethnography in the Global Interregnum." In *Bombay Brokers,* edited by Lisa Björkman, 1–46. Durham: Duke University Press, 2021.

Björkman, Lisa. "The Ostentatious Crowd: Public Protest as Mass-Political Street Theatre in Mumbai." *Critique of Anthropology* 35, no. 2 (2015): 142–65.

Björkman, Lisa. *Pipe Politics, Contested Waters: Embedded Infrastructures of Millennial Mumbai.* Durham: Duke University Press, 2015.

Björkman, Lisa. *Waiting Town: Life in Transit and Mumbai's Other World-Class Histories.* Ann Arbor, Mich.: Association for Asian Studies, 2020.

Björkman, Lisa, and Michael Collins. "Publics." In *Bombay Brokers,* edited by Lisa Björkman, 297–306. Durham: Duke University Press, 2021.

Bohannan, Paul. "The Impact of Money on an African Subsistence Economy." *Journal of Economic History* 19, no. 4 (1959): 491–503.

Böhme, Gernot. *The Aesthetics of Atmospheres.* Edited by Jean-Paul Thibaud. London: Routledge, 2017.

Bombay Aman Committee. *Justice Denied—Why? The Srikrishna Commission Report and the Maharashtra Government's Responce.* Mumbai: Maktaba Faraan, 1998. http://www.unipune.ac.in/snc/cssh/humanrights/04%20COMMUNAL %20RIOTS/A%20-%20%20ANTI-MUSLIM%20RIOTS/06%20-%20MAHA RASHTRA/m.pdf.

Bombay Municipal Corporation (BMC, @mymbc). "Hon'ble Chief Minister Mr Uddhav Thackeray Appreciated the #StreetDesigns by the Winning Teams from #MumbaiStreetLab, @CMOMaharashtra Encouraged Developing the Vision of Safe, Inclusive & Accessible Streets in Mumbai." X, December 27, 2019. https://x.com/hashtag/MumbaiStreetLab?src=hashtag_click.

Bonilla, Yarimar. *Non-sovereign Futures: French Caribbean Politics in the Wake of Disenchantment.* Chicago: University of Chicago Press, 2015.

Bonilla, Yarimar, and Jonathan Rosa. "#Ferguson: Digital Protest, Hashtag Ethnography, and the Racial Politics of Social Media in the United States." *American Ethnologist* 42, no. 1 (2015): 4–17.

Bordoloi, Satyen K. "[4K] हम कागज़ नहीं दिखायेंगे (Hum Kagaz Nahi Dikhaenge) —Varun Grover." YouTube video, December 27, 2019. https://www.youtube .com/watch?v=y_eAhzWoSto.

Boyle, Danny, dir. *Slumdog Millionaire,* 2008.

Breckenridge, Carol A. *Consuming Modernity: Public Culture in a South Asian World.* Minneapolis: University of Minnesota Press, 1995.

Butler, Judith. *Bodies That Matter: On the Discursive Limits of Sex.* New York: Routledge, 2011.

Butler, Judith. *Notes Toward a Performative Theory of Assembly.* Cambridge, Mass.: Harvard University Press, 2015.

Cameron, Deborah, and Don Kulick. *Language and Sexuality.* Cambridge: Cambridge University Press, 2003.

"Cancellation of Fadnavis' Rally Hint at Changing Scenario." *Business Standard,* February 18, 2017. https://www.business-standard.com/article/pti-stories/can cellation-of-fadnavis-rally-hint-at-changing-scenario-cong-117021800716_1 .html.

Carse, Ashley. "Keyword: Infrastructure: How a Humble French Engineering Term Shaped the Modern World." In *Infrastructures and Social Complexity,* edited by Penny Harvey, Casper Bruun Jensen, and Atsuro Morita, 45–57. London: Routledge, 2016.

Central Government of India. The Citizenship (Registration of Citizens and Issue of National Identity Cards) Rules, 2003. Accessed on June 7, 2023. https://ruralindiaonline.org/en/library/resource/the-citizenship-rules-2003/.

Chandavarkar, Rajnarayan. *Imperial Power and Popular Politics: Class, Resistance, and the State in India, 1850–1950.* Cambridge: Cambridge University Press, 1998.

Chandhoke, Neera. "Revisiting the Crisis of Representation Thesis: The Indian Context." *Democratization* 12, no. 3 (2005): 308–30.

Chaturvedi, Swati. *I Am a Troll: Inside the Secret World of the BJP's Digital Army.* New Delhi: Juggernaut Books, 2016.

Chowdhury, Nusrat Sabina. "Figurative Publics: Crowds, Protest, and Democratic Anxieties." *The Immanent Frame.* February 19, 2020. https://tif.ssrc.org/2020/02/19/figurative-publics-introduction/.

Chowdhury, Nusrat Sabina. *Paradoxes of the Popular: Crowd Politics in Bangladesh.* Stanford: Stanford University Press, 2019.

Chumley, Lily. "Qualia and Ontology: Language, Semiotics, and Materiality: An Introduction." *Signs and Society* 5, no. S1 (2017): S1–20.

Clough, Patricia Ticineto. Introduction to *The Affective Turn: Theorizing the Social,* edited by Patricia Ticineto Clough and Jean Halley, 1–33. Durham: Duke University Press, 2007.

Cody, Francis. "Metamorphoses of Popular Sovereignty." *Anthropological Quarterly* 93, no. 2 (2020): 57–88.

Cody, Francis. *The News Event: Popular Sovereignty in the Age of Deep Mediatization.* University of Chicago Press, 2023.

Cody, Francis. "Publics and Politics." *Annual Review of Anthropology* 40, no. 1 (2011): 37–52.

Cooper, Timothy P. A. "'*Live* Has an Atmosphere of Its Own': *Azadari,* Ethical Orientation, and Tuned Presence in Shi'i Media Praxis." *Journal of the Royal Anthropological Institute* 28, no. 2 (2022): 651–75.

Corbridge, Stuart, and John Harriss. *Reinventing India: Liberalization, Hindu Nationalism and Popular Democracy.* Cambridge, UK: Polity Press, 2000.

Dalton, Russell J. *Democratic Challenges, Democratic Choices: The Erosion of Political Support in Advanced Industrial Democracies.* Oxford University Press, 2004.

Davis, Richard. "The Iconography of Rama's Chariot." In *Contesting the Nation: Religion, Community, and the Politics of Democracy in India,* edited by David Ludden, 27–54. Philadelphia: University of Pennsylvania Press, 1996.

Dayan, Daniel, and Eihu Katz. *Media Events: The Live Broadcasting of History.* Cambridge, Mass.: Harvard University Press, 1992.

Debord, Guy. *Society of the Spectacle.* Translated by Donald Nicholson-Smith. New York: Zone Books, 1995.

Deodhar, Neerja. "What Happens at a Pro-CAA Rally in Mumbai." *Firstpost*, December 20, 2019. https://www.firstpost.com/india/what-happens-at-a-pro-caa-rally-in-mumbai-chants-about-vd-savarkar-incendiary-slogans-and-praise-for-delhi-police-7806331.html.

Derrida, Jacques. "Signature Event Context." In *Limited Inc*, translated by Samuel Weber and Jeffrey Mehlman, 1–23. Evanston: Northwestern University Press, 1988.

Desai, Manmohan, dir. *Roti*. 1974.

Deshpande, Abhinay. "Mumbai Dasara Rallies Become a Free for All, Shinde and Uddhav Hurl Barbs at Each Other." *The Hindu*, October 5, 2022. https://www.thehindu.com/news/national/other-states/mumbai-dasara-rallies-become-a-free-for-all-shinde-and-uddhav-hurl-barbs-at-each-other/article65973280.ece.

"Despite Note Ban, Cash Is King in Last Leg of Poll Drive." *The Times of India*, February 18, 2017. https://timesofindia.indiatimes.com/city/mumbai/despite-note-ban-cash-is-king-in-last-leg-of-poll-drive/articleshow/57214082.cms.

Dickey, Sara. "The Politics of Adulation: Cinema and the Production of Politicians in South India." *Journal of Asian Studies* 52, no. 2 (1993): 340–72.

Disch, Lisa, Mathijs van de Sande, and Nadia Urbinati, eds. *The Constructivist Turn in Political Representation*. Edinburgh: Edinburgh University Press, 2023.

"Don't Put Labels of Caste and Creed on Nationalism (राष्ट्रीयभक्तीला जाती-धर्माचे लेबल लावू नका)." *Saamna*, January 5, 2020.

Dutt, Nirupama. "'Hum Kya Chahte? Azaadi!': Story of Slogan Raised by JNU's Kanhaiya." *Hindustan Times*, March 4, 2016. https://www.hindustantimes.com/punjab/kanhaiya-kumar-s-azadi-chant-not-a-gift-from-kashmir-separatists-but-from-feminists/story-K7GQNzhzE1Z8UFBDGVYh6J.html.

Dutta, Sweta. "Face of the Jamia Protests: 22-Year-Old Aysha Renna Says She Will Be Back on the Streets Soon." *Mumbai Mirror*, December 17, 2019. https://mumbaimirror.indiatimes.com/mumbai/cover-story/face-of-the-jamia-protests/articleshow/72780285.cms.

Eco, Umberto. "Semiotics of Theatrical Performance." *Drama Review* 21, no. 1 (1977): 107–17.

Eisenlohr, Patrick. "Latency, Media Practices, and the Right to the City in Shi'i Mumbai." Draft essay, n.d.

Elam, J. Daniel. "Hong Kong: 'When We Burn You Will Burn with Us.'" *Public Books*, November 26, 2019. https://www.publicbooks.org/hong-kong-when-we-burn-you-will-burn-with-us/.

"Election Card Is Proof of Citizenship: Court." *The Times of India*, February 15, 2020. https://timesofindia.indiatimes.com/india/election-card-is-proof-of-citizenship-court/articleshow/74144034.cms.

Engineer, Irfan. "Politics of Muslim Vote Bank." *Economic and Political Weekly* 30, no. 4 (1995): 197–200.

Eshwar and Anjali Palod. "Gaddar vs Khuddar: Uddhav's Dussehra Rally High on Emotions; Shinde Aces Optics." *The Quint,* October 6, 2022. https://www .thequint.com/news/politics/shiv-sena-uddhav-thackeray-eknath-shinde -dasra-dussehra-melava-rally-2022-shivaji-park-mmrda-mumbai-legacy -war-bal-thackeray.

Esposito, John L., ed. "Jamaat-i Islami of India." In *The Oxford Dictionary of Islam,* 156. Oxford University Press, 2003.

Esposito, John L., and Natana J. DeLong-Bas. *Women in Muslim Family Law.* Syracuse: Syracuse University Press, 2001.

Fadnavis, Devendra (@Dev_Fadnavis). "What a Pity! Now Separatist Tendencies Get a Government Advocate. Jayantrao, This Vote Bank Politics Is Not Expected from You. Kashmir Has Already Been Freed from Discrimination and . . . (1/2)." X, January 7, 2020. https://x.com/Dev_Fadnavis/status/12144 34986213826561?ref_src=twsrc%5Etfw.

"Fadnavis Attacks Maha Govt on Loan Waiver, CAA, Muslim Quota." *Business Standard,* March 14, 2020. https://www.business-standard.com/article/pti-sto ries/fadnavis-attacks-maha-govt-on-loan-waiver-caa-muslim-quota-12003 1400927_1.html.

Fazili, Sana. "'Kisi Ke Baap Ka Hindustan Thodi Hai': Remembering Poet Rahat Indori and His Words on Inclusive India." *News18,* August 11, 2020. https:// www.news18.com/news/buzz/kisi-ke-baap-ka-hindustan-thodi-hai-remem bering-poet-rahat-indori-and-his-words-on-inclusive-india-2777129.html.

Ferguson, James. *Presence and Social Obligation: An Essay on the Share.* Chicago: Prickly Paradigm Press, 2021.

Fisch, Max Harold. *Peirce, Semeiotic, and Pragmatism: Essays by Max H. Fisch.* Edited by Kenneth Laine Ketner and Christian J. W. Kloesel. Bloomington: Indiana University Press, 1986.

"For and Against (समर्थन आणि विद्रोही)." *Maharashtra Times,* December 29, 2019.

Frank, Jason. "Beyond Democracy's Imaginary Investments." *The Immanent Frame.* February 19, 2020. http://tif.ssrc.org/2020/02/19/beyond-democracys -imaginary-investments/.

Frank, Jason. "The Living Image of the People." *Theory & Event* 18, no. 1 (2015). https://muse.jhu.edu/article/566086.

Fraser, Nancy. "Rethinking the Public Sphere: A Contribution to the Critique of Actually Existing Democracy." *Social Text* 25/26 (1990): 56–80.

Freedom House. "India: Freedom in the World 2022 Country Report." Freedom House. 2022. https://freedomhouse.org/country/india/freedom-world/2022.

Freitag, Sandria B. *Collective Action and Community: Public Arenas and the Emergence of Communalism in North India.* Berkeley: University of California Press, 1989.

Friedland, Paul. *Political Actors: Representative Bodies and Theatricality in the Age of the French Revolution.* Ithaca: Cornell University Press, 2002.

Fujii, Lee Ann. "Shades of Truth and Lies: Interpreting Testimonies of War and Violence." *Journal of Peace Research* 47, no. 2 (2010): 231-41. https://doi.org/ 10.1177/0022343309353097.

Gajara, Dhairya. "Bombay HC Lawyers Read Preamble Outside Court." *The Hindu,* January 20, 2020. https://www.thehindu.com/news/cities/mumbai/bom bay-hc-lawyers-read-preamble-outside-court/article30610402.ece.

Gal, Susan. "Contradictions of Standard Language in Europe: Implications for the Study of Practices and Publics." *Social Anthropology* 14, no. 2 (2006): 163–81.

Gal, Susan, and Judith T. Irvine. *Signs of Difference: Language and Ideology in Social Life.* Cambridge: Cambridge University Press, 2019.

Gandhi, M. K. "The 'Quit India' Speech," August 8, 1943. http://www.mkgandhi .org/speeches/qui.htm.

Gayer, Laurent, and Christophe Jaffrelot. "Muslims of the Indian City: From Centrality to Marginality." In *Muslims in Indian Cities: Trajectories of Marginalisation,* edited by Laurent Gayer and Christophe Jaffrelot, 1–22. New York: Columbia University Press, 2012.

Geertz, Clifford. *Negara: The Theatre State in Nineteenth-Century Bali.* Princeton: Princeton University Press, 1981.

Gershon, Ilana. "Media Ideologies: An Introduction." *Journal of Linguistic Anthropology* 20, no. 2 (2010): 283–93.

Geschiere, Peter. *Witchcraft, Intimacy, and Trust: Africa in Comparison.* Chicago: University of Chicago Press, 2013.

Ghai, Riti. "Citizenship (Amendment) Act: Why CAA in 2024 Could Be Different from CAA in 2019–20." *Economic Times,* March 12, 2024.

Ghertner, D Asher. "India's Urban Revolution: Geographies of Displacement beyond Gentrification." *Environment and Planning A: Economy and Space* 46, no. 7 (2014): 1554–71.

Ghertner, D Asher. *Rule by Aesthetics: World-Class City Making in Delhi.* Oxford: Oxford University Press, 2015.

Giridharadas, Anand. "The Real Battleground of 2024 Is Emotion." *The.Ink,* January 17, 2024. https://the.ink/p/the-real-battleground-of-2024-is?utm_source =post-email-title&publication_id=70374&post_id=140743950&utm_campaign =email-post-title&isFreemail=true&r=2xo6e&utm_medium=email

Goffman, Erving. "Footing." In *Forms of Talk,* 124–59. Philadelphia: University of Pennsylvania Press, 1981.

Goffman, Erving. *Frame Analysis: An Essay on the Organization of Experience.* Boston: Northeastern University Press, 1986.

Goffman, Erving. "The Nature of Deference and Demeanor." *American Anthropologist* 58, no. 3 (1956): 473–502.

Goffman, Erving. *The Presentation of Self in Everyday Life.* New York: Doubleday, 1959.

Gregory, Christopher A. *Gifts and Commodities.* London: Academic Press, 1982.

Gupta, Akhil. *Red Tape: Bureaucracy, Structural Violence, and Poverty in India.* Durham: Duke University Press, 2012.

Gupta, Anupam. "Dissecting the Ayodhya Judgment." *Economic and Political Weekly* 45, no. 50 (2010): 33–41.

Gupta, Radhika. "There Must Be Some Way out of Here: Beyond a Spatial Conception of Muslim Ghettoization in Mumbai?" *Ethnography* 16, no. 3 (2015): 352–70.

Gupta, Swati, Omar Khan, and Ahmer Khan. "Protests Spread across India over New Citizenship Law Which Excludes Muslims." *CNN,* December 16, 2019. https://www.cnn.com/2019/12/15/india/india-protests-assam-delhi-citizen ship-intl-hnk/index.html.

Habermas, Jürgen. "Popular Sovereignty as Procedure." In *Deliberative Democracy: Essays on Reason and Politics*, edited by James Bohman and William Rehg, 35-65. Cambridge, Mass.: MIT Press, 1997.

Habermas, Jürgen. *The Structural Transformation of the Public Sphere: An Inquiry into a Category of Bourgeois Society.* Translated by Thomas Burger. Cambridge, Mass.: MIT Press, 1989.

Habermas, Jürgen. *The Theory of Communicative Action.* Translated by Thomas McCarthy. Boston: Beacon Press, 1984.

Hansen, Kathryn. "The Indar Sabha Phenomenon: Public Theatre and Consumption in Greater India (1853–1956)." In *Pleasure and the Nation: The History, Politics and Consumption of Public Culture in India,* edited by Rachel Dwyer and Christopher Pinney, 76–114. New Delhi: Oxford University Press, 2001.

Hansen, Thomas Blom. "Politics as Permanent Performance: The Production of Political Authority in the Locality." In *The Politics of Cultural Mobilization in India,* edited by John Zavos, Andrew Wyatt, and Vernon Marston Hewitt, 19–36. New Delhi: Oxford University Press, 2004.

Hansen, Thomas Blom. *Wages of Violence: Naming and Identity in the Postcolonial Bombay.* Princeton: Princeton University Press, 2001.

Hansen, Thomas, and Christophe Jaffrelot. "Introduction: The Rise to Power of the BJP." In *The BJP and the Compulsions of Politics in India,* edited by Thomas Blom Hansen and Christophe Jaffrelot, 1–21. New Delhi: Oxford University Press, 2001.

Hansen, Thomas Blom, and Oskar Verkaaik. "Introduction—Urban Charisma: On Everyday Mythologies in the City." *Critique of Anthropology* 29, no. 1 (2009): 5–26.

Hardt, Michael, and Antonio Negri. *Multitude: War and Democracy in the Age of Empire.* New York: Penguin, 2004.

Hardy, Kathryn. "Anil Prakash: Amplifier of Cinema-Industrial Connections." In *Bombay Brokers,* edited by Lisa Björkman, 315–21. Durham: Duke University Press, 2021.

Harikrishnan, Charmy. "Anti-CAA Protests: People Hold Up Constitution as the Only Document That Matters." *Economic Times,* January 26, 2020. https://eco

nomictimes.indiatimes.com/news/politics-and-nation/anti-caa-protests
-people-hold-up-constitution-as-the-only-document-that-matters/article
show/73618451.cms.

Harriss, John, and Craig Jeffrey. "Depoliticizing Injustice." *Economy and Society*
42, no. 3 (2013): 507–20,

Hay, Colin. *Why We Hate Politics.* Cambridge, UK: Polity, 2007.

Herzfeld, Michael. *Cultural Intimacy: Social Poetics in the Nation-State.* 2nd ed.
New York: Routledge, 2005.

"He Who Is Afraid Is Already Dead, so Don't Be Afraid." *Mumbai Urdu News,*
January 5, 2020.

Hirschkind, Charles. *The Ethical Soundscape: Cassette Sermons and Islamic
Counterpublics.* New York: Columbia University Press, 2006.

Horkheimer, Max. "Traditional and Critical Theory." In *Critical Theory: Selected
Essays,* translated by Matthew J. O'Connell, 188–243. New York: Continuum,
1982.

Howes, David. "Multisensory Anthropology." *Annual Review of Anthropology* 48,
no. 1 (2019): 17–28.

Hymes, Dell. "Models of the Interaction of Language and Social Life: Toward
a Descriptive Theory." In *Intercultural Discourse and Communication* 4–16.
Hoboken, N.J.: Wiley, 2005.

IITB4Justice (@IITB4Justice). "The #OccupyGateway Protest Is Going on in
Full Swing. We Are Calling Everyone to Come and Join." X, January 5, 2020.
https://x.com/i/status/1213950343572148224.

Indian Express. "Shaheen Bagh's 'Dadi' in Time Magazine's List of 100 Most
Influential People." YouTube video, September 23, 2020. https://www.youtube
.com/watch?v=zeJfcEr3GOM.

"India Sees Six-Fold Jump in Voters since 1951; Total Electorate on January 1 Is
over 94.50 Crore." *The Hindu,* February 5, 2023. https://www.thehindu.com/
news/national/india-sees-six-fold-jump-in-voters-since-1951-total-electo
rate-on-january-1-is-over-9450-crore/article66473978.ece.

India Today. "Watch the Most Creative Posters against CAA and NRC." YouTube
video, December 21, 2019. https://www.youtube.com/watch?v=i56RvyNJf6g.

Irvine, Judith T. "Shadow Conversations: The Indeterminacy of Participant Roles."
In *Natural Histories of Discourse,* edited by Michael Silverstein and Greg
Urban, 131–59. Chicago: University of Chicago Press, 1996.

Ivanov, Vyacheslav. "Heteroglossia." *Journal of Linguistic Anthropology* 9, nos. 1/2
(1999): 100–102.

Jaffe, Alexandra. "Indexicality, Stance, and Fields in Sociolinguistics." In *Sociolinguistics: Theoretical Debates,* edited by Nikolas Coupland, 86–112. Cambridge:
Cambridge University Press, 2016.

Jaffrelot, Christophe, and Gilles Verniers. "The BJP's 2019 Election Campaign:
Not Business as Usual." Contemporary South Asia 28, no. 2 (2020): 155–77.

Jaffrelot, Christophe, and Gilles Verniers. "A New Party System or a New Political System?" *Contemporary South Asia* 28, no. 2 (2020): 141–54.

Jain, Kajri. *Gods in the Time of Democracy.* Durham: Duke University Press, 2021.

Jones, Caroline A. "The Mediated Sensorium." In *Sensorium: Embodied Experience, Technology, and Contemporary Art,* edited by Caroline A. Jones, 5–49. London: MIT Press, 2006.

Jonsson, Stefan. "Populism without Borders." The Immanent Frame, March 4, 2020. https://tif.ssrc.org/2020/03/04/populism-without-borders/.

Kachru, Yamuna. "Hindi–Urdu–Hindustani." In *Language in South Asia,* edited by Braj B. Kachru, Yamuna Kachru, and S. N. Sridhar, 81–102. Cambridge: Cambridge University Press, 2008.

"Kanhaiya Kumar Speech at JNU." *Hindustan Times,* YouTube video, March 8, 2016. https://www.youtube.com/watch?v=pxcE7LhrqQc.

Kapur, Devesh, and Milan Vaishnav, eds. *Costs of Democracy: Political Finance in India.* Oxford: Oxford University Press, 2018.

Kaur, Kanchan. "A Review of the Fake News Ecosystem in India and the Need for the News Literacy Project." *Przegląd Politologiczny* 4 (2019): 23–29.

Kaur, Raminder. *Performative Politics and the Cultures of Hinduism: Public Uses of Religion in Western India.* London: Anthem Press, 2005.

Keane, Webb. "Money Is No Object: Materiality, Desire, and Modernity in an Indonesian Society." In *The Empire of Things: Regimes of Value and Material Culture,* edited by Fred Myers, 65–90. Santa Fe, N.Mex.: School of American Research Press, 2001.

Keane, Webb. "On Semiotic Ideology." *Signs & Society* 6, no. 1 (2018): 64–87.

Keane, Webb. "Semiotics and the Social Analysis of Material Things." *Language & Communication, Words and Beyond: Linguistic and Semiotic Studies of Sociocultural Order* 23, no. 3 (2003): 409–25.

Keane, Webb. "Signs Are Not the Garb of Meaning: On the Social Analysis of Material Things." In *Materiality,* edited by Daniel Miller, 182–205. Durham: Duke University Press, 2005.

Keane, Webb. *Signs of Recognition: Powers and Hazards of Representation in an Indonesian Society.* Berkeley: University of California Press, 1997.

Keane, Webb. "Voice." *Journal of Linguistic Anthropology* 9, nos. 1/2 (1999): 271–73.

Khan, Saheed Ahmad. "Government Accused of Continuously Lying about NPR and NRC." *Inquilab,* January 5, 2020.

Khanna, Rhoit. "How Modi, Ambani, and 'Entitlement' Have Usurped People's Power." *The Wire,* March 12, 2024. https://thewire.in/society/how-modi-ambani-and-entitlement-have-usurped-peoples-power.

Khapre, Shubhangi. "Why BJP Only a Spectator in the Grand Sena Shows." *Indian Express,* October 6, 2022. https://indianexpress.com/article/political-pulse/why-bjp-only-a-spectator-in-the-grand-sena-shows-8191596/.

Kidambi, Prashant. "Housing the Poor in a Colonial City: The Bombay Improvement Trust, 1898–1918." *Studies in History* 17, no. 1 (2001): 57–79.

Kidambi, Prashant. *The Making of an Indian Metropolis: Colonial Governance and Public Culture in Bombay, 1890–1920.* London: Routledge, 2007.

Kidangoor, Abhishyant. "India's Narendra Modi Broke Ground for a Controversial Temple of Ram. Here's Why It Matters." *Time,* August 4, 2020. https://time.com/5875380/modi-ram-temple-ayodhya-groundbreaking/.

Kitschelt, Herbert, and Steven I. Wilkinson, eds. *Patrons, Clients and Policies: Patterns of Democratic Accountability and Political Competition.* Cambridge: Cambridge University Press, 2007.

Kress, Gunther, and Theo van Leeuwen. *Multimodal Discourse: The Modes and Media of Contemporary Communication.* Oxford: Oxford University Press, 2001.

Kunreuther, Laura. *Voicing Subjects: Public Intimacy and Mediation in Kathmandu.* Berkeley: University of California Press, 2014.

Kuroda, Ken. "Shankar: Delivering Authenticity." In *Bombay Brokers,* edited by Lisa Björkman, 208–15. Durham: Duke University Press, 2021.

Kusters, Annelies. "Deaf on the Lifeline of Mumbai." *Sign Language Studies* 10, no. 1 (2009): 36–68.

Laclau, Ernesto. "Power and Representation." In *Emancipation(s),* 84–104. London: Verso, 1996.

Lefort, Claude. *The Political Forms of Modern Society: Bureaucracy, Democracy, Totalitarianism.* Cambridge, Mass.: MIT Press, 1986.

"Maharashtra: Murmurs of Discontent Grow over Induction of Defectors into BJP." *Hindustan Times,* February 16, 2024. https://www.hindustantimes.com/india-news/maharashtra-murmurs-of-discontent-grow-over-induction-of-defectors-into-bjp-101708076698786.html.

"Maharashtra: No Detention Centre Will Be Set Up in State under NRC, CAA, Says Uddhav." *Indian Express,* December 24, 2019. https://indianexpress.com/article/cities/mumbai/maharashtra-no-detention-centre-will-be-set-up-in-state-under-nrc-caa-says-uddhav-6181964/.

"Maharashtra: No Need to Be Scared of CAA, NRC & NPR, Government with You, Says Sanjay Raut." *Indian Express,* January 5, 2020. https://indianexpress.com/article/cities/mumbai/maharashtra-no-need-to-be-scared-of-caa-nrc-npr-government-with-you-sanjay-raut-6200060/.

"Maharashtra: Reciting Preamble Mandatory in Schools Starting January 26." *The Times of India,* January 21, 2020. https://timesofindia.indiatimes.com/india/maharashtra-reciting-preamble-mandatory-in-schools-starting-january-26/articleshow/73495410.cms.

"Maharashtra's Lesson Is 'Daro Mat . . .': Sanjay Raut to Citizenship Act Protesters." *NDTV,* January 5, 2020. https://www.ndtv.com/india-news/maharashtras-lesson-is-daro-mat-sanjay-raut-to-citizenship-act-protesters-2158910.

Makne, Eknath. "BMC Polls: Fits and Starts to the Final Frenzy." *DNA India,* February 13, 2012. https://www.dnaindia.com/mumbai/report-bmc-polls-fits-and-starts-to-the-final-frenzy-1649834.

Mankikar, Sayli Udas. "Cashing In on the Election Fever." *Hindustan Times,* February 2, 2012. https://www.hindustantimes.com/mumbai/cashing-in-on-the-election-fever/story-GQEoXWMq2okcfJcnbKlL6M.html.

Mansbridge, Jane. "Clarifying the Concept of Representation." *American Political Science Review* 105, no. 3 (2011): 621–30.

Mathur, Nayanika. *Paper Tiger: Law, Bureaucracy, and the Developmental State in Himalayan India.* Cambridge: Cambridge University Press, 2015.

Maurer, Bill. "The Anthropology of Money." *Annual Review of Anthropology* 35, no. 1 (2006): 15–36.

Mauss, Marcel. *The Gift: The Form and Reason for Exchange in Archaic Societies.* Translated by Ian Cunnison. London: Cohen and West, 1966.

Mazzarella, William. "Affect: What Is It Good For?" In *Enchantments of Modernity: Empire, Nation, Globalization,* edited by Saurabh Dube, 291–309. New Delhi: Routledge India, 2009.

Mazzarella, William. "The Anthropology of Populism: Beyond the Liberal Settlement." *Annual Review of Anthropology* 48, no. 1 (2019): 45–60.

Mazzarella, William. "Internet X-Ray: E-Governance, Transparency, and the Politics of Immediation in India." *Public Culture* 18, no. 3 (2006): 473–505.

Mazzarella, William. *The Mana of Mass Society.* Chicago: University of Chicago Press, 2017.

Mazzarella, William. "The Myth of the Multitude, or, Who's Afraid of the Crowd?" *Critical Inquiry* 36, no. 4 (2010): 697–727.

Mazzarella, William. "Political Incarnation as Living Archive: Thinking with 'L' in a Revolutionary Time." Paper prepared for Wenner-Gren Symposium #162, "Populism: Anthropological Approaches." March 20–26, 2023, Sintra, Portugal.

Mbembe, Achille. "The Banality of Power and the Aesthetics of Vulgarity in the Postcolony." *Public Culture* 4, no. 2 (1992): 1–30.

McGregor, R. S. *The Oxford Hindi-English Dictionary.* Oxford: Oxford University Press, 1993.

Michelutti, Lucia. "The Vernacularization of Democracy: Political Participation and Popular Politics in North India." *Journal of the Royal Anthropological Institute* 13, no. 3 (2007): 639–56.

Mid-Day (@mid_day). "Uddhav Thackeray's Shivaji Park Dussehra rally." Video by @AshishRane2, X, October 5, 2022. https://x.com/mid_day/status/1577642560566493185.

Mines, Mattison. *Public Faces, Private Voices: Community and Individuality in South India.* Berkeley: University of California Press, 1994.

Mirror Now. "Uddhav Thackeray vs Eknath Shinde: How Dussehra Festival Became a Political Faceoff in Maharashtra." YouTube video, October 7, 2022. https://www.youtube.com/watch?v=7QkHYCvIYfU.

"Miscommunication or Empty Chairs? After Reaching Venue, CM Fadnavis Cancels Rally." *Indian Express,* February 19, 2017. https://indianexpress.com/article/cities/pune/after-reaching-venue-cm-fadnavis-cancels-rally-4532256/.

Mitchell, Lisa. *Hailing the State: Indian Democracy between Elections.* Durham: Duke University Press, 2023.

Mitchell, Lisa. "'To Stop Train Pull Chain': Writing Histories of Contemporary Political Practice." *Indian Economic & Social History Review* 48, no. 4 (2011): 469–95.

Modak, Sadaf. "Women, Transpersons Protest against CAA." *Indian Express,* January 3, 2020.

Moores, Shaun. *Interpreting Audiences: The Ethnography of Media Consumption.* London: Sage, 1993.

Morris, Charles. *Foundations of the Theory of Signs.* Chicago: University of Chicago Press, 1938.

"Mumbai Anti-CAA Protest: At August Kranti Maidan Today, 2,000 Security Personnel on Guard." *Indian Express,* December 19, 2019. https://indianexpress .com/article/cities/mumbai/citizenship-amendment-bill-act-2019-protests -caa-cab-mumbai-august-kranti-maidan-6174208/.

"Mumbai Civic Polls: Social Media Is the New Door-to-Door." *Hindustan Times,* February 18, 2017. https://www.hindustantimes.com/mumbai-news/social -media-campaign-is-good-business-during-elections/story-QyRl4lamjse9n kt9ytmGaM.html.

Mumbai Police (@MumbaiPolice). "Dear Mumbaikars, Azad Maidan Is the Designated Place for All Agitations in South Mumbai as per Hon. HC Instructions. However Some Agitators Gathered at an Important South Mumbai Location for a Long Duration without Any Permission. (1/4)." X, January 7, 2020. https:// x.com/MumbaiPolice/status/1214413951099736064.

"Mumbai Police Clamping Down on Anti-CAA Protests?" *SabrangIndia,* February 1, 2020. https://www.sabrangindia.in/article/mumbai-police-clamping -down-anti-caa-protests.

Nakassis, Constantine. *Onscreen/Offscreen.* Toronto: University of Toronto Press, 2023.

Nasikh, Imam Bakhsh. "Hae laya na koi qasid-e-dilbar kaaghaz." Rekhta.org. https://www.rekhta.org/ghazals/haae-laayaa-na-koii-qaasid-e-dilbar-kaagaz -imam-bakhsh-nasikh-ghazals?lang=ur.

Naylor, Brian. "Read Trump's Jan. 6 Speech, a Key Part of Impeachment Trial." *NPR,* February 10, 2021. https://www.npr.org/2021/02/10/966396848/read -trumps-jan-6-speech-a-key-part-of-impeachment-trial.

NDTV. "Team Thackeray vs Team Shinde at Big Dussehra Rallies | Breaking Views." YouTube video, October 5, 2022. https://www.youtube.com/watch?v= 1rAxFhioO9Y.

"Newly-Convened Alliance Underscores Potential Impact of CAA-NRC on Dalits, Adivasis." *The Wire,* January 16, 2020. https://thewire.in/rights/caa-nrc -dalits-adivasis-obcs.

Nigam, Aditya. "Staging the 'People' in Three Recent Movements." *India Seminar,* no. 756, August 2022. https://www.india-seminar.com/2022/756/756-02%20 ADITYA%20NIGAM.htm.

Nikas, "Pro-Bolsonaro Riots Laid Bare Threat to Brazilian Democracy." *New York Times,* January 9, 2023. https://www.nytimes.com/live/2023/01/09/world/brazil-congress-riots-bolsonaro#brazil-riots-jan-6-misinformation-social-media.

"No Question of Linking CAA to NRC: Union Minister Ravi Shankar Prasad—India Today." *India Today,* December 17, 2019. https://www.indiatoday.in/india/story/no-question-of-linking-caa-to-nrc-union-minister-ravi-shankar-prasad-1629020-2019-12-17.

"'Not about Muslims Alone, but All Indians.'" *Indian Express,* December 28, 2019.

Orsini, Francesca, ed. *Love in South Asia: A Cultural History.* Cambridge: Cambridge University Press, 2006.

Outlook. "Danger of Deification." *Outlook,* April 4, 2016. https://www.outlookindia.com/magazine/story/danger-of-deification/296875.

Palshikar, Suhas, and Rajeshwari Deshpande. *The Last Fortress of Congress Dominance: Maharashtra since the 1990s.* New Delhi: SAGE Publishing India, 2020.

Pandey, Gyanendra. *Routine Violence: Nations, Fragments, Histories.* Stanford: Stanford University Press, 2022.

Pandit, Ambika. "Muslim Population in 2023 Estimated to Be 20 Crore: Lok Sabha." *The Times of India.* July 21, 2023. https://timesofindia.indiatimes.com/india/muslim-population-in-2023-estimated-to-be-20-crore-lok-sabha/articleshow/101996898.cms.

Papailias, Penelope. "Witnessing in the Age of the Database: Viral Memorials, Affective Publics, and the Assemblage of Mourning." *Memory Studies* 9, no. 4 (2016), 437–54.

Parmentier, Richard J. "Money Walks, People Talk: Systemic and Transactional Dimensions of Palauan Exchange." *L'Homme* 162 (2002): 49–79.

Parry, Jonathan, and Maurice Bloch. "Introduction: Money and the Morality of Exchange." In *Money and the Morality of Exchange,* edited by Jonathan Parry and Maurice Bloch, 1–32. Cambridge: Cambridge University Press, 1989.

Parth MN. "JNU Violence: WhatsApp Groups Tied to ABVP Show Members Were Circulating Plans to Attack; Group Denies Role in Campus Raid-India News." *Firstpost,* January 6, 2020. https://www.firstpost.com/india/jnu-violence-whatsapp-groups-tied-to-abvp-show-members-were-actively-circulating-plans-to-carry-out-attacks-group-denies-role-in-campus-raid-7866701.html.

"Parties Condemn Violence at JNU: Congress Blames 'Fascists,' BJP 'Forces of Anarchy.'" *Indian Express,* January 6, 2020. https://indianexpress.com/article/india/parties-condemn-violence-at-jnu-congress-blames-fascists-bjp-forces-of-anarchy-6201315/.

Pathak, Ankur, and Aman Sethi. "The Real Story behind Modi's Blooming Romance with Bollywood." *HuffPost,* October 20, 2019. https://www.huffpost

.com/archive/in/entry/narendra-modi-ranveer-singh-bollywood-bjp-selfie -ranbir-kapoor-alia-bhatt-vicky-kaushal_in_5cd0211de4b0548b735d1615.

Patil, Jayant (@Jayant_R_Patil). "Devendraji, It's 'Free Kashmir' from All Dis- criminations, Bans on Cellular Networks and Central Control. I Can't Believe That a Responsible Leader like You Trying to Confuse People by Decoding Words in Such a Hatred Way. Is It Losing Power or Losing Self Control? #JNUViolence." X, January 7, 2020. https://x.com/Jayant_R_Patil/status/1214 420467504816128.

Pemmaraju, Gautam. "Dalvi: Speaker of Cities." In *Bombay Brokers,* edited by Lisa Björkman, 286–96. Durham: Duke University Press, 2021.

Pernau, Margrit, and Imke Rajamani. "Emotional Translations: Conceptual His- tory beyond Language." *History and Theory* 55, no. 1 (2016): 46–65.

Piliavsky, Anastasia. Introduction to *Patronage as Politics in South Asia,* edited by Anastasia Piliavsky, 3–37. Cambridge: Cambridge University Press, 2014.

Piliavsky, Anastasia, and Judith Scheele. "Towards a Critical Ethnography of Polit- ical Concepts." *HAU: Journal of Ethnographic Theory* 12, no. 3 (2022): 686–700.

Pinney, Christopher. "Introduction: Public, Popular, and Other Cultures." In *Pleasure and the Nation: The History, Politics and Consumption of Public Cul- ture in India,* edited by Rachel Dwyer and Christopher Pinney, 1–34. New Delhi: Oxford University Press, 2002.

Pitkin, Hanna F. *The Concept of Representation.* Berkeley: University of Califor- nia Press, 1972.

Platts, John Thompson. *A Dictionary of Urdu, Classical Hindi, and English.* Lon- don: W. H. Allen & Co., 1884. https://dsal.uchicago.edu/dictionaries/platts/.

Plotke, David. "Representation Is Democracy." *Constellations* 4, no. 1 (1997): 19–34.

"Protest against UP Police 'Atrocities.'" *Indian Express,* January 3, 2020.

"Punekars' Siesta Forces Chief Minister Devendra Fadnavis to Cancel Meeting." *The Times of India,* February 18, 2017. https://timesofindia.indiatimes.com/ city/pune/punekars-siesta-forces-chief-minister-devendra-fadnavis-to-can cel-meeting/articleshow/57224453.cms.

Punwani, Jyoti. "BMC Election 2017: Why Asaduddin Owaisi Makes Us Uneasy." *Mumbai Mirror,* February 3, 2017. https://mumbaimirror.indiatimes.com/oth ers/sunday-read/why-asaduddin-owaisi-makes-us-uneasy/articleshow/56 845823.cms.

Punwani, Jyoti. "Mumbai's Muslims and 'Friends.'" *Economic and Political Weekly* 47, no. 34 (2012): 16–18.

Punwani, Jyoti. "'My Area, Your Area': How Riots Changed the City." In *Bombay and Mumbai: The City in Transition,* edited by Sujata Patel and Jim Masselos, 235–65. Oxford: Oxford University Press, 2003.

Punwani, Jyoti. "Remembering City's Exuberant Morchas." *Mumbai Mirror,* Octo- ber 10, 2020. https://mumbaimirror.indiatimes.com/mumbai/other/remem bering-citys-exuberant-morchas/articleshow/78583951.cms.

Punwani, Jyoti. "'Sena Is Now Part of Secular Coalition Govt,' Says Jamaat-e-Islami-Hind." *Mumbai Mirror,* January 4, 2020. https://mumbaimirror.india times.com/mumbai/other/sena-is-now-part-of-secular-coalition-govt/arti cleshow/73093057.cms.

Punwani, Jyoti. "'Thank You, Uddhavji': Exuberance of Mumbai's CAA Protest Showed Why City's Muslims Are Welcoming of the 'New' Sena." *Firstpost,* December 21, 2019. https://www.firstpost.com/india/thank-you-uddhavji-ex uberance-of-mumbais-caa-protest-showed-why-citys-muslims-are-welcom ing-of-the-new-sena-7811001.html.

Punwani, Jyoti. "25 Years On, Children of the Bombay Riots Have Forgiven the Culprits—But They Haven't Forgotten," *Scroll.in,* December 6, 2017. https:// scroll.in/article/860413/25-years-on-children-of-the-bombay-riots-have -forgiven-the-culprits-but-they-havent-forgotten.

Punwani, Jyoti. "What Was Sanjay Raut Doing at a Jamaat Rally?" *Rediff.com,* January 5, 2020. https://www.rediff.com/news/column/what-was-sanjay-raut -doing-at-a-jamait-rally/20200105.htm.

The Quint. "Symbol of Resistance: How Bilkis Dadi Made It to TIME's Top 100." Facebook, September 24, 2020. https://www.facebook.com/watch/?v=77665 4029733986.

Radcliffe-Brown, Alfred Reginald. "On the Concept of Function in Social Science." *American Anthropologist* 37, no. 3 (1935): 396.

"Ram Mandir-Babri Masjid Case Verdict, as It Happened: Highlights." *The Times of India,* November 9, 2019. https://timesofindia.indiatimes.com/india/ayod hya-babri-masjid-ram-mandir-case-verdict-highlights-supreme-court-de clared-verdict-on-ram-janmabhoomi-case/articleshow/71978918.cms.

Rao, Ursula. *News as Culture: Journalistic Practices and the Remaking of Indian Leadership Traditions.* New York: Berghahn, 2010.

Rao, Ursula, and Vijayanka Nair. "Aadhaar: Governing with Biometrics." *South Asia: Journal of South Asian Studies* 42, no. 3 (2019): 469–81.

Rizzo, Salvador. "President Trump's Crowd-Size Estimates: Increasingly Unbelievable." *Washington Post,* November 19, 2018. https://www.washingtonpost .com/politics/2018/11/19/president-trumps-crowd-size-estimates-increas ingly-unbelievable/.

Roberts, Nathaniel. *To Be Cared For: The Power of Conversion and Foreignness of Belonging in an Indian Slum.* Berkeley: University of California Press, 2016.

Rotman, Andy. "Baba's Got a Brand New Bag: Indian Jute Bags and Exotic Others." In *5 Year Plan: Literary Supplement,* edited by Aaron Sinift, 31–55. Jaipur: Krishna Printers, 2010.

"Saamana Stands by Girl with Free Kashmir Poster." *Nagpur Today,* January 9, 2020. https://www.nagpurtoday.in/saamana-stands-by-girl-with-free-kashmir -poster/01091112.

Sadadekar, Chetna. "For Residents of Jogeshwari Chawl 1993 Riots Is Now a Distant Memory." *Mid-Day,* November 10, 2019. https://www.mid-day.com/mum

bai/mumbai-news/article/mumbai-for-residents-of-jogeshawari-chawl
-1993-riots-is-now-a-distant-memory-22063178.

Sahlins, Marshall David. *Stone Age Economics.* New Brunswick, N.J.: Transaction, 1972.

Saldanha, Alison, Pranav Rajput, and Jay Hazare. "Child-Lifting Rumours: 33 Killed in 69 Mob Attacks since Jan 2017. Before That Only 1 Attack in 2012." *IndiaSpend,* July 8, 2018. https://www.indiaspend.com/child-lifting-rumours-33-killed-in-69-mob-attacks-since-jan-2017-before-that-only-1-attack-in-2012-2012/.

Samervel, Rebecca. "Election Card Is Proof of Citizenship: Court." *The Times of India,* February 15, 2020. https://timesofindia.indiatimes.com/india/election-card-is-proof-of-citizenship-court/articleshow/74144034.cms.

Sarkar, Arita. "BMC Polls: AIMIM's Strong Chances in Mumbadevi and Byculla." *Indian Express,* February 21, 2017. https://indianexpress.com/article/cities/mumbai/bmc-polls-aimims-strong-chances-in-mumbadevi-and-byculla-4535393/.

Saward, Michael. *The Representative Claim.* Oxford: Oxford University Press, 2010.

Schaefer, Donovan. "The Promise of Affect: The Politics of the Event in Ahmed's *The Promise of Happiness* and Berlant's *Cruel Optimism.*" *Theory & Event* 16, no. 2 (2013).

Schaffer, Frederic Charles. "Introduction: Why Study Vote Buying?" In *Elections for Sale: The Causes and Consequences of Vote Buying,* edited by Frederic Charles Schaffer, 1–24. Boulder, Colo.: Lynne Rienner, 2007.

Schechner, Richard. *Between Theater and Anthropology.* Philadelphia: University of Pennsylvania Press, 1985.

Schechner, Richard. *Performance Studies: An Introduction.* London: Routledge, 2020.

Schechner, Richard. "Rasaesthetics." In *The Senses in Performance,* edited by Sally Banes and André Lepecki, 10–28. New York: Routledge, 2012.

Schumpeter, Joseph A. *Capitalism, Socialism, and Democracy.* London: Routledge, 2003.

Scott, James C. *Comparative Political Corruption.* Englewood Cliffs, N.J.: Prentice-Hall, 1972.

Scott, James C. "Corruption, Machine Politics, and Political Change." *American Political Science Review* 63, no. 4 (1969): 1142–58.

"Secularism, Democracy, and Fascism." Jamaat-e-Islami Hind. March 18, 2022. https://jamaateislamihind.org/eng/secularism-democracy-and-fascism/.

Sen, Moumita. "Between Religion and Politics: The Political Deification of Mahishasur." *Religion* 52, no. 4 (2022): 616–36.

Sen, Moumita, and Kenneth Bo Nielsen. "Gods in the Public Sphere: Political Deification in South Asia." *Religion* 52, no. 4 (2022): 497–512.

Sengupta, Shuddhabrata. "Vision Mixing: Marriage-Video-Film and the Video-Walla's Images of Life." In *Image Journeys: Audio-Visual Media and Cultural Change in India,* edited by Christiane Brosius and Melissa Butcher, 279–307. New Delhi: Sage, 1999.

Shaikh, Mohammed Uzair. "BMC Election Results 2017: Asaduddin Owaisi's AIMIM Wins 2 Seat; Samajwadi Party's Raees Shaikh Wins Nagpada." *India .com,* February 23, 2017. https://www.india.com/news/india/bmc-election-re sults-2017-asaduddin-owaisis-aimim-wins-2-seat-samajwadi-partys-raees -shaikh-wins-nagpada-1864433/.

Shaikh, Zeeshan. "Protest against Violence at JNU: Why Mumbai Police Removed Protesters from the Gateway of India." *Indian Express,* January 8, 2020. https:// indianexpress.com/article/cities/mumbai/protest-against-violence-at-jnu -why-mumbai-police-removed-protesters-from-the-gateway-of-india-620 5377/.

"Shiv Sena MP Sanjay Raut Assures Muslims of Safety in Maharashtra." *Mumbai Mirror,* January 5, 2020. https://mumbaimirror.indiatimes.com/mumbai/ other/mp-raut-assures-muslims-of-safety-in-maharashtra/articleshow/731 04478.cms.

Singh, Rajiv. "'Pappu' Connects with Consumers; Becomes Darling Salesman for Marketers." *Economic Times,* August 15, 2011. https://economictimes.india times.com/industry/services/advertising/pappu-connects-with-consumers -becomes-darling-salesman-for-marketers/articleshow/9606316.cms?from =mdr.

Singh, Ritu. "Amit Shah's Epic 'Aap Chronology Samajh Lijiye' Triggers Hilarious Meme-Fest on Twitter." *India.com,* December 28, 2019. https://www.india.com/ viral/amit-shahs-epic-aap-chronology-samajh-lijiye-inspires-a-hilarious -meme-fest-on-twitter-3891733/.

Spencer, Jonathan. "Post-colonialism and the Political Imagination." *Journal of the Royal Anthropological Institute* 3, no. 1 (1997): 1–19.

Srivastava, Kanchan. "Is Your 'Bai' on Long Leave? Blame the 'Neta.'" *DNA India,* February 7, 2012. https://www.dnaindia.com/mumbai/report-is-your-bai-on -long-leave-blame-the-neta-1646848.

Stiegler, Bernard. "Telecracy against Democracy." *Cultural Politics* 6, no. 2 (2010): 171–80.

Strassler, Karen. *Demanding Images: Democracy, Mediation, and the Image-Event in Indonesia.* Durham: Duke University Press, 2020.

Suneetha, A. "The Real Debate on Arbitrary Talaq Is Happening within Muslim Communities Themselves." *The Wire,* December 9, 2016. https://thewire.in/ gender/triple-talaq-debate-allahabad-cout-aimplb-bmma-muslims.

Taneja, Anand Vivek. "'Hindustan Is a Dream': Urdu Poetry and the Political Theology of Intimacy." *Public Culture* 34, no. 1 (96) (2022): 71–98.

Tawa Lama-Rewal, Stéphanie. "Political Representation in India: Enlarging the Perspective." *India Review* 15, no. 2 (2016): 163–71.

Thapar, Romila. *Our History, Their History, Whose History?* Chicago: University of Chicago Press, 2024.

Thapar, R. "What History Really Tells Us about Hindu-Muslim Relations." *The Wire*, January 18, 2023. https://thewire.in/history/what-history-really-tells-us -about-hindu-muslim-relations.

"There's No Mainstream Voice Representing Urban Youth: Zoya Akhtar on 'Gully Boy,'" *Business Standard*, February 13, 2019. https://www.business-stan dard.com/article/pti-stories/there-s-no-mainstream-voice-representing -urban-youth-zoya-akhtar-on-gully-boy-119021300745_1.html.

The Times of India (@TOI+). "In Protest of #CAA, #NRC and #NPR, Lawyers Read the Preamble of the Constitution of India Outside Bombay High Court." X, January 20, 2020. https://x.com/TOIPlus/status/1219206773397049352.

Times Now (@TimesNow). "Mehak Mirza Prabhu issues a video statement defending her 'Free Kashmir' poster." X, January 7, 2020. https://x.com/Times Now/status/1214420543132200960.

Tormey, Simon. "The Contemporary Crisis of Representative Democracy." *Parliament of Australia Website.* October 2016. https://www.aph.gov.au/About_ Parliament/Senate/Powers_practice_n_procedures/pops/Papers_on_Parlia ment_66/The_Contemporary_Crisis_of_Representative_Democracy.

"Uddhav Thackeray's Brother Jaidev Shares Stage with Maharashtra CM Eknath Shinde at Dussehra Rally." *The Tribune,* October 5, 2022. https://www.tribune india.com/news/nation/uddhav-thackerays-brother-jaidev-shares-stage-with -maharashtra-cm-eknath-shinde-at-dussehra-rally-438454.

Turner, Victor. *The Anthropology of Performance.* New York: PAJ Publications, 1987.

"Uddhav, Jagan Rule Out NRC Exercise in Their States." *The Hindu.* December 23, 2019. https://www.thehindu.com/news/national/other-states/no-caa -nrc-in-maharashtra-uddhav-tells-muslim-leaders/article61603430.ece.

UNESCO. "Ramlila, the Traditional Performance of the Ramayana." 1987. https:// ich.unesco.org/en/RL/ramlila-the-traditional-performance-of-the-rama yana-00110.

Urban, Greg. "Metasemiosis and Metapragmatics." *Linguistic Inquiry* 2 (2006): 401–7.

Urbinati, Nadia, and Mark E. Warren. "The Concept of Representation in Contemporary Democratic Theory." *Annual Review of Political Science* 11, no. 1 (2008): 387–412.

Vaishnav, Milan. "Indian Women Are Voting More Than Ever. Will They Change Indian Society?" Carnegie Endowment for International Peace, November 8, 2018. https://carnegieendowment.org/2018/11/08/indian-women-are-voting -more-than-ever.-will-they-change-indian-society-pub-77677.

Vasudevan, Ravi. "The Melodramatic Mode and the Commercial Hindi Cinema: Notes on Film History, Narrative and Performance in the 1950s." *Screen* 30, no. 3 (1989): 29–50.

Vats, Vaibhav. "Liberation Square: How Shaheen Bagh Offers a Model for the Future." *The Caravan,* January 31, 2021. https://caravanmagazine.in/books/politics-shaheen-bagh-model-for-the-future.

Vazeer, Khwaja Mohammad. "Sar miraa kaat ke pachhtaaiyegaa." In Daftar-e-Fasahat (Matba Mustafai, Lucknow): 29 (1847). Rekhta.org. https://www.rekhta .org/ghazals/sar-miraa-kaat-ke-pachhtaaiyegaa-khwaja-mohammad-vazeer -lakhnavi-ghazals?lang=ur.

Velamur, Sumanya Anand. "Religion-Marked Spaces and Memories of Violence in Mumbai: Inhabiting and Remembering." Doctoral thesis, University of Bergen, 2022.

Venkataramakrishnan, Rohan. "Who Is Linking Citizenship Act to NRC? Here Are Five Times Amit Shah Did So." *Scroll,* December 19, 2020. https://scroll.in/article/947436/who-is-linking-citizenship-act-to-nrc-here-are-five-times -amit-shah-did-so.

Verma, Rahul, and Melvin Kunjumon. "The Political Hot Potatoes on Which Urban India Disagrees with the BJP." *Livemint,* February 13, 2024.

Verma, Rahul, and Melvin Kunjumon. "Support for BJP Reaches Fever Pitch; INDIA Alliance Has Few Takers: Survey." *Livemint,* February 11, 2024.

Viswanath, Rupa. "Commissioning Representation: The Misra Report, Deliberation and the Government of the People in Modern India." *South Asia: Journal of South Asian Studies* 38, no. 3 (2015): 495–511.

Waghorne, Joanne Punzo. *The Raja's Magic Clothes: Re-visioning Kingship and Divinity in England's India.* University Park: Penn State University Press, 1994.

Wajihudin, Mohammed. "Sanjay Raut to Speak at Jamaat's Anti-CAA, NRC Function in Mumbai." *The Times of India,* January 3, 2020. https://timesofindia .indiatimes.com/city/mumbai/sanjay-raut-to-speak-at-jamaats-anti-caa-nrc -function-in-mumbai/articleshow/73078867.cms.

Warner, Michael. "Publics and Counterpublics." *Public Culture* 14, no. 1 (2002): 49–90.

Wedeen, Lisa. *Ambiguities of Domination: Politics, Rhetoric, and Symbols in Contemporary Syria.* Chicago: University of Chicago Press, 2015.

Wedeen, Lisa. *Peripheral Visions: Publics, Power, and Performance in Yemen.* Chicago: University of Chicago Press, 2008.

"Who's Afraid of a Song?" *Indian Express,* January 3, 2020. https://indianexpress .com/article/opinion/editorials/whos-afraid-of-a-song-faiz-ahmed-faiz-iit -kanpur-6197024/.

"A Wildfire of Student Discontent across the Country." *Loksatta,* January 7, 2020.

Williams, Raymond. *Keywords: A Vocabulary of Culture and Society.* New York: Oxford University Press, 1985.

Wit, Joop W. de. *Poverty, Policy, and Politics in Madras Slums: Dynamics of Survival, Gender, and Leadership.* New Delhi: Sage, 1996.

Wortham, Stanton, and Angela Reyes. *Discourse Analysis beyond the Speech Event.* London: Routledge, 2015.

Xiang, Biao. "Introduction: Suspension: Seeking Agency for Change in the Hyper-mobile World." *Pacific Affairs* 94, no. 2 (2021): 233–50. https://pacificaffairs.ubc.ca/articles/introduction-suspension-seeking-agency-for-change-in-the-hypermobile-world/.

Yadav, Yogendra. "Electoral Politics in the Time of Change: India's Third Electoral System, 1989-99." *Economic and Political Weekly* 34, nos. 34–35 (1999): 2393–99.

Young, Iris Marion. *Inclusion and Democracy.* Oxford: Oxford University Press, 2002.

Index

LISA BJÖRKMAN is associate professor at the University of Louisville and the author of *Pipe Politics, Contested Waters: Embedded Infrastructures of Millennial Mumbai, Waiting Town: Life in Transit and Mumbai's Other World-Class Histories,* and *Bombay Brokers.* Lisa is also research associate at the Max Planck Institute for Social Anthropology in Halle.